Complete Idiot's Numerology Reference Card

These five numbers reveal both the inner and the outer you.
Below are the formulae for finding each of these numbers.

Your Five Core Numbers

DESTINY NUMBER
Add together the
numbers of your
birth name.

LIFE PATH NUMBER
Add together the
numbers of your
birth date.

PERSONALITY NUMBER
Add together the
consonants of your
birth name.

MATURITY NUMBER
Add together your
Life Path Number
and your Destiny Number.

SOUL NUMBER
Add together the
vowels of your
birth name.

Your pinnacles and challenges can help you understand your highs and lows.

Your Pinnacles

First Pinnacle: month of birth plus day of birth

Second Pinnacle: day of birth plus year of birth

Third Pinnacle: 1st Pinnacle plus 2nd Pinnacle

Fourth Pinnacle: month of birth plus year of birth

Your Challenges

First Challenge: month of birth minus day of birth

Second Challenge: day of birth minus year of birth

Third Challenge: 1st Challenge minus 2nd Challenge

Fourth Challenge: month of birth minus year of birth

Pythagoras, the father of mathematics and numerology, assigned each letter in the Arabic alphabet a number.
You'll be using the letter chart below to convert the letters of your name into numbers to use the formulae above.

Your Personal Years, Months, & Days

YEAR
Add birth month + birth day + current year

MONTH
Add calendar month + personal year

DAY
Add personal month number + calendar day

Letters and Numbers

1	2	3	4	5	6	7	8	9
A	B	C	D	E	F	G	H	I
J	K	L	M	N	O	P	Q	R
S	T	U	V	W	X	Y	Z	

alpl
bool

Every number has a specific meaning. Here are keywords for each of the 9 numbers, to help you understand what these meanings are.

Number 1
Beginning
Individual
Independence
Leadership
Determination
Strong-willed
Innovative
Courageous

Number 2
Feminine
Compromise
Sensitive
Receptive
Harmonious
Balanced
Patient/Loving
Cooperative

Number 3
Self-expression
Joy-bringer
Creative
Enthusiastic
Imaginative
Inspirational
Gift of words
Optimism

Number 4
Planner/Manager
Solid/Stable
Security
Traditional
Practical
Hard work
Systematic
Cautious

Number 5
Freedom
Change/Variety
Unconventional
Rebellious
Progressive
Resourceful
Magnetic/Sexual
Quick thinking

Number 6
Nurturing
Responsibility
Family
Duty
Marriage/Divorce
Love/Romance
Service/Community
Beautification

Number 7
Solitary/Loner
Mystical/Deep
Philosophical
Analytical
Intuitive
Perfectionist
Specialization
Skeptical

Number 8
Power/Mastery
Money/Materialism
Success/Abundance
The Boss/Authority
Vision
Organization
Recognition
Achievement

Number 9
Completion
Perfection
Compassion
Brotherhood
Spirituality
Forgiveness
Multi-talented
Reward

KEY WORDS

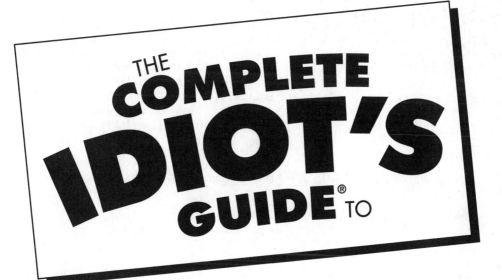

THE
COMPLETE
IDIOT'S
GUIDE® TO

Numerology

by Kay Lagerquist and Lisa Lenard

alpha books

Macmillan USA, Inc.
201 West 103rd Street
Indianapolis, IN 46290

A Pearson Education Company

International Standard Book Number: 0-02-863201-X
Library of Congress Catalog Card Number: Available upon request.

01   00   99   8   7   6   5   4   3   2   1

Interpretation of the printing code: The rightmost number of the first series of numbers is the year of the book's printing; the rightmost number of the second series of numbers is the number of the book's printing. For example, a printing code of 99-1 shows that the first printing occurred in 1999.

Printed in the United States of America

Note: This publication contains the opinions and ideas of its authors. It is intended to provide helpful and informative material on the subject matter covered. It is sold with the understanding that the authors and publisher are not engaged in rendering professional services in the book. If the reader requires personal assistance or advice, a competent professional should be consulted.

The authors, book producer, and publisher specifically disclaim any responsibility for any liability, loss or risk, personal or otherwise, which is incurred as a consequence, directly or indirectly, of the use and application of any of the contents of this book.

Alpha Development Team

Publisher
Marie Butler-Knight

Editorial Director
Gary M. Krebs

Associate Managing Editor
Cari Shaw Fischer

Acquisitions Editors
Amy Gordon
Randy Landenheim-Gil

Development Editors
Phil Kitchel
Amy Zavatto

Assistant Editor
Georgette Blau

Production Team

Book Producer
Lee Ann Chearney/Amaranth

Development Editor
Alana J. Morgan

Production Editors
Robyn Burnett
Christy Wagner

Copy Editor
Susan Aufheimer

Cover Designer
Mike Freeland

Photo Editor
Richard H. Fox

Illustrator
Kathleen Edwards

Cartoonist
Brian Mac Moyer

Book Designers
Scott Cook and Amy Adams of DesignLab

Indexer
Angie Bess

Layout/Proofreading
Angela Calvert
Mary Hunt

Contents at a Glance

Appendixes

Contents

Appendixes

Foreword

Numerology, the study of the spiritual qualities of numbers and letters, has been one of the greatest gifts in my life. Using the guidance of this ancient knowledge, I changed my life forever in 1972 when I selected a new last name for myself after my divorce. In one of those amazing synchronicities upon which you reflect years later, I was guided to make the acquaintance of a woman named Ruth Drayer in Santa Fe, New Mexico. In a casual conversation, I mentioned to Ruth that I had had a persistent thought for the last few months that I ought to change my name. I didn't want to take back my maiden name and had not made any real move to find a new one. Ruth said, "Oh, if you're going to change your name, you ought to use numerology to harmonize the new name with your birth date in order to create the best Destiny for that birth date."

I had never heard of this system, but I was eager for Ruth to work out my chart. We started with my birth name and birth date, and when I saw her simple, handwritten chart, a light literally went on in my head! I was fascinated to see that there is a blueprint of our destiny hidden within the energies of our name and birthday. I selected my last name, Adrienne, because I had always liked the sound of it, and I had given it to my daughter as a middle name. Spelling it Adrienne instead of Adrian happened to coincide to the total numbers in my birth date—so that was the best choice.

Without a doubt, the name I now have, Carol Adrienne, which totals to the number 11—has opened up my life path in ways I could never have believed possible. Little did I realize then—being a novice to the system—that the 11 put me on a path, while very challenging, that has given me my livelihood, success, and insight into the mysteries of the spiritual quest. For this I am forever grateful.

Throughout the years, the accuracy of the numbers has been astounding. Numerology, I found, explains the various personalities within different families. It can also highlight the possible attractions and conflicts between couples.

For me, numerology has provided confirmation of life decisions about when to move, change jobs, start new projects, buy property, be patient, and even find a mate or get pregnant. Over the years, I've received many letters and phone calls from people who report that events unfolded right in line with the advice of the numbers.

I am delighted to be able to recommend *The Complete Idiot's Guide to Numerology* by Kay Lagerquist and Lisa Lenard because it is one of the clearest and easiest books on numerology that I have read. They obviously love their subject, and this book is so well written and well laid out, that the reader will have no trouble immediately putting the information to use. I didn't want to put it down, even though I know the subject well! I felt as if the authors were chatting with me by the fireside.

Without a doubt, numbers influence our lives. If we open our eyes to this hidden spiritual knowledge, we have within our grasp a priceless intuitive tool. For example, one of the most fun uses of numerology is to add up the numbers in your house or apartment. I'll never forget one day during a very, very challenging part of my life when I was being treated for breast cancer, going through a divorce, starting a full-time counseling practice, moving, and having financial problems.

I was standing in the shower and realized that my house number, 2078, not only added up to 8 (money and legal matters), but also represented every number of my karmic lessons (karmic lessons are the missing numbers of your name—I had no letters for the numbers 2, 7, or 8 in my name). No wonder, I thought, that things were a bit dicey here!

My next house number was 1015, which added up to 7. This new house gave me a time of healing, a good place to write in solitude, and a simple life. I then moved to 6641, adding again to 8, but also representing my 6 Heart's Desire, 6 Destiny, and the 41 of my birth year. I had incredible success in that house, and have since moved on to another 8 house (314), which continues to provide me a space to work at home, work in publishing (as a writer), enjoy success, and make good money—all characteristics of the number 8.

It's all in the numbers. Read on and find out what you came here to do.

Carol Adrienne, Ph.D.

Carol Adrienne, Ph.D., an international workshop facilitator and master numerologist, is the author of the best-selling *The Purpose of Your Life, The Numerology Kit,* and co-author with James Redfield of *The Celestine Prophecy: An Experiential Guide.*

Introduction

Every number tells a story—and the story it tells is the story of you. And the best thing about numerology is that all you need to know is your birth name and your birth date—it's that simple. From those two pieces of information, you'll create your numerology chart.

Basically, your numerology chart consists of 5 core numbers: your Life Path Number, your Destiny Number, your Soul Number, your Personality Number, and your Maturity Number. Taken together, these 5 numbers paint a singular portrait of who you are—both the secret you and the you who everyone else sees.

There are also numbers all around us, and we'll show you how to find your personal days, months, and years, as well as how to live in the house that's right for you. With numerology to guide you, you can direct your life by the numbers.

How to Use This Book

You don't need a thing to go with this book except for the two facts we've already mentioned—your birth name and birth date. We've even provided key words for each number and a letter conversion chart on the tearout card that's in the front of this book. We know you won't read it cover to cover, but will instead figure out your core numbers and go straight to those chapters. That's fine with us, but we'll bet you'll want to learn more about the other numbers once you read about your own.

This book is divided into six parts:

Part 1, "What Is Numerology?" introduces you to numerology and how numerology works. We show you how you can use numerology to help you live in the flow—in harmony with the universe.

Part 2, "A Closer Look at Numbers 1 Through 5," takes an in-depth look at the numbers 1, 2, 3, 4, and 5, and shows the positive and negative aspects of each number as well as its interpretation.

Part 3, "A Closer Look at Numbers 6 Through 9, Master Numbers, and Karmic Numbers," takes an in-depth look at the numbers 6, 7, 8, and 9, and includes the positive and negative aspects of each number and an interpretation of each. We'll also introduce the master numbers, 11, 22, and 33, and the karmic numbers, 13, 14, 16, and 19, as well.

Part 4, "Getting Personal with the Numbers," is where you'll learn about the first 3 of the 5 core numbers—the Life Path Number, the Destiny Number, and the Soul Number—where you can discover your purpose in life and your heart's desire.

Part 5, "Putting Your Numbers to Work for You," reveals the last 2 of the core numbers, your Personality and Maturity Numbers, as well as your Pinnacles and Challenges, and how to find your own personal years, months, and days. Here we take you into the discovery of what governs the second half of your life, the theme for each year, and what challenges you'll face.

Part 6, "Living by the Numbers," shows you how to apply numerology in your everyday life—from your bank accounts to your dreams!

Extras

In addition to all this, we've scattered boxes throughout the text with definitions, tips, warnings, and fascinating tidbits to help you understand and learn more about numerology. Here's what to look for:

Merlin's Notes

Merlin the Magician used numerology for character analysis as well as foretelling the future. We chose Merlin as a symbol of a wise wizard who used metaphysics to harness the energy of the universe and to understand its mysteries.

By the Numbers

These boxes define numerology terms so that you can speak the language of numbers.

Easy as 1-2-3

With these simple tips, learning numerology really *is* as easy as 1-2-3!

Sixes and Sevens

Take care when you come across one of these cautionary boxes—it can help you avoid making numerological errors.

Acknowledgments

From Lisa: Thanks, as always, to book producer Lee Ann Chearney of Amaranth for her vision and masterminding, and to the editors and production staff at Alpha/Macmillan—for everything. I cannot imagine having written this book without the wisdom and patience of Kay Lagerquist, who has taught me not only about numerology but about faith and trust. Once again, I also give love and thanks to Bob and the dogs—and to Kait, who's now so far away.

From Kay: Thanks to Lisa, the consummate supportive writer, for her encouragement (it takes a lot of encouragement to write a 30-chapter book on numerology!), for without her sense of humor and spark, this book might have been as dull as dirt. I, too, would thank Lee Ann Chearney of Amaranth for her courage in producing this book and bringing the sacred information of numerology out in a user-friendly format to mainstream U.S.A. and the rest of the world to read, enjoy, and, hopefully, put to use.

A special thanks to my daughter Anna-Stina for choosing to incarnate as a 3 soul and a 3 personality so that I might learn the true essence of the creative spirit, to say nothing of the unquenchable enthusiasm for life.

Last, I want to thank all those who have gone before us to blaze the metaphysical trail, especially the ladies of the Numerical Institute of California, Dr. Juno Jordan, and the many authors who have contributed to the current body of literature that now exists about this fascinating subject.

I have had the privilege of working with two unique groups of numerology students for the past six years now. As a group they have willingly examined all aspects of numerology. For the Seattle group, I would like to thank Susie, Beth, Cherie, Jeanne, Theresa, and Judy. From the Whidbey Island group, I want to thank Nancy, Betsy, Andy, Cynthia, Paula, and Charlene. They have funded me with a vast reserve of stories and experience about living with the numbers. I would especially like to thank Nancy for all those late-night e-mails and endless hours of proofreading, chapter after chapter. To my friends, clients, and special friend Bill, who have been patient and understanding while I essentially "vanished" for five months to write this book with Lisa, I extend a heartfelt thanks.

Special Thanks to Carol Adrienne

We were thrilled and delighted when Carol Adrienne, numerologist and co-author of *The Celestine Prophecy: Experiential Guide* and the best-selling *The Purpose of Your Life*, agreed to write our foreword. We were still more thrilled when she e-mailed us about her delight with our book—and attached the fabulous foreword you see here. We've since both begun intriguing correspondences with Carol. But then, numerology, as you'll soon discover, is often the beginning of beautiful friendships. Carol—thanks.

Special Thanks to the Technical Reviewer

The Complete Idiot's Guide to Numerology was reviewed by an expert who double-checked the accuracy of what you'll learn here, to help us ensure that this book gives you everything you need to know about numerology. Special thanks are extended to Nancy Robert.

Trademarks

All terms mentioned in this book that are known to be or are suspected of being trademarks or service marks have been appropriately capitalized. Alpha Books and Macmillan USA, Inc. cannot attest to the accuracy of this information. Use of a term in this book should not be regarded as affecting the validity of any trademark or service mark.

Part 1
What Is Numerology?

Have you got a favorite number? Does one certain number keep popping up in your life? There is a reason. Numbers have meanings. Did you know that each number has a vibration as well as a distinct energy pattern? Even your birthday and your name have meaning. Your life is made up of numbers, which tell the story of the journey of your life. In addition, your numbers tell you how to get the most out of life. It's time to learn exactly how numerology works, and how it can help you live successfully, happily, and in harmony with others.

Chapter 1

Foundations of Numerology

In This Chapter

➤ Numerology is the language of numbers

➤ Your name and birthday have meaning

➤ Numerology can help you understand transition and change

➤ Numerology tells your cosmic code

What lies behind us and what lies before us are small matters compared to what lies within us.

—Ralph Waldo Emerson

Trying to figure out your life? Curious about your future? Who isn't? There are many ways to wisdom—and to the heart—and numerology is one of the most intriguing. You may have already heard of astrology, the Tarot, or palmistry, which are also methods of knowing yourself and your future.

Numerology is one more metaphysical science, but it's the least known. As an accurate, easy-to-use system for divining the future, however, numerology may prove an easy way for you to find some wisdom of your own. What, for example, if we told you your birthday means something? Or that your name will reveal your destiny?

The ancient metaphysical science of numerology has unlocked the mysteries of life for over 2,500 years. Today, numerology continues to be a profound tool for discovering who you are, where you're headed, and who you might become.

By the Numbers

Numerology is the study of the significance of names and numbers.

What Is Numerology?

Numerology is the language of numbers, as well as a system of relating numbers and names to teach us about the human condition.

You can think of numerology as the science of number vibrations, with each number having its own vibratory influence. Based on the belief that a person comes into this life on a certain date, with a certain name, numerology uses numbers to tell who a person is and what the map is for his or her life.

What Numerology Can Do for You

Not only does numerology tell us about ourselves, it gives us information about the people around us. In fact, numerology can help you

➤ Understand transitions and changes.

➤ Learn more about the psychological conditions around you.

➤ Make sense of the cycles in your life.

➤ Identify your challenges.

➤ Use your talents and gifts to your best advantage.

Plus, numerology is easy—there are no theorems, equations, or difficult calculations. All you'll ever have to do to learn what your numbers are is add (and, occasionally, subtract).

Predicting by the Numbers

According to Juno Jordan, the "grandmother" of modern numerology, "Everything is named or numbered, but few people are conscious of the degree to which names and numbers influence their experience, progress, and communication."

Numerology is the study of what names and numbers mean and is based on the idea that your birth name and birth date paint a detailed portrait of who you are and what your potentials and challenges have been and will be.

Once you've learned what your numbers have to say about you, in fact, you'll have a convenient map for your life—both to show you the best roads and to keep you from ending up on the dead-end.

A Plan for Life

You play a unique and special role in the scheme of things, and numerology is a system for knowing both your plan for your life and the game plan for your time here on Earth. We've all been given a choice—to go through life aware and conscious, or to do so unaware and unknowing. With numerology, you can unlock the gems of wisdom available to you so that you can live consciously—aware of the plan.

Whether it's an architectural blueprint or a Feng Shui floor plan, we look to symbols to add meaning and vision to our lives. Numerology, as a system of symbols, is as simple as the numbers in your birthday and the letters of your name.

Not So Ancient History

The science of names and numbers, as numerology has been called, has its roots in the ancient cultures of Greece, China, Rome, and Egypt, and it also has ties to the Hebrew Kabbalah. As we move forward into the Aquarian Age, numerology emerges as an important tool for understanding and self-knowledge, as you will see. But let's start at the beginning.

By the Numbers

Feng Shui is the ancient Chinese art of placement, based on the belief that a home or building is a definable map of energy influencing our daily lives.

The Father of Math—and Numerology

Pythagoras, a 6th-century B.C.E. Greek mathematician and mystic, is considered one of the fathers of numerology. Based on his precepts that nature is a set of numerical relationships, that divine law is defined and accurate, and that all of this can be computed through mathematics, he developed the "science of names and numbers."

Merlin's Notes

Pythagoras didn't explore only numerology. He's also considered the father of modern mathematics (remember the Pythagorean theorem?) and is responsible for the first known exploration of musical harmony. Interestingly, he connected his two main interests together into a concept called "The Music of the Spheres." According to this theory, everything vibrates to its own special harmony. The higher an object's vibration, the more spirit force it contains, hence the more positive its nature. When the rate of vibration is lower, however, the object contains less force, and so is more negative in its action. When taken all together, the vibration of everything great and small becomes the music of the spheres. The "celestial music" that is heard by some may be because the numbers that make up their vibratory field are those of a higher frequency, such as master numbers.

It was Pythagoras's belief that numbers were the source of form and energy in the world that led to his system of numbers. Pythagoras based his theory of numbers on the idea that the numbers 1 through 9 are symbolic representations of the nine stages of the human life cycle.

Mrs. L. Dow Balliett

In early 1900, an ardent student of the Bible, Pythagoras, Plato, and other philosophers, introduced her own unique teaching of the system of numbers. Credited with originating Western numerology, Mrs. Dow Balliett pioneered teachings that were spiritual in nature, and focused on awakening people to the knowledge of themselves as divine beings.

Mrs. Balliett (back in the days when this was how "ladies" preferred to be addressed) was an influential speaker in the New Age Thought Movement and was a profound influence on one Dr. Julia Seton (who was also the mother of Juno Jordan). Dr. Seton is credited with modernizing the name of the study of numbers into "numerology."

One of Mrs. Balliett's teachings is shown in the following illustration.

The Balliett diagram.

This circle represents the pattern of vibration of numbers. It begins with the 1, 2, and 3, and builds in intensity to the 8 and 9, with the highest vibration being the master number 11, and the center the master number 22. (We'll be discussing the master numbers in detail in Chapter 14, "The Master Numbers 11, 22, and 33: Potent Potential.") Not surprisingly, Mrs. Balliett's teachings were rooted in the Pythagorean theory.

Dr. Juno Jordan and the California Institute of Numerical Research

In the early 20th century, some 2,500 years after Pythagoras lived, a group of women in southern California began to explore his theories in earnest. Led by Dr. Juno Jordan, these women studied every aspect and nuance of numerology for 25 years. According to Dr. Jordan, they studied "Every phase of the science of names and numbers: testing, proving, and disproving." Dr. Jordan herself continued to teach numerology until she passed away, two months before her 100th birthday, in 1984.

Every authority on numerology today is grounded to one degree or another in these women's findings. Some authorities try to "liberate" themselves from the teachings, some are straight "party line," and some just flat out change them, saying their information was channeled.

We believe that Juno Jordan, along with her California Institute of Numerological Research colleagues, as well as a number of modern-day numerology experts such as Carol Adrienne—who wrote the foreword for our book—have much to offer us, and we've found their information to be both straightforward and reliable.

Easy as 1-2-3

One of the most important things to remember about numerology from the outset is that it's a symbolic system. This means that the numbers, in and of themselves, do not make things happen. At the same time, however, as Dr. Juno Jordan herself pointed out, "NUMBERS DO NOT LIE."

Numerology Today

Numerology's been enjoying a renaissance of late, and that should be no surprise—it has much to offer in the way of personal knowledge we can use today.

At the close of the 20th century and beginning of the 21st, people have become aware of their own personal powers—to visualize, manifest, and materialize—and in the search to expand those powers, they've sought to understand their own potentials as well. It's no wonder the science of numbers is experiencing a rebirth. After all, much wisdom and insight can be gleaned from the knowledge of your personal numbers.

By the Numbers

Archetypes, according to psycho-analysis pioneer Carl G. Jung, are myths and stories that belong to the collective unconscious and explain the unexplainable. These archetypes have common links to us all.

Today's scientists tell us everything in the universe vibrates and has energy, and that somehow all of this energy is connected. So is it any wonder then that a system which is about the energy of numbers is finding its way into our lives? We think not. In fact, it's most fitting for the times.

Archetypes and Numbers 1 Through 9

Because the numbers 1 through 9 are the primary numbers of the numerology system, we thought it might be helpful to look at the meaning of each number in terms of an *archetype*.

It will help if you think of each of the numbers 1 through 9 as progressive steps through the cycles of human life, each of which can be understood as a certain type of archetypal behavior. To assist you in your understanding of each number, we've made a list for you of the meaning of each number and its archetypal correlation.

Numbers and Their Archetypes

Number	Meaning	Archetype
1	Independence	Leader, warrior
2	Harmony	Peacemaker
3	Self-expression	Joy bringer, cheerleader
4	Build	Builder, manager, worker
5	Change	Rebel, risk taker, free spirit
6	Nurture	Counselor, teacher, caregiver
7	Inner focus	Wizard, researcher, spiritual seeker, scientist
8	Power	C.E.O., chief, general, authority
9	Service	Healer, mystic, global reformer, philanthropist

Numerology and Myth

Myths are filled with stories of individuals searching for their destiny, seeking answers to the riddle of love, and longing for insight about solving their daily problems. Numerology can serve a similar purpose in your life, and, for that reason, we'll be using myths from various cultures, including our own, throughout this book to illustrate some numerological concepts.

While today we look to a therapist to solve the mystery of relationship, or consult a financial advisor to guide us to a secure plan for our lives, there's not really anyone to tell us about ourselves. Where, for example, can we get insight into who we are, or find out if we're on the right track? Eventually, nearly every one of us comes to wonder if we're missing something. Is there more meaning to this life than the daily grind?

If you've ever asked if there's a plan for your life, or if there's a way to know what the future holds, our answers are yes and yes: Numerology holds the key. Like myths, numerology can help you place the story of your life against a more universal backdrop.

Your own personal story is a kind of myth—and your numbers help to tell your story. Further, it's not one number alone that will allow you to see the beauty of your being; it's the cluster of numbers that reveals the singular brilliance of who you are.

Once you know your own numbers, you will be able to understand how you fit against the backdrop of a universe filled with the stories of other bright lights—human stars. In the next section, we'll show you the first step toward discovering your own special light.

By the Numbers

Myths are stories using archetypal images that often tell of a person's quest to access spiritual power. Myths reflect how an individual relates to the universe or his or her culture.

Looking for the Light

Numerology is a system of numbers and vibrations, and you have your own personal set of numbers that symbolically represents the vibration that's the essence of you. Not only is your birthday filled with numbers, your name reveals a whole set of numbers telling of the themes of your life. You might think of these numbers as components of your "light," or, to put it another way, the energy you put out.

Oh, My Stars

The next step after thinking of yourself as energy—a light—that beams forth your radiance, is to think of each of your numbers as a star of light. When we put together the chain of stars that makes up your light, we can see the full spectrum of light that is you.

Sixes and Sevens

When your "light" is on, you express the positive aspects of a number. When your "light" is off, you may have the tendency to live in fear and express the negative (possibly because you don't know that you have numbers and that they can help you!). We'll show you the meanings of each of the numbers in your life, and discuss in depth the interpretation of each number. Then, it's up to you to let your light shine!

Your star crystal.

Easy as 1-2-3

You are a set of numbers—energies that together create your own special light.

Imagine yourself as a star crystal which is made up of a set of unique numbers which in turn are merely vibrations of energy. You could think of this as your cosmic code. Using your own numbers, we've created a star chart just for you, and we're going to show you how to identify your numbers. When you finish this book, you'll be able to fill in all the missing pieces and see your own personal star crystal.

Your "numerology profile," as your set of numbers is called, is made of many numbers. The most significant ones are called core numbers. There are *5 core numbers* in anyone's numerology profile.

Your Numerology Profile

Number	Formula
Life Path Number	Your birth date numbers
Destiny Number	Letters of your birth name
Soul Number	Vowels from your birth name
Personality Number	Consonants from your birth name
Maturity Number	Name + birthday numbers

A Star Chart for Your Numbers

Once you learn your 5 core numbers, you can fill in the blanks in the following star chart. Then, from our lists of archetypes and numbers, choose the archetype that matches your number. When you're finished, you'll have a chart of the star crystal that is you. Read on to learn more about how to let your own special starlight shine bright.

We've created a chart for you to enter your own personal numbers and archetypes, but first we want to show you a sample of what a star chart looks like. As you work your way through this book, you'll be able to fill this chart in, so you may want to tab this page for future reference.

Each number is a star itself, and all together your numbers create a star crystal—the unique "light" that is you.

By the Numbers

The **5 core numbers** of a numerology profile are the Life Path Number, Destiny Number, Soul Number, Personality Number, and Maturity Number.

A sample star chart.

My Life Path Number
My Life Path Archetype is _____

WRITE YOUR NUMBER INSIDE THE APPROPRIATE STAR

CORE STARS

My Maturity Number
My Maturity Archetype is _____

My Destiny Number
My Destiny Archetype is _____

My Personality Number
My Personality Archetype is _____

My Soul Number
My Soul Archetype is _____

My Birthday Number
My Birthday Archetype _____

11

Your Cosmic Code

You've got a special set of numbers that are the cosmic code for your lifetime on this earth. Your own vibrational pattern is composed of this unique set of numbers.

Your personal cosmic code might look like this:

7 7 3 4 6 5

Or, your code might look like the numbers in the next illustration.

The numbers of the star chart.

My Life Path Number
My Life Path Archetype is _Rebel_

5

CORE
STARS

4
My Maturity Number
My Maturity Archetype is _Builder_

7
My Destiny Number
My Destiny Archetype is _Wizard_

7
My Personality Number
My Personality Archetype is _Wizard_

3
My Soul Number
My Soul Archetype is _Cheerleader_

6
My Birthday Number   _Teacher_
My Birthday Archetype ————

What are your numbers? Unlike a complex computer program or a difficult math calculation, your number code is simple. All you need comes from two things:

➤ Your birth name
➤ Your date of birth

Star Power: ER *Characters by the Numbers*

To get you started on understanding some basic meanings of the numbers right off the bat, we thought we'd begin by assigning numbers 1 through 9 to the cast of characters from the popular television program, *ER*. Each of these characters is a modern-day archetype of the nine numbers we consider primary. Let's see how this plays out.

ER **Characters by the Numbers**

ER Character	Archetype	Number	Meaning
Dr. Mark Green	Independence	1	Independent, stands alone, leader of ER staff
Jeanie Boulet	Harmony	2	Soft-spoken, plays a supportive role, reluctant to speak up, nurse practitioner
Dr. John Carter	Self-expression	3	Humorous, challenged to say what's in his heart, ruled by his emotions
Dr. Carrie Weaver	Build	4	Manager, bean counter, concerned for policy, controlling, rigid, has a health challenge
Dr. Doug Ross	Change	5	Rebel, unconventional, wants his freedom, hard to make commitments
Nurse Carol Hathaway	Nurture	6	Nurturing, caring, the lover, responsible for all the nurses, mothers the clinic
Dr. Peter Benton	Inner focus	7	Silent, aloof, scientific researcher, introvert, but wise
Dr. Donald Anspaugh	Power	8	Chief, head honcho, large ego, has the power
Dr. Elizabeth Corday	Humanitarian	9	Brings global wisdom (from England), intuitive, brings the attitude of tolerance to this small world of healers

Putting the Numbers to Work

Throughout this book, you'll find end-of-chapter exercises to help you put the numbers to work for you. You'll probably want to buy a notebook journal for this purpose, although we've provided spaces for you here as well.

13

We know you're eager to get started, so we're going to begin with an easy number you can find right this minute: your Birthday Number. This number, quite simply, is the sum of the digits of the day you were born.

By the Numbers

In numerology, all numbers are **reduced** to a single digit by adding their digits together. The number 27, for example, would be reduced as 2 + 7 = 9. The only exceptions to this are the master numbers 11, 22, and 33.

Let's say you were born February 7th. That would mean that your Birthday Number is 7. But what if you were born February 13th? If that's the case, you *reduce* the 13 by adding its digits together: 1 + 3 = 4. So, your Birthday Number would be a 4.

There are actually 31 Birthday Numbers, each with a specific meaning, but each has a base number as well. Once you've found your Birthday Number, you can, if you wish, go to Chapter 16, "Your Birthday Number: A Gift for Yourself," where we've devoted a whole chapter to Birthday Numbers, and find out just what this deceptively simple number reveals about you.

Okay, what's your Birthday Number? Write it in the cake in the following illustration.

The Least You Need to Know

➤ Numerology is a way of understanding your potentials and challenges.

➤ Numerology is a symbolic system of numbers and names.

➤ Your numbers are a star crystal showing the pattern of your essence.

➤ Begin to keep a numerology journal notebook of your own.

➤ You can find your Birthday Number.

Chapter 2

What Numerology Can Do for You

In This Chapter

➤ Understanding the number energy for yourself

➤ Numbers have meanings

➤ Letters have meanings, too

➤ Some simple numbers you can use now

Enough history! We know you really want to know what numerology can do for you. We like to think of numerology as a way of exploring all the various aspects of your self and your environment.

Just as your wall mirror reveals your outer image, the mystical mirror of numerology can disclose your inner self. Did you know that everyday things like your phone number, your address, your first name, and even your age have significance? Numerology can teach you a secret code for unlocking the mystery hidden in the numbers surrounding your life.

Numerology Works Like Feng Shui

No, numbers don't have power over you. However, it's important to realize there's more at work in a person's life than just what you see. Numbers, as symbols, contain two major elements:

➤ A vibrational frequency that magnetizes certain energy—like a magnet

➤ A potential for spiritual attraction and connection

Just as Feng Shui shows a map of the natural flow of energy in the living spaces of your house and the things you place in it, your personal numbers create a template for the energy in your life. Just as the principles of Feng Shui give you the ability to change the energy in your home or office, and thereby change your life, numerology can help you understand how to live in accordance with your own natural energy or how to change it.

Easy as 1-2-3

Your personal numbers are a source of strength and healing that invite you to step up to a higher level of awareness. In fact, the study of numbers is one key to interpreting the forces of your outer world in order to better understand your inner self.

What this means is that once you become aware of the principles of numerology and the meanings of the numbers, you'll have a code to change the energy surrounding your life to a harmonious vibration that allows you to reach your highest potential.

More Than Mere Numbers

Numerology is concerned with the primary numbers 1 through 9 and their symbolic meanings, which we'll explore in depth in Parts 2 through 4 of this book, where we'll also discuss the unique master numbers 11, 22, 33 and the karmic numbers, 13, 14, 16, and 19.

By the Numbers

As with all the metaphysical sciences, numerology subscribes to the concept of **reincarnation,** which is the belief that the soul is reborn into different physical incarnations, all of which are interconnected karmatically.

The science of numerology shares certain beliefs with other metaphysical sciences, including astrology, Tarot, palmistry, and handwriting analysis. Some of those shared beliefs include:

1. Your birth date has a definite effect on your life.

2. A person is born into a certain life at a certain time with a certain name, all of which influence their life.

3. Nothing happens by chance.

4. People have *reincarnated* into this life for spiritual growth.

Numerology helps us to

➤ See ourselves more clearly.

➤ Realize our talents and strengths.

➤ Identify our limitations.

➤ See how to best accomplish our destiny.

In addition to all that, numerology can help us discover what lessons we came to learn in this lifetime—and when it's best to take action and when it's not.

Not only does numerology tell us about ourselves, it can illuminate our understanding of others in our lives as well:

➤ For parents, numerology can help you understand why your children are the way they are and the best ways to encourage their growth.

➤ For mates, numerology explains personality quirks, what your partner truly desires in life, and how best to achieve harmony in relationships.

➤ For teachers, numerology is a way to understand your students as unique individuals.

➤ For businesses, numerology gives insight into employees and partners and offers counsel about productive periods as well as slowdowns.

Merlin's Notes

The beauty of numerology is that you don't have to study long before insights begin to come. That's because, of all the metaphysical sciences, numerology is the easiest to learn! Perhaps its simplicity is why it's not as widely known as its cousins, astrology and Tarot. After all, we live in an age when people seem to believe that the highest value goes to the most complex—and simplicity is undervalued or even discounted. As you will come to see, numerology's beauty is in its straightforward simplicity.

We think the value of numerology is how well it works. But we'll let you be the judge as you try it for yourself.

The End All—Be All

It's our belief that no one science of this nature gives the whole picture, and so, numerology need not be studied alone. Each metaphysical science offers a unique, specialized focus of self-discovery, and, while numerology can stand alone, it can be enhanced when used in conjunction with other disciplines. All that you are or anyone is, and how any two individuals will do as mates, is told only in part through one of the metaphysical sciences.

Easy as 1-2-3

An in-depth, insightful look at the issues of our lives needs to be viewed from a multi-layered approach of numerology + astrology + the Tarot + psychology + mind/body medicine, all of which are systems of knowing. By putting them together, you have the *complete* picture. At the same time, though, without numerology (or any of the other aspects), the picture isn't complete.

By the Numbers

Your **Soul Number** reveals what you long for in your heart of hearts. Your **Destiny Number** refers to your purpose and direction in life. Your **Life Path Number** reveals your natural gifts and talents that will allow you to fulfill your destiny.

Numerology is an excellent resource if you want insight into the 5 core parts of yourself, your challenges, and for living intentionally, fully conscious of who you are, and the direction for your highest potential.

Numbers as Mirrors

Numerology gives us a mirror to the soul. In the numbers 1 through 9, we find all the experiences life can present. We become privy to the *Soul Number* of each individual, as well as the *Destiny* and *Life Path Numbers*. Such information is considered to be sacred knowledge and is tremendously valuable to those who wish to make the journey. These numbers reveal a direction, a map for achieving happiness and success in your life.

The More You Know, the More You Grow

We study numerology to become aware of who we are and to discover our potential. The numbers affirm who we are. One of numerology's greatest gifts is that it teaches us tolerance and acceptance of others, as well as who we are ourselves. As your self-awareness increases, you'll achieve a more objective view of your life, and from this you can make better choices for how to live it.

Follow the Numbers

Numerology is a comprehensive system from which you will learn the following:

➤ **Your Life Path Number:** Your own special path that you walk in this lifetime. This number shows the natural gifts and talents that will allow you to fulfill your destiny.

➤ **Your Destiny Number:** The purpose and direction of your life. This number represents your calling and mission in life.

➤ **Your Soul Number:** This is your heart's desire and your inner motivation, and reveals what you long for in your heart of hearts.

➤ **Your Personality Number:** This number shows how others see you. It is the outer look you wear and how others define you.

➤ **Your Maturity Number:** This number shows the direction for the second half of your life. It represents the "true you," as you begin to live in harmony with your inner and outer selves.

➤ **Your Life Lesson Numbers:** These are the numbers which are not present in your name. They tell of the lessons you're meant to learn to advance your personal and spiritual growth.

➤ **Your Pinnacles:** These are the four phases of your life that point the way to your highest achievements.

➤ **Your Challenges:** These are the four doors through which you must pass to reach your highest attainments. The numbers representing the four doors define the difficulties and challenges you must confront.

➤ **Your Major Cycles:** These are the three divisions of your life that tell of the major themes governing your time here on Earth. These three numbers help to give meaning and focus to your pinnacles and challenges.

➤ **Your Personal Year:** This number tells you where to focus your energy for each year. The Personal Year Number indicates what you must face and accomplish to live in harmony with the natural flow of the year.

➤ **Your Personal Months and Days:** These numbers tell you what to expect and how to organize around coming events, and identify the theme for each month or day.

➤ **Your Birthday Number:** This number indicates a special talent you possess. It also shows a particular lesson you're trying to learn in this lifetime.

We're going to teach you how to find all this personal information and more, but first, we will need to address the basics of numerology.

Alphabet Soup

Whenever we calculate a word, such as your name or street name, or when we want to discover the meaning of a word, we assign numerical values to letters of the alphabet. Here is a handy conversion chart you'll find useful as you calculate your own chart. You'll also find this chart on the tearout card at the front of this book.

Letters and Their Numbers

1	2	3	4	5	6	7	8	9
A	B	C	D	E	F	G	H	I
J	K	L	M	N	O	P	Q	R
S	T	U	V	W	X	Y	Z	

You may want to tab this page to refer to as you read this book. But, hard as it may be to believe right now, eventually, you'll memorize the number for each letter. It just takes practice!

Easy as 1-2-3

As you know from English class, the letter "y" may be considered a vowel or consonant, depending on the word or name. For a full discussion of the use of the letter "y," refer to Chapter 19, "Your Soul Number: The Heart of the Matter."

Let's say your first name is Hillary. Using the letter chart, find the corresponding numbers for each letter of your name:

$$H = 8$$
$$I = 9$$
$$L = 3$$
$$L = 3$$
$$A = 1$$
$$R = 9$$
$$Y = 7$$

_____

$$40 = 4 = 0 = 4$$

When you add up all of the numbers, you will see that 40 is the total for Hillary.

Unless you arrive at one of the three master numbers (that is, 11, 22, or 33), you reduce any two-digit sum by adding the numbers together. In this case, the sum for Hillary is 40, or 4 + 0 = 4, so the name Hillary is a 4.

Numerology Rule #1

Reduce numbers to a single digit. Add all numbers together to get a single number.

Following rule #1, if you were born on the 14th of the month, add 1 + 4 to get the reduced number 5. You've got a 5 birthday!

Now let's look at the meaning of the name Hillary. Hillary carries the abilities of the 4, which we'll be discussing in Chapter 8, "The Number 4: A Solid Foundation." Hillary adds up to a 4, so we know that certain things are true about her. For example, because the 4 is the archetype of the builder, you can expect that she'll want to build her life around security and permanency. All that she undertakes is done to build toward something. She can work hard, but has a high need for security, and therefore can be controlling and rigid. She has excellent abilities to organize and manage projects. We get to know all that—and more—from one number!

> **Numerology Rule #2**
>
> Don't reduce master numbers! Our master numbers are 11, 22, 33. They tell of special attributes (which we'll discuss in depth in Chapter 14, "The Master Numbers 11, 22, and 33: Potent Potential").

Numbers Have Meanings

The key to numerology is: Each number has a specific meaning. While we'll give our in-depth analysis of each number in Parts 2 through 4 of this book, for now, here's a number "cheat sheet" for handy reference.

Numbers Cheat Sheet

Number	Key Words and Concepts
1	Beginning, independence, innovation, leadership, masculine principle
2	Harmony, unity, relationships, cooperation, feminine principle
3	Saying one's truth, imagination, optimism, happy, creative expression
4	Building, formation, hard work, endurance, seriousness
5	Change, progressive, resourceful, unrestricted, versatility
6	Balance, nurturing, service oriented, responsibility and duty, family focus, marriage and divorce number, domestic vs. work issues
7	Inner analysis, research, science minded, solitude, wisdom, spiritual focus, investigates the mysteries, the mystical, the metaphysical
8	Authority, power, finances, business, successful, material wealth, organization, self-mastery
9	Endings, vision, tolerance, transformation, spiritual consciousness, cosmic teachings, global awareness, perfection

Master Numbers

11	Master of inspiration, idealism, visionary; brings light to the world; a leader with spiritual consciousness, reformer of world problems, wants to uplift
22	Master builder, visionary; knows how to plan and execute large projects; wants to bring spiritual principles into the material world; powerful skills of manifestation; humanitarian
33	Teacher of teachers, master of compassion, master of healing through love

continues

Numbers Cheat Sheet (continued)

Number	Key Words and Concepts
Karmic Numbers	
10	Renewal, rebirth, karmic completion, mastery
13	Reworking karmic laziness through discipline
14	Reworking karmic abuse of freedom through order and stability
16	Reworking karmic abuse of responsibility and love through spiritual rebirth
19	Reworking karmic abuse of power through learning to stand up for oneself and at the same time to value interdependence

Simple Numbers You Can Use Now

Using the letter chart and the numbers cheat sheet above, you can find some simple numbers to use right this minute! Not only does the name of your street translate into a personal numerological message, your country reveals a message, too.

The Street Where You Live

The street on which you live may be a number or a name, but either way, it has meaning. The full meaning of your place of residence is made up of both the house number and the street name or number. However, the house number has the strongest influence, and we'll discuss that in the next chapter. But first, let's look at the street where you live.

To discover the meaning of either the name or the number of a street, we add it up.

For a named street:

Easy as 1-2-3

To figure the street name, use what is actually on your street sign. Look for Rd. vs. Road, Ave. for Avenue, and Ln. for Lane, for example.

1. Write the name out, exactly as it appears on your street sign.
2. Assign the corresponding numbers from our letter chart.
3. Add the numbers together.
4. Reduce the numbers by adding them together until you reach a single number.
5. Check the meaning of the number on your handy number cheat sheet.
6. Watch for master numbers 11, 22, and 33.

For example, Log Cabin Rd. (use Rd. instead of Road if it is written that way on the sign) corresponds to:

Log = 367 = 16 = 7

Cabin = 31295 = 20 = 2

Rd = 13 = 4

Taking the final sums of Log, Cabin, and Rd., you get:

7 + 2 + 4 = 13

1 + 3 = 4

Sixes and Sevens

Karmic numbers give us a chance to go back and get it right. Each karmic number has a special theme and task. As you read this book, you'll want to pay attention to your own karmic numbers: 10, 13, 14, 16, 19. Their lessons are those you're destined to learn.

Log Cabin Rd. is a 4 street. But in fact, Log Cabin Rd. is a 13(4) street. It's a karmic number. Lots of hard work there! Karmic work!

For a numbered street use the number only, not the words "Road" or "Street" or any other letters on the street sign. Look at this example:

23rd St. = 2 + 3 = 5

We might say then, that 23rd Street is a 5 street—lots of change here!

Okay, let's try a famous one. How about the street in front of the White House?

Pennsylvania Avenue:

P	E	N	N	S	Y	L	V	A	N	I	A		A	V	E	N	U	E	
7	5	5	5	1	7	3	3	1	5	9	1		1	3	5	5	3	5	= 74 = 11

So, Pennsylvania Avenue equals 11, which is a master number. This famous street is a place where leadership will be required, tension runs high, and peacemaking is the order of the day.

Your P.O. Box

P.O. boxes have numbers, too, and the number on your post office box is just one more number your life vibrates to. If you don't like what's going on, change the number!

Here's an example. Brittany has a P.O. box numbered 147. We add these numbers together: 1 + 4 + 7 = 12. Then we add the 12 together, 1 + 2, to get the reduced number 3. Brittany has a "3" mailbox. This box number says she should get fun mail and have lots of communications from friends.

This is just one of the numbers Brittany would want to be aware of. If a number, such as this 3, is repeated in her phone number, house address, or office number, she would want to take note of the influence of the 3 in her life. Does this number enhance or present a challenge to her 5 core numbers (which we'll be discussing in Chapters 16 through 22)? Too much of any one number can be hard to live with.

Your Hometown

By now, you've probably figured out that cities or towns have their own numbers, too, which can tell what you can expect to find there. Think of the possibilities: If you're planning a move, you might want to consider the number of the city, town, or state. What can this city offer you? Can you live up to its requirements? What will you have to give up or gain in this city, town, or state?

You could also use these numbers to find out if the number of your hometown resonates with who you are. Or, you could find out a city or state's number before you planned your vacation, depending on what kind of vacation you wanted. No matter what your need, the story's in the numbers!

Each city or town has its own purpose and destiny as shown by its numbers. Some of the questions to ask after finding out the number for your hometown include:

➤ Does your city match any of your numbers?

➤ Is the city's number one of your karmic lessons?

➤ Is the number of this town the same as your Life Path Number? You will have good success when your environment is the same number as your Life Path.

➤ Is the number the same as your Destiny Number, Soul Number, or Maturity Number?

Easy as 1-2-3

The state where you reside also has a number, and so does your town or city. It pays to be aware of the influence the numbers have on your life.

If any of these numbers match your numbers, then it's a good bet that this is a good place for you to be. After all, life will be easier for you if you harmonize where you live with your natural energy.

How does your hometown match up with your *core numbers?*

No, we're not suggesting you move if your town, city, or state number doesn't match one of your core numbers! However, by discovering these numbers, you will know the requirements and demands that are placed on your life by living where you do. Is your town compatible with you? The town, city, or state number tells if the energy there supports you, allows you to grow, fosters your success, or is just a start-up town for you.

Most metaphysical folks would say you're living where you are for a reason. Figure the numbers to learn the answer—and see if you agree.

Universal Law #1

Nothing happens by chance. Everything happens for a reason.

For an example, let's look at the state of Washington to find its number:

W A S H I N G T O N

5 1 1 8 9 5 7 2 6 5 = 49 = 13 = 4

This 4 number tells us that if you live in the state of Washington, you can expect to find people who are hardworking, practical, honest, serious, realistic, determined, and cautious. They might also be a bit stubborn, rigid, and security-conscious. Risk-taking is not their favorite thing.

If you were to live in this state, you would want to know this information. Obviously, if you are the party type and like the laid-back life, you might want to relocate!

Country Names

Some numerologists believe that even a country's name has significance. For example, the name America, which the United States is often called, vibrates to the number 5 (go ahead, add it up!), and anyone with a 5 in his or her core numbers would find living in the U.S.A. compatible with its risk-taking, freedom-loving nature.

Here's a sampling of several country numbers. See for yourself if any of these numbers fit your impression of that country.

Countries by the Numbers

Country	Number	Quality
England	7	Reserved
Australia	3	Friendly
Japan	6	Duty to family
America	5	Freedom
Sweden	6	Family focused

Your Phone Number

As with other numbers in your environment, your phone number has meaning that should not be ignored.

To understand your telephone number, you'll want to refer to interpretations in the Number Cheat Sheet appearing earlier in this chapter.

When calculating your phone number, you'll be using only the three-digit prefix and the last four digits, not the area code. For example, to figure the phone number 371-3381, add all the numbers together and then reduce your sum to a single-digit number. The total number here is 26 so we reduce it to 8.

Now, look at the Number Cheat Sheet for the meaning of the number 8. This 8 phone number brings an attraction for money and authority!

There are two layers to consider in examining your phone number:

1. The last four digits have the most significance. Add together these last four digits to find a single number. Let's look again at our example:

    ➤ 3381 are the last four digits

    ➤ 3 + 3 + 8 + 1 = 15

    ➤ Then reduce to a single digit: 1 + 5 = 6

Easy as 1-2-3

Numbers in your environment, such as your address and phone number, have meaning. Understanding those meanings can help you move through life smoothly and wisely and help you to live in sync with all aspects of your life.

Sixes and Sevens

When calculating your phone number, use *only* the three-digit prefix and the last four digits, *not* the area code!

The significant number for this phone number is 6. Checking out the meaning of the 6 reveals that this phone number will bring responsibility and caring and nurturing of others, as well as advising and problem solving. It may also be that there will be a lot of family issues handled over this phone number. The person at 371-3381 may find that many of the phone calls are about family (6 is the total of the last four digits) and money (8 is the total of all seven digits).

2. The second layer is to consider the meaning of the individual numbers in the final four digits of your phone number. Our sample number, 3381, has two 3s, an 8, and a 1. On this phone number, there will be lots of communication, possibly emotional discussions (3s). There will also be challenging moments with those you consider to be in authority (8), as you say your truth and establish your own sense of power (3 and 8). The 8 and the 3 in combination also suggest that you might have a tendency to be extravagant and spend money over the phone. Cut up those charge cards now! The 1 here reveals that you will be given opportunities to stand up for yourself and be self-reliant. All of this while you work with the family and responsibility issues of the 6!

And you thought choosing a phone number was no big deal!

What about the other numbers in the phone number? Here's the scoop:

➤ **The Area Code.** This is a widespread collective number shared by all of the people in your area. Because it's widespread, its effect is general, unlike the specific set of four numbers you can choose for your phone number. For this reason, the area code is not used to calculate your phone number meaning.

➤ **The Prefix.** This number refers to your local area and, again, has only general significance. While the prefix is part of your phone number and wants to be figured in, the number that counts most is found in adding together the last four digits. The prefix is used in figuring the total vibrational force of your phone number.

Your Apartment Number

Not only does your phone number have influence in your life, but your apartment or house number adds or subtracts to the harmony of your life as well. Let's consider the apartment number first. The entire next chapter will be devoted to house numbers.

Usually, there are two addresses for an apartment. One is the building address, the other is the actual apartment number. Both numbers have significance. Figure each one separately, and then add the numbers together to reach a final total, and, as before, reduce to a single number. The number that will have the most influence will be the number of your apartment. For the meaning of the apartment number, you can use the meanings for house numbers, which we discuss in the next chapter.

Remember, if you're living in an apartment, your apartment number tells what is expected of you personally, under that number.

Easy as 1-2-3

Speaking of choosing a phone number: Yes, you can choose one. You have more control over your phone number than you do over a house or apartment number. Most phone employees are friendly and helpful. You can pick your number or choose an alternate. It's the last four digits that count most.

Easy as 1-2-3

If your apartment has a letter as well as a number, or is just a letter, use the letter conversion table shown earlier in this chapter to convert it to a number. For example, apartment 3B equals a 5, because B is a 2, and 3 + 2 = 5.

The Least You Need to Know

➤ You can learn to understand your own energy through numerology.

➤ Numbers have meanings that reflect areas of your life.

➤ Every letter has a number.

➤ You can add up your phone number to see if it rings true.

➤ The numbers of your address can help you understand where you live.

Apartment or House, It's the Number That Counts

Some people swear by the number on their house. In fact, one of Kay's colleagues considered it the sole deciding factor when she made a move. If you're a very busy career type with a good deal of stress, for example, a 5 house isn't the place for you. If you're having financial difficulties, move into an 8 house or apartment. And, if you're in a place in your life where you want to focus on studying or working on your spiritual path, a 7 house is perfect.

Whether for an apartment or a house, it's important to calculate the number *before* you move in. Naturally, there are many considerations in choosing a home, but the house's energy is important and should resonate to your own personal energy. A house's numerology is an important factor in living your life consciously!

Figuring the House Number

If you live at 421 Long Ears Lane, both the house number and the street name affect you. The same is true if you live on a numbered street. However, the number on the house will have the strongest effect. For a quick review of how to figure the street number and street name, turn back to Chapter 2, "What Numerology Can Do for You," where we walk you through the particulars of calculation. However, it is the number on the house that will have the strongest effect.

House numbers tell the essence or energy of the house. The street tells the essence of the neighborhood. When the number of the house is reduced to a single digit, that number tells of the characteristics of the house and what goes on there.

To get you started on seeing how this works, here's a sample address: 5717 16th N.E.

First, we figure the house number like this:

$5 + 7 + 1 + 7 = 20$

When we reduce this 20 to a single number, we find the house number is $2 + 0 = 2$. This 2 house, then, tells us that sharing and cooperation will be important for people who live here.

Next, the street number is figured:

$1 + 6 = 7$

So 16th is a 7-kind of street: quiet, private, everyone pretty much keeping to themselves.

$N.E. = 5 + 5 = 10 = 1$

Together then, 16th (7) N.E. (1) as a street bears the energy of the 8. This is a street where money is made (good for real estate!), but you will be surrounded by independent, private neighbors.

See? It's easy.

Anytime your address has a letter on it, convert the letter to a number using the handy letter chart. For example: 578C Sunlight Beach Rd.

Here's how to calculate this house. First, the number:

$5 + 7 + 8 + 3$ (for C) $= 23$

The 23 is then reduced to a 5 $(2 + 3)$. The 5, then, is the number of this house.

Next, calculate the street name separately. This gives you the neighborhood's number.

S	U	N	L	I	G	H	T		B	E	A	C	H		R	D
1	3	5	3	9	7	8	2		2	5	1	3	8		9	4 = 70

Reduced, $7 + 0 = 7$. So, we have another 7 neighborhood, but with a 5 house. The 5 house will be full of activity, much coming and going, and full of change. In fact, it will probably be a bit too active for the rest of the quiet, refined 7 street!

The Number of an Address

The home's base number (the reduced number) is only part of the energy of the home. The numbers that make up the house's address are important as well. Using our 587C Sunlight Beach Rd. address, we notice that the house number is comprised of a 5, a 7, an 8, and a 3 (the C). From these numbers, we note the following:

➤ The 5 is active, the 7 reclusive, the 8 brings success and money, and the 3 brings social and creative influences.

➤ The busy 5 main energy of this house is enhanced and accelerated by the 8 and the 3.

➤ The 7 allows for research or study at the house, but rest and retreat will be overshadowed by the more dominant, active energy of the 5, 8, and 3.

Needless to say, if you need quiet to study or just to be yourself, forget this house!

Easy as 1-2-3

Occasionally, a house will be renumbered. If that happens, the change in numbers will also change the energy field of a home.

No Number—Only a Name

If you live in a named house, work out the letter-number equivalents and reduce them to a single digit number. For example:

M	A	R	S	H		H	O	U	S	E	
4	1	9	1	8		8	6	3	1	5	= 46

Reduced, 4 + 6 = 1. So Marsh House is a place of independent, creative energy, where leadership will be learned.

By the Numbers

The **base number** is the final reduced single digit you get after adding together all of the numbers of any name or address.

The Meanings of House Numbers

Once you've got the *base number* of your house, you can begin to understand the numerology of your home. In the remainder of this chapter, we'll discuss the individual aspects of each house number.

The Number 1 House

This is a house for independent, self-reliant people. The 1 house will encourage individuality, courage, determination, and integrity for those who live there. It's an excellent house for a person who wants to undertake an individualistic creative venture. If you want to follow your own instincts, this is the house for you.

The 1 house will foster leadership and solo undertakings. If you've been unduly weighted down with caretaking of others, this 1 house would be a good choice—if you're ready to be number one again.

The Challenge of a 1 House

You might feel isolated or alone in this house, even if there are others in the house. If you are the dependent type, a 1 house can be very challenging: It will require you to become independent. Also, learning to be patient might present a challenge living here. You've got to want to be independent in a 1 house. Patience might present a challenge living here. Another challenge might be: In this 1 house, there are all chiefs and no Indians!

Key Aspects Fostered in a 1 House

➤ Independence

➤ Courage

➤ Honesty

➤ Activity

➤ New beginnings

➤ Innovation

➤ Individuality

➤ Leadership

➤ Independence

Easy as 1-2-3

When a person lives in a 2 house, he or she begins to grow in awareness of the subtle, small aspects of life. Sensitivity is heightened here, and this is a great house to develop your intuition and psychic abilities, and to pay attention to the subtle energies of gardens, art, music, and magic.

The Number 2 House

The 2 house is a quiet house, excellent for two people who want to share space. In fact, this is a house for sharing anything, because a strong desire for peace and harmony pervades this home. An aggressive, impatient person won't do well in this house, because the 2 house demands patience and encourages sensitivity and gentleness. In addition, it will require attention to detail and a willingness to cooperate.

People who live in a 2 house can be very connected because they will become strongly tuned in to their energy and feelings. This is a good house for the growth of a partnership or marriage—it's not a house for someone who wants to live alone. The 2 is at its best with companionship.

The Challenge of a 2 House

There might be a tendency in a 2 house to collect things—too many things. How many seashells or salt shakers does any one house need, after all? Also, any form of conflict or discord will challenge those who live under the vibration of this house.

At its extreme, the 2 vibration can find people nitpicking or being critical (after all, the 2 pays attention to detail, right?). A 2 house insists on balance in relationships.

Key Aspects Fostered in a 2 House

➤ Patience

➤ Cooperation

➤ Warmth

➤ Tact

➤ Attention to details

➤ Sensitivity

➤ Balance of opposites

The Number 3 House

Here's a fun house where you can feel positive about your life, because enthusiasm and charm permeate the 3 house. We would expect to find abundant creativity here. This house encourages expression of oneself: communication, creativity, and emotions. This is a home where you expand your vision for life.

Here you'll find a natural affinity for the positive, which naturally leads to positive results. A 3 house is conducive to generating creative, sexual, and spiritual energy. Your social life is going to expand in this 3 house. Romance flourishes in a 3 house but expects truth and loyalty.

The Challenge of a 3 House

The challenge here has to do with getting *too* excited, *too* enthusiastic, and having *too* many friends: The challenge of the 3 house is to not scatter your energies. A 3 house is sometimes messy, which is sometimes called "creative chaos." This house will drive a person with strong 4 energy nuts. You'd better expect to live with lightheartedness in this house!

Sixes and Sevens

There's a tendency with the 3 to play now and pay later, so a keen eye on finances will be necessary. Remember, all that entertaining can add up fast! In addition, spontaneous, impulsive action can be a challenge with the 3 house as well.

> **Key Aspects Fostered in a 3 House**
>
> ➤ Creativity
> ➤ Openness
> ➤ Optimism
> ➤ Happiness
> ➤ Radiance
> ➤ Friendships
> ➤ Imagination
> ➤ Enjoyment of life

Easy as 1-2-3

People who live in a 4 house will find it easier to be steady, loyal, well respected, and grounded. This is a great home for planting your roots—and seeding your dreams.

Easy as 1-2-3

Cars have numbers, too. Check your license plate. KJR 618, for example, tells us that this car carries the energy of the 9—a rewarding car for the owner. You shouldn't get crazy with things like your license plate number—or any other number. Just have fun with it. The serious numbers are coming later in the book!

The Number 4 House

This is the house to have if you want security and stability: A 4 house brings wholeness, down-to-earth living, and practicality. It's a good place to build a solid foundation for your future, because this house wants order and economy.

The 4 house lends itself to steady employment for those who live there. In addition, people or groups who are working toward a common goal will find the 4 house a good match as well.

This is a house to build toward something, and, if you're interested in gardening or earthiness, the 4 house is for you. Family matters and the affairs of relatives will demand that you use common sense and practical management if you live here. Last, a 4 house has a serious kind of vibration, and so will be a haven for those who aren't afraid of hard work and discipline.

The Challenge of a 4 House

Sometimes, living in a 4 house can feel like life is too much work. There might be a tendency to hoard at this house, or to become rigid and inflexible. Loosen up—you've got other numbers in your life to help you out. How about a perky little 3 car? Or a 3 phone number?

One might want to be cautious in moving into a 4 home, and should accurately assess the amount of work it will require to maintain this particular house. The 4 is about hard work, after all, and under the 4, it's just not going to go away.

Key Aspects Fostered in a 4 House

➤ Security

➤ Plans for the future

➤ Organization

➤ Discipline

➤ Groundedness

➤ Thriftiness

➤ Hard work

The Number 5 House

If you feel stuck, this is the house for you. The 5 house is one of activity, movement, and change. There will be lots of out-of-town trips, a constantly ringing phone (the 5 is the number of sales and networking), and the hustle and bustle of an extremely busy schedule.

The 5 house is a hub of activity. It lends itself to stimulating communication and the gathering of experiences and information—especially about ethnic cultures.

Routine is hard to establish and hold in a 5 house, and change is the constant. The coming and going of many people, as well as sudden or unexpected changes, will keep life anything but dull.

A 5 house encourages resourcefulness, enterprise, and promotion of oneself. Variety is the norm here—which sometimes leads to chaos and hectic living. Conditions rarely remain the same over a long period in this house. Many a romantic fling takes place in a 5 house, because people who live here will have enhanced magnetism, impulsiveness, enthusiasm, and will be more talkative and possibly more competitive. It would not surprise anyone who knows numbers to find a fast-talking, enthusiastic salesperson living here.

Easy as 1-2-3

People who live here will enjoy life through its pleasures (read this as *wine, women ...* you know the rest!), or through the thrill of being on the leading edge of new trends, owning the latest gadget, or being "in the know" of progressive thinking.

The Challenge of a 5 House

Life can sometimes feel like a chaotic whirlwind in this home. More than likely, there will be a tendency to make snap decisions here, but because your instincts will be sharpened, your decisions could be right on. Even so, you might want to slow down and deliberate before you make that decision.

It may be hard to feel rested in this house, and if you're planning to be celibate—move on—this house isn't for you. Last, because of the pervasive element of change, this 5 house may have a high turnover in occupants.

Key Aspects Fostered in a 5 House

➤ Nonconformity
➤ Change
➤ Variety
➤ Activity
➤ Personal magnetism
➤ Gregariousness
➤ Sales
➤ Publishing
➤ Risk taking

Easy as 1-2-3

The 6 house is the home of the gardener, especially for one who loves to beautify the home and grounds with lots of flowers. Make this a place of beauty and love, for that's the natural vibration of the 6.

The Number 6 House

Nesting and family interests mark this house, so this is a great house for raising a family. Love of children, pets, animals, and family traditions are classic for this house number, and it's also good for those wanting to develop their artistic abilities.

Money, comfort, and good things are attracted to this house when life is lived out of good will and a humanitarian spirit. In addition, this is an excellent home for homeschooling or for a counselor who works at home, because the energy of a 6 house is warm, caring, and nurturing. Close, loving relationships will come to life in this house.

The Challenge of a 6 House

The idea of giving and nurturing can get out of balance here: You could give too much to others and too little to yourself, trapping you in a sacrificing role. This is not balanced and under a 6 vibration, you will be challenged to correct the situation.

Duty and responsibility will be ever present in a 6 house, so if you rebel at responsibility, this isn't going to be your first choice for a house. However, the 6 house will teach the lessons of responsibility—so maybe you should stick around after all.

Key Aspects Fostered in a 6 House

➤ Beauty

➤ Children

➤ Balance

➤ Love

➤ Nurturing

➤ Domesticity

➤ Teaching

➤ Counseling

➤ Service

➤ Responsibility

The Number 7 House

The 7 house is a retreat, a sanctuary for those who need to rest, recuperate, contemplate, or do inner work. For those reasons, it's a perfect house for someone who wants to be alone, meditate, and seek divine inspiration. Education, learning, and research profit here, too, and the 7 house will be enjoyable for the writer, scientist, or student, because this house lends itself to focused investigation.

Success in this house is attained through knowledge, skill, and specialization. The 7 vibration enhances intuition, dreams, telepathic communication, spiritual development, and metaphysical studies. This is the house for a very private person.

The Challenge of a 7 House

This is not the home for those who want to attain material wealth or advancement in the business

Sixes and Sevens

If partners are to live together in a 7 house, both should expect lots of aloneness and aloofness. However, pairs of contemplative, introspective souls will do very well here.

world. It's also a difficult home for marriage, partnership, or roommates. The 7 wants to be alone, basically, so this isn't the house for someone who can't live alone or wants to entertain regularly.

Key Aspects Fostered in a 7 House

- ➤ The inner life
- ➤ Solitude
- ➤ Analysis
- ➤ Contemplation
- ➤ Recuperation
- ➤ Specialization
- ➤ Privacy
- ➤ Eccentricity
- ➤ Study or research

The Number 8 House

If you're ready to get the material side of your life in order, move into an 8 house. This house will encourage organization, vision, and management of financial matters, and through discipline and vision, you can achieve a position of power while living in an 8 house.

The 8 brings recognition and respect in the community for your good work, and success and financial abundance are possible under this house's vibration. Good judgment will be called for, as well as strength and decisiveness.

This is not a truly domestic home, but instead is often a place of business activity. People of authority, money, businesslike minds, and success will be attracted to an 8 house, because power, money, and success are the three hallmarks of the number 8. The 8 is also the number of self-mastery, so in this house, you may find that your spiritual beliefs enhance your material achievement.

The Challenge for an 8 House

Under the 8 vibration, money goes out as money comes in. Usually, there are big expenses in an 8 home—no wonder you need to attract big money! The challenge is to stay focused and organized as you work toward abundance.

Careful management of finances, honesty, and integrity, as well as justice, are all called for as you learn to live under the powerful vibration of the 8. This is not the house for the spendthrift—poor financial management under this vibration will bring disaster.

Key Aspects Fostered in an 8 House

➤ Material prosperity

➤ Authority

➤ Leadership

➤ Self-mastery

➤ Business

➤ Good judgment

➤ Achievement

➤ Sound money management

The Number 9 House

This is a home for the compassionate and the tolerant, a great space for the humanitarian. If you have no racial or social prejudices, are philanthropic, or have a burning desire to help the world, this is the house for you. The 9 vibration allows you to see the possibilities, to see beyond limitations and oppression. This is a home for broadminded thinkers. You'll find rewards for past efforts in this house.

The 9 house is a good place to complete something, heal a wound, or pass on your deep understanding to others. Intuition, dreams, healing, spiritual pursuits, the arts, drama, philosophy, and even metaphysical teachings will all be sources of inspiration to those who live at this 9 house. When you live in a 9 house, you'll find people and money drawn to you for your humanitarian outlook, your compassion, and your wisdom.

The Challenge of a 9 House

Passionate, dramatic emotions may be fully expressed in the 9 house. Because 9 rules intense feelings, we might expect to see this intensity unleashed in a passionate display of emotions. A marriage or relationship may experience difficulties if it's too limiting.

The 9 also signifies detachment and impersonal love, because the energy is focused on the larger picture. In an effort to see the greatest good for the greatest number, you may fail to see the individual you're living with. The 9 is a very powerful number that exacts powerful feelings and lessons for those under its influence.

Easy as 1-2-3

Did we mention that business addresses work the same way as house and apartment numbers? Why not figure out the number for where you work, and then look to the house number for its meaning?

Key Aspects Fostered in a 9 House

➤ Selflessness

➤ Completions and endings

➤ Release

➤ Tolerance

➤ Wisdom

➤ The arts

➤ Passionate feelings

➤ Good fortune

Finding the Number of Your House

Throughout this book, we'll be providing you with exercises to help you find your own numbers. So let's begin with finding out what number your house represents.

On the first line write down the your address. That's the number and name of your street address: Note that if your street name is a number, you should write down *only that number*. For 23rd Street, for example, write down only 23 and ignore all the other letters.

My address is: _____

Next, translate each letter in your street name to a number, and on the following line write down each number directly under the letter it corresponds to:

Street name letters:

_____

Corresponding numbers:

_____

Now, add all the numbers together and reduce to a single-digit number. Write that number here.

My Street Number is:

_____

Or:

If you have only numbers in your street name, add the numbers together here, then reduce to a single number:

My Street Number is:

_____

So, what's the number of your house? Read about it in this chapter and see what the numbers of your house have to tell you.

Merlin's Notes

We realize you often have no choice in the address of your home. So we want you to know that every number vibration has its own beauty, and that the number on your house or apartment is exactly what you need at this time. We believe there are no accidents in where you live. You'll gain valuable insight from the number on your house, which will help you to orchestrate a fulfilling life. Remember, the more you know, the more you grow. Knowledge is power.

Universal Law #2

Life happens as it should. There are no mistakes.

The Least You Need to Know

➤ Your house number can tell you a lot about your house's energy.

➤ You can use the meaning of your house number to determine which activities are best for your house.

➤ The challenge of each house number can make certain activities more difficult.

➤ You can find your own house number and its meaning.

Chapter 4

Learning to Read Between the Numbers

> **In This Chapter**
>
> ➤ The philosophy behind numerology
>
> ➤ How to add those numbers together
>
> ➤ Learning the reducing plan that's best for you
>
> ➤ The nine-year growth cycle
>
> ➤ The Universal Year
>
> ➤ A chart of your own

Everything's got a philosophy behind it, and numerology's no exception. Once you understand why we use numbers to explore ourselves, you'll be ready to learn how to add some of your own numbers together.

In this chapter, we'll be showing you how to do just that. We'll discuss different methods of reducing the numbers, and then we'll look at the nine-year growth cycle we all go through again and again throughout our lives.

The Philosophy Behind Numerology

The universe is based on the fundamental reality that all things are related, and within that underlying notion of unity, all things are energy. It's our relationship to this energy that defines our lives. Numerology is about the relationship of numbers and their influence on our lives.

The act of giving something or someone a name isn't a superficial act; it comes from our intuitive feel or connection to this person or object. Numerologists maintain that each of us carries the perfect name—a name that reflects our inner nature. Even if you argue that your name or date of birth are a matter of chance, or even that they were an accident, you'll most likely agree that your name and your birthday have an effect upon your life.

Numerology, as one of the metaphysical sciences, is a search for understanding. Even though it's ancient in its origin, it's enormously useful in its application to the search for direction in present-day life.

Different Strokes for Different Folks

If you pick up any of the numerology books in a bookstore today, you'll find the authors calling the 5 core numbers by other names. What's important is that even though there may be different names for these 5 core numbers, all of them are figured the same way. We're all really talking about the same thing—some folks just call them something else.

> **Numerology Rule #3**
>
> The most important numbers in numerology are the core numbers.
> There are 5 of them.

The 5 Core Numbers and How to Figure Them

The Number	What It Represents	How to Get It
1	Soul Number	Add together the vowels of name
2	Destiny Number	Vowels + consonants of name
3	Personality Number	Add together the consonants of name
4	Life Path Number	Month + day + year of birth
5	Maturity Number	Birth name number + date of birth numbers

So that you don't become confused by all the different names for the core numbers, we've devised a handy table to sort this out. Here's a list of the 5 core numbers and what they've been called in various numerology books.

Core Numbers Names Table

What We Call It	Other Names Used
Soul Number	Heart's Desire Motivation Number Soul Urge Self-Motivation Number Individuality Number The Inner Self
Destiny Number	Expression Number Self-Expression Number Mental Number Outer Self
Personality Number	Self-Image Number Heart Self Quiescent Self
Life Path Number	Destiny Number Vocational Number Birth Force
Maturity Number	True-Self Number Reality Number Realization Number Ultimate Goal Power Number

One thing that has remained consistent is the name for the Birthday Number: Everyone seems happy to call the number of the birthday just that! When we talk about the Birthday Number, we're referring to only the day of your birth—such as the 6th or the 29th.

Just as there are different views about what to call the 5 core numbers, there are different philosophical approaches to the study of numerology. Numerology as a study might be approached from a variety angles. However, because it's called the "science of names and numbers," we shouldn't be too surprised to find a large part of what goes on to be focused on name analysis.

In fact, some numerologists specialize. Here are some of the different specialties found in the study of numerology:

➤ Names analysis

➤ Biblical numerology

Sixes and Sevens

Your Date of Birth Numbers (plural) refer to the month, day, and year you were born. Your Birthday Number (singular) is the day you were born—just the day. Don't get mixed up!

➤ Character analysis

➤ Spiritual numerology

➤ Predictive numerology

➤ Numerolinguistics (the language of numbers)

Spiritual Numerology—It's Our Way

Spiritual numerology is based on the premise that we're more than the physical manifestation of our collective gene pool—we are spirit. Spiritual numerology suggests that the interpretation and analysis of numbers emphasizes growth of higher consciousness, and shows how to use the numbers to grow in your awareness and advance spiritually.

By the Numbers

A way to frame an individual's journey on Earth as one of meaning and purpose, **spiritual numerology** is based on the idea that each of us carries a set of vibrations, a blueprint for our life. This blueprint can be discovered from a numerology chart.

Sixes and Sevens

We might also look to see if you're carrying any of the karmic-debt numbers, which are 13, 14, 16, and 19. These numbers give insight into unfinished business you have from a time before—or, as we like to say, "in another life."

Spiritual awareness means being tuned to the larger picture, to the idea that there's a greater plan, awareness, and source than ourselves, and that the numbers hold symbolic information that spell out a path of spiritual guidance.

Spiritual numerology embraces the idea of reincarnation; that is, that the soul is ongoing, while the physical body is temporary. The idea, then, would be that you are a soul having a physical experience in this lifetime. It also suggests that your soul was somewhere else before it came here to this lifetime (incarnation).

Now, if your soul was somewhere else before, what was it doing? Spiritual numerology would say that your soul was learning and growing, getting ready for your time on Earth now. This information is revealed in the Soul Number.

In spiritual numerology, we also look to see what karmic debts you came in to this life with. These would be lessons you were unable to finish in previous lives, or even lessons you refused to learn (for a variety of reasons). We look to the karmic-lesson numbers for information about how you might re-learn or finally learn what your soul needs to grow and advance. These numbers are the ones that are absent in your birth name.

When working with karmic-debt numbers, a person is given another opportunity in this life to complete relationships, health issues, previous abuses of love, and power. We'll be covering the karmic-debt numbers in more detail in Chapter 15, "The Karmic Numbers 10, 13, 14, 16, and 19: Lessons to Be Learned."

Spiritual numerology is only one approach to this fascinating subject, and, as there are different approaches, there are differences of opinion about how to figure the numbers. If you're interested in exploring one of the other approaches, you can check out some of the books listed in Appendix A, "Further Reading."

Pick a Number, Any Number

The math for numerology is really quite simple: You either add or subtract.

The main idea behind the manipulation of the numbers is to find the single base number. This base number is usually a reduced number that comes from a double-digit number, but the single number will tell the story—unless of course, it's a master number. (We'll get to that in a few pages.) The method for adding the numbers is indeed the most controversial question in numerology.

The trick is how you add the numbers together. Bet you didn't know there was more than one way to add!

Numerologically, there are essentially four ways to add the numbers:

1. Add across.
2. Reduce as you go.
3. Add down.
4. Add double digits.

Let's look at each of these individually, so you can see the differences for yourself.

Method #1: Adding Across

One way to add the numbers is to add straight across. When figuring your house number, this is fine to use. But if you're adding your birthday numbers to determine your Life Path Number, the simple "add-straight-across" method can lead to problems.

Let's use the example of July 6, 1944. If you're adding the Date of Birth Numbers (we're talking about *all* of your Birthday Numbers), you might think to add them like this:

$$7 + 6 + 1 + 9 + 4 + 4 = 31$$

$$3 + 1 = 4$$

The single number 4 is the base number (also called the reduced number). The reason we don't like to use this method for finding Date of Birth Numbers is that when the add-straight-across method is used, you lose the chance of finding master numbers, which is the case in our example, as you'll see.

> **Numerology Rule #4**
>
> Don't add all the numbers straight across! The numbers within a number are important as well, as you'll find out as we calculate your core numbers later in the book.

Let's look at the July 6th birthday when it's reduced before it's added. When we do this, it reveals a master number! To do this for July 6, 1944, you'll first reduce 1944. (July is a 7 and the day is a 6, so no reduction is necessary for those numbers.)

To find the year's reduced number, add the numbers together: 1 + 9 + 4 + 4 = 18. Now, you'll reduce again, to arrive at the single-digit number 9 (1 + 8). Once you have reduced the year number, add all the reduced numbers together (but remember, 7 and 6, in this case, don't need to be reduced). Add: 7 + 6 + 9 = 22. Our new way of writing the sum of this date of birth will be 22/4.

Easy as 1-2-3

We endorse Method #2, reducing as you go. It ensures the discovery of master numbers.

Voilà! A master number. As we said before, you would have missed it using the add-straight-across method.

Method #2: Reduce First, Adding Together

Another method for adding numbers is to reduce as you go along.

Here's an example to illustrate this method. The date of birth December 16, 1972, might be written like this: 12 + 16 + 1972. If reduced first, it looks like this: 3 + 7 + 1 = 11/2.

Reducing before you add is fast. Some numerologists swear by this system, and it's certainly the easiest method for beginners. Notice in our example that we have uncovered yet another master number, the 11. We'll be explaining what that means in a few paragraphs.

We recommend reducing as you go. It's faster—and you carry less weight (something we all desire!).

> **Numerology Rule #5**
>
> Don't lose your master numbers!

Watch for master numbers when reducing to a final number. Remember, the numbers 11, 22, and 33 have special meanings.

Method #3: Adding Down

A third method for calculating numbers is to set it up like a little math problem.

For example, to figure the date of birth March 17, 1982, we would write it like this:

$$1982$$

$$17$$

$$\underline{+\ 3}$$

$$2002$$

Then, we'd reduce 2002 to the base number 4 (2 + 0 + 0 + 2 = 4). This method reveals that the Life Path Number for this birthday is 4.

We use this method as a tie-breaker, when trying to determine if the Life Path Number is really a master number. We would use Method #2 first, then try Method #1, and last of all try Method #3, to see if two of the three methods give us the same answer.

Here is an example: Betsy thinks she might have a master number birthday. Her birthday is February 12, 1941. Let's see how to use the different methods to determine if she has a master number or not.

Method #1, adding straight across, we find:

2 + 12 + 1941 = 20

Not a master number.

Method #2, reducing first, then adding together, we find:

2 + 3 (1 + 2) + 6 (1 + 9 + 4 + 1 = 15 or 6) = 11/2

This *is* a master number.

Method #3, adding down, we find:

1941 + 12 + 2 = 1955 (1 + 9 + 5 + 5) = 20

Again, not a master number.

Therefore, we would conclude that Betsy doesn't have a master number after all. We can only be sure if we use all three methods to verify. Just remember—you want two out of three methods to agree to get a true master number.

Of course, it's necessary to try all three only if you're working with a master number.

Method #4: Double-Digit Adding

This method is almost the same as the second method. When adding your Date of Birth Numbers or Name Numbers, hold on to the double-digit number when adding.

For example, in the birthday November 22, 1908, we would not reduce first. Instead, we hold on to the double-digit numbers and write it like this: 11-22-1908. Remember, November = 11.

Next, we reduce 1908 to 18, and then add it up: 11 + 22 + 18 = 51. Then, we reduce the double-digit total: 5 + 1 = 6.

By holding on to the double digits, you can see what numbers lie behind the total (the 5 and the 1 are what are influencing the 6, in other words), and what numbers are making up the total. In our example here, it's pretty important, because this person is dealing with two master numbers (11 and 22) in his date of birth!

Reducing Is Not a Diet Plan

No matter which method you choose, you'll have to add your numbers together and then reduce. The reduced number gives the simple, base number from which an interpretation can be made.

Choose the method that feels right for you. Try them all and see which one gives you the most information. Don't be dismayed by all of these choices. This is one of the most important decisions you'll make in your study of numerology.

If you're not sure, start with Method #2 and reduce first. The more you work with the reducing methods, the easier it will be to find which one works for you. Just like diets—sooner or later, you find that one works for you!

The Lowest Common Denominator

When writing a master number, you'll have two numbers to consider (the master number and the reduced number). A master number is written like this:

➤ 11/2 for the master number 11

➤ 22/4 for the master number 22

➤ 33/6 for the master number 33

In a master number, the lower number is equally as important as the higher number.

Whether you're working with a master number or any other double-digit number, you'll be interested in the reduced number. If it's a 22/4, for example, you'll want to interpret both the 22 and the 4. But if you're looking at the number 27, you'll be mainly interested in the reduced number 9 of that number.

Double Digits

Some numerologists give a lot of credence to the double-digit number, too. This is because a number with two or three digits gives added information to the base number in consideration. Double digitizers write these numbers as 21/3, 17/8, or 103/4. Both the single base number and the double number are considered for analysis. For example, let's look at the 15.

When we reduce 15, we'll of course add the 1 + 5 to find the base number 6. Now, let's say you wanted to know your Life Path Number. You would add up the numbers of your date of birth, say, November 9, 1975, and, reducing as you go, find that it adds up to a 15/6.

The number 6 tells us that you'll have a path to walk in this life that will bring responsibility, duty, nurturing, and care for others. However, if you look at the 15, you would note that both the 1 and the 5 are to be considered; they show how you'll go about your Life Path 6 duties. In other words, you may be facing responsibility and duty, but will want to be independent (the 1) about the way you go about these duties, and will also demand freedom from time to time (the 5).

It's actually much more simple than it might appear at first glance. First, look to the reduced number for your interpretation. Then, look at the double-digit number to see what else is involved. If working with the double-digit number is too much, too soon, and you're not ready for it, just concentrate on the single number—there's plenty there!

Now that you've got the basics of how to figure your numbers, it's time to see what these numbers can tell you.

Easy as 1-2-3

In considering the numbers that make up the single base number, you'll gain insight into the underlying concerns or the direction that is given when looking at the double-digit numbers involved.

What Do the Numbers Mean?

Each number, 1 through 9, has a distinct meaning and message, and the master numbers, 11, 22, and 33, also have important news. Let's look briefly at how to use these numbers. Note that we'll discuss each number separately and in depth in Parts 2 and 3 of this book.

What Do You Want to Know?

The most important numbers to know are your 5 core numbers, which we showed you earlier in this chapter.

Remember, you can find the meaning of your name and date of birth using numerology. Your *birth name* alone is composed of 3 of the core numbers: the Soul Number, Destiny Number, and Personality Number.

Your *date of birth* numbers give you a wealth of information. They tell you another of your core numbers, the Life Path Number. But still more, your date of birth numbers also tell you what lesson you're working on at a particular age, what your potential is for achievement, what the theme is for each year of your life, and what's influencing you as you live out each year. Best of all, to discover all this information about yourself, all you have to do is add!

> **Numerology Rule #6**
>
> From your date of birth, you'll find core number 4, the Life Path Number.

When you add your date of birth numbers and your birth name together, you get the last of the core numbers, the Maturity Number (also called the Reality Number or the True Self Number)—you know, the "real you."

> **Numerology Rule #7**
>
> Add your name and birth date together to get core number 5, your Maturity Number.

How, you say, can I add my name to my birthday? There are no numbers in my name! Ah, yes, but there are.

The Numbers Behind the Letters

Remember that when Pythagoras first devised the system of numerology, he noted that everything in the world is made up of numbers, and so applied numbers to the Arabic alphabet. Using the numbers 1 through 9, he came up with a chart (see the "Letters and Their Number" chart in Chapter 2, "What Numerology Can Do for You") that allowed him to decipher the meaning of any name. In fact, not only could he decipher names, but words, which could then be considered for their underlying meanings.

Once Pythagoras had the numbers to figure a person's name, he had a tremendous tool for seeing into the hidden essence of a person, and so it was thought that anyone who knew this method of decoding a name could see into the soul of a person. That's why this information was carefully guarded and taught only in the Mystery Schools to devoted students who were sworn to secrecy.

Numerology began to surface again in the early 1900s, however, as we discussed in Chapter 1, "Foundations of Numerology," and became popular as a useful meta-physical tool for human potential and growth. Today, all of us can use this not-so-ancient system to uncover the meaning of our names. Now that you have the code, you can uncover the hidden messages in your name.

Easy as 1-2-3

Here's an example of how to find a word's meaning from its letters:

L I G H T
3 9 7 8 2 = 29 = 11/2

No surprise there! "Light" vibrates to the energy of the master number 11, which is all about illumination!

The Nine-Year Growth Cycle

We'll be using numbers 1 through 9 throughout this book. Why? Because numerology is based on the prime numbers 1 through 9. In fact, a nine-year-cycle rhythm is very important to a *numerological cycle* called the *Pinnacles*. The philosophy behind this is that all the experiences we can have in a lifetime are symbolized in the numbers 1 through 9.

Western Numerology Numbers 1 Through 9

In this book, we're using Western numerology, in which the numbers 1 through 9 have definite, unique, symbolic meanings that correspond to the evolution of a person's life. These meanings are basically very simple:

➤ 1: Beginning

➤ 2: Connecting

➤ 3: Creating

➤ 4: Building

➤ 5: Changing

➤ 6: Nurturing

➤ 7: Reevaluating

➤ 8: Expanding

➤ 9: Completing

We all move through the cycle of numbers, from 1 to 9, over and over again, throughout our lives.

By the Numbers

A **numerological cycle** is a nine-year cycle that happens again and again in one's lifetime, but with a different theme ruling the cycle each time. **Pinnacles** and their corresponding **Challenges** define the four major phases (and themes) of a lifetime—in nine-year chunks.

Nine-Year Cycles

Numerologically, your life is operating on repeated nine-year cycles. Every year has a number, and each number has a particular meaning. This meaning is your theme for that year (called your *Personal Year*). In nine years you will have completed a specific cycle, which also has a specific lesson to be learned. In addition to the Personal Year, there are four Pinnacles to a lifetime, and 4 Challenges, that are figured in nine-year cycles.

As an example, the beginning of the new millennium, it can be argued numerologically, was actually in 1999. That's because if you add the numbers 1 + 9 + 9 + 9 together, you'll get the single digit 1. This number 1 is the beginning of a nine-year cycle which will end in 2007.

By the Numbers

Your **Personal Year** identifies which year in the nine-year cycle you are in now. It's figured by adding your birth month and day to the current year. We discuss the Personal Year in Chapter 25, "Your Personal Year: For Every Time There Is a Season."

This means that the first cycle of millennium 2000 actually begins with a 1 year in 1999 and ends with a 9 year in 2007. A new cycle will begin in year 2008, when it's a 1 year again. See? Kind of got the idea? Everything comes together in nine-year cycles.

By the Numbers

The **Universal Year,** the reduced number for any given calendar year, is the energy under which the entire Earth is vibrating for that year.

Easy as 1-2-3

Remember, the 1 Universal Year is the first year of a nine-year cycle. By the way, you can't have a 0 year, even if it feels like it!

You'll see how it works for you personally when we discuss your Personal Years in Chapter 21, "Your Maturity Number: Your Mid-Life Message." In fact, all of your numbers work together to create a map for your life, complete with signposts and markers.

The Universal Year

The *Universal Year* is, quite simply, the calendar year. For instance, if the year were 1999, all of the planet Earth would operate under the 1.

To figure the Universal Year, just add the numbers together. For example: $1 + 9 + 9 + 9 = 28$. Reduce 28 and you will find it is a 1 ($2 + 8 = 10$, then reduce again $1 + 0 = 1$). This means that the whole planet is functioning under the vibration of the number 1 Universal Year.

What does it mean to be in a 1 Universal Year? It's a time of new beginnings, a time for starting over and planning for the future. It's a time to stand up, to feel confident, persevere, be assertive, take charge, and get results. We would say, then, that this is what would influence all of us at a collective level, globally and locally, in a 1 Universal Year, and represents the energy that would surround us. However, don't confuse this with your Personal Year, because that's another story.

Zero Ain't for Nuthin'

The number 0 shouldn't be ignored. It represents an energy that's unformed and pregnant with potential: After all, it's full and empty at the same time. In fact, the 0 is the symbol of an open channel to higher forces.

We see the zero in numbers like 10, 240, and even 2000.

Interestingly enough, in fact, the year 2000 has *three* zeros. There's power in these zeros: We won't see three of them for another thousand years (kind of like watching your odometer roll over).

Sometimes, we find a 0 on the Challenge Number. (We'll be discussing this number in detail in Chapter 22, "Predictive Numerology: Future Forecasts.") It's thought that those who have a 0 Challenge Number are old souls.

When you have a 0 behind a number, the idea is that this 0 magnifies the number ahead of it. If, for example, you have a 10 birthday (such as the 10th), the 0 magnifies the 1. You might be independent, ambitious, a leader, in other words, but you're also working the issue of courage, and all of these qualities and issues are magnified by the 0.

Figuring a Chart

Now that you know how to add the numbers, have an idea of the philosophy of numerology, and have a few basics under your belt, let's put this stuff to work.

We thought you'd like to figure your own numerology chart, so we've provided you with a sample chart. If you really get into it, and want to do charts for your sweetie, child, boss, or whomever, photocopy the chart and keep on figuring!

Before we begin, there are a few pointers we want you to have.

The Name You Were Born With

When figuring a chart, you'll be working with the name you were born with. We're talking about the name on your birth certificate or your given name, even if you don't like it or never use it. Numerology is working with your very essence, which means your original, pure vibration. We can only get that with your original name.

There are lots of wonderful stories about names given out at birth, like, Carol vs. Carole where the "e" was left off the birth certificate and she went through 50 years of her life thinking she was someone other than who she really was; or a baby in a hospital given another baby's name. (Lisa recalls a story about a woman who insisted her child was already named. She was named "F-e-m-a-l-e." "It's right there on her birth certificate," the woman insisted.)

The philosophy behind using the name given at birth is that there are no mistakes. It follows that the name given to you at birth was not a mistake. However, clerical errors do occur and if this is the case for you, use the original birth name that was intended for you. Just be sure to check the spelling!

The numerology school of thought goes something like this: You were given the very name you got because it is the correct set of vibrations you will need to achieve your destiny, to work on your karmic lessons, and for your soul to express itself fully in this lifetime.

It's also thought that you selected your parents when you were back in "soul land," and they agreed to be a channel for your birth and life on Earth. The name that was decided for you was meant to be, or was an intuitive moment your parents had. Even if you were named after your great uncle Alfred III, the point is: Your name is not a mistake.

> **Universal Law #3**
>
> All things happen according to a Master Plan or Master Design. We all have free will by the choices we make about how we live the Master Plan.

Adopted Names and Name Changes

When you don't know your original name, you'll figure your chart with the name you were given at adoption, because this name is the essence or vibrational pattern you grew into.

So, what if you don't know your birth name? You simply will figure a chart for the adopted name. However, if you should have both a birth name and an adopted or changed name, then use the original for the pure essence of your numbers. Then figure another chart for the name you came to live by. This second chart will show who you have become.

Sixes and Sevens

Even if you've changed your birth name, dropped it, or gone to great lengths to have the "correct" name put on your birth certificate, you'll still need to use your original intended name to figure your numerology chart.

Not surprisingly, the question of a married name is often brought up. The married name is figured separately from your original birth name, and shows what energy or lessons you added to your life during the period you carried that name.

All of your basic core numbers remain the same as they were at birth. The married name is what energy you drew to you—that you needed in order to learn the next step. Always figure your married name separately from your birth name.

What Your Birthday Says About You

Your Birthday Number is the number of the day of the month you were born. Unlike your name, it cannot be altered. Note that your Birthday Number is not one of your core numbers, but its influence is potent all of your life, and it's particularly potent between your 28th and 56th birthdays (which we'll discuss in depth in Chapter 20, "Your Personality Number: See Me, See You," when we explore your Major Cycles).

Your birthday greatly influences your Life Path. It identifies some special talent you possess. It's also thought that your birthday is a number to consider in helping you choose the right career path. And, it concerns the whole middle period of your life: your productive years or the "flowering."

A Chart of Your Own

Let's start simple. (But before you get going tear out our letter/number chart on the tearout card in the front of this book. It will help you convert letters to numbers.) You need two things for your numerology chart: your birth name and your date of birth. On the first line, write your birth name.

Your birth name: _____ = Destiny.

On the second line, assign the appropriate number to each letter of your name.

Your birth name converted to numbers:

_____

Figure each name separately. Reduce each word to one number, then add each number together. This is your Destiny Number. Write that number here:

My Destiny Number:

_____

Now write down your date of birth on the following line.

Your date of birth numbers: Month _____ Day _____ Year _____ = Life Path _____

Reduce each of these numbers to a single digit, and then add them together. This is your Life Path Number. Write that number here:

Life Path Number:

_____

There. You've got the beginnings of your numerology chart. In Appendix B, we've provided you with a complete numerology chart, but this is a good beginning for exploring your personal numbers.

The Least You Need to Know

➤ Numerology believes that all things are related.

➤ Remember to reduce the numbers first, and then add them across.

➤ You'll soon find the reducing plan that's best for you.

➤ The nine-year growth cycle is a cycle we all go through again and again.

➤ The Universal Year is a number that everyone on Earth vibrates to.

➤ You can create a chart of your own.

Part 2

A Closer Look at Numbers 1 Through 5

Numerologists believe that each number has its own special meaning and archetype. The number 1, for example, being first, naturally likes to lead, while the number 5— smack in the middle—is often a turning point and change catalyst. In between are the balancing of the 2, the creative principle of the 3, and the practicality of the 4.

The Number 1: In the Beginning

If you want to light a fire under a project, get a 1 on board. She'll begin it with flare and a burst of enthusiasm. The 1 assesses what needs to be done with the speed of light and then executes the plan in about the same amount of time, all the while ordering everyone around. She means no harm—she's just into the power of her 1 energy. The drive and focus she'll bring to the job—any job—are hallmarks of the number 1.

One (1) is the number of new beginnings. It always signals a new time is about to begin, that new opportunities can be expected, and that all will be done with courage and the intent to get the job done, because the 1 symbolizes taking action.

Maybe you won't be able to tell a 1 what to do—but you won't find him waiting for anyone to tell him what to do either. In fact, while you may still be talking, the 1 will be long gone, already into the thick of the action.

By the Numbers

The **1** is the number of initiation and action, the self-motivated leader.

Easy as 1-2-3

Aries, the astrological equivalent for the number 1, represents the independent, headstrong initiator.

Leader of the Pack

What makes a leader? Knowing what one wants, having the courage to go to the head of the pack, having strength of will, and having the wit, intelligence, and quickness to execute the plan.

Independent and headstrong, the 1 is both ambitious and determined. Never afraid to try something new, the 1 will "boldly go where no one's gone before"—but seldom "goes with the flow."

Key Words, Colors, and Gemstones

Traditionally, every number has certain words and colors associated with it, as well as a gemstone, an astrological sign, a Tarot card, and even some flowers. It's important to bear in mind that each of these should be thought of as an association or mnemonic device, rather than a definitive symbol that's cast in concrete. Still, we think these associations can be very helpful and hope they'll help you learn each number's meaning quickly.

The Number 1

Key Words	Colors	Gemstone	Sign
Beginning	Red	Ruby or garnet	Aries
Individual	Flame		
Independence			
Leadership			
Pioneering spirit			
Determination			
Creative thinking			
Strong-will			
Innovation			
Courage			
Initiation			

In addition, there are other things to consider with their relationship to the number 1:

➤ **Tarot cards:** The Magician, the Aces
➤ **Flower:** Lily for purity, purple lilac for first emotions of love, sage for esteem

Merlin's Notes

Tarot cards, another metaphysical tool, present a symbolic picture of the elements of life. The Tarot deck is divided into two parts: the Major Arcana and the Minor Arcana. The Magician card, key 1 of the Tarot's Major Arcana, has the ability to create his own reality, and sometimes represents the need to find a new direction in life. Similarly, the act of creating one's own reality is very much in the domain of the independent, self-directed 1.

The Aces in all four of the suits of the Tarot are represented by a perpendicular Cup, Wand, Pentacle, or Sword. The meaning remains the same for all four: A new beginning is foretold.

The Number 1's Symbol

The symbol of the 1 is a perpendicular line, standing alone, which signifies truth and separateness. It's said that Pythagoras considered the 1 to be the creative power, and the line between heaven and Earth.

The symbol of the 1 is a perpendicular line.

The Number 1's Meaning

The 1 is part of the sacred cycle that includes the first 3 numbers:

➤ **Number 1:** Creation

➤ **Number 2:** Assimilation

➤ **Number 3:** Expression

It's also part of a three-stage action of the mind or way of thought formation:

➤ **Number 1:** Impression

➤ **Number 2:** Re-impression

➤ **Number 3:** Expression

The basic meaning of the 1 is energy in a state of perpetual motion. The 1 has the power to create, develop, and govern all things pertaining to this earthly life, like the Tarot card, the Magician. The 1, however, requires a complete overcoming of self before it attains its highest success.

A number 1 person will mingle with the world, but is never really one of "them." If you vibrate to the 1, whether it's your Birthday Number, Pinnacle, Challenge, Personal Year, Soul Number, Destiny, Life Path, Personality, or True Self Number, you must learn through personal experience that everything gained—until self is overcome—comes through difficulty.

Easy as 1-2-3

The letters of the 1 are A, J, and S.

The 1 has to overcome self-absorption, self-interest, and selfish focus. To do this the 1 has to realize that to love without thought of holding out for what one gets in return is what allows the 1 to become a happy individual, rather than a separate, lonely one.

Life with the 1

As with all the numbers, life with the 1 can bring both blessings and challenges. The 1's insistence on action can mean it won't tolerate any dillydallying, and its strong opinions can sometimes make it contrary. A 1, however, won't care much if others find him or her contrary or forceful, because both of those are very much a part of who a 1 is.

The Blessing

The blessings of the 1 are its confidence, creativity, and vital energy, as well as its feisty, independent spirit. People with strong 1 influence in their charts will find it easier than any other numbers to learn how to be in touch with their divine centers, as well as to organize both their inner and outer lives in accordance with Divine Law.

You can think of the 1 as energy that begins all action, who leads the way to a new direction.

The Challenge

The weak side of the 1 is lack of self-esteem, self-consciousness, and the struggle to believe in the higher self. The 1 needs to learn to believe that he or she is capable of meeting the challenges of life, to have courage, and to be determined—even when there's doubt within.

The Lesson

The lesson of the number 1 is that this person will be required to overcome the negative expressions of self to attain his or her highest success. This is most prominently seen in the opinionated 1 who offends everyone with tactless, strongly stated opinions.

The 1's aggressiveness, for example, is often a cover for its alone-ness and lack of self-confidence. The lesson for the 1 is that it must seek the right environment in which its strengths can thrive. You've got to put the 1s in with the grounded 4s, or the head-honcho 8s, rather than the timid 2s, or the idealistic dreamer 9s. Not patient themselves, 1s need to learn to surround themselves with people more patient than themselves (6s have lots of patience), who at the same time will not be afraid to stand up to the 1 when necessary.

Merlin's Notes

We've chosen Anthony Edwards' character, Mark Green, from the TV show *ER* to illustrate the essence of the 1. Mark is the capable, independent doctor who will stand up for his principles, even if it means going against his best friend, Doug Ross, or colleague Carrie Weaver. While innovative and strong, he remains the assertive leader of this infamous emergency room staff.

Archetypes, Heroes, and Stars

Take a moment to think of all the 1 people you run across every day. Are there movie stars, heroes, characters from fables, or even friends or relatives who remind you of the character traits of the 1? We've provided space for you to write down these names and traits. After you've done so, think about those people. That's the energy of the 1!

The Number 1's Archetypes, Heroes, and Stars

_____

_____

_____

_____

Higher Ground

Spiritual numerologists believe that each number represents a universal principle, which is a step in the cyclical evolution of all things. Every number vibrates to an inner meaning, and it should be no surprise that the 1 vibrates the spirit of all things, as if the 1 were the "spirit" of the organization, or something was done with the right "spirit." It's the independent spark of the 1 that's so inviting.

Juno Jordan, the "grandmother" of modern numerology, called the 1 the "intelligence to move where all is dark and void" and to make a beginning. The 1 is the number of the oneness of all, as well as symbol of the basic self, and spirit made manifest in the self.

Spiritual Essence of the 1

The number 1 symbolizes the spirit at the center of all things. It stands for "spirit." Which, we should note, is not the same as the "soul": Spirit is the masculine spiritual principle, the fire, or the spark; and soul is the feminine spiritual principle.

The French say it is "l'esprit de coeur," or "the spirit of the heart," and in America we say she is a "spirited one." The 1 is the essence of the vital, pulsating imprint of beginning energy, which penetrates all things which are about to be brought into reality. This new beginning comes complete with a spark of spirit.

Esoteric Meaning of the 1

The 1 represents the prime masculine principle, the *yang*, which in turn signifies the law of polarity. Masculine, active, forceful, courageous, and powerful are all aspects of the yang polarity.

By the Numbers

Yin and yang represent the two sides of every whole, according to Oriental tradition. Yin represents female energy, while yang represents male energy. In numerology, odd numbers are considered to be yang, while even numbers are yin.

The oriental symbol of yin and yang represents the oneness of all (the 1) through duality (the 2), creating wholeness and unity.

A Closer Look at the 1

Individualistic, innovative, and original, nothing's going to get by the 1. Understanding the 1's need to be first goes a long way toward understanding its tendency to push everyone else out of the way to get there. Similarly, understanding all the nuances of the 1 can help you learn to live with its forcefulness—whether you're the 1, or someone you love (or don't!) is.

Positive Expression and Negative Expression

Every number's got its plusses and minuses so it's up to each individual to choose what to express. "Forcefulness" can cross the fine line into "aggression," for example, or "determination" can become "dominance."

The 1 is a clear leader, but this means it can sometimes be, well, bossy. At the same time, because it's such a quick decision maker, the 1 can seem impulsive or even reckless. The 1 can also tend to cross the line from courage to bravado when it feels threatened. Much of its negative expression, in fact, arises out of fear.

It's important to remember that the 1 can't wait for anyone, so when it must wait, its negative expression can't help but rise to the surface. Understanding the 1's need to get results can help the 1 learn that pushiness and demands won't always win the day.

The Positive and Negative Expression of the Number 1

Positive	Negative
Strong	Aggressive
Capable	Know-it-all
Individualistic	Demands own way
Innovative	Impulsive
Leadership	Dominant
Self-determined	Self-interested
Strong opinions	Headstrong
Establishes solid identity	Conceited
Initiates	Wants instant gratification
Gives willingly of self	Self-centered
Strikes out alone	Defiant
Courageous	Willful
Keen perception	Impatient
Starts new ideas	Stubborn

Cosmic Vibration

The cosmic vibration is the energy a number gives off. The energy of the 1 is pushing, driving, and determined action, the universal masculine principle. The name of the cosmic game here is action, action, and more action.

> **Universal Law #4**
>
> The number 1 is the universal principle of action or activity. It affirms "I act."

Unique Abilities

The world is wide open to the 1, literally a place full of unlimited opportunity just waiting for the 1's talents and innovation. Among the 1's unique abilities are

➤ Single focused concentration.

➤ Courage to pioneer new ideas.

➤ Determination.

➤ Direction.

➤ Seeking new opportunities and expanding horizons.

➤ Goal-orientation.

➤ Having an excellent memory.

➤ Natural leadership.

Sixes and Sevens

As Lisa, with her 1 Life Path Number, will tell you, 1s tend to jump first—and then check to see if there's water in the pool. This also means that they often don't understand others' seemingly "slow" decision-making processes—even if that decision takes only a few minutes. So far, Lisa's survived relatively unscathed from her many leaps. If you're a 1, you probably know about bungee jumping into new projects, commitments, or investments.

Not a physical laborer, the 1 lives on the mental plane. The creative 1 strives for originality in its thinking and has the courage to be original—the "pioneer." Action-oriented 1s are also good in business, and can do well with finances when it's about the good of others rather than personal prestige.

The 1 is especially qualified to head up just about anything—as long as there are others there to keep the ball rolling once the 1 has got it started: 1s like to start it, but not to stick around and manage it. The 1 is a thinker and planner, quick-witted and ready to start NOW!

Relationships

Despite its ability to stand alone, the 1 can make a good friend, and often uses its sense of humor to get over the rough spots (quickly!). The 1 is also a good conversationalist, often using wit, intelligence, and insight to spice up favorite topics. But in groups, the

1 will stand apart, it doesn't really like people it doesn't know. In the end, the 1 remains a loner at heart, because the 1 considers him- or herself different from the others.

When seeking relationships, the 1 looks for attractiveness in others, as well as a strong personality, strength of character, and a self-confidence that can match its own. The 1 doesn't like boredom, anything ordinary, or anyone who demands too much of it—the 1 likes to be the person doing the demanding!

At the same time, the 1 is very sensitive to other's approval or criticism, and if it senses any disapproval, no matter how minor, it may become angry and resentful. A little praise will go a long way with a 1—but the 1 needs to remember that praise is a two-way street, not a one-way alley!

The 1 likes to be in charge, so it can appear bossy, and it needs a mate of a strong character who's warm, patient, and capable of standing on his or her own. Love and affection are very important to the 1, and in fact the 1 won't reach its potential unless it's understood at home.

The Misunderstood 1

When the 1 is not understood, it can be a great loss for both the 1 and for those in the 1's life. With a little understanding, insight can be gained into how to handle the 1.

If you've ever read one of those lists in a women's magazine of positive male traits that are interpreted as negative female traits, you already know what it's like to be a misunderstood 1.

The following list gives some examples of the different ways that the traits of the 1 can be interpreted.

The Traits of the 1

Positive Spin	Negative Spin
Tough	Aggressive
Forceful	Pushy
Determined	Willful
Knows his mind	Opinionated
Self-aware	Egotistical
Clever	Know-it-all

We could go on, of course. The point is, the 1 doesn't like to be told what to do, so leadership is a natural channel for the 1. In addition, when the 1 doesn't understand itself (or when others aren't understanding), it can become shy, vacillating, self-conscious, or even reticent to express its opinion and its more natural bold, decisive, confident self.

What's Important to the 1

Approval, activity, and ambition are of primary importance to the 1. In addition, the 1 prefers to work alone and likes to be the one exploring and trying out new things. The 1 needs to be creative and to lead and is often the trendsetter or future forecaster.

The 1 also values obedience, spirit, the new, independence, and principle. The 1 prefers cleanliness and order, and simply can't understand others' messes, as you'll find out next.

What Offends the 1

The 1 is offended by anything that seems haphazard. Carelessness, lack of logic, inattention to order—all of these are contradictory to the 1's natural need to go straight from point A to point B.

The 1 is drawn to loveliness, so is naturally offended by vulgarity or what it views as coarseness. The 1 doesn't like what it deems to be ugliness, whether in other people or in the larger world, and it tends to turn its back on such things rather than face them. Lack of artistry or creativity, indifference to order and principle, or sheer carelessness, are all offensive to the 1.

You and the Number 1

It's time to use your journal to keep track of your numbers. Use the following list to decide how important the number 1 is in your own numerology chart.

➤ I have the number 1 as my Soul Number. Destiny Number. Personality Number. Life Path Number. Maturity Number. (Circle which of your numbers are 1s.)

➤ The number 1 is ___ is not ___ present in my 5 core numbers. (Check one.)

➤ The 1 is not a strong number in my chart; therefore, I do not need further study on this number. Yes ___. No ___. (Check one.)

➤ The 1 is a strong number in my chart and I need further study on this number. Yes ___. No ___. (Check one.)

The Least You Need to Know

➤ The 1 is the number of self-determination.

➤ 1s are both original and inventive.

➤ Action and independence are key 1 words.

➤ The 1 likes to lead, but not to follow.

The Number 2: Balancing Act

If you want a patient, supportive, detailed team player, get a 2 on your staff. The 1 may stand alone, but the 2 is the number of companionship and cooperation. Gentle and sensitive, the 2 seeks the balance and harmony the 1 forgets in its hurry to meet the goal.

Sometimes, working with the 2 can be like walking on eggs—a balancing act, but once you understand both the positive and negative aspects of this number, you'll be well-equipped to build your dream team. The 2 wants to cooperate and relate.

Two Heads Are Better Than One

The saying, "Two heads are better than one" neatly sums up the basic principle of the 2: it's at its best when it's working with others. Cooperation is the hallmark of the 2, and, not surprisingly, it's the number of the diplomat and the mediator, as well as the joiner (the woman who belongs to Librarians United, the PTA, and Secretaries for Peace).

By the Numbers

The **2** gravitates toward living in peace, finding harmonious solutions, and, most important, finding sensitive partnerships. It seeks to live without discord.

While the 2's patience may sometimes look like laziness to non-2s, 2s know that "slow and steady wins the race." Whether it's through patience or its unique ability to see both sides of any situation, the 2 will be noted for its capacity for giving comfort to all.

Key Words, Colors, and Gemstones

As with every number, the 2 can be associated with certain key words, colors, and gemstones, as well as astrological, Tarot, and flower symbols. We're providing those associations here to help you learn just what the energy of the 2 represents.

The Number 2

Key Words	Colors	Gemstone	Sign
Feminine	Orange	Moonstone	Libra
Gentle	Salmon	Gold	
Unified	Peach		
Sensitive	Gold		
Receptive			
Harmonious			
Balanced			
Patient			
Cooperative			
Loving			
Relationship-conscious			
Compromise			

Easy as 1-2-3

The number 2's astrological equivalent, Libra, is represented by the scales, which weigh balance and equality.

As we discussed in the previous chapter, there are other things to consider with the number 2:

➤ **Tarot card:** High Priestess—as a symbol of heightened sensitivity, intuition, and balancing the dualities of life.

➤ **Flower:** White jasmine for amiability, white lilac for modesty, hibiscus for delicate beauty, mimosa for sensitivity, and the pansy for shyness.

The Number 2's Symbol

The symbol of the 2 is parallel lines, which represents the duality in nature:

➤ Day/night

➤ Male/female

➤ Yin/yang

➤ Positive/negative

➤ Hot/cold

➤ Life/death

➤ Youth/age

➤ Disease/health

➤ Poverty/wealth

➤ Joy/sorrow

➤ War/peace

➤ Friends/enemies

The symbol of the 2 is two parallel lines.

As you can see by the various dualities in the illustration, the 2 governs one thing in relationship to another, and this includes, of course, your relationships as well.

The Number 2's Meaning

The meaning of the 2 is to cooperate, to harmonize and merge. Following the leader of the 1, the 2 is born to follow. The 2's greatest strength is its love of peace, and it will go far to persuade others that their battles are not worth fighting.

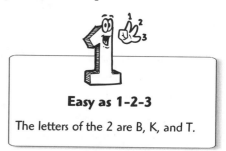

Easy as 1-2-3

The letters of the 2 are B, K, and T.

Life with the 2

As it is with all the numbers, life with the 2 can bring both blessings and challenges. The 2's knack for arbitration can make it too considerate, and its consideration of others can result in fear of rocking the boat. You'll have to talk long and hard and then listen well to get the 2 to tell you what's wrong.

The Blessing

The 2 is much blessed. It possesses a finely tuned sensitivity, and is excellent at mediation and drawing people together for peaceful resolution. The 2 takes life slowly—soothing, arbitrating, mediating, and balancing as it goes.

As the first feminine number, the 2 naturally seeks the perfect balance between any opposition, and allows seeds to gestate until they're ready to form. The 2 will let things evolve, unlike the 1, who will push to make it happen.

In addition, the 2 has an excellent sense of timing, knowing just when to bring up that delicate issue. Blessed by an innate sense of rhythm and harmony, the 2 has natural musical ability as well, and seeks a harmonic rhythm for all.

The Challenge

The main challenge for the 2 is figuring out how to be seen as cooperative without ignoring its own independence and personal needs.

A second challenge is that the 2 will always wait until the "right time"—and so sometimes misses opportunities. And finally, there's the challenge of not getting caught in indecisiveness.

Twos are so sensitive to the issue of cooperation that they often struggle against having to stand alone or having an opposing opinion. Standing alone is not a 2 strength—standing together is.

The Lesson

Because it's so sensitive, the 2 often places others first, and so the lesson for the 2 is to not be a doormat for others, to be true to itself, and to speak up with tactfulness. Until this lesson is learned, the 2 will find itself again and again in situations where this lesson presents itself, so it's important for the 2 to learn how to stand up for itself.

Merlin's Notes

The Archetype of the number 2 is the Peacemaker, and the Power Behind the Throne. We've chosen Princess Diana as the symbolic representation of the number 2 energy. As you may recall, Princess Diana used her place in the world (as the power behind the throne) to forward various causes for the greater good. We are also reminded of the television show *ER*'s character, Jeanie Boulet. She embodies the essence of the 2 energy—soft-spoken, feminine, and supportive.

Archetypes, Heroes, and Stars

Take a moment to think of all the 2-kind of people you might know. Has there been a supporting actress you recall who exemplifies this number 2 energy? Do you know someone personally who's the "power behind the throne"? Are there any unsung heroes in your town? What famous person can you think of who fits the profile of the 2? We've provided space for you to write these people down. After you've done so, think about what they mean. That's the energy of the 2!

The Number 2's Archetypes, Heroes, and Stars

_____

_____

_____

_____

Higher Ground

Spiritual numerologists believe that each number represents a universal principle, another step in the cyclical evolution of all things. Every number vibrates to an inner meaning, and it should be no surprise that the 2 vibrates to the energy of the unity of duality.

Endowed with an inner light that loves peace, the 2 has a unique insight into right and wrong—because it understands the true relationship between human and spirit.

Spiritual Essence of the 2

The spiritual essence of the number 2 is Unity. The 2 seeks unity with life's principles and laws. The 2 is the builder of all relationships, the unification of 2 opposites into a whole.

Esoteric Meaning of the 2

The 2 represents the prime feminine principle, yin, which in turn signifies the law of polarity. Feminine, gentle, receptive, sensitive, and spiritual are all aspects of the yin polarity.

Where the 1 is aggressive, the 2 is passive, waiting rather than forging ahead. Similarly, where the 1 exudes energy, the 2 is calm and patient, and, unlike the 1 who needs to be dominant, the 2 is content to stay in the background.

A Closer Look at the 2

Romantic, artistic, and considerate, the 2 can sometimes be indecisive or moody. Understanding the nuances of the 2 can help you live with your favorite 2. To truly understand the 2, it's important to consider both the positive and negative aspects of this number.

Positive Expression and Negative Expression

Every number's got its plusses and minuses, and as you study the 2's, you'll notice how much they're really two sides of the same coin. Where's the line between cooperative and conciliatory, for example? When does "good at details" spill into nit-picky?

The 2 can be adaptable—but that means it can sometimes be a pushover. The 2 can be compliant, but it can sometimes be weak as well. It's important to remember that both the positive and negative expression of the 2 arise out of the 2's great desire to live in peace with all. Understanding this need can help the 2, and you, achieve that peace without forfeiting self-respect.

The Positive and Negative Expression of the Number 2

Positive	Negative
Feminine	Passive
Gentle by nature	Subordinate
Artistic	Conciliatory
Romantic	Can suffer from depression
More mental than physical	Can be deceitful or malicious
Prone to collecting and gathering	Nit-picky
Strongly intuitive, even psychic	Critical
Loves beauty and order	Indecisive
Emotionally receptive	Fearful of what others say or think
Understanding	Timid
Good at details	Shy
Poised	Alone
Adaptable	Divided
Compliant	Weak
Loving	Self-deprecating
Persuasive	Dependent
Supports the leader	
Kind	
Considerate	
Relating	
Blending opposites	

Cosmic Vibration

It should be no surprise that the cosmic vibration, or energy pattern of the number 2, vibrates to its own unique harmony. Slower, more subtle, lit from within, the 2 wishes to merge, which makes it both receptive and supportive.

The 2 is patient and peaceful, yet has a heightened sensitivity to light, sound, and energy. The 2 finds the harmony in all things, and dwells in both beauty and things of the spirit.

Unique Abilities

Even the 2 has abilities that are uniquely its own. When your 2 energy is strong, you can be sure you're

➤ Patient.

➤ Moderate in your tastes.

➤ Rhythmical.

➤ A natural channel for cosmic energy (able to pick up those intuitive vibes).

➤ Super-sensitive.

The 2 is especially qualified to collect, sort, assemble, or put together just about anything, and they love to do these things. In addition, the 2 brings the feminine principle of receptivity and support into relationships, negotiations, and work situations.

Relationships

If you're looking for a healthy relationship, you can't do better than a 2. The 2 is an excellent partner: faithful and affectionate, as well as careful with money. Not surprisingly, 2s like their partners to demonstrate love physically, and may constantly seek reassurance and encouragement.

The 2 is cultured, charming, and gracious, and so makes a wonderful host or hostess. On the other hand, the 2 can be shy and self-conscious, and is dependent by nature. Above all, companionship is essential to 2s, and they don't stand alone well.

Sixes and Sevens

Twos can become possessive of people and/or things. They can be jealous (with their super-sensitivity, they pick up on every vibe), but they dislike arguments, and are always the first to want to kiss and make up. Still, when a 2 is hurt by criticism, it may behave as if it's mortally wound. When this happens, the 2 can become nit-picky and critical, because *its world must be in balance* for the 2 to feel right with it.

The Misunderstood 2

Poor 2! Because of its extreme sensitivity, indecisiveness, and avoidance of conflict at all costs, it can sometimes be seen as weak. Remember, too, that the 2 is dependent by nature, and therefore needs partnership to fulfill its function. In our strongly assertive, aggressive American culture, this can be mistaken for frailty, when in reality, it's the much-needed sensitivity and gentleness that saves us from ourselves.

What's Important to the 2

The 2 loves all things beautiful, and this love of aesthetic appearance means not only that they adore the nicer things in life, but that they'll create this for others as well. The 2's love of beauty allows it to grow and be in harmony with the world around it.

In addition, groups and organizations are important to the 2. There's also a desire for precision and exactness, and the 2s are often the tidy polishers of every last detail. Fastidious, orderly, neat, and clean, the 2 will see that every last detail and fact is gathered and placed into its proper place.

What Offends the 2

With its love of peace and harmony, the 2 would seem to be a number not easily offended, but in fact the opposite is true. Anything that threatens perfection and unity offends the 2, and that includes disagreements, conflict, to be hurried, sloppiness of detail, and even anything unclean.

The 2 doesn't like forcefulness or people with a lack of tact. It also shies away from directness and boastfulness, and may retreat rather than deal with someone's unreasonable demands.

You and the Number 2

It's once again time to use your journal to keep track of your numbers. Use the following list to decide how important the number 2 is in your own numerology chart.

➤ I have the number 2 as my Soul Number. Destiny Number. Personality Number. Life Path Number. Maturity Number. (Circle which of your numbers are 2s.)

➤ The number 2 is ___ is not ___ present in my 5 core numbers. (Check one.)

➤ The 2 is not a strong number in my chart; therefore, I do not need further study on this number. Yes ____. No ____. (Check one.)

➤ The 2 is a strong number in my chart and I need further study on this number. Yes ____. No ____. (Check one.)

The Least You Need to Know

➤ The 2 is the number of the team player.

➤ The 2's symbol represents duality in nature.

➤ Spiritually, the 2 is the number of unity.

➤ The 2 is a great partner and host/hostess.

The Number 3: Keeping It Light

After the leadership of the 1 and the sensitivity of the 2, it's time for a little fun, and the 3 is just the number for the job. We like to think of the 3 as the cheerleader of numerology: bubbly, enthusiastic, and full of creative energy.

Quick and clever, the 3 can bring light humor to any situation, which makes 3s fun to be around and an inspiration to all. In fact, the optimism of the 3 can be contagious—are you ready?

"I Came upon a Child of God ..."

Forever young, no number brings more joy than the 3. This is the number of creative self-expression, of the optimistic happy spirit, of enthusiasm and imagination. Juno Jordan, in her book, *The Romance in Your Name,* called the 3 a "child of God," because it's gifted with a seemingly magical power to bring that which has never been before into being. It's the creative power of the 3.

The numbers 1 through 9 divide into groups of kindred numbers. These groups are called concords, and the 3 belongs to the concord of 3-6-9, where the artistic, inspirational, and spiritual are naturally its realm. All three of these numbers are considered emotional in nature, but the 3 is the most emotional of them, probably because of its emotive, dramatic flair.

By the Numbers

The **3** is the number of creativity and joyful self-expression.

Lucky in love, lucky in money, lucky in the opportunities life seems to offer, the 3 comes by its enthusiasm naturally. With a 3 around, a party will never be dull—and the food, wine, and decorations will always be the best, too.

Key Words, Colors, and Gemstones

In the following table you'll find the key words, colors, and gemstone for the number 3. We've also given its astrological and Tarot card associations and even some flowers.

The Number 3

Key Words	Color	Gemstone	Sign
Self-expression	Yellow	Topaz	Leo
Joy bringer			
Creative			
Enthusiastic			
Imaginative			
Inspirational			
Gift of words			
Optimism			
Childlike			
Happy spirit			

Easy as 1–2–3

Leo, the astrological equivalent for the number 3, has the same creative, fun-loving spirit and desire to shine its charm upon the world.

Also important to consider are:

➤ **Tarot card:** The Empress—the ultimate creative force.

➤ **Flowers:** Yellow jasmine for happiness and elegance, larkspur for lightness and levity, lily of the valley for the return of happiness.

The Number 3's Symbol

The symbol of the 3 is that three-sided figure, the triangle. The triangle adds a third dimension, a fulcrum, to the balance of the 2, and so a much-needed middle between the beginning and the end.

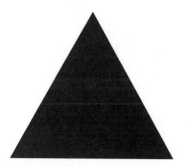

The symbol of the 3 is a triangle.

In addition, the 3 is the number of the eternal triangle, which means it will probably have more than one interest—in both love and life!

The Number 3's Meaning

The 3 represents the creative principle, as well as a variety of trinities, such as

➤ Past, present, future.

➤ Mother, father, child.

➤ Birth, life, death.

The creative principle of the 3 governs both the act of creation and the act of procreation, which translates to both spiritual and sexual creative power.

Easy as 1-2-3

The letters of the 3 are C , L, and U. Note that these letters together spell L-U-C, not surprising for this luckiest of numbers!

Life with the 3

As it is with all the numbers, life with the 3 can bring both blessings and challenges. The 3 is known for its tendency toward faddishness and its intoxicating love of luxury. It may be less well-known for its self-centeredness and laziness.

Still, nothing keeps this happy number down for long, as you'll see from its blessings.

The Blessing

Three (3) is a happy spirit, blessed with humor, optimism, and enthusiasm for life—after all, it's a joyful energy.

The 3 is lucky in both money and opportunity; so lucky, in fact, that it takes its luck for granted. The 3 will never wonder where its next meal, next dollar, or next job is coming from. When it needs something, it will be there.

Blessed with an uncanny knack for being in the right place at the right time, luck favors the 3 in everything.

The Challenge

There are several challenges for the 3, mainly to find appropriate channels for its creativity, enthusiasm, and exuberance. The 3 is also challenged to keep the spirit of the inner child alive, and so of course needs playful, positive relationships and environments.

The biggest challenge for the 3 by far is to learn to communicate straight from the heart. The 3 needs to find the words to match the emotions, to find the courage to utter the words, and to capture the feelings with words.

The Lesson

The lesson for the 3 is to stay in the moment and not scatter its energy. The 3 must live in joy in order to uplift and inspire others. In addition, the 3 must learn that laughter and humor are healing agents.

Merlin's Notes

We've chosen two women to represent the 3 character: Sarah Ferguson (you may know her as "Fergie"), past Duchess of York and ex-wife of the royal Prince Andrew; and the Academy Award-winning Gwyneth Paltrow (you may remember her from the movie, *Shakespeare in Love*). Both of these women represent the joy and happiness the 3 brings to all around them. It's for their effervescence, openness, and enthusiasm that we call these women the essence of the number 3. Picture their smiles: don't they just make you want to smile, too? Also, Dr. Carter of the television show *ER* embodies the humor, enthusiasm, and warmth of the 3. In addition, he represents the core element of the 3: using words to cut to the heart and feeling of a situation.

Archetypes, Heroes, and Stars

Take a moment to think of all the 3-kind of people you can think of. Are there other movie stars who remind you of the 3? How about characters from fables or tales—or from your own life? We've provided space for you to write down these characters. After you've done so, think about what they mean. That's the energy of the 3!

The Number 3 Archetypes, Heroes, and Stars

_____

_____

_____

_____

Higher Ground

Spiritual numerologists believe that each number represents a universal principle, another step in the cyclical evolution of all things. Every number vibrates to an inner meaning, and it should be no surprise that the 3 vibrates to the energy of creativity.

As Juno Jordan put it, "The number 3 dreams—visualizes in its mind's eye—speaks the word and dreams come true." The 3 is the number of imagination made concrete, of visions made real.

Spiritual Essence of the 3

The spiritual essence of the 3 is bringing that which has never been into being, the power of creativity in all its forms. The essence of the 3 is a natural sweetness, an inner beauty, and a bubbling enthusiasm that creates joy for all to share.

Esoteric Meaning of the 3

To Pythagoras, the 3 represented the meaning of excellence, because not only did it have a beginning, but a middle and an end as well.

The 3 is often used as a magical aspect in fairy tales, such as

➤ 3 wishes.

➤ 3 riddles.

➤ 3 guesses.

➤ 3 chances.

➤ 3 doors.

A Closer Look at the 3

Creative, exuberant, expansive, and lighthearted as it is, still, the 3 does have its darker side—although it's not nearly so dark as some other numbers'. Understanding the nuances of the 3 can help you to understand the fine lines between its positive and negative expressions and keep everything light and happy.

Positive Expression and Negative Expression

Even the 3 has its pluses and minuses, so its expansive nature can lead to scattered energy, its sociability to nonstop chatter, and its childlike playfulness to childishness.

Other numbers may find the 3 just too lighthearted—all play and no work (to turn an aphorism on its head). Playful 3 may never get around to the work in fact—but it also won't understand what all the fuss is about.

The Positive and Negative Expression of the Number 3

Positive	Negative
Expressive	Prone to exaggeration
Imaginative	Gossipy
Expresses emotions	Gets caught up in fads and fantasies
Gift of words	Selfish
Artistic	Self-centered
Optimistic	Talks too much—nonstop chatter
Joyful	Scattered energy
Humorous	Untidy, cluttered
Lighthearted	Moodiness
Inspirational	Critical
Expansive	Becomes negative
Loves creativity	Childish
Good communicator	Has delusions of grandeur
Vitality	Lazy
Childlike playfulness	Too outspoken
Fun	Insincere
Witty	Gushy
Humorous	Frivolous
Sociable	Wasteful
Brilliant—as in shines brightly	Impractical

Cosmic Vibration

The vibrational energy of the 3 is excitable, enthusiastic, and exuberant. Intensely creative, the 3 can sometimes be hyper, insisting on everything immediately.

The 3 can be inspirational with its insights and feeling, and, while its strength is to be creative and incubate ideas, it depends on other numbers to put those ideas into form.

Flooded with exuberance, bubbling with joy, the 3 can be a very intense energy when there's no appropriate channel for this effervescent energy. In fact, when the 3 has no outlet for its creative, engaging energy, it becomes chaotic, disorganized, involved in trivial matters, or depressed.

Unique Abilities

The 3 is clever, learns quickly, and has a keen mind. The 3 has the unique ability to bring in levity or a light note, no matter how heavy the occasion.

Fun, playful, touched by the fire of enthusiasm, and uniquely creative, the 3 is a joy to be around.

The 3 makes a good speaker and may have dramatic ability. It also has a gift with words and is often a wordsmith.

Relationships

The 3 dislikes being in subordinate positions and wants to be one jump ahead of everyone else. It can be shrewd, original, observant, and a hard worker, and this combo is what allows the 3 to rise in the world. Note, however, that the 3 can also have a sharp tongue (after all, its forte is expressing itself!).

In relationships, 3s are warm, generous, impulsive, and loyal. They're extremely good company—witty, entertaining, and fun to be with. The talent to be a pleasing hostess or host, entertaining, a good conversationalist, and colorful with a touch of drama, all come together to make the 3's life exciting and lively.

As we've suggested, the 3 is full of feeling, and an ever-flowing exuberance floods this person. The 3 has a strong need to create and beautify, and will do best where there is a channel for this expression.

In a narrow or limited field of activity, especially where the imagination is restricted, or where the 3 is required to be practical on a constant basis, the spirit of the 3 will be damaged and lead to much unhappiness.

Sixes and Sevens

Once a 3 has decided a relationship is over, that's it. The 3 will end it and not look back.

By way of example, Kay's daughter has a 3 Soul Number and a 3 Personality—she's a 3 through and through, you might say. Kay says, "I always thought she needed to be drugged or something to get her emotions under control. She's very expressive and dramatic, to say the least." She has pursued drama, dance, music, and is very creative. She goes all out to decorate for a dinner party—complete with the hand-designed napkin holders and centerpieces that are to die for.

Now in her mid 20s, she owns her own business doing faux finish painting. "She's the most fun person to be with of anyone I know—except when she's in a mood. She's just so '3'!" By the way, she just happens to be a Sagittarius as well.

The 3 has a drive, an urge, an insatiable thirst to add beauty, feeling, and emotion to all it does. The 3 wants to be popular, and in fact needs to feel loved to allow its spontaneous, creative energy to emerge. While it is flirtatious, the 3 also has a deep capacity to give and receive both love and affection.

Merlin's Notes

The 3 wants the best life has to offer, and thinks nothing of what others might call "frivolous expenses," such as designer sunglasses, lobster or filet minion at the chicest restaurant in town, or a case of that classic wine (just for the investment, of course). In fact, the 3 looks extravagant to others; but to the 3, it's about the joy of living and the flair for life, and the 3 will pour all of its considerable energy into attaining this kind of life.

Luckily, the 3 has an attraction for money—in fact, it's considered the luckiest number of all. While the 3 isn't a laborer, it does possess the talent and skills to attain its desires without hard work. In fact, the 3's love of ease, luxury, pleasure, and social ambitions means it may not always use its abundant creative energy in constructive, productive ways.

The 3 has an enthusiastic way of talking, is very articulate, and through its enthusiasm, inspires others to help or take part in just about anything. When used negatively, the 3 can use that same energy to point out its displeasure, and don't be surprised if it is delivered dramatically!

More Relationships

Naturally playful and spontaneous, as a partner, the 3 is the most fun person imaginable. Still, you can count on those emotions to surface, and not in a predictable pattern. In fact, the 3 can be moody, emotive, euphoric—or anything in between. After all, this number is the pulse of life itself, so the current runs strong and full. In fact, there are those (like the 4) who will want to suppress this energy.

The 3 is the number of the eternal triangle, so watch out! It will more than likely have more than one interest—and more than one admirer. Not surprisingly, the 3 can be flirtatious, too. It's also very conscious of what's said, both to the 3 and about the 3.

Because 3s have vivid imaginations, for children with 3s in their core numbers, it's important they not have their imaginations suppressed or be told of weaknesses, unlovely features, or handicaps. This helps to keep those active imaginations focused on the positive. In fact, parents of 3s are well advised to protect this 3 spirit. After all, it's the pulse of life.

The Misunderstood 3

Playful 3 may be criticized for messiness, but it's always a creative mess. Other numbers may look down on the 3 for its childlike spirit and playfulness, especially by the more serious 4, introverted 7, or the business-minded 8.

What's Important to the 3

Nothing's more important to the 3 than to be free to use its imagination to beautify and create. Whether its energy is used to make hand-crafted Valentines, have a stimulating conversation, or make an inlaid tile fire pit, the 3 needs to express itself.

What Offends the 3

Eternal optimist that it is, the 3 doesn't necessarily get offended, but it can have its childlike spirit dampened. Among the attitudes that can cause this are

➤ Criticism.

➤ Judgmentalism.

➤ Uncreative approach or lack of appreciation of the creative effort.

➤ Diminishment of spontaneity, creative drive, or enthusiastic expression.

You and the Number 3

It's time to use your journal to keep track of your numbers. Use the following list to decide how important the number 3 is in your own numerology chart.

➤ I have the number 3 as my Soul Number. Destiny Number. Personality Number. Life Path Number. Maturity Number. (Circle which of your numbers are 3s.)

➤ The number 3 is ___ is not ___ present in my chart. (Check one.)

➤ The 3 is not a strong number in my chart; therefore, I do not need further study on this number. Yes ____. No ____. (Check one.)

➤ The 3 is a strong number in my chart and I need further study on this number. Yes ____. No ____. (Check one.)

The Least You Need to Know

➤ The 3 is the number of joy and creativity.

➤ The 3's symbol is the triangle.

➤ The 3 is witty and humorous.

➤ The 3 loves both parties and the finer things in life.

The Number 4: A Solid Foundation

The solid, stable 4 understands the value of good, honest labor, and isn't afraid to do what it takes to get the job done. Sober-minded and respectable, you can think of the 4 as the "grownup" of the numbers.

Someone's got to be disciplined and dedicated, and the 4 handles these tasks like the solid character it is. You can depend on the 4, and if you're a 4, "Dependability" may well be your middle name.

Stability Matters

Where the 3 may have had "fun, fun, fun 'til her Daddy took the T-bird away," the 4 is Daddy personified—serious and cautious. The 4 is steeped in tradition, practical, and respectable, a manager you can rely on, providing a solid foundation on which you can always stand.

Stability matters to the 4, so it can't understand others' more frivolous ways. A 4 puts in a hard day's work, stays between the lines (all four of them), and respects both rules and convention. Sober and true, the 4 is practicality personified.

The 4 is also efficient and well-organized, which is another aspect of its discipline and concentration. Trustworthy, honest, straightforward, and, well, square, the 4 is an Eagle Scout all grown up.

Key Words, Colors, and Gemstones

As with all of the numbers, we'd like to introduce you to the 4 by showing some of its key word, color, and gemstone equivalents, as well as astrological, Tarot, and flower associations. We hope these will help you understand the energy of the 4.

The Number 4

Key Words	Color	Gemstones	Sign
Planner	Green	Jade, emerald	Taurus
Solid			
Stable			
Traditional			
Practical			
Hard work			
Order			
Conventional			
Cautious			
Patriotic			
Respectable			
Builder			
Construct			
Manage			
Form			
Security			

Also important to consider are:

➤ **Tarot Card:** The Emperor.
➤ **Flowers:** Bluebell for constancy, nasturtium for patriotism.

The Number 4's Symbol

The symbol of the number 4, not surprisingly, is the square. Equal sides of equal lengths, strong, solid, and true, the square and the 4 go hand in hand.

The symbol of the 4 is the square.

The Number 4's Meaning

The 4 represents the principle that creates form and foundation for plans, dreams, ideas, patterns, philosophies, thoughts, and feelings, and gives form to things, as well as stabilizes and structures them.

Universally, we see the 4 as

➤ 4 seasons: spring, summer, autumn, winter.

➤ 4 directions: north, south, east, west.

➤ 4 elements: fire, earth, sir, water.

➤ 4 aspects of self: physical, mental, spiritual, emotional.

➤ 4 human functions: sensation, feeling, logical thought, intuition (these are the basis of the Myers-Briggs Personality Inventory).

➤ 4 aspects of matter: mineral, gaseous, animal, vegetable.

Note that all of these foursomes serve to bring form and structure to their respective group—that's what the 4 is all about.

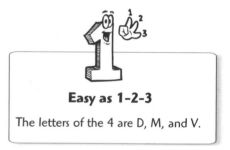

Easy as 1–2–3

The letters of the 4 are D, M, and V.

Life with the 4

As it is with all the numbers, life with the 4 can bring both blessings and challenges. The 4's discipline, for example, can cross over into rigidity, while its knack for organization can translate into control.

The Blessing

The 4 has endurance, dedication, and discipline, and so, can naturally bring order to chaos. It also has the know-how to manage a business or a home and create order in its life—or, for that matter, in anyone else's.

The Challenge

The challenge for the 4 is to not be rigid but resilient, to see the need for structure but not be inflexible. Its best use is to help form something as a foundation for life, rather than a box that restricts growth. In addition, it's always a challenge for the 4 to not be controlling (after all, things must fit into the plan).

The Lesson

The lesson for the 4 is to be flexible, and not be so inflexible that it forces all life into a box, hence restricting growth for itself and those around it.

Fours tend to see life as restricted and narrow because they follow the rules and are bound by the policy, and so think that the plan is cast in cement. They forget that life in between the narrow lines, or living in the rut, is a rut of their own making. Hence, they're presented with the lesson over and over: Look outside the box; get out of the rut, take a risk, take a chance, and be creative with your options.

Those of us who don't have 4 as a core number can't understand this kind of dogged adherence to doing things. Besides being rigid, the 4 is stubborn as well, so most often will argue that it's not being inflexible. Most of the rest of us will give up and leave the 4 to its fixed ways, which is precisely why the 4 will remain stuck—no one sticks around to help the 4 see a less rigid way of doing things. In fact, you've got to be a 4 yourself to wade through the stubbornness and narrow thinking that can be so much a part of the 4!

Merlin's Notes

Again drawing from the TV show *ER*, Dr. Carrie Weaver is our candidate for the archetypal 4: controlling, rigid about the rules, traditional, and following hospital policy even if she offends her friends and colleagues. Typical 4 that she is, Carrie can't seem to see beyond the rules and regulations. Film examples of archetypal 4s include "all work and no play" characters such as Aidan Quinn's character in *Legends of the Fall* and the ship designer in *Titanic*, while you'll find some good literary samples in Larry McMurtry's Captain Woodrow Call and Tony Hillerman's Lt. Leaphorn.

Archetypes, Heroes, and Stars

Do you know someone who's a practical manager? Someone who's always on time, knows where you left your keys (even when you don't), keeps the gas tank above one-quarter full, files things not only alphabetically but promptly, and can patiently and efficiently add up that column of numbers? If so, you know a 4. Of course, if we've just described you, chances are, you *are* a 4!

Now, take a moment to think of all the 4-type people you know. Are there movie stars or characters from stories and fables (or from your own life) who embody the characteristics of the 4? We've provided space for you to write those names and traits down. After you've done so, think about what they mean. That's the energy of the 4!

The Number 4 Archetypes, Heroes, and Stars

_____

_____

_____

_____

Higher Ground

Spiritual numerologists believe that each number represents a universal principle, another step in the cyclical evolution of all things. Every number vibrates to an inner meaning, and it should be no surprise that the 4 vibrates to the energy of spirit made manifest into matter, or, putting things into law, system, and order.

Juno Jordan, the grandmother of modern numerology, says the 4 is "the foundation upon which all things stand to sustain life." The 4 is the number of forms, and brings everything down to Earth.

Spiritual Essence of the 4

The essence of the 4, spiritually, is the point at which spirit is brought into matter, and the spirit of the 1 and the creative expression of the 3 finally find form in the 4.

Esoteric Meaning of the 4

The 4 orders time and space into practical use for human living. It's the idea that things that were only a part of the realm of light (such as spirit and creativity) move into physical form. The 4 is a heavier, more dense form of energy, which allows one to feel grounded.

A Closer Look at the 4

Steady, calm, enduring, and tenacious, the 4 can sometimes seem, to put it bluntly, awfully dull. Does "all work and no play" make 4 a dullard? Let's take at look at the positive and negative expressions of the 4, and see where its strengths—and weaknesses—lie.

Positive Expression and Negative Expression

Every number's got its plusses and minuses, and for the 4, it's no laughing matter. That's because the 4 is the most serious of the numbers, which can sometimes make the 4 seem downright boring.

Sure, the 4 can be a calm in a storm, and its determination has saved more than one flightier sort, but it can also be stubborn and stern. Understanding its need for order and security can help the 4 keep from becoming entirely without joy, or worse, becoming suspicious and insecure.

The Positive and Negative Expression of the Number 4

Positive	Negative
Steady	Boring
Calm	Slow
Practical	Stubborn
Industrious	Severe depression
Enduring	Joyless
Application	Gloomy
Methodical	Suspicious
Determination	Repressive
Serious	Insecure
Protective	Fixed opinions of right and wrong
Tenacious	
Secure	

Cosmic Vibration

The cosmic vibration, or energy pattern, of the 4 is that it arranges, constructs, builds, maintains, carries out, systematizes, creates order, shapes, molds, plans, and manages—all with a calm, steady hand.

Unique Abilities

Well-organized, the 4 can always see the best ways to set up systems. In addition, the 4 keeps efficient systems, whether it's an appointment book, calendar, road map, or bookkeeping method. The 4 has great discipline, stamina, and "stick-to-it-iveness," as well as the gift of concentration.

Relationships

The 4 can be considered rather dull, but in fact, what we have here is a down-to-earth, respectable, trustworthy, precise person who takes life seriously. The 4 can be depended on to deal with problems systematically, work hard, and manage a situation—any situation—quite well.

Not surprisingly, 4s are devoted, thoughtful, faithful, and considerate partners. They're also home lovers, who manage financial affairs well, and usually don't live beyond their means. A 4 can always be counted on to be reliable, and, yes, predictable. A nice 4 bonus is that it always cleans up its own messes!

If you let the 4 set up systems such as organizing those closets, the 4 will not only order it, it will label and alphabetize it, too! In fact, the entire 4 home will be neat and tidy, with boxes and containers for everything.

The 4 has been called both the "salt of the earth" and the "pillar of the community" because it's the backbone of any organization, family, or marriage. You can count on your 4 to be reliable, consistent, and punctual, and to manage the task at hand.

The 4 will tend to see things in a common-sense manner. Born to build, the 4 loves to create permanent and lasting things, whether it's a marriage, a system, a job position, or building a company from the ground up. Note, however, that the 4 is not an originator. It needs and depends on others, such as the 1, the 3, and the 8, for inspiration.

The 4 won't get carried away with emotion or imagination; we'll just leave that to the 3. The 4 does, however, have high standards of honesty and courage, and succeeds in what it does through hard knocks and responsibility.

The 4 will find it can't work for selfish purposes, so it can always be called upon to take care of others' stuff—especially if something is left unfinished. At the same time, the 4 manages its own affairs with thrift and practical judgment, but needs to evaluate its own self-worth. That's because the 4 usually undervalues the work that it does.

Even though the 4 is the workhorse of the numbers, don't confuse hard work for security. The 4 has a high need for security—in business, in marriage, and in the right to be itself. With its excellent ability to evaluate value and worth (not

Sixes and Sevens

The 4 can get so caught up in doing things or managing details that it can become rigid. Sometimes the 4 can't see the forest for the trees, gets stuck in a rut, and becomes just plain boring. In fact, the 4 can sometimes get so stuck and rigid that a rule becomes cast in stone. When this happens, the 4 can make life harder than it need be—for both themselves and those around them. Still, the serious 4 will always dig in, head down, and methodically work on the project until it's finished.

Easy as 1-2-3

The 4 always needs something to build, construct, fix, mend, or arrange, and is able to conform to systems and establish order. For all these reasons, the 4 makes a good partner. Besides, 4s are neat and tidy (it's that need to make order!).

just its own), as well as to estimate and appraise, the 4 seeks recognition as a useful, efficient partner.

Fundamentally, the 4 is serious and conscientious, has strong opinions about right and wrong, likes to plan, and looks forward to results. At the same time, the 4 doesn't like to be "ordered" or "told" what to do, but rather has the need to feel in control.

The 4 is willing to do the hard work with family, in-laws, business tasks, and daily living, as long as it feels it's respected, and its own rights are honored.

The 4 doesn't like to be hurried, and moves slowly and methodically. In fact, the 4 needs to work to quicken its thinking, and needs to experience action to learn adaptability (from the 5, of course).

The Misunderstood 4

Like Carrie Weaver of *ER*, a 4 person is often misunderstood in its need to follow the rules, create order, and do what's right. Even when the situation calls for bending of the rules, out of fear of being in the wrong, or feeling insecure, the 4 will remain rigid, failing to see up over the edges of its rut.

The 4 often makes things harder than they need to be. The 2, 6, and 8 will have more tolerance for what the 4 is trying to do—it's the odd numbers (such as the 5 that Doug Ross represents) that have problems with the 4—they think the 4 is odd.

The 4 might deviate from the original game plan if it feels secure, can see an alternative plan, and isn't told to "lighten up." "Might," we said; the 4 *might*.

What's Important to the 4

Above all, the 4 values order and discipline. A MAN, A PLAN, A CANAL, PANAMA (which, incidentally, with 4-like efficiency, reads the same forward and backward) could be said about a 4.

The 4 values efficiency, whether it's with time or money, and will always have the most practical approach to a situation.

What Offends the 4

It should come as no surprise that efficient 4 is offended by

➤ Chaos.

➤ Wastefulness.

➤ Inefficiency.

➤ Goofing around.

➤ Not taking the job seriously.

If the 4 is standing in a long check-out line, it will wonder why they don't open another register. If it sees someone taking four steps when he or she could have taken two, number 4 will point out to the person how many steps were wasted. The 4s are the efficiency experts of the world—we're lucky to have them around, even if they can be trying!

You and the Number 4

It's time to use your journal to keep track of your numbers. Use the following to note the 4s in your own numerology chart.

➤ I have the number 4 as my Soul Number. Destiny Number. Personality Number. Life Path Number. Maturity Number. (Circle which of your numbers are 4s.)

➤ The number 4 is ___ is not ___ present in my chart. (Check one.)

➤ The 4 is not a strong number in my chart; therefore, I do not need further study on this number. Yes ___. No ___. (Check one.)

➤ The 4 is a strong number in my chart and I need further study on this number. Yes ___. No ___. (Check one.)

The Least You Need to Know

➤ The 4 is the number of stability.

➤ The 4 has a strong respect for tradition.

➤ A builder of foundations, the 4 believes in security.

➤ No number is more reliable and true than a 4.

The Number 5: You Shall Adapt!

When it comes to the number 5, change is the name of the game. Sure, change brings the excitement of discovering the new and the unexplored, but it also requires risk and challenge.

"Variety is the spice of life" might be the 5's motto—but if you've got any 5s in your core numbers, you already know that things are seldom dull.

Everybody Changes

All things in life change and the life of the 5 is no exception. Those who carry the number 5 in the Life Path, Destiny, Soul, Personality, Maturity, or Birthday position will be intimate with the notion of change—in fact, it's probably been the constant in their lives. Change brings with it the opportunity for adventure, excitement, stimulation, and curious exploration—and these are all trademarks of the number 5.

By the Numbers

The **5** is the number of change and exploration. Nothing stays the same for long with the 5 around.

Magnetic, risk-taking 5s will make sure to stir up the action if things seem to be getting a little dull, and, not surprisingly, you can count on the 5 to be the life of the party—so long as he or she sticks around.

Key Words, Colors, and Gemstones

Like every number, the 5 has some key words, colors, and gemstones to help you remember its unique qualities. Plus, it's got the astrological sign of Gemini, so you know that "changeable" will be a 5's middle name.

The Number 5

Key Words	Color	Gems	Sign
Freedom-loving	Turquoise	Aquamarine	Gemini
Change		Turquoise	
Risk-taking			
Variety			
Progressive			
Resourceful			
Magnetic			
Forever young			
Quick-thinking			
Curious			
Promotion and sales			
Investigative			
Publication			
Communication			
Generalist			
Free spirit			
Rebel			
Sensual			
Unconventional			

Also important to consider are:

➤ **Tarot Card:** The Hierophant—rebelling against the status quo.

➤ **Astrological Equivalent:** Gemini—communicative, interactive, curious, adaptable, uses the mind to explore options.

➤ **Flowers:** Ranunculus for radiant charms, gardenia for sensuality.

The Number 5's Symbol

The symbol of the 5 is the pentagram, such as in the five-pointed star. The 5 also is symbolically represented by the hand, with its five fingers.

The 5 is also the symbol for humanity, as there are five human senses, and, in fact, when a human figure is stretched out, a line joining the head to the arms and legs forms a pentagram.

Easy as 1-2-3

Changeable Gemini and the number 5 are "two of a kind"—one thing you can expect for certain with either is to expect the unexpected.

The symbol of the 5 is the pentagram.

The Number 5's Meaning

The 5 is the number of chance and change, and it rules the physical and any kind of movement. This number is almost always linked with sensuality and the five senses, and so is about immersing oneself in the pleasures of the physical world as a means of exploration, discovery, and free will.

The lesson that goes with this meaning is to not lose oneself overindulging in these pleasures. The 5 seeks freedom and adventure, craving to know what's out there, who's got it, and who doesn't, and so, of course, the 5 is also the number of the progressive minded.

Easy as 1-2-3

The letters of the 5 are E (5), N (1 + 4 = 5), and W (2 + 3 = 5). Not surprisingly, these letters spell "new."

Life with the 5

Five folks are adventurers who love to try anything new. Not surprisingly, travel is especially exciting to the 5, whether it's meeting new people, visiting different cultures, or just living in different surroundings. The 5 knows how to adapt. Fives are people of many talents—clever, resilient, and creative. In fact, it's their quick thinking and resourcefulness that's particular to the number 5.

In business, a 5 is an excellent asset because he or she is a rapid thinker, has a fertile mind and a gift with words, and possesses a keen perception of public opinion and need. The 5 can also administrate or head up a company, not because the 5 has true executive ability, but because he or she is good at getting others to act. No matter what the business, the 5 loves to gather information, juggle multiple tasks, and be in the heart of the action.

Fives are naturals in advertising, marketing, networking, sales, and promoting an individual's talent. They can sell anything to anyone because they're "good talkers." They're also good at giving speeches, like to help others, are full of ideas for improvement, and like to use their multi-talented bags of tricks to show people how to do things.

Sixes and Sevens

Because this free spirit is often attracted to the glitz and the multiple opportunities it finds in the world, the 5 can fail to incorporate the traits that give structure to his or her life: stability, dependability, and permanence. (Where is that 4 when you need it?)

Easy as 1-2-3

Fives are lucky with future events, often getting that lucky break because they're not afraid to take a chance, gamble on the future, or take a risk—unlike the perfectly planned, security-conscious 4.

Still, too many changes, too many interests, or too much freedom can bring chaos to the life of the 5. In fact, chaos is always hovering around the 5 anyway. Whether it stems from a lack of discipline or an inability to apply his or her talents to anything substantial, it usually brings on the downside of the 5—uncertainty, unreliable income, possible failure, and loss.

The 5 loves to travel, because movement is its operative principle. Of course, the 5 also loves physical activity of any kind (5's the aerobic number), and prefers fast-paced living so it can use its quick, creative mind. Needless to say, monotony is death to a 5 and impatience is its Achilles' heel.

The Blessing

Fives are blessed with pep, energy, speed, enthusiasm, wit, and excellent powers of observation. They have a magnetism that stems from their enthusiastic, curious response to life and the people in it. People are just drawn to the 5, and it's thought that a 5 is forever young for these qualities.

The Challenge

The challenge for the 5 is to not get lost in physical desires or scatter his or her potential and end up with nothing to show for the 5's many talents. The 5 person must learn to focus and make a meaningful existence by using freedom in a productive manner.

The Lesson

The main lesson for the 5 is the constructive use of freedom, and it needs to learn to do things in moderation. The 5 also needs to learn from others' mistakes so that the 5 doesn't have to try everything for him- or herself. Basically, this number has come to learn how to stick to it, to establish structure, and to create stability, so that the 5 can truly enjoy the freedom he or she so desperately desires.

The Lingo

Above all, 5s love freedom and are curious. Let's look at the nature of these two words more closely to see what the lingo of the 5 has to say about these people.

Curious

➤ Unafraid of new experiences, lands, people, languages

➤ Intellectually curious

➤ Voracious reader

➤ Wants to be up on trends—to be "in the know"

Freedom loving

➤ Abhors dullness and routine

➤ Desires freedom of thought and action

➤ Seeks freedom of worship—looking to the unconventional, unrestricted expression of spirituality

➤ "Don't make me commit" attitude about relationships

➤ Supports the law of change

➤ Can change partners often in looking for "greener grass"

Archetypes, Heroes, and Stars

The 5 is the wanderer, promoter, change agent, and wheeler-dealer of numerology, and so its archetypes are all those bad-boy film stars from James Dean to Brad Pitt. Another good example of a 5 is the recurring character of Q on *Star Trek: The Next Generation*. This omnipotent being likes nothing better than to materialize into Captain Picard's life and promote change for all aboard the *Enterprise*.

Merlin's Notes

Doug Ross of *ER* exemplifies the number 5 in his constant struggle with commitment and authority, as well as his difficulty in following the rules. While we adore his free-spirited approach in trying to help his patients, we can see where he gets himself into trouble. Always the rebel, Doug and the 5 personality will seek alternative ways to live in the world of rules, policy, and commitment. As avid *ER* viewers know, Doug's bucking of authority finally got him in too much trouble—and he's now moved on to greener pastures, off the series!

Higher Ground

The 5, the midpoint in the numbers 1 through 9, is the symbol of the freedom to change, represents the vitality and energy of life itself, and is the point of transition in life. As the pivotal point between the 1 and the 9, the 5 allows change to take place in the original idea established by the 1, the beginning.

Sixes and Sevens

Even though a 5 may lean toward speculative business endeavors, this is not necessarily a good thing for the 5 due to the 5's gullible nature, attraction to the fast-paced action, and innate love of change. A person with a Destiny 5, a Life Path 5, or a 5 Pinnacle, more often than not, will have uncertain finances, unstable income, and more change on the way.

Spiritual Essence of the 5

The essence of the 5 is the spirit of change, and it's meant to help us all bring about change, learn to live without fear, take risks, and break up old patterns. It should come as no surprise that we all experience the 5 at some point in our lives, either through one of the 5 core numbers, or through the Personal Year Number.

Esoteric Meaning of the 5

The 5 causes each human life to mirror the laws of nature, to allow for change and adaptability in life. The energy of forward movement is what drives the number 5. Remember, too, that the 5 is the symbol of the five-pointed star, which is said to be the symbol of humankind.

A Closer Look at the 5

Fives are drawn to metaphysics, the occult, and the philosophical as methods of investigating the mystery of life. These are, after all, just one more way to satisfy the

5's curiosity. At the same time, however, the 5 can be introverted and private about these matters in spite of his or her worldly interests.

Fives are happiest when they feel they're being useful through promotion of an individual or issues of public welfare.

Fives are interested in all the latest health tips, diets, psychological programs for improving emotional well-being, as well as yoga or meditation groups. The 5 needs to be up on the latest trend, thinking, or avant-garde approach.

If 5 is your Destiny Number, you may find yourself in lines of business that involve speculation, money-making schemes, or any line of work that is designed to get quick results. Five is the gambler at heart—the one who's willing to take risks and shortcuts.

Positive Expression and Negative Expression

Adventurous, versatile, adaptable, the 5 can sometimes become restless or too hasty in his or her decisions. In addition, because it's a high-spirited number, the 5 may possess a bad temper, speak sharply or out of place, or be just plain discontented if the going gets dull.

Understanding the 5's need for adventure and change can help keep the 5's negative expression from becoming dominant. After all, remember, 5s are nothing if not versatile.

The Positive and Negative Expression of the Number 5

Positive	Negative
Adventurous	Conceited
Excellent traveler	Lustful
Adaptable	Unstable
Spirited	Restless
Versatile	Discontent
Good at sales	Sharp speech
Curious	Temper flares
Progressive minded	Too many irons in the fire
Deals with change easily	Hasty
Energetic	Impatient
Attracts the opposite sex	Impulsive
Good communicator	Lacks application
	Moody
	Addicted

Cosmic Vibration

The cosmic energy pattern of the 5 is that it frees up, changes, adapts, quickens, energizes, expands, and creates.

Unique Abilities

The 5 has the unique ability to find things out and can uncover, investigate, and gather information exceptionally well, due to the 5's curious nature.

A 5 person is multi-talented, and this number is often called the "Jack (or Jill) of all trades." With all these talents, the 5 will experience freedom with the abundance of opportunities this number brings. Needless to say, life can be very exciting with a 5.

Easy as 1-2-3

The 5 would make a great private eye or FBI agent—except the 5's just not secretive enough. We'll leave the FBI to the number 7—the private one.

Relationships

Fives are affectionate and loving, loyal and sympathetic. The 5 has more extremes of temperament than any of the other numbers (yes, even more than the 3). This is due to the 5's restless nature, and the constant ups and downs of his or her life.

Fives are secretly afraid of failure but they're careful not to communicate their fear to others. Sensual, earthy people, 5s possess great elasticity of character, and, as born gamblers, they're always ready to take a chance. When being negative, 5s can be hurtful, conceited, promiscuous, lustful, irresponsible, or rebellious.

Merlin's Notes

It's a given that life is never dull with the 5. The 5's life and yours will be shaped and directed by the demand for personal freedom and independence, the desire to escape, and the inability to tolerate boredom. It will probably be best if you just accept that life with a 5 is going to be full of the unexpected. Where other numbers might be daunted by this kind of life, the 5 will always bounce back with clever, witty perceptions, resourcefulness, and the energy to move forward.

Fives like to be one of the gang—to know many people. Fond of the opposite sex, you know that if you're a 5, you can expect that the opposite sex is attracted to you.

However, making a commitment or being bonded in the bliss of holy matrimony may be a long time coming because, first and foremost, the 5 fears losing freedom. If you do manage to marry a 5, don't be surprised to find the marriage breaking up if it becomes dull or boring (just keep it hot, honey!).

Housekeeping or any domesticity is not the 5's gig, either. After all, they're not very interested in repeated routine or binding responsibility. Be sure to consider these things before signing on the dotted line with a 5 (and that includes business partnerships, too). If a 5 has 4, 2, or 8 in his or her chart, the 5's freedom-loving traits will be more grounded and stable. In fact, when a 5 has an active, entertaining, useful life, he or she will be a happy and protecting companion.

A 5 gets into hot water when his or her temper, impatience, and impulsive nature are without training or education, or are improperly channeled. The 5's haste, lack of discipline, and quickness with words can bring on quarrels, accidents, and legal troubles if the 5 hasn't developed patience, understanding, and discipline.

Another irritating little habit of the 5 is to take credit for something another has achieved, simply because the 5 once helped guide the other person. A 5 can be very unappreciative of all he or she has received and that others have done on the 5's behalf. A 5 is more dependent on others than he or she wishes to admit (you've gotta be if "Change" is going to be your middle name). Once the 5 learns to appreciate and share the responsibility, this lively, fired-up energy will delight you, but only until tomorrow, when things will change again.

The Misunderstood 5

The 5 won't be the originator, but is quick with observations. As we've said, we see *ER*'s Doug Ross as the misunderstood 5—no one knows his pain—as he tries to save the lives of children (that's his mission, is it not?) at the expense of hospital liability, Carol's clinic, and his friend Mark's reputation. He's misunderstood because he's only trying to help.

Recall, of course, that Doug Ross also had an earlier reputation that he's trying to live down. Those years of irresponsibility, quick, easy sex, and me-first-ism are also very 5-like, but when the 5 means well, as Doug does, he can't understand why others don't understand his good intentions.

What's Important to the 5

The 5 loves freedom, lack of restriction, and change. As long as there's variety, the 5 is happy and challenged. It's when the going gets slow that the 5 gets going.

What Offends the 5

Here are some things that offend the 5:

➤ To be told he or she can't change it.

➤ To be told he or she is inflexible.

➤ To be discounted for his or her resourcefulness.

➤ To not be recognized as a hero—after all, the 5 was trying to help change things.

➤ To be labeled or boxed in.

You and the Number 5

Do you have a 5 in your chart? It's time to take out your numerology journal and see if the 5 is an important part of you. Use the following list to decide how important the number 5 is in your own numerology chart:

➤ I have the number 5 as my Soul Number. Destiny Number. Personality Number. Life Path Number. Maturity Number. (Circle which of your numbers are 5s.)

➤ The number 5 is ___ is not ___ present in my chart. (Check one.)

➤ The 5 is not a strong number in my chart; therefore, I do not need further study on this number. Yes ___. No ___. (Check one.)

➤ The 5 is a strong number in my chart and I need further study on this number. Yes ___. No ___. (Check one.)

The Least You Need to Know

➤ The 5 is the number of change and adaptability.

➤ The symbol of the 5 is the five-pointed star or pentagram.

➤ Spiritually, the 5 is the number of learning to take risks.

Part 3

A Closer Look at Numbers 6 Through 9, Master Numbers, and Karmic Numbers

Naturally, the higher numbers resonate to higher frequencies, and in the 6 through 9, you'll find everything from the nurturing of the 6 through the universal compassion of the 9, with the analysis of the 7 and the executive ability of the 8 in between. Then there are the master numbers that resonate to still higher frequencies, and the karmic numbers that present some lessons all their own.

Chapter 10

The Number 6: We Are Fam-i-ly

In This Chapter

➤ The number of nurturing and understanding

➤ Just like your mom

➤ Love and marriage

➤ Duty and responsibility

Generous, sympathetic, self-sacrificing, caring: sound like anyone you know? Some numerologists call the 6 the ultimate nurturer, and once you've read this chapter, you may well agree. Whether you're looking for fresh-baked brownies or a shoulder to cry on, the 6 may be the number you need.

The 6 is also the number of love and marriage, which, as the old song reminds us, "go together like a horse carriage." In fact, if everything were up to the 6s, everything would go together like a horse and carriage, because the 6 is the number of balance and evenhandedness.

If You Want *Our* Advice ...

You can always look to the 6 to create a sense of family. With hot cocoa, warm blankies, and fresh-baked cookies, this is a nurturing number you can always cozy up to.

Got a problem? Take it to the 6, who will give you sympathy and understanding. Got a question? You can be sure the 6 will have some good solid advice.

Key Words, Colors, and Gemstones

When it comes to responsibility, no one does it quite like the 6. Here are some key words, colors, and gemstones to help you understand just what the 6 represents, as well as its astrological equivalents—Cancer and Libra.

The Number 6

Key Words	Colors	Gemstones	Signs
Nurturing	Royal blue	Pearl	Cancer
Responsibility	Indigo	Sapphire	Libra
Family			
Duty			
Balance			
The marriage and divorce number			
Love			
Romance			
Loves to beautify			
Love of animals and children			
Service to others			
Community			
Harmony (like the 2)			

Also important to consider are:

➤ **Tarot Card:** The Lovers—the card of love and romance and making commitments in these matters. This card desires balance in all relationships.

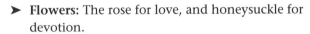

➤ **Flowers:** The rose for love, and honeysuckle for devotion.

By the Numbers

The **6** is the number of nurturing, sympathy, and understanding.

The Number 6's Symbol

Two symbols for the 6 are the heart and the double triangle (the triangle, you'll recall, is the symbol for the 3). The 6 is the double triangle (two 3s), or the six-pointed star, also know as the Star of David.

The symbol of the 6 is the heart, the double triangle, or the six-pointed star.

The Number 6's Meaning

It's said that if you look carefully at the way the number 6 is written, you'll notice it has a fat little belly that is pregnant with love. In fact, the 6 represents love: romantic love, passionate love, mother love, and tender love. This number also rules marriage and domestic happiness, and represents the heart of things, where the love resides, and where love is nurtured. Whether it's a community project, tending to animals, or educating children, the 6 will see that it's all done with love.

The 6 is considered the number of the "Cosmic Mother." In family concerns, the 6 is the loving parent at the center (usually the mother) who is the hub of the wheel, nurturing, loving, supporting, and nursing the family. More important, the 6 loves it—although the 6 can sometimes get a little too motherly for the 1, the 5, and the 7.

Life with the 6

The 6 is romantically inclined and leans toward the ideal in matters of the heart, therefore the 6 is likely to have has some ideal notions about marriage partners. For this reason, the 6 can find it hard to have a partner live up to his or her high standards about how the ideal partner "should" be—and we emphasize "should" because 6s are big on shoulds.

Everything in a 6's life must be harmonious, for this number, above all else, requires balance in its life. If there should be a quarrel or disruption, a 6 will have an urgent desire to put things right in the home. That's because the home is the nest for the 6, and if there's any discord there, trust the 6 to rush in to set it right.

Easy as 1-2-3

The number 6's astrological equivalent shares the energy of two signs: Cancer and Libra. Cancer is the sign of the nurturer, caring, family focused, who loves to create a safe haven and cozy nest. Libra's energy reflects the number 6 also with its love of beauty, balance, and harmony.

Easy as 1-2-3

The letters of the 6 are F (6), O (15 = 1 + 5), and X (24 = 2 + 4). The letters of the 6 are particularly easy to remember, because they spell out the word "fox."

Merlin's Notes

The 6 is thought to be ruled by the planet Venus, which is very appropriate because 6s, with their love of beautiful homes and lovely objects, have a very Venusian outlook on life. Sixes are artistic and imaginative, too, with excellent senses of color, and they're often known for their musical and vocal talent, with many having very pleasing voices. Note that the planet Venus is associated with the astrological sign Libra, a sign that takes harmony and balance very much to heart.

Six is also called the marriage and divorce number because the 6 brings deep matters of the heart to bear upon one's life. If 6 loves, it will be a deep, committed love, not the flirtatious love attraction of the 3, or the sensual love affair of the 5. It will be the deeply felt "real" love of marriage (well, as real as an idealized love can be, anyway). This is devotion at its best.

If one's marriage has no "heart" left, however, the 6 becomes the number of divorce. It's not unusual to find people getting married or divorced in a 6 year—but more on that in Chapter 24, "Your Personal Year: For Every Time There Is a Season," where we discuss the Personal Year.

A 6 will spend much of his or her leisure time planting flowers, remodeling, or doing home projects, preferably with his or her spouse. These are the homebodies—and no one can nest like a 6.

The number 6 governs counseling and teaching and people will be drawn to the 6 for advice or problem solving—talents at which this number excels. It's not unusual to find a 6 with a home-based business, especially a therapist or counselor whose clients will not only get loving advice, but will be nurtured by the environment of the caring 6.

Sixes are very responsible, and, in fact, are often responsible for other people's stuff where there's no need to be. It's this desire to put others before themselves, their nurturing nature plus their need to be responsible, along with a strong sense of duty that leads 6s to over commit and then find they're out of balance in their lives.

The Blessing

The blessing of the 6 is that he or she is wise and lives according to guidance from the heart. The ability to make a full commitment, to take on great sums of responsibility, and to execute it competently and with love is the blessing of the 6. But the 6's greatest gift is his or her loving nature.

The Challenge

The challenge of the 6 is to not be the long-suffering martyr and to remain realistic in matters of the heart. If you're a 6, your challenge is to learn not to sacrifice so much of yourself that you have nothing left to give or no heart to love.

Archetypes, Heroes, and Stars

The 6 is the number of the heroine, that is, of the mother who will sacrifice herself in order to see that all goes well for her children. Do you remember, for example, the movie starring Sally Fields, *Not Without My Child,* in which she married an Iranian man in the United States, and when he took her and their daughter back to Iran for a visit, he suddenly made it clear that he'd never intended to return to the United States? The whole movie is about what Sally's character must do to get herself out of Iran—but she won't go without her child. This is a great example of the mother sacrificing herself for her child—and of the energy of the 6.

Merlin's Notes

Our *ER* archetype for the 6 is nurse Carol Hathaway, the nurturing, self-sacrificing, and caring persona that the 6 personifies. She lovingly cares for her patients, opens a clinic for those who can't afford health care, and, of course, is the lover in the Doug 'n' Carol duo.

But a still better archetype can be found in Greek mythology. When Demeter, the goddess of all that grows, lost her only daughter Persephone to Hades, the god of the underworld, the world went barren with her grieving. Not until Zeus arranged a deal with Hades, where Demeter could have Persephone for one half of the year, did the earth once more become fruitful—but of course, 6 that she was, Demeter had to sacrifice her child for the other half of the year. Sixes give up a lot for their family and loved ones.

Higher Ground

The 6 desires to bring harmony, peace, justice, and truth to all experiences in life. The 6 embodies the perfected sense of balance, as represented by the six-pointed star, which is made up of two triangles.

Spiritual Essence of the 6

As the number of perfected balance, the 6 is the essence of spirituality and love. In fact, it's the unification of the spiritual world with the material world through love, and the 6 is thought to be spiritually protected.

Esoteric Meaning of the 6

The vibration of the 6 is the energy of service and responsibility—to be the humanitarian caretaker of the community, and the provider for humanity. The life of the 6 will be filled with giving to others.

A Closer Look at the 6

A closer look at the positive and negative aspects of this number will help you solidify an understanding of the challenges and attributes of the 6. As with all of the numbers, a person with a 6 number is free to choose whether to live the positive or negative expression of this number.

Positive Expression and Negative Expression

Even the 6 has its downside, and it can be clearly seen in some of the 6's classic traits. The 6's willingness to give, for example, can lead to martyrdom, while the 6's desire to help his or her family can make the 6 meddlesome, or worse, interfering. Still, if the 6 emphasizes his or her positive expression, the 6 can turn negativity into more of the good he or she has to give.

The Positive and Negative Expression of the Number 6

Positive	Negative
Proud	Unrelenting
Loving	Interfering in family matters
Honest	Unforgiving
Straightforward	Stubborn
Giving	Unresponsive to reason
Generous	Codependent
Comforting	Martyr
Sympathetic	Set in own ways
Harmonious	Argumentative
Balanced	
Humanitarian	
Serving	
Responsible	
Understanding	

Cosmic Vibration

The cosmic vibration of the 6 is to nurture, give, serve, comfort, understand, be warm and abundantly loving, and to protect those the 6 cares for.

Unique Abilities

The 6 is one of the money numbers, where money flows toward the 6 through service to others, not from personally motivated gain. In fact, the 6 is a great business number, especially for a cottage industry or a home-based business—or for any service-based business. Sixes will pour their hearts and souls into a business and nurture it to success as if it were a child.

The most unique ability of the 6 is his or her capacity to love, nurture, and serve others. No other number holds a candle to the 6 on this note, and the 6's warmth and comfort can be felt in the simple rush to pour you a hot cup of tea, close the blind from the glaring light, or bring you of a blanket to ward off the cold. The 6 will establish a cozy home, complete with good food and warm hearth, close, loving relationships, and beautiful working environments.

Relationships

To love and be loved is the 6's deepest desire. Without love, a 6 won't reach the soul satisfaction or the heights of success the 6 is capable of. In addition, 6s need approval and praise. They crave it: Feeling appreciated is essential to the 6. If a 6 isn't receiving appreciation, don't be surprised to see him or her looking elsewhere for companionship or work—in fact, count on it!

This number is, however, subject to flattery and influenced strongly by the kind word or flattering remark. The 6 can go blissfully off in the wrong direction just with a note of praise, which is a contradiction of character in this otherwise strong, responsible number. Of course, the fact that the 6 already has an idealized notion of love isn't too helpful in this situation, either. In short, we might find the 6 falling in love and devoting his or her life to someone who flatters and only appears to love him or her. But don't be fooled—the 6 longs for and can deliver heart-connected love.

Learning to receive is one of the hardest tests for the 6. The 6 is so competent at giving that others are either intimated in their efforts to give back, or feel they're not needed. But don't be confused, in reality, the 6 needs you: to love and to praise him or her!

Sixes and Sevens

Sixes must learn to not only give, but to receive, which will restore balance to the devoted life of the 6. A 6 must learn to give him- or herself praise and to extend appreciation to those in his or her life. While this won't substitute for the much-desired approval the 6 seeks from others, it will begin to bring back into the 6's life the equally needed balance.

When a wrong or injustice is being committed, trust the 6 to speak "the truth," in an honest, straightforward manner, which, in fact, usually comes out bluntly. The 6 is the champion of the underdog—is it any wonder that we find 6s naturally drawn to social work, community restoration projects, and children's education? I suppose we shouldn't be surprised that Hilary Rodham Clinton has a 6 Destiny Number and has devoted much of her professional life to defending children's rights and education.

Speaking of education, the 6 is always the teacher for the 6 has a natural propensity to instruct others. The 6 also has strong interests in reform and principles, or any kind of instruction along the lines of emotions or spiritual longings of the soul. This number is a natural for homeschooling, and you may find, whether you want it or not, that in your relationship with the 6, you are the recipient of many a lesson.

Merlin's Notes

Home, family, and children form the background of the 6 because 6s are loyal, devoted, generous, and oh-so loving. There's a natural love of luxury, beautiful things, and the good things in life, and the 6 will indulge him- or herself, friends, and family, all in a generous spirit of love. Some of those more freedom-loving, independent souls might not be so happy with this much love, mothering, or attention; in fact, they might feel smothered by the attentions of the 6. In addition, when it comes to love, the 6 can be completely blind to the faults of others—the 6 can see no wrong where his or her heart and affection have been pledged.

Oh, have we mentioned this yet? The 6 has a strong desire to protect his or her loved ones, and considers them wee ones all, be it husband, wife, child, or furry little critters.

As you might have guessed, the 6 is capable of sacrificing—so much so that he or she becomes a martyr, weighed down by the burden of responsibility, duty, and concern for others. After a long many years of living in this manner, the 6 may find health challenges moving into his or her life. We believe that the recently identified health issues of fibromylagia and chronic fatigue syndrome belong to the 6-type of consciousness. After all, these are the caregivers of the world.

Even though 6 is the marriage number, sometimes we will see a 6 fail to marry. When this happens we might look to one of the following as the cause:

➤ High ideals about marriage and love

➤ Early disappointment in love

➤ A deep sense of loyalty to father, mother, or family due to a well-established sense of duty and responsibility

However, love may come late in life for the 6 as a reward for a life of service and sacrifice.

Sixes have firm convictions, a strong sense of right and wrong and what is just and fair, and they don't like to be contradicted or crossed. They're slow and deliberate in thought and action, retreating when hurried into promises or action.

Sixes also tend to worry a lot about all manner of things, most of it unnecessary. It's one way the 6 can feel responsible—just keep worrying about things as a way to keep the issue warm, protected, and cared for. We know, it's crazy, but the 6 is crazed when it comes to being responsible. The worry is that someone might think he or she doesn't care!

Ultimately, 6s must learn to love themselves—to be loyal, thoughtful, sensitive, and caring toward themselves. Then they will not dispense love from a diminishing well, but become a well of love itself from which all may drink.

In a funny way, 6s must learn to care not so much for others but more for themselves. They get confused sometimes.

The Misunderstood 6

In the 6's desire to be loved and to love, to care for others and be responsible, the 6 may not be seen as the strong, resilient force it truly is. In fact, for those who do not understand "coming from the heart," the 6 may be seen as egotistical or weak. In the 6's desire for beauty and love, he or she can idealize romance and marriage, and find it hard to live in the realistic day-to-day life (of dreary burden, said the 6). The 6 may put unrealistic demands on his or her partner, or find it hard to have a marriage partner because of the 6's ideal standards.

What's Important to the 6

Some of the things that are important to the 6 include

➤ Loyalty.

➤ Things being fair.

➤ Not mistreating the underdog.

➤ Calm.

➤ Peacefulness.

➤ A comfortable home.

➤ Things must be adorned with grace and beauty.

The 6 requires that routine and personal affairs be kept in order, and above all, needs tranquillity at home.

What Offends the 6

Sixes are offended by

- ➤ Noise and confusion.
- ➤ Undependability.
- ➤ Not to be of service.
- ➤ Unhappiness in the outer world.
- ➤ Unattractive environments.
- ➤ Being hurried or rushed.

You and the Number 6

It's time to take out your numerology journal and determine if you have any 6s in your star chart. Use the following list to find out how important the 6 is in your own life.

- ➤ I have the number 6 as my Soul Number. Destiny Number. Personality Number. Life Path Number. Maturity Number. (Circle which of your numbers are 6s.)
- ➤ The number 6 is ___ is not ___ present in my chart. (Check one.)
- ➤ The 6 is not a strong number in my chart; therefore, I do not need further study on this number. Yes ___. No ___. (Check one.)
- ➤ The 6 is a strong number in my chart and I need further study on this number. Yes ___. No ___. (Check one.)

The Least You Need to Know

- ➤ The 6 is the number of the family and mothering.
- ➤ The 6's symbol represents the heart.
- ➤ The 6 is symbolized by the balanced six-pointed star.
- ➤ Spiritually, the 6 is the essence of love.
- ➤ The 6 is the number of nurturing, giving, and understanding.

The Number 7: Perception and Wisdom

Contemplative and private, the 7 is considered the most mystical of the numbers. In fact, the 7 likes nothing better than to be holed up with a favorite book in that funky old rocker inherited from great-grandma.

At the same time, this is also the number of the researcher and philosopher, because with all that time alone, the 7 can't help but dig deeply and think things over. While others may consider the 7 eccentric, in fact, the 7's too busy observing them to care what they think!

Looking to the Inner Self

No other number likes so much time alone, so it should come as no surprise that the 7 is the number of anyone whose work requires solitude and contemplation. Whether a scholar or a computer geek, the 7 will always seek the heart of the matter—and won't be satisfied until he or she knows his or her answer is the perfect one.

Key Words, Colors, and Gemstones

"Solitude" and "mysticism" are just the tips of the iceberg when it comes to the 7. Here are some key words, colors, and gemstones for you to remember the 7 by, as well as its astrological signs.

The Number 7

Key Words	Colors	Gemstones	Signs
Solitary	Violet	Amethyst	Pisces
Mystical	Purple	Alexandrite	Virgo
Philosophical			Scorpio
Analytical			
Private			
Deep			
Contemplative			
Selective			
Skeptical			
Perfectionist			
Inventor			
Loner			
Observant			
Eccentric			
Reserved			
Intuitive			
Specialization			
Researcher			
Interested in metaphysics, occult mysteries			
Science or technology oriented			
Rest and rejuvenation			
Inner wisdom			
Purification			
Spiritual			

Also important to consider are:

➤ **Tarot Card:** The Hermit—silent counsel, wise, seeks truth. The solitary Hermit needs to withdraw to meditate and seek wise counsel for himself.

➤ **Flowers:** Lavender for silence, rose-scented geranium for preference and discernment.

The Number 7's Symbol

The sacred symbols of the 7 are the seven-branched Tree of Life, the seven chakras, the ziggurat (ladder) to Heaven with its seven steps, and the triangle (the 3) above the square (the 4) that represents cyclic time in the cosmos and the life of man. This is also the symbol of the Masonic apron. In addition, the 7 is represented by yet another star: the seven-pointed star.

Bearing in mind that the 7 is often considered the most mystical of numbers, it's easy to see that the symbols of the 7 often connect heaven and Earth in some way.

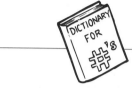

By the Numbers

The **7** is the number of solitude and mysticism. It's here you'll find both the philosopher and the analyst.

The symbols of the 7 are the seven-pointed star and the triangle above the square.

The Number 7's Meaning

The 7 is often associated with magical powers, perhaps because it's a number that deals with all things deeply, as opposed to the number 5, which deals with things generally. The 7 is the summoning to move inward and discover the universal laws of nature and the connection to the mysteries of life.

The Lingo of the 7

Among the concepts associated with the 7, you'll find

➤ 7 days of the week.

➤ 7 days in each Moon phase.

➤ 7 colors in the spectrum.

➤ 7 notes on the musical scale.

➤ 7 energy centers known as chakras.

Easy as 1-2-3

The number 7's astrological equivalent is found in three signs. Pisces represents the search for spiritual wisdom, Virgo's energy mirrors the 7's analytical and scientific nature as well as the tendency toward perfectionism, and Scorpio shares the traits of the 7's need for depth, meaning, and privacy.

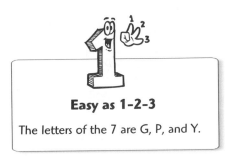

Easy as 1-2-3

The letters of the 7 are G, P, and Y.

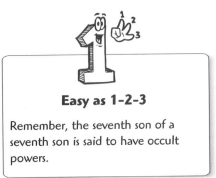

Easy as 1-2-3

Remember, the seventh son of a seventh son is said to have occult powers.

Here are still more things associated with the 7:

➤ The seven petals of the lotus flower, as shown with the Buddha sitting in the middle of the flower, are said to represent his teachings: the creative spirit and the origin of all things (nature and human), which are met with creative action (of the seven planets, the original planetary influences).

➤ The seventh day (the day of rest).

➤ There numerous references to the number 7 in the Bible, where the 7 was considered the perfect number and the number of God.

Matthew 18:21–22: When Jesus was asked how many times one should forgive he said "seventy times seven."

Book of Revelation: Here there are many references to the 7: Seven Churches, Seven Angles, Seven Seals, Seven Lamps, Seven Plaques, a beast with Seven Heads, Seven Stars (the Pleiades).

Life with the 7

Sevens are solitary by nature and love to do things alone, whether it's to think, meditate, contemplate—or just stare at the wall. A 7 is quiet, and likes it that way—the better to think and study. In addition, 7s are rejuvenated by the outdoors and by being in nature.

The 7 will choose things that are refined or unusual in some way, and is especially drawn to antiques or things from the past, such as a claw-foot round table or a roll-top desk (but how many antique hand planers does one need?), as well as things that are distinctive, such as Grandma's cameo brooch or volumes of rare books.

You'd better love being by yourself if you team up with a 7. Not only will you be alone, but if you're with the 7, he or she will be silent much of the time. Don't expect a "Good morning" from a 7, for example, because morning is an especially quiet time. That's when the 7's thinking about the day, a dream last night, or that book the 7's reading.

The 7 finds "soul" in all things. While the 7's not necessarily religious, more often than not he or she will seek alternative spiritual avenues. More than anything, the 7 makes holy the experience of life.

The 7 simply does not do the ordinary; the 7's unusual, even eccentric. Nothing is accepted at face value, and all must be scrutinized, but after all, the 7 is the student of life with a scholarly attitude, never satisfied until he or she has found a way to link the known to the unknown. The 7 is also the number of the skeptic, so the 7 will have to check things out. The 7 is most often the investigator, scientist, inventor, or occultist.

Merlin's Notes

A 7's ideas about religion are often unorthodox. The 7 may even invent a religion of his or her own (we'd bet that David Koresh of Waco fame had a 7 somewhere in his chart). The 7 is drawn to philosophical thought, spiritual law, esoteric literature, metaphysics, or any system that offers insights into the mysteries of life. This is your major thinker, analyzer, and observer, whose purpose in life is to discover inner wisdom, and in fact the 7 seems to see the realities of unseen power and the wisdom of the ages.

The 7 is the number of specialization, which is to say that the 7 delves deeply into specific areas of interest and becomes a kind of expert. Eventually, people come to the 7 for wisdom, not only for the specialized field of study, but for the insights and understanding the 7 has about life itself.

The 7 is excellent in jobs that require analysis, factual research, keen observation (lots of bird watchers are 7s), an inventive approach, or technical data—just so they can do the job alone! Sevens are not team players, but rather will seek an out-of-the-way location where the job can be executed with slow, methodical precision, careful thought, and of course, their usual intuitive wisdom. And pul-eeeze! No airheads as job mates!

As a parent, the 7 will often be distant and removed, with more interest in the education of the children than playing with them on a day-to-day basis. When we say "interested in their education," we're talking about both academic education and their philosophical education; after all, thinking about things is the 7's specialty.

Sevens make wonderful teachers but their approach is more professorial and scientifically based. Of course, teaching kids about nature is a natural for a 7, since the 7 has a spiritual and physical bond with the outdoors and nature.

The Blessing

The 7 opens the door to higher knowledge and understanding of the mystery of life. Sevens are blessed with great dedication and a keen sense of observation and insight.

The 7 is also blessed with a great reserve of inner wisdom, and in addition, is gifted with a superb analytical mind. Other 7 blessings are

➤ The blessing of being at peace in solitude.

➤ The blessing of a sense of connectedness to the unseen world.

➤ The blessing of a contemplative approach to life.

The Challenge

The challenge of this inward 7 is to have friends, a marriage, or any relationship with another human being. The 7's inward pursuit leaves him or her with viewpoints that may bear no resemblance to those of their peers, so not only is the 7 silent and aloof, but now the challenge is to find someone who thinks like the 7 does—in an unorthodox manner, unusually, and with insightful notions. The greatest challenge for the 7 is to learn to deal with aloneness, and to not let the desire for solitude turn into loneliness and isolation.

The Lesson

Sevens have to learn to not take their search for perfection to the extreme—in other words, to not be such perfectionists. They also must learn to find love, affection, and tenderness by reaching out into the world.

Archetypes, Heroes, and Stars

Mythology both ancient and modern is filled with 7 types. Think of the tall, dark stranger, the solitary horseman (remember Alan Ladd in *Shane?* "Come back, Shane!"), any character played by Clint Eastwood, and many of Gary Cooper's roles as well (such as Robert Jordan in *For Whom the Bell Tolls*).

Merlin's Notes

Peter Benton of *ER* is a classic number 7. Introverted, aloof, distant, and silent (as well as often brooding), he's mainly interested in scientific research, or the technical approach. Because he's completely lacking in warmth, others find him unapproachable. Of course, it's all too obvious to us, the viewers, that he needs love and affection so that he might learn to bring that to his bedside ministration of his patients, to say nothing of the improvement it might make on his private life!

The solitary scholar—like the Hermit of the Tarot deck—who goes off on his own to contemplate what he knows and what he doesn't, as well as the solitary, contemplative hero of W. Somerset Maugham's classic *The Razor's Edge* are 7 archetypes as well.

Higher Ground

When the 7 shows up in a person's chart, it calls for retreat and reevaluation. This number says it is the time to go within, for it's concerned with understanding knowledge on a higher level. This is the stage in the human cycle where it's time for introspection and analysis; it's a call to know oneself and life in the deepest way.

Under the influence of the 7, it is time to be alone, time to contemplate. As author and numerologist Juno Jordan tells us, "Now calm, serene in meditation and contemplation, it [the 7] looks out upon established facts and beholds in visions and dreams the realities of unseen power." The 7 is the number of inner wisdom.

Spiritual Essence of the 7

The essence of the 7 is the point where an individual reflects upon the spiritual nature of things and investigates, analyzes, and intuits inner wisdom. It's the quest to discover the inner landscape of one's life and place it in relationship to larger, higher truths.

Esoteric Meaning of the 7

Seven is a number that is indivisible, and it represents the perfection of the God energy. The number 7 has been called the Christ consciousness number as well. No matter what you call it, however, this is the number that represents the triumph of spirit over matter.

A Closer Look at the 7

Introverted, quiet, thinking all the time, the 7 is often distant and removed from normal human relations. Needless to say, this is not the social number—leave that to the 5 or the 3. No, this is the number of the loner, the hermit, the monk, or the one who spends zillions of hours ensconced in a project involving research, analysis, or philosophical pursuit. As we have said before, the 7 actually prefers to be alone with his or her books, computer, catalogs, and resource guides.

Nerds, computer whizzes, librarians, professors, or anyone who specializes in being alone will no doubt reveal a 7 nestled in their personal numbers.

Sevens may have very distinct eating habits, choosing particular foods or diets. This is because the 7 has a strong instinct for purification and perfected health.

The 7 operates on a different wavelength than others, and comes to his or her own individual solutions, does things his or her own way, and is not too adaptable.

The 7 is sometimes described as odd (by those who aren't 7s, of course). Remember, the 7 rules the unusual, so don't be surprised to find your 7 choosing clothes, food, and a lifestyle that does not follow the hip trend.

Positive Expression and Negative Expression

Solitary or reserved? The 7 is actually both, and each word is actually one side of the same coin. When it comes to the positive and negative expression of the 7, in fact, it may be hard to tell the difference between "discerning" and "critical."

The Positive and Negative Expression of the Number 7

Positive	Negative
Refined	Aloof
Distinctive	Dreamy
Quiet	Depressed
Thinker	Moody
Investigator	Cynical
Keen observer	Perfectionist
Educated	Loner
Scholarly	Withdraws
Researching	Suspicious
Discerning	Critical
Skilled with hands	Shrewd
Loves solitude	Reserved
Intelligent	Hard to get to know
Philosophical	Silent
Wise	Lack of generosity
Charming	Skeptical
Dry wit	Out of touch with humanity
Specializes	Unsympathetic

Cosmic Vibration

The energy of the number 7 is withdrawing, concealing, focusing inward, perfecting, and leaving the material world to turn to the world of spiritual understanding, philosophical contemplation, or analytical thought. Its vibration is silent; that is, meditative, contemplative, reflective, and resting. The 7's energy is spent on inner seeing, whether to examine, analyze, or intuit.

Unique Abilities

Most 7s have a high degree of intellect, and some will demonstrate talent in fields of science, research, or technology. Sevens are great with computers or in any field where data needs to be collected and analyzed. You might see a 7 as a forensic specialist, for example, because of the 7's ability to investigate with the careful and keen observation.

Sevens might be found as archaeologists, deep sea divers, numerologists, or detectives, or involved in spiritual studies—in other words, wherever in-depth study or deep analysis is involved. They're dedicated to their study/research, always wanting to uncover the hidden answers. To a 7, in fact, knowledge is power, and most 7s will be educated in some area where they've been called to investigate in a specialized way.

If technology or science is not the path followed, then you'll often find the 7 doing spiritual, metaphysical, or philosophical work. The 7's unique gift lies in the fact that he or she is dedicated to searching for understanding of human life in relation to a larger universe.

Relationships

As we've said, the 7 prefers to be alone, although most 7s do get lonely. In fact, that's their own private paradox. "Private," of course, is the 7's byword, and they can be secretive. Certainly, they tend to be silent, reserved, and introverted. Luckily, a person is not just one number; others numbers in the chart help to balance out all of this introversion.

Merlin's Notes

When it comes to money, 7s may have little or no money sense and often live beyond their means—much to the horror of their mates. Sevens earn money from specialized fields—they're not the generalists like the 5, but instead know a subject in depth, which brings money and recognition.

If you're going to live with a 7, you'll want to know that solitude is very important. The 7 needs a great deal of time alone—to meditate, think, reexamine, or rejuvenate. The 7 isn't comfortable with lots of people, especially people he or she doesn't know. Actually, the 7 does best in one-to-one situations rather than in groups.

The 7 can be depressed, moody, aloof, cynical, and generally hard to get along with. The 7 does, however, possess great depth of feeling (depth is the operative word with the 7—the 7 does *all* things in depth). Sevens are passionate, sincere, understanding, and wise but also innately shy and reserved.

Sevens are very individualistic, in fact, maybe even eccentric. The main point is they are unusual. Not particularly domestic and definitely not a caretaker (leave that to the 6), the 7 is the educator. In terms of giving, once the 7 has been convinced, he or she will give generously to a worthy cause.

As you might suspect, this is not an easy marriage number. A 7 will want to find someone who can give him or her lots of space and time alone, and someone who understands the 7's silent ways.

Quiet and reticent to participate, the 7 finds it difficult to express his or her thoughts and is even less able and willing to express emotions, unless there is a 3, 6, or 9 also in the chart.

Merlin's Notes

Although quite charming and persuasive, the 7 just doesn't do well making small talk and is consequently confused by the social scene. Remember, the 7 does things in depth—and that includes trying to entertain friends from out of town. While the 7 may wax poetic on the nuances of thermal dynamics and decoding binary systems, ask the 7 to converse with your guests at a dinner party about the neighbors' affair, and you can forget it! There will be silence.

The 7 has little interest in frivolous or foolish wastes of time, or what he or she deems a waste of time. Your 7 can come across as cool, dignified, and aloof, but underneath is a mystical being. Remember, the 7 relies on his or her intuitive guides more than the 7 may wish to acknowledge.

If you want a partner who will figure out the system, reroute the wiring, or set up your latest computer program, a 7 is the one to get. If you like mellow, unassuming, spiritual perspectives, you'll love being with a 7! Marriages based on spiritual beliefs and deeper issues will bring happiness.

The Misunderstood 7

Even as a child, a 7 might be considered "strange," keeping secrets, off by himself (usually in nature), always observing and watching. As an adult, a 7 has a hard time trying to fit in. Unlike most of its peers, the 7 will be misunderstood and may have difficulty finding someone who understands his or her solitary, distant ways.

Even though the 7 may be hard to get to know, he or she gets lonely, too. Remember, the 7 needs understanding—but will have a difficult time asking for companionship or help. Just remember, the 7's private; so if you can respect the 7's need for privacy, can carry on an intelligent conversation, and show an interest in the 7's all-time favorite subject (nature), you just might find a sincere, dedicated friend who will let you in to his or her sanctuary. Of course, if you're another 7, no problem!

What's Important to the 7

Here are some of the things that are important to the 7:

➤ Time alone

➤ A library

➤ Solitary retreats

➤ A cabin in the woods, a place on the beach, or a hideaway in the mountains; in short, a place to be alone with nature

➤ Work that allows for research or study

➤ Privacy

➤ The search for truth and wisdom

➤ Old gardens, pictures, antiques—anything mellowed by time

➤ To analyze, dissect, examine, and consider

What Offends the 7

Among the things that offend the 7 are

➤ Prying.

➤ Superficiality.

➤ Noise and confusion.

➤ A house filled with crowds of people.

➤ The realities of life.

➤ Imperfection.

You and the Number 7

Now that you've learned about the 7, it's time to take out your numerology journal to find out if you've got this number in your chart. Use the following list to find out how important the 7 is in your own numerology chart.

➤ I have the number 7 as my Soul Number. Destiny Number. Personality Number. Life Path Number. Maturity Number. (Circle which of your numbers are 7s.)

➤ The number 7 is ___ is not ___ present in my chart. (Check one.)

➤ The 7 is not a strong number in my chart; therefore, I do not need further study on this number. Yes ___. No ___. (Check one.)

➤ The 7 is a strong number in my chart and I need further study on this number. Yes ___. No ___. (Check one.)

The Least You Need to Know

➤ The 7 is the number of solitude and contemplation.

➤ The 7's symbol represents the connection between heaven and Earth.

➤ Spiritually, the 7 is the number of inner wisdom.

➤ The 7 is a loner and is sometimes considered eccentric.

Chapter 12

The Number 8: Getting Down to Business

In This Chapter

➤ The number of leadership

➤ Recognition and achievement

➤ The organizer and manager

➤ Money and materialism

After the introspection of the 7, the 8 comes on like gangbusters. This is the number of leadership and leaders, organization and organizations.

If it has anything to do with making money, chances are it has something to do with the 8. That's because this is the number of wealth and abundance, as well as the material aspects of life.

Mastery's the Name of the Game

Where the 7 works within, the 8 takes it back out into the world and expands it. At its best, the 8 is a master of personal power, money, and business. The 8 was born to be the boss.

If there's a General or C.E.O. in the room, chances are this person has an 8 somewhere in his or her chart. That's because the 8 is the number of natural leadership and power. Where there's an 8, in fact, everything will always run shipshape.

Key Words, Colors, and Gemstones

Everything about the 8 points to money and success, and its key words are no exception. In addition, we've provided colors and gemstones to help you remember this masterly number, which is also associated with the practical sign of Capricorn.

The Number 8

Key Words	Colors	Gemstones	Sign
Power	Pink	Diamonds	Capricorn
Money	Rose	Rose quartz	
Success			
The boss			
Business			
Vision			
Organization			
Recognition			
Achievement			
Financial management			
Strength			
Authority figure			
Mastery			
Expansion			
Materialism			
Wealth			
Abundance			
Manifestation			
Harvest			

By the Numbers

The number 8 is the number of personal power, materialism, and the boss.

Also important to consider are:

➤ **Tarot Card:** Strength—the strength to harness the elements of power for self-mastery.

➤ **Flowers:** Hollyhock for ambition, camellia for excellence and mastery.

The Number 8's Symbol

The figure 8, the symbol for the number 8, is believed to represent the joining of the two spheres, heaven and

Earth. The 8 is also represented by the double square (as in two 4s) and the infinity sign, which is the 8 lying on its side.

The 8's Meaning

The 8 represents the achievement of material success, position, and power. Not surprisingly, 8s have great successes or great failures—with nothing in between. The 8 is the vibration of power and the authority to guide and direct, and 8s are invested with drive and ambition to succeed and make material gain.

The 8 isn't always a fortunate personal number, and people who are 8s often face losses and humiliations in their lifetimes. With relentless dedication to work, however, they'll find themselves in positions of power and authority. Wise, enduring, and exceptionally tough, 8s can go the long haul it often takes to reach the top.

Easy as 1-2-3

The astrological equivalent of the number 8 is Capricorn, which seeks to organize and manage physical reality, and shares the same energy around power. Both the 8 and people with Capricorn prominent in their charts must learn to use power wisely and not be dominant or controlling.

The symbol of the 8 represents the joining of two spheres.

Life with the 8

Eights must have a "shoulder to the wheel" at all times—they have to give everything their all. Shortcuts, greed, or abuse of any position of authority will lead to loss, failure, and more karmic debt when you're an 8.

An 8 needs a goal and a plan to give direction to this powerful energy. Unlike the 6 or the 9, the 8 isn't motivated by humanitarianism, but rather by the love of work and the thrill of successfully attaining a worthy goal.

Eights often have an interest in secret societies where there's structure, organization (especially a hierarchical ladder to climb), and mystical training (Masonic Order, anyone?). They're also interested in the mental sciences (psychology, metaphysics, ancient philosophies), the study of character, vocational analysis, and, of course, business organization. The 8's biggest interest is in money and what it can do—the 8's the king (or queen) of making money.

The Blessing

Eights are blessed with the ability to size up any situation and create a plan for execution, and it's their ability to organize and see the larger picture, as well as the smaller details, that brings about the achievements and success for which the 8 is known.

In addition, 8s are blessed with the strength and courage to undertake large projects, financial risks, and the management of large organizations.

The Challenge

The challenge is for the 8 to resist the drive to live for money and to be consumed by the acquisition of wealth. The 8 is also challenged to utilize his or her executive abilities without ordering, intimidating, or dominating people.

The Lesson

Many 8s have come to learn the correct use of power, and so will learn to believe in their own personal power without dominance or intimidation. Many situations will arise to help the 8 learn about becoming his or her own authority. The major lesson is empowerment—claiming and utilizing the 8's own gift of power.

Archetypes, Heroes, and Stars

For archetypes, heroes, and stars, we've chosen several figures who characterize the qualities of the 8. From *ER,* Dr. Donald Anspaugh symbolizes the head honcho, the powerful authority who's often brusque, impatient, and egotistical. As the leader, however, he's efficient in the execution of his duties and successfully manages the hospital as a business so that it is a viable financial institution as well as a place of healing.

In addition, a number of movie stars exemplify the energy of the number 8. All of the following people have 8 Life Path numbers:

Jane Fonda	12-21-1937
Tommy Lee Jones	9-15-1946
Carrol O'Connor	8-2-1924
Warren Beatty	3-30-1937
Barbra Streisand	4-24-1942

Other famous people bearing the number 8 are:

➤ In sports: Muhammad Ali, Joe Namath, Jesse Owen

➤ In leadership roles: Neil Armstrong, Melvin Belli, Lyndon Johnson, Ulysses S. Grant

➤ In outstanding contributions to history: Edgar Cayce, John D. Rockefeller IV, Andrew Carnegie, and the first lady of soul, Aretha Franklin

138

With his November 25, 1960 birthday, John F. Kennedy Jr. had an 8 Destiny. Clearly, his 8 Destiny was reflected by his personal power, his presence, vision, and his easy access to wealth.

Merlin's Notes

If you're looking for a film archetype for the 8, look no further than the roles played by actor Michael Douglas. His portrayal of characters such as Gordon Gecko, the meanie in *Wall Street,* personify the work-to-get-ahead characteristics of the 8.

Higher Ground

Until mastery is achieved, much of the energy of the 8 is spent on achieving wealth and grandeur, but mastery comes after the 8 emerges from this long struggle with the material world, through awareness of a higher purpose. Once the 8 is on to the laws of higher consciousness, he or she then truly becomes a powerful being, with his or her own personal power in balance, and can utilize the skills of mastery. This is when the 8 has become adept, drawing successfully upon the laws of manifestation and abundance.

Spiritual Essence of the 8

The spiritual principle that rules the 8 is: You will reap what you sow. The 8 is bound by the laws of karma and is challenged spiritually to walk in the realms of power without creating new karma or avoiding old karmic debts.

The 8's power is not manmade, but rather belongs to the higher principle of bringing the infinite into the finite in harmonious balance. Spiritually, the 8 is charged with the responsibility of working with integrity to build a world of the future that is aligned with higher consciousness and serves all of mankind, not just for personal profit or recognition.

The 8's process, at the highest level, may be one of materializing wealth and following a path of power, achievement, and success, but the 8's reward is ultimately the satisfaction of a job well done.

Esoteric Meaning

The number 8 is said to be the number of the force that exists between terrestrial order (the square) and external order (the circle). The 8 has a dual nature (one circle on top

Sixes and Sevens

The 8 is a double number, both masculine and feminine. Its masculine qualities are strong, active, and demanding, while its feminine qualities are passive and capable of being molded. It's thought that together this is the formula for bringing the Divine into the material, hence the resultant abundance and harvest. If, however, these two are separated or opposed, then the result is sorrow and destruction.

of another), which represents degeneration and regeneration. Not surprisingly, complete reversals are an ever-present possibility with this number.

It's thought that the 8 has Divine awareness that has been learned through many past lifetimes. Further, it is believed that, intuitively, the 8 has knowledge of the great mysteries—secrets of the occult and metaphysical sciences.

Because the 8 is invested with a natural power that stems from an inherent understanding of universal principles, the 8 is required to participate in the world of form (our material world), honoring what the 8 inherently knows: All power, wealth, success, and achievement come from a power greater than the 8's. When the 8's ego leads, forgetting that he or she is not the *power,* then failure, destruction, and reversal of fortunes often follow. Balance must be restored.

Undisputedly, the 8 is the number of money, power, and success. It's just that the 8 can't take all the credit.

A Closer Look at the 8

The 8 cements dreams and visions together. The 8 expands the ideas of the 3, the hard work of the 4, and the reevaluated theories of the 7. Taking all of these, the 8 creates a larger plan that will serve the greater good. The 8 provides order, knowledge, supervision, stability, and the know-how to expand into the next level to make the dream a reality. The 8's task is great and its burdens are many.

The 8 has the potential to become noble, greatly respected, a fine judge of character and potential, and a master of life's forces.

Eights like to theorize (like the 7), and want to discover motive and feelings behind human action (like the 6). Often, the 8's part, and part of its power, is that of the wise counselor and director, without prejudice or illusions. These are hard-won achievements in the life of an 8.

As we've said before, much of the 8's energy is spent on achieving wealth and grandeur, but the 8 isn't lucky in money like the 3, 6, and the 9. Sure, the 8 loves money, and his or her personal ambition pulsates with the desire to be wealthy, powerful, and recognized for this success, but all of these may fail unless the 8 heeds the higher calling.

Eights must work with integrity and must incorporate spiritual wisdom (found in the 7). When this is done, they'll find they have unusual opportunities given to them placing the 8 as an authority.

Money comes through efficiency, excellent mental powers, and good judgment. Money also comes from work well done, unceasing effort, mental concentration, outstanding ability, mastery, integrity, and *right action.*

The 8 wants to know about life and its relationship to the Divine purpose and is attracted to musical instruments, arts, and antiques.

Positive Expression and Negative Expression

Tough or ruthless? Tenacious or obstinate? When it comes to the ruling mastery of the 8, it's no easy task dividing the positive from the negative. Here are some words to prove it:

By the Numbers

In Buddhist teachings, it is believed that one must take **right action** (do the right thing) in accordance with the laws of the universe and in keeping with the highest good for all.

The Positive and Negative Expression of the Number 8

Positive	Negative
Tough	Ruthless
Tenacious	Obstinate
Capable	Unscrupulous
Successful	Haughty
Good money manager	Overbearing
Interest in metaphysics	Dominant
Demonstrates integrity	Jealous
Unprejudiced	Demanding
Competent	Guilt ridden
A leader	Driven
Visionary	Materialistic
Excellent instincts	Egotistical
Business minded	Prejudiced
Mastery level work	Overly ambitious
Dependable	Has money difficulties
Performs with excellence	Demands recognition
	Represses others
	Strains to attain
	Impatient
	Explosive anger
	Intentionally intimidating
	Know-it-all
	Manipulative
	Self-righteous

Cosmic Vibration

The cosmic vibration of the 8 involves the energy of

➤ Directing.

➤ Arbitrating.

➤ Judging.

➤ Planning.

➤ Supervising.

➤ Leading.

➤ Strenuously driving.

➤ Being intensely active.

Easy as 1-2-3

Eights have executive abilities that are unique to them—even if they don't know it. Just have an emergency to find the true colors of your 8: He or she will take charge and bring the situation under control.

Easy as 1-2-3

Known for a strong personality, the 8 likes to be around important people, big houses, good clothes, and also likes to make a good appearance (especially when he or she can do it with a bit of drama and flair).

Unique Abilities

Eights are excellent judges of character and have a unique gift for seeing a person's potential. Even though an 8 may be powerful, the 8 also has the ability to be fair and to see both sides of a situation.

The 8 is also proficient at relating feelings and facts, and is a natural as an efficiency expert. Business is the 8's forte, and the 8 has a knack for building up run-down businesses and turning them into successes. The 8 is especially good in fields of industry, commerce, government, politics, real estate, spying, and even literature.

You'll find that 8s have unusual amounts of courage, strength, and self-control. Like the 7, the 8 has keen skills of observation. The 8 is also dependable, trustworthy, of an outstanding character, and is often known locally for his or her good works.

Relationships

Consider marriage carefully when dealing with an 8—it will pay to give great attention to financial security, because the 8 is money-conscious. In fact, the 8 can be generous and understands money as a tool for achieving a dream or a plan, but at the same time, the 8 doesn't like to be subordinate because he or she likes to be the boss.

As a driving force, the 8 may try to be all things to all people. After all, intense action is the daily diet of the 8, and he or she is always doing business, whether in his or her head or in bed. Because the 8's naturally a doer, others depend on the 8. Who wouldn't? The 8 wants to be the boss, is good at organizing, and knows how the money game works—you'd just better not want to be the leader, too! In fact, an 8 needs "Indians." There's already a "chief"— and it's the 8.

The energy of the 8 is honest and frank, and the 8 lets you know where you stand. When push comes to shove (and you won't be the one doing the pushing), the 8 speaks honestly, bluntly, and—more often than anyone would like—severely. In addition, the 8 has a temper and can show it, especially when it comes to inefficiency and repeated mistakes. Fortunately, however, the 8's anger blows over quickly.

The 8's driving need for purpose and goals can be overwhelming in a close relationship. With an 8, there will always be rules, a "right" way to do things, and a procedure to follow. Remember, this is the "General" archetype—the 8 needs troops to direct. But the 8 also needs admiration and love for the reward of all his or her efforts and achievements.

The 8 needs to slow down and look at the real value of those dear to him or her. In love, marriage, and romance, this one's loyal but not sentimental—the 8's too busy for that. The 8 will love deeply (all the while watching the clock to see when his or her next appointment is, or if this display of affection is taking too long). We must remember, to the 8, time is money.

Sixes and Sevens

Even though the 8 looks powerful to the outside world, the 8 needs encouragement at home to claim his or her true power, which is its authentic self. In this way, there won't be so much effort exerted to "prove" that he or she has power. But, with encouragement, the 8 understands his or her own power and the connection to something larger in the universe than his or her own ego.

If the 8's lesson is to learn to use its incredible power, then the home front needs to be a place where power is not an issue. Don't expect the 8 to get home for dinner often, for the 8's a true workaholic. The 8 wants at all costs to accumulate prosperity symbols—they're a sign of 8's success. Still, the 8 will build you a castle and an empire of lasting importance because the 8 builds for permanence.

In keeping with new paradigms for the new millennium, the 8 needs to work on achieving more win-win situations and fewer competitive, hard-driven bargains. Most of the other numbers have a hard time living with the 8, and two 8s together can make fireworks with all those power struggles. However, if an 8 has learned to accept his or her own power and feels secure in his or her achievements, and has developed a higher consciousness, the 8 will find that he or she can afford to be more magnanimous in his or her gestures of love, time, and participation at home.

Life becomes happier when the 8 learns to

➤ Deal with people patiently.

➤ Realize he or she can be intimidating.

➤ Find time to express love, sweetness, and appreciation.

➤ Share the abundance of the world around him or her.

➤ Recognize that others know things, too.

Remember, in all relationships, an 8 will have to take responsibility to remain balanced in all that he or she says, does, and doesn't do. For an 8, balance (remember that symbol) is the key.

The Misunderstood 8

The 8 drives and pushes to be the best, to be ahead, and to be on top, because somewhere underneath is a feeling that he or she isn't good enough, won't get there in time, isn't seizing the opportunity, or could be doing more. Often, this demanding 8 is more critical of his or her own efforts, than anyone from the outside. With all this inner dialogue going on, no wonder the 8 barks out orders.

Most 8s are self-made, and in that arduous pursuit, they often forget that there really is a tender, warm, caring human in there who needs to be reminded that he or she is human and needs to be loved, too. If you're an 8, we'd recommend a good 6 to be your partner.

What's Important to the 8

We'll bet you already know what's important to the 8, but we'll list it here anyway:

➤ Money

➤ Achievement

➤ Success

➤ Power

➤ Organization

➤ Efficiency

➤ Competence

➤ Toughness

What Offends the 8

Among those things that offend the 8 are

➤ Inefficiency (like the 4, who's a cousin—two 4s make an 8).

➤ Mismanagement of money.

144

➤ Lack of money.

➤ Being told he or she is wrong.

You and the Number 8

So how 8 are you? It's time to take out your numerology journal and see if and where the 8 appears in your chart. Use the following list to find out.

➤ I have the number 8 as my Soul Number. Destiny Number. Personality Number. Life Path Number. Maturity Number. (Circle which of your numbers are 8s.)

➤ The number 8 is ___ is not ___ present in my chart. (Check one.)

➤ The 8 is not a strong number in my chart; therefore, I do not need further study on this number. Yes ___. No ___. (Check one.)

➤ The 8 is a strong number in my chart, and I need further study on this number. Yes ___. No ___. (Check one.)

The Least You Need to Know

➤ The 8 is the number of power and success.

➤ The 8's symbol represents two spheres joined together.

➤ Spiritually, the 8 is the number of learning to live with power without sowing more karmic debt.

➤ The 8 is the number of leaders and generals.

The Number 9: And, in the End ... the World

We began with the 1—the beginning, the leader—and now we close with the 9, which represents closure and completion, and the humanitarian. Just as the 1 will always be out in front, the 9 will always make sure that things are finished, tying up all the loose ends into a tidy package of loving universal perfection.

The 9 is a highly spiritual and intuitive number, so if we seem to use loftier terms than usual as we discuss this number, that's the reason why. Still, the 9 isn't without its dramatic, human side, as you'll soon see.

Completion of the Cycle

Now we come to the last and greatest number of the cycle—the number 9. This is a high potency number, with the energy of all the previous numbers infused into it. It's the number that signifies the end of things, but at the same time, it also suggests mastery.

Key Words, Colors, and Gemstones

Nine is the number of completion. In the following table, we've provided colors and gemstones to help you remember this number, which is also associated with the sign of Scorpio, Pisces, and Aquarius.

The Number 9

Key Words	Colors	Gemstone	Signs
Completion	White	Opal	Scorpio
Perfection	Clear		Pisces
Compassion			Aquarius
Universal brotherhood			
Forgiveness			
Reward			
Money attraction			
Dramatic			
Multi-talented			
Universal love			
Sensitive			
Humanitarian			
Benevolent			
Artistic			
Highly intuitive			
Spiritual			
Healer			
Idealism			
Transformative			
Philanthropic			
Fortunate			

By the Numbers

The **9** is the number of completion and transformation.

Also important to consider are:

➤ **Tarot Card:** The World—the Major Arcana card that completes the journey, promising universal healing and forgiveness.

➤ **Flowers:** Michaelmas daisy for farewell, magnolia for grief, red poppy for consolation, rosemary for remembrance, woodbine for fraternal love.

The Number 9's Symbol

There are two symbols for the number 9: 3 triangles, or the Scepter and the Orb. The 9 is also believed to be the sacred number of the pyramids.

One of the symbols of the 9 is three triangles.

The Number 9's Meaning

The 9 represents the process of understanding the true value of life and the human experience and their subsequent connection to the Divine. Gifted with the intuitive, spiritual, and emotional power to embrace the human condition, the 9 will serve mankind out of a great love for his or her fellow humans.

The 9 is a number that contains the energy of all the other numbers, and so it represents the 8 steps around the cycle of life, plus the motionless center (the 9). It is thought that the 9 symbolizes the pinnacle of mental and spiritual attainment.

Some of the 9s in life include

➤ 9 muses.

➤ 9 months to deliver a full-term baby.

➤ "Nine Elected Knights" in freemasonry which includes 9 roses, 9 lights, and 9 knocks in their ritual.

➤ 9 steps in the pyramids.

The 9 is also the most important number in Feng Shui, as the number of perfection and the central energy of that system.

Easy as 1–2–3

The number 9's astrological equivalent is shared by three signs: Scorpio reflects the emotionally intense, deeply transformational nature of the 9, while Pisces shares the intuitive, sensitive, healing properties of the 9. And finally, Aquarius and the number 9 are the qualities of the humanitarian, utopian visionary, and the philanthropist.

Life with the 9

It's not uncommon to find the 9 marching in civil rights demonstrations, working for the World Hunger Project, or helping with welfare reform: It's their concern for the betterment of all people on this earth that lives in the soul of the 9. That's because the 9 is the number of compassion, tolerance, and philanthropy. Nines are both inspired and inspiring, and some are exceptionally gifted artistically. In addition, they're enterprising, imaginative, and quick thinking.

For the 9, there has to be a soul realization that love equals giving, and through understanding and acceptance of all people without prejudice or thought for oneself, personal love, purposefulness, and abundance will begin to build up in the 9's life. This in turn brings spiritual protection and great reward, both emotionally and materially.

The 9 is the number of reward for all the hard work done in numbers 1 through 8, and the rewards are both material and spiritual. At some point in the life of the 9, he or she realizes that his or her soul's expression is vital to living a whole and balanced life. You could think of the 9 as the 6 grown wiser and much more tolerant—but the 9's also more emotional. In fact, the 9 rules the emotions, which can be experienced in the extreme. You'll find vacillation from intense anger to great tolerance, from passionate outcries to detached observation, from outrageous jealousy to sympathetic understanding.

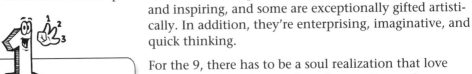

Easy as 1-2-3

What the 9 learns from the 8 is that reward isn't gained through ambition, recognition, power, or money. There's more to life, the 9 realizes: There's spiritual attainment and inner confidence, both of which have far-reaching benefits. Just look what happened as we moved from the 1980s (the 8 embodies power, money, and ambition) to the 1990s (the 9 manifests the search for spiritual connection, global concern, and unparalleled prosperity).

The 9 is learning to surrender. The 9 will be involved in completing unfinished tasks and learning not to take it personally when something is over, but instead understanding how this ending fits into the larger picture, as well as the Divine plan for mankind (this is the number of endings, after all). When the 9 "gets it," the endings begin to look like beginnings, and then the 9 can focus on what's coming next, instead of what is in the past.

Merlin's Notes

The 9 has the ability and desire to work for global consciousness, international business, and understands things on a large scale. The 9 has a great passion for wanting to make the world a better place because of his or her efforts, and has a deep-seated love for people that kindles the philanthropic, humanitarian outreach that's characteristic of the 9. Not surprisingly, the 9 is the universalist.

Nines understand that life has been a series of lessons teaching them about the full spectrum of the human drama, so that they can develop a high degree of compassion and tolerance. While a 9 may start out being intolerant, that's not hard to understand because the 9 is an idealist and a perfectionist. Still, the 9's life lesson will be to develop tolerance for all people regardless of race, creed, or color. This number is here to learn and to live selflessly, giving loving service to mankind.

When 9s come of age, they'll be able to acknowledge pain, grief, misery, suffering, and poverty as conditions of this planet. It's then that they'll be able to live in joy, love, beauty, and mystical understanding. Nines want to show everyone a better way, and get involved where they shouldn't. In fact, 9s can attract volumes of worries and problems.

Nines are unusually artistic or involved with the arts, especially at the philanthropic level (such as being the large donor for the symphony's annual fundraising project, or chair for the statewide Young Writers' Contest).

There's a kind of aristocratic air about the 9: The 9 is stately, worldly, and may well be wealthy.

The Blessing

The blessing of the 9 is that it has the ability to restore its position, to redeem itself from failure and loss, and to reestablish success. This, of course, is metaphorically the process of death and rebirth, or endings bringing beginnings. It's also related to the astrological sign of Scorpio, who is said to be able to rise from the ashes. As the number of transformation, the 9 has a great deal of power to regenerate.

The Challenge

The challenge of the 9 is to love unconditionally and to live with an open heart. Lessons may be learned through tears and pain as well as moments of great joy and ecstasy. Health issues can challenge the 9 because of its highly sensitive and emotional constitution.

Nines have to open their hearts to urges to be intolerant, possessive, unsympathetic, selfish, or greedy. To balance this challenge, the 9 needs to turn these negative energies into creating a talent for sympathetic understanding, inclusiveness, compassion, selfless service, and trust in the universe to deliver her just reward.

The Lesson

Lessons for the 9 include learning

> ➤ To accept, forgive, and let go.
> ➤ To learn to detach.
> ➤ To open his or her heart to all, regardless of labels.
> ➤ That its most valuable asset is a heart filled with love big enough to melt resistance.
> ➤ To love and forgive itself.

More than anything, the 9 must learn that it's been given a generous heart, an array of talents, a belief in the basic goodness of mankind, a deep love of humanity, and a deep understanding of the universal laws of divine order. Along with these priceless gifts, the 9 must realize it's meant to serve and promote universal brotherhood.

Archetypes, Heroes, and Stars

When we thought about who is a 9 type of character, we couldn't help but think of Mother Teresa, who had a 9 Life Path, and who symbolized compassion and caring at its highest level. A more modern example might be television and film personality Oprah Winfrey, who's generous, warm, and global in her thinking, as well as genuinely concerned for the lives of people everywhere.

Other familiar 9s are Luke Skywalker, who has a 9 Destiny, Mahatma Gandhi, with a 9 Life Path (10-2-1869), and Charles Lindbergh (2-4-1902) with a 9 Life Path as well. In the arts category, we find that Elvis Presley had a 9 Life Path (1-8-1935).

Merlin's Notes

Not surprisingly, film and literature are filled with 9 types, those whose selfless compassion for humanity comes before themselves. One example is Levin, in Tolstoy's masterpiece, *Anna Karenina*. Another, more contemporary example, can be found in many of the characters played by Kevin Costner, such as the hero of *Dances with Wolves*. And Luke Skywalker's 9 Destiny should come as no surprise.

Higher Ground

With the number 9, it's a time to finish, draw to a close, complete—and then to let go. In fact, the 9 rules the principle of surrender, "letting go and letting God." This is the higher ground of living with faith in a divine plan.

Spiritual Essence of the 9

The 9 symbolizes spirit as a fully conscious energy, that is, wisdom attained. The power of the 9 is the fusion of a fully conscious spirit with the material world.

In addition, it's the kundalini force of yoga, symbolizing the surge of energy from the base of the spine to the brain. (If you look at the way the 9 is written, it looks like a spinal cord curving up to a head.) The goal of the 9 is universal love for all, carrying forth its spiritual wisdom into all human experience on earth.

Esoteric Meaning

In the Chaldean system of numbers, an older numerology system, the number 9 wasn't used because it was thought to be the number of God. Instead, the Chaldeans based their system on numbers 1 through 8. In modern numerology, the 9 is included in the system of numbers because it is thought to include the energy of all of the numbers 1 through 8, thus giving it great power.

The number 9 is both powerful and potent, and, because it's privy to the wisdom of spiritual law, it's conscious of the needs of mankind and has the talent to bring these two together in a living testimony to the oneness of all life. The 9 also has the power to choose to live with a higher purpose or to suffer the grief and pain of separation from what it intuitively and psychically knows.

The 9 understands that there's only one people, one religion, one race, one nation, and one creed—in other words, the universal oneness of all mankind. The service of the 9 is to promote, in small and large ways, the brotherhood of mankind.

Forgiveness is the key for the 9, and this is its life lesson: to forgive all wrongdoing and intolerance and become impartial, impersonal, and detached from its emotions so that it can live with compassion and purpose.

A Closer Look at the 9

The 9 rules worldly concerns such as international business and moves in wide circles. Its energy should be used to educate, comfort, and protect mankind, and work for the betterment of the planet.

It's not unusual to find the 9 financially well-off. This is the number of reward, an attraction for money, and good fortune. When a 9 is wealthy, no doubt the 9 will be involved with numerous charitable organizations, especially in the arts.

Positive Expression and Negative Expression

There are two sides to the 9, and they're exemplified by the yin and yang of selflessness versus martyrdom. In order to give you an idea of this number's multi-faceted nature, here are some words that typify its positive and negative expression.

The Positive and Negative Expression of the Number 9

Positive	Negative
Selfless	Martyr
Generous	Smothering
Sees possibility	Ambivalent

continues

The Positive and Negative Expression of the Number 9 (continued)

Positive	Negative
Compassionate	Greedy
Tolerant	Too idealistic
Highly aware of the beauty of life	Impulsive
Acknowledges pain, grief, misery as part of the cycle of life	Gullible Stresses what others should do
Benevolent	Perfectionist
Highly intuitive	Melodramatic
Mystical	Clings to the past
Creative	Takes life personally
Forgiving	Closes heart to pain
Charitable	Attracts loss and suffering
Understanding	Emotional extremes
Magnetic	Prejudice
Charming	Intolerant
Wealthy	Insensitive
Has good fortune	Accident prone
Idealistic	

Cosmic Vibration

The cosmic vibration of the 9 is

➤ Loving.

➤ Caring.

➤ Magnetic with money.

➤ Completing.

➤ Ending.

➤ Releasing.

➤ Transforming.

➤ Forgiving.

Unique Abilities

The 9 has an unusual ability to attract assistance and opportunities for success. This is also known to be the number that attracts money and fortune. Look at the following:

M	=	4
O	=	6
N	=	5
E	=	5
Y	=	7

$$27 = 9$$

The caution is: It's said that 9s can make a fortune and lose it more than once in a lifetime.

Relationships

The father is often a strong influence in the life of the 9. There can be both misunderstandings that influence the young 9 and the influence of love and happiness stemming from the father. Later in the 9's life, the 9 will play father and mother of the world and be the cosmic parent.

Merlin's Notes

To position oneself for personal love, ego gratification, or for monetary gain brings with it the possibility of disappointment and loss, especially in affairs of love. Love, in fact, must come from a place of greater good than personal gain or personal gratification. For a 9, love must be linked to a higher purpose. In fact, when the 9 learns to do so, the 9 very well may be a benevolent leader, like Mahatma Gandhi (a 9 Life Path) or Martin Luther King (a 9 Soul Number).

Unhappy emotions are not uncommon—remember, the 9 rules moving to the extremes of emotion. The 9 may fluctuate between ecstasy and depression, and many 9s are manic depressive or bipolar (possibly because they're struggling to reconcile their notions of an idealized vision for the planet with the reality they see all around them).

At the same time, 9s are charming and can show great sympathy, warmth, and understanding. They're usually well-liked and are good companions who love life. Still, the 9's personal charisma and the necessary development of the notion of detachment may make the 9 seem inconsistent and difficult to understand.

Nines love with great passion and intensity and experience sorrow and pain with great intensity, too. Love fades when the object of the 9's affection fails to live up to his or her idealized version of perfection, (Lisa, who has three 9s in her chart, comments, "That's for sure ..."). Sometimes, too, the 9s will sacrifice those they love until they awaken to higher possibilities.

Nines love home, family, and friends. In relationships, happiness will be found when the 9s place all others' needs before their own and remember that giving must be done for the sheer pleasure of giving. The 9 is also romantic and attracted to beauty and lovely surroundings. Creative and sensitive to color, the 9 often has well-developed artistic expression as well.

When you have a relationship with a 9, you'll have to give him or her plenty of space. You may find you share your home with Peace Corp trainees or volunteers for Houses for Humanity. Generous and loving, the 9 will give time to worthy causes of social concern. The 9's personal life will be mixed with love for humanistic projects, and those at home may find themselves fending for themselves while number 9 is off crusading for whales, seashores, or refugees of the human kind.

Easy as 1-2-3

It wouldn't be unusual to find new friends from foreign countries or representatives of liberal causes sharing the dinner table with the 9, for the 9 is global in its thinking. The 9 has strength of character, inner wisdom, and strong intuition, but at the same time, the 9 needs love and approval to do his or her best work.

Lest you become confused, just remember: This is your basic air-fairy, dreamy, mystical, holistic warm spirit, who wants to make life better for everyone.

The 9 is spiritual, romantic, emotional, magnetic, efficient, responsible, cooperative, and often an independent leader. With the 9's broad outlook on life, the 9 is at his or her best when the 9 has a sense of purpose, balance, and emotional control. As renowned numerologist Juno Jordan says of the 9, "Being the highest number on the scale of human experience, it cannot transgress the principles of inner grace and spiritual living."

Undeveloped 9s appear meek, shy, vacillating, looking upon the dark side of things, fearful, or longing for something but don't know what. When they're like this, they need an understanding guide and a helping hand. At the same time, however, the 9 needs to develop its own individuality.

What makes the difference in the life of a 9 is

➤ Living with faith in something larger, a belief in a Divine Plan.

➤ Having confidence in him- or herself.

➤ Having love for fellow humans.

➤ Forming solid structures and foundations to stand on.

The 9 is the number that learns there's great satisfaction in giving. The healing aspect of the 9's energy is felt when the 9 gives of him- or herself from this loving space and shines his or her considerable warmth and understanding on those seeking assistance.

A certain amount of detachment is essential for the 9. The 9 is learning to contain his or her emotions, idealistic notions, utopian dreams, and intense love for the humane causes, the world's wrongs, and the down and out. Nines need the steady hand of the 4, the nurturing of the 6, and the objective analysis of the 7 to help them through.

The Misunderstood 9

Nines have a problem making decisions quickly—they can be vulnerable or impressionable. They can seem distant, abstract, or yearning for something unattainable, but then, as we know, the 9 is rooted in idealism.

Sixes and Sevens

Because 9 is a high-potency number, it's important that stimulants and habit-forming substances be curtailed. It's very hard for the 9 to break habits or for anyone to reform him or her. Change can come only from transformation and a spiritual alliance with a higher power.

Sixes and Sevens

A 9 might be mistaken for a bleeding heart, a pushover, or someone to be taken advantage of, because its loving concern for the good of all can make the 9 overly generous or gullible.

Its emotional response to things might cause others to discount the 9's feelings. Many people will run from such intense emotional expression. For the 9, life can seem traumatic: The 9 experiences what he or she feels so intensely because the 9's highly sensitive and intuitively connected.

A 9 is always picking up on more than meets the eye, and it's really challenging to have such a keen sense of the beauty of life, and then to see poverty, bombings, and children starving. They continuously learn the lesson of surrender—to let go and leave that which cannot be fixed to a higher source or greater plan than can be seen from the vantage point of the emotional 9. Unless you understand compassion, you cannot understand the 9.

What's Important to the 9

Some of the things that are important to the 9 are

➤ Beauty.

➤ Love.

➤ Human causes.

➤ Giving.

➤ Creative and artistic expression.

What Offends the 9

You probably won't be surprised to learn that the 9 is offended by lack of compassion, ugliness, selfishness, and black velvet paintings. Especially the black velvet paintings.

You and the Number 9

Do you have a 9 in your numerology chart? It's time to get out your numerology journal and note your 9s. Use the following list to find out how important the 9 is in your own numerology chart.

➤ I have the number 9 as my Soul Number. Destiny Number. Personality Number. Life Path Number. Maturity Number. (Circle which of your numbers are 9s.)

➤ The number 9 is ___ is not ___ present in my chart. (Check one.)

➤ The 9 is not a strong number in my chart; therefore, I do not need further study on this number. Yes ___. No ___. (Check one.)

➤ The 9 is a strong number in my chart, and I need further study on this number. Yes ___. No ___. (Check one.)

The Least You Need to Know

➤ The 9 is the number of universal compassion.

➤ The 9's symbol represents the uniting of all humanity.

➤ Spiritually, the 9 is the number of returning to one's higher self.

➤ The 9 is both creative and intuitive.

Chapter 14

The Master Numbers 11, 22, and 33: Potent Potential

In This Chapter

➤ The master numbers reveal increased potential

➤ The 11: self-illumination through spiritual inspiration

➤ The 22: self-mastery through self-enterprise

➤ The 33: self-awareness through selfless service

In this chapter, we'll be addressing three master numbers, 11, 22, and 33, each of which is a number requiring a particular kind of mastery. The 11 requires self-illumination through spiritual inspiration; the 22, self-mastery through self-enterprise; and the 33, self-awareness through selfless service.

As you'll learn, each master number reveals a particular kind of potential, as well as increased responsibilities. Have you got master numbers in your numerology chart? It's time to find out.

Mastering Your Numbers

Each of the *master numbers* is called by an esoteric name which gives insight into its purpose and shows how it's meant to serve its time on Earth:

➤ The 11 is the Spiritual Messenger.

➤ The 22 is the Master Builder.

➤ The 33 is the Master of Healing Energies Through Love.

By the Numbers

The numbers 11, 22, and 33 are called **master numbers** because they are considered to have more potential than the other numbers. The 11 is considered the most intuitive of all of the numbers, the 22 is considered the most powerful of all of the numbers, and the 33 is thought to be the most loving of all the numbers.

Master numbers are double-digit numbers that repeat themselves and at the same time come from a single root number. For example, 11 is a master number in which the 1 is repeated or in which there are two 1s present. At the same time, the reduced number of the 11 is 2 (1 + 1 = 2)—and the 2 is an equally present vibration in this number.

For these reasons, we write all master numbers by representing the double-digit number first and then the reduced root number with it. The following chart shows how.

How to Write Your Master Numbers

Master Number	Write As
11	11/2
22	22/4
33	33/6

It's Not Easy Being a Master Number

All of the master numbers indicate an opportunity for learning and integrating spiritual information. This learning, however, often comes through trials, tests, or stressful circumstances. The bottom line is, if you're using spiritual, philosophical, universal, or metaphysical principles, you're operating at the master number level, which we call working with the higher vibration of the master number (11, 22, or 33). If, however, you're focusing yourself on ego, the material world, or negative energies, then you're working within the confines of the lower vibrations of the master number (2, 4, 6). This is only the case with master numbers.

Easy as 1-2-3

There are as many master numbers as can be configured from repeating the numbers 1 through 9. All of the following are considered master numbers: 11, 22, 33, 44, 55, 66, 77, 88, and 99. We have included a list of the meanings of all of the master numbers at the end of this chapter, however, we'll be confining our discussion to the three most commonly found numbers: 11, 22, and 33.

Numerologists believe that, for all of the master numbers, you've made a kind of contract (back when you were still in spirit form) to come back and help humankind in this lifetime. In fact, all of the master numbers have volunteered to come back to assist the world in moving to a higher place—kind of like teaching assistants—low pay for teaching the same courses as the regular faculty, but doing it because they want to learn more.

Spiritual Gifts

Master numbers indicate spiritual gifts that make them highly sensitive to intuition, extrasensory perception, and the world of higher guidance, including celestial beings, other life realities, and universal spiritual law. Master numbers have a greater ability to be in touch with their own higher guidance, because they're more fully developed spiritual souls (when they are listening).

The only problem is, lots of master number people don't live up to their spiritual potential, partly because it's so hard just to live this life. These highly sensitive individuals must be in balance in all areas of their lives—all of the time.

This requirement for balance extends to the physical, emotional, and mental aspects of their lives, and, quite frankly, it's a tall order. The idea is that living in a balanced way will allow them to be able to use the spiritual realm on the material plane. A master number 11, for instance, would be constantly struggling to live up to the energy of the 11, all the while being pulled by the energy of the 2. The point is this: The effort demands a great deal of self-mastery.

In other words, any master number's natural spiritual affinity has to find its place in our world of violence, negativity, materialism, and personal gratification. When it does, it can bring much needed knowledge to a soul-weary world. At the same time, however, for the master number to live in our world is very difficult emotionally, mentally, and physically. This means those who carry a master number are constantly having to adjust, filter, fine-tune, and remember his or her spiritual origins.

Another reason why it's hard to live with a master number is because the ideals and goals of master vibrations are high and the master number's inner guidance is developed enough to be a strong presence. This causes the master number person to lean toward perfection and to live in a heightened state of awareness, which means that person is not always able to accept what he or she sees.

The master numbers have been called "testing" numbers, where life seems to be a series of tests to live up to, so that they can demonstrate all that

Easy as 1-2-3

Master number individuals are thought to be old souls who carry much wisdom and spiritual knowledge, which has been learned through many lifetimes. The master numbers carry wisdom of the mysteries of life and death.

Sixes and Sevens

The gifts of the spiritually attuned master numbers create tension, extreme restlessness, illness, and physical problems if their energies aren't channeled into service to humankind (remember the soul contract?). It doesn't matter what form the service takes; it's just that it must be a service that in some way will help humanity elevate its consciousness toward living with spiritual awareness.

161

they know and have the potential to be. Master numbers have an innate ability to help others overcome their challenges, as well as an extraordinary ability to assist with the challenges of humankind. We like to think of master number people as a kind of light, a very bright star shining among all the rest of us "stars."

What Master Numbers Share in Common

As you'll see, it's quite a responsibility to be a master number! While each master number has unique characteristics (which we're going to discuss in a few pages), they share the following:

➤ Vibrations of tremendous power and energy

➤ The innate ability to achieve fame

➤ The need to work on a large-scale level to bring about greater good to humanity

➤ The demand for self-mastery

➤ The responsibility for the great power master numbers possess

➤ Idealism

➤ High creativity

➤ Natural leadership ability

➤ The frequent need to be alone, to recharge, to find their spiritual center once again, and to detoxify

➤ The mission to serve in their own way, in their own field

➤ High introspection and sensitivity

Merlin's Notes

For all master numbers, the journey in this lifetime is into themselves, seeking the spiritual power that is part of their higher guidance, and learning control over their lesser nature: for the 11, to control the 1 and 2; for the 22, to control the 2 and the 4; for the 33, to control the 3 and 6.

➤ The need to constantly control their direction

➤ The expectation that they will do more and set higher standards than the average person

➤ Extremes in emotions

➤ The need to perform personal tests of mastery, including experiencing both the positive and negative characteristics of their master number

The Master Number 11: The Illuminator

The meaning of the number 11 is "Spiritual Messenger." In the ideal, the master number 11/2 is on a journey to find its own truth (illumination), using spiritual inspirations as a guiding light, and then bringing these illuminations to others to help raise spiritual awareness on the planet. You might say the 11 is born to bring spiritual insights (messages) to Earth.

Key Words, Colors, and Gemstones

Intuitive, sensitive—and very enthusiastic—it's no surprise that the 11/2 is associated with bright colors and translucent gems and metals. The following table provides key words, colors, and gems to help you begin to understand just what this master number is all about.

By the Numbers

The 11/2 master number, the illuminator, includes all of the qualities of the 1 and the 2. (Refer to Chapters 5 and 6 for an in-depth look at these qualities.)

The Master Number 11

Key Words	Colors	Gemstones/Metals
Intuitive	Silver	Platinum
Sensitive	Glossy white	Silver
Very bright		Mother of pearl
Enthusiastic		
Creative		
Inspirational		
Revelation		
The Illuminator		
The Spiritual Messenger		
Uplifts humanity		
Brings light to humanity		
Nervous energy		
Visionary		

continues

The Master Number 11   (continued)

Key Words	Colors	Gemstones/Metals
Loves the spotlight		
Impractical		
Leadership		
Seeks spiritual truth		
Spiritual teacher		
Peacemaker		
Negotiator		

Easy as 1-2-3

The master number 11/2's astrological equivalent is shared by two signs—two types of energy. Sagittarius represents the inspired, enthusiastic truth-seeker, while Aquarius shares the idealistic reformer and humanitarian qualities.

Sixes and Sevens

Not surprisingly, the demands of the 1 are often at odds with the demands of the 2. No matter what, though, the 11/2 is very sensitive to all within its radar, and, more often than not, is shy and nervous, and lives with intense emotions.

Also important to consider are:

➤ **Guardian Angel:** Uriel—Uplifting and inspirational, Uriel guides you back to the truth and nurtures balance.

➤ **Astrological Equivalent:** Sagittarius/Aquarius.

Mastery Through Spiritual Illumination

As we have said before, numerologists write the master number 11 as 11/2 to honor both the energies of the 11 and the 2, and both play an integral part in the story of this master number. In addition, the 11 combines all of the traits of the 1—twice over, and at the same time includes the traits of the 2.

How these two numbers play out together is the real story of the 11/2 master number. You might think of this number as two 1s, which embody individuality, the pioneering spirit, leadership, solitude, and independence; and a 2, which personifies companionship, team spirit, harmony, and peace.

The master number 11/2 is sensitive, dreamy, and idealistic, and it will often have revelations born out of its own experiences with life and the constant search for truth about the mystery of life. Elevens love to delve into the hidden mystery behind any of the many challenges they're called to face, whether it's the mystery of relationships, money, or the work world. While 11/2s can participate in the social world (the 2 is good at this), they really live more on the inside than in the external world.

It's the test of the soul of the 11/2 to learn to live honestly and with integrity. This master number loves the spotlight and it's not unusual to find people with 11/2s gaining fame. Bill Clinton, for example, carries two 11/2s in his chart—in his Soul Number and his Life Path Number—and we'd say that he, for one, has had more than a few tests in a journey toward spiritual illumination.

Merlin's Notes

Even though an 11/2 finds itself in the spotlight, sometimes the fame this number acquires is for the wrong reasons. After all, both Hitler and Mussolini had 11 prominently in their names. Remember, a master number is very powerful: How one chooses to use that power is part of what the soul is learning. Even though the 11/2s have come to help the human race, they're faced with choosing how to use their power. An 11/2 calls for an individual to live by spiritual standards—or self-destruction can be the outcome.

Learning to Surrender to Higher Ideals

One can't *seek* recognition with any of the master numbers; rather, these are the humanitarian numbers and require one to *surrender* to higher ideals. The 11/2 must live in truth, which is revealed through life's lessons. Their most rewarding opportunities will come from living and teaching truth as they see it, the truths they've discovered along the road.

The 11/2s are intense, and at times electrifying. In fact, they can have trouble with nervousness because the 11 is a highly intense vibration. At the same time, 11/2s have great courage and are highly creative.

The 11/2s are humanitarians to the bone—it arises from their very souls. Perhaps it's the 2 in this number that brings their unique ability to bring peace through negotiations. It's not surprising, then, to find that Henry Kissinger and Anwar Sadat both share an 11/2 Life Path Number.

The Pathway for the 11/2

The pathway for 11/2s is often hidden, and they must stumble along until their inner worlds are securely established and then taken out into the outer world. The stress is having to stay centered and balanced at all times because there's a tendency to swing

Easy as 1-2-3

Because of its heightened sense of intuition, the 11/2 has excellent insights into personal situations as well as to issues of the larger world. In fact, this is often the number of someone who's psychic.

from extremes. This number has the capacity to see the broad picture, to see the vision, to hold the dream—but it must find an outlet where it can be an active participant in the vision.

The 11/2s are inspirational leaders, however, only when they draw on their cosmic knowledge through profound intuitive abilities. They're leaders only when their vibrations are raised to the two 1s. If an 11/2 doesn't respond to the higher vibration, the 11/2 will be working at the lower vibration of the 2, in a position of supporting others. While this is an excellent outlet for the energy of this number, the 11/2 can't play the supporting role forever: The 11 is born to lead and to bring spiritual truths to people, as the master teacher.

As we've suggested, the 11/2 is a bright light with a spiritual message. In fact, the word "light" adds up to 11/2:

L	=	3
I	=	9
G	=	7
H	=	8
T	=	2

$$11 = 2$$

Weaknesses of the 11/2

The 11/2 walks the fine line between greatness and self-destruction. This number can be given over to fear and phobias or soar to the heights of the enlightened. The 11/2's growth and stability lie in the acceptance of his or her unusual gift for intuitive understanding and spiritual truths. In fact, the 11/2 must learn to live with faith: This is where the 11/2's peace is made.

Here are some of the more famous 11/2s:

The Inspired Ones:

➤ Claude Debussy

➤ Wolfgang Amadeus Mozart

➤ Nikolai Rimsky-Korsakov

➤ Jules Verne

➤ Antonio Vivaldi

The Negotiators for Peace:

➤ Henry Kissinger

➤ Anwar Sadat

➤ James Schlesinger

➤ Matthew Fox

In the Spotlight:

➤ Princess Diana

➤ Charles, Prince of Wales

➤ Bill Clinton

➤ J. Paul Getty

➤ Whoopi Goldberg

➤ Katharine Hepburn

➤ Jacqueline Kennedy Onassis

Merlin's Notes

While the 11/2 can have great strength, it's all too often insecure. It's the combination of the 1 with the 2 that accounts for the insecurity. The 1 is about the self, and self-confidence and self-reliance are two key features of this number, and when we double the vibration of the 1 to 11 (and couple it with a 2, which is usually concerned with how they are being perceived), then it emphasizes the positive and negative aspects of the number: It sometimes shows up as crisis in confidence. So one of the struggles for the master number 11/2 is to learn to believe in itself.

The Master Number 22: Master Builder

The meaning of the master number 22 is "Spiritual Master in form." The 22/4 has the unique ability to see the large picture, the details, and the spiritual principles needed to execute all of these into concrete form. This number builds things for humanity.

Key Words, Colors, and Gemstones

The 22/4 doesn't just build—it builds big. Once you begin to learn the key words, colors, and gemstones for this master number, you'll begin to understand why.

The Master Number 22

Key Words	Color	Gemstone/Metal
The Master Builder	Red gold	Rose gold
Master organizer		
Master planner		
Visionary		
Large undertakings		
Spiritual		
Practical idealism		
Dreams into reality		
Ambitious		
Intuitive		
Inspired		
Methodical		
Disciplined		
Natural leader		
Confident		
Wise		
Hardworking		
Honest		
Competent		

Easy as 1-2-3

The astrological equivalent for the master number 22/4 is shared by three signs. Capricorn reflects the ability to create form and structure of the 4, Libra brings the sensitivity and balance of the 2, and Virgo brings the vision for wholeness and hard work.

Also important to consider are:

➤ **Astrological Equivalent:** Capricorn/Libra/Virgo.

➤ **Guardian Angel:** Jamaerah—the angel of manifestation, who opens space for visions to manifest.

This master number combines all of the traits of the 2—twice over—and at the same time includes the traits of the 4. As with the 11/2, it's how these two numbers play out together that's the real story of the 22/4. You might think of this number as two 2s, which embody high sensitivity, intuition, harmony, and relationships; and 4, which represents hard work, discipline, practicality, building, organization, bringing things to form.

For the master number 22/4, the demands of the 2 must blend with the 4, and this is its struggle and its glory. Like the other master numbers, the 22/4 has a heightened sensitivity that gives it a unique ability to sense things, but also, when out of balance, causes health issues.

Mastery Through Self-Enterprise

The 22/4 has exceptional organizational ability. That's because the 22/4 has the balance of a focused mind and the highest ideals and brings both to any project or undertaking. The 22/4 is a natural leader, and can use esoteric wisdom to achieve tangible results. This master number has the desire to build big projects or set big goals—and the lesson is to use these desires to bring greater good to all.

By the Numbers

The master number **22/4** includes all of the qualities of the numbers 2 and 4. (Refer to Chapter 6, "The Number 2: Balancing Act," and Chapter 8, "The Number 4: A Solid Foundation" for an in-depth look at these qualities.) It's the number of the Master Builder.

Merlin's Notes

The 22/4 is interested in ideas and fields of work that result in forward movement and the evolution of humankind. These people want to make use of their talents to build something of lasting value that is splendid and uplifting. A 22/4 should choose a field that requires ultra-specialization, for it's in this area that both success and satisfaction will be gained.

The 22/4 is inspired to apply cosmic principles of metaphysics and spiritual and philosophical teachings to the physical and material world, and in this way invent new ways to apply these age-old principles.

Meet the Master Builder

The 22/4 loves to build systems, programs, projects, and organizations that are useful, practical, and uplifting. Naturally, this master builder is highly creative, and is delighted to create something that calls for order, planning, and bringing people to a higher sense of awareness in the process.

The 22/4s are intuitive, natural leaders, and they're creative, much like the 11/2, except that they're better adapted to the world and know better how to deliver the same truths in a more acceptable practical language. Life for the 22/4 is more solid than that of the 11/2, partly because the 22/4 is able to bring into tangible form the ideas the 11/2 can only dream of. With its practical know-how and ability to organize and plan, in fact, the 22/4 manifests dreams.

Sixes and Sevens

The 22/4 master number is an even higher vibration of the 11/2; after all, it's twice the energy. Instead of two 1s, it is two 2s. That means it has greater potential, and a greater struggle to stay in balance.

It's the mission of the 22/4 to elevate its body and make it conscious of the oneness of mind, body, and spirit. This number carries the root number 4, which governs health. For this reason, it's not uncommon to find 22/4 with weak bodies, who have to work on their health, or, at the very least, improve their health using progressive, spirit-honoring methodologies.

Sometimes, 22/4s feel as if they live in two worlds or two realities—the slow, everyday world of details and problems; and the inspired world of creativity, where everything and anything is possible. This master number is very connected to the earth and loves to work with its hands, yet at the same time is equally connected to the world of universal law, spiritual principles, and other world possibilities.

Sixes and Sevens

It's important to remember that the 2 plays a very important part in master number 22/4, because it's the number of the double 2 (as in 22). Therefore, the qualities of the 2 must be honed and perfected with this number, and life will bring the 22/4 many opportunities to be patient, tactful, willing to wait, polish the art of persuasion, be supportive, and become intimate with the perimeters of living a life of balance (physically, emotionally, mentally, and spiritually). Yet most important, the 22/4 learns to become an expert at improving relationships of all kinds. All of this then becomes part of the 22/4's service to mankind.

Attributes of the 22/4

The 22/4 is the number of someone who is serious, hardworking, loyal, and supportive. Like all of the master numbers, 22/4s feel things deeply, but don't get caught up in unproductive dreaming. Instead, the dreams of the 22/4 are based on facts and practical usefulness. After all, these are the master doers, and they're willing to work hard to achieve their vision for mankind.

Interestingly, the root of the 22 is the 4, the number of hard work—and the word "work" adds up to a 22:

W	=	5
O	=	6
R	=	9
K	=	2
		___
		22

The 22/4 can function well in arenas that allow for a broad perspective, encompass national and international interests, and promote universal understanding, peace, and higher consciousness.

Weaknesses of the 22/4

Like all of the master numbers, the 22/4 is very sensitive. Because 22/4s have the tendency to be involved in large projects, they can feel over-whelmed when too many obstacles are present, and when this happens, the 22/4 may need to resort to the vibration of the 4 to regain a sense of groundedness.

Remember, master numbers are a very high vibration and require balance of the mental, physical, and emotional body. A 22/4 can become a workaholic, so he or she must stay disciplined about achieving balance and then use his or her powerful energy to build wonderful things that contribute to the general welfare of all.

Sixes and Sevens

If the powerful energies present with 22/4 are abused by indulgence in grandiose dreams of self-glorification, then the 22/4 will lower his or her vibration to the mundane level of the 4 and become the workhorse, bean counter, or laborer, instead of the enterprising spiritual leader this number promises.

Here are some of the more famous 22/4s:

Visionaries and Luminaries:

➤ General Colin Powell

➤ Ron Howard

➤ Woody Allen

➤ Vince Lombardi

➤ James Mitchner

➤ Mike Nichols

➤ Issac Stern

➤ Luciano Pavorotti

Master Builders:

➤ Bill Gates

➤ Rory Gates (son of Bill Gates)

➤ P.T. Barnum

➤ J.D. Rockerfeller III

➤ Frank Sinatra

➤ Winston Churchhill

Leaders of Cosmic Principles for a Material World:

➤ Yogi Maharishi

➤ Pope Paul I

➤ Swami Sachitanada

➤ Stephen Covey (Principle Centered Leadership)

By the Numbers

The master number **33/6** carries two 3s and reduces to a 6. Therefore it carries all of the qualities of the 3 and the 6. (Refer to Chapter 7, "The Number 3: Keeping It Light," and Chapter 10, "The Number 6: We Are Fam-i-ly," for an in-depth look at these qualities.)

The Master Number 33: Master of Healing Love

The meaning of the number 33 is "Master of Healing Energies Through Love." This number is on the journey of discovering its powerful healing energy through an open heart and unconditional love. Through love and example, the 33/6 awakens others to its depth and understanding of how to make spiritual truths work in the material world.

Key Words, Colors, and Gemstones

Altruistic and selfless—those are just two of the key words that begin to describe the 33/6. We've provided colors and gemstones to help you understand this deeply felt master number, too.

The Master Number 33

Key Words	Color	Gemstone
Intuitive	Deep sky blue	Lapis lazuli
Visionary		
Sensitive		
Selfless service		
Ministering		
Avatar		
Altruistic		
Caring		
Nurturing of the spirit		
Mystical		
Sympathetic		
Tenderhearted		
Emotional		
Protective		
Forgiving		

Key Words	Color	Gemstone
Loving		
Mercy		
Crusader for justice		
Cosmic parent		
Teacher of teachers		

Also important to consider are:

➤ **Astrological Equivalent:** Cancer/Pisces.

➤ **Guardian Angel:** Michael—the angel of protection who is dedicated to the preservation of the spiritual destiny of each soul.

Mastery Through Giving

For a long time, the 33/6 was thought to be the highest master number there was, signifying the highest human consciousness possible. Because of this, the number 33 has been elevated to nearly divine status, and called the number of the *avatar*. However, with the expansion of human consciousness, we now allow for other master numbers beyond the 33.

The 33/6 is a champion of the underdog, and exudes compassion, love, and empathy. This master number willingly gives of itself, lending encouragement and heartfelt understanding to all who need help. It's thought that the 33/6 has Christ-like qualities of sacrificing itself for the sake of others. However, because of their tenderheartedness and sensitivity, 33/6s can easily be swept into the despair of others, feeling the deep pain of the world.

The 33/6s are highly emotional and can find themselves in emotional distress from their heartfelt identification with those in need. Like all master numbers, the 33/6 will need to master balance and detachment (but with a caring attitude). These are not easy lessons for this number. Because it's made up of two 3s, this number experiences a double dose of emotional expression.

Easy as 1-2-3

The master number 33/6's astrological equivalent is shared by two signs: Cancer and Pisces. Cancer rules the heart, the emotional aspect of the human experience which is represented by the 6, while the creative, expressive, mystical, self-sacrificing, healing energy of Pisces reflects the energy of the double 3.

By the Numbers

Avatar is a Sanskrit term meaning "descent." In Hinduism, an avatar is thought to be a human incarnation of the Divine who mediates between people and God. Krishna, an East Indian deity, is considered the most perfect expression of the Divine, and so an avatar. In popular usage, this word is used to indicate a person or program of superior spiritual achievement in consciousness development.

Plus, with the number 6 (3 + 3) as its root number, it carries the weight of self-imposed responsibility for the welfare of others.

The Prime Directive of the 33/6

The prime directive of the 33/6 is to benefit, serve, and administer to as many people as possible. Because of the strong presence of the need to right injustice and human rights, those with this number are often found caring for the elderly or the handicapped, or in some from of service which benefits humanity. This number is exemplified by Elizabeth Kübler-Ross, whose life work is devoted to teaching and helping others understand the process of death and dying.

This number would like to heal all with its love.

Attributes of the 33/6

This master number has a special gift of working with humility and is unaffected by the power it has. If you're a 33/6, many will perceive the light that glows from you and will gladly follow you: Your faith and love show them the way. You see beyond the situation to the good in all people, regardless of color, race, or creed. In fact, you're Love personified.

Weaknesses of the 33/6

The greatest challenge for the 33/6 is to focus his or her emotions on higher goals in tune with spiritual laws, rather than trying to solve each and every problem of humanity. This master number is here to learn detachment, to express love and kindness, and to willingly respond to the needs of others. If the 33/6 remembers the universal principle, "everything happens for a reason, and there is a divine plan for all of life," then the 33/6 will lessen his or her stress and restore balance. In this way, the 33/6 will find direction for his or her own spiritual growth.

Sixes and Sevens

Because the number 6 is carried within this master number 33/6, there will be a tendency to be burdened and overly responsible. This is where the 33/6 gets out of balance.

The 33/6s may have trouble distinguishing where their service is truly needed due to their confusion over hearing someone's story and deciphering fact from fiction. They will learn that they can't be all things to all people. Remember, 33/6s have come to learn mastery for themselves through loving service, and they must always strive for balance, emotionally and spiritually.

Clear expression of the 33/6's own needs and a willingness to let others be responsible for their own "stuff" is part of what the 33/6 is here to learn. Sacrifice is valuable only as long as there is still a "self" left to do the sacrificing. The 33/6 may be the "Cosmic Parent," and the Master of Healing Energy, but, like all parents and healers, the 33/6 must hold some back for him- or herself.

The lesson of healing with love is to love yourself first and to heal yourself first, so that you may truly be of service to mankind.

Here are some of the more famous 33/6s:

The Expressive Ones:

- ➤ Meryl Streep
- ➤ Robert DeNiro
- ➤ Richard Dreyfuss
- ➤ Francis Ford Coppola
- ➤ Fred Astaire
- ➤ Pearl Bailey
- ➤ Mikhail Baryshnikov
- ➤ B.B. King
- ➤ Linda Ronstadt
- ➤ Bonnie Raitt
- ➤ André Segovia

Leaders of Compassion:

- ➤ Elisabeth Kübler-Ross
- ➤ Dale Carnegie
- ➤ John Bradshaw
- ➤ Dag Hammarskjold
- ➤ Christopher Reeve
- ➤ Steven Spielberg

A Final Note on Master Numbers

With all of the master numbers, it's important to remember that these are not indications of perfection, nor do they have greater significance than the other numbers. All master number people have come here to learn mastery and at the same time to fulfill an agreement to help the human race.

All of the master numbers are challenged to live according to spiritual principles and higher consciousness. Most will have numerous tests and challenges to overcome in an effort to develop their mastery. With each master number, there is also a calling to become a leader, or a model of living awareness and reconciliation of the spiritual world with the material world.

Not all those with master numbers are sterling folk. Some have taken the path of least resistance, showing disregard for the humanistic and spiritual principles. In fact, it's not uncommon to find alcoholics, drug addicts, or vagrants among those who share master numbers. For some, the higher vibration is too much of a challenge, and, having free will, they'll choose not to rise to challenge. Others choose to disregard their original contract to help advance the race this time around. These choices create karmic debt, which is no escape but merely a postponement. We devote an entire chapter to discussing karma and karmic debt next.

Anytime you see a 2, 4, or 6 as one of your numbers, check to see if you have mistakenly reduced a master number. For all of you with master numbers doing your work out there helping all of us move forward in the universal scheme of things, we say blessings to you. We thought you might be curious about the other master numbers as well, so we have included a complete list of master numbers and their meanings.

Complete Chart of Master Numbers

11/2 Spiritual Messenger and Master of Illumination

> The test of this number is to develop honesty and integrity. Its challenge is what it has to teach the world. The 11/2 can only teach from its own experience, and, if it is out of integrity with itself, it cannot trust what it knows and cannot teach what it has learned.

22/4 Master Builder

> The challenge with this number is to develop positive and constructive use of energy. The test is to develop patience, discipline, and determination to bring spiritual consciousness in the material world through manifestation.

33/6 Master of Healing Energies Through Joyful Love and Service

> The challenge for this number is to learn to focus one's emotional attention on spiritual goals. The test is to learn that service and responsibility are joyful experiences when done from a loving heart.

44/8 Master of Material and Spiritual Power

> The challenge for this number is to develop self-control and perseverance while organizing time and talents. The test is to make the best spiritual use of the material abundance that comes naturally to this number.

55/1 Master of New Thought Forms

> As non-conformists, people with this master number's challenge and test is to expand spiritual consciousness to new spiritual insights that come from new patterns of thought. These thought patterns include mental activities such as healing, astral projection, mental telepathy, clairvoyance, and prophecy.

66/3 Master of Cosmic Love

The challenge and test of this master number is for personal transformation through suffering and sacrifice so that one's energy and love can be available to all nations and all people for teaching and sharing of wisdom.

77/5 Master of Spiritual Energies

The challenge for this master number is to achieve enlightenment and inner wisdom and transmute it into cosmic love through personal application. The test requires one to spiritualize the material world and materialize the spiritual into the world, which then brings about change and transforms old concepts into new concepts. All of this is to be done for all souls here on Earth.

88/7 Master of Material Reform

This master number is a karmic vibration that brings the opportunity and challenge for a new awakening that aligns the use of power and authority with the spiritual universe to link and reform the affairs of the material world with the spiritual laws of the universe.

99/9 Master of Universal Compassion and Love

This master number will learn the spiritual strength of the great avatars of the past in order to endure and sustain the crucifixion of the self that must take place in order to bring forth full transformation of this powerful vibration. The challenge and achievement inherent in this number is to assume great burdens for humanity, sacrificing the self. The demand is for health and purity of mind and body so that he or she may give love purely as the most potent healing force of the universe. We may not see this number in a name until well into the new millennium.

The Least You Need to Know

➤ The master numbers are the numbers of those who have come to this life with special purposes.

➤ The 11/2 is the inspirational leader.

➤ The 22/4 is the master builder.

➤ The 33/6 is the healer through love.

➤ Numbers 44/8, 55/1, 66/3, 77/5, 88/7, and 99/9 are master numbers we don't see very often.

The Karmic Numbers 10, 13, 14, 16, and 19: Lessons to Be Learned

Chapter 15

In This Chapter

➤ Karmic lessons and karmic debts

➤ Your karmic lessons: What's not in your name?

➤ The 10 represents rebirth and completion

➤ The 13 represents work to do

➤ The 14 represents temptation

➤ The 16 represents the abuse of love

➤ The 19 represents the abuse of power

Do you seem to pick the same kind of guy over and over? Or, do you never seem to learn to save money—even though you're often on the brink of bankruptcy?

The last of the numbers we'll be defining for you are the karmic numbers. These numbers represent life lessons you haven't yet learned, and which you are destined to repeat over and over until you do learn them. Knowing what your karmic numbers are can help you understand why you have the patterns you do—and then help you break them as well.

What Is Karma?

Karma is the belief that one reaps what one sows. In esoteric literature, karma is thought of as the universal law of cause and effect, which is played out over many cycles of rebirth, and so the playing out of karma can take place over many lifetimes.

Obviously, this belief system subscribes to the notion of reincarnation: The soul of an individual is reborn, again and again, into different physical bodies, and karma is worked out through each incarnation. In addition, there is both *good* karma and *bad* karma.

Karma is a term used to designate thoughts or actions of the past which show up in the present and require retribution, or, to put it colloquially, "payback time." The idea is that all life is connected, and so, what you do, say, and think will eventually come home to roost.

While the word karma comes from Eastern philosophy, we have a similar saying from our culture: "What goes around, comes around." Basically, both mean the same thing: that there is some labor of the soul that has to be righted. Karma is a belief that says, quite simply, each of us is responsible for our actions and thoughts.

By the Numbers

Karma, whether good or bad, is a playing out of the universal cause and effect, which takes place over many lifetimes of the reincarnated soul.

Karmic Debt

First, we want to introduce you to the idea of karmic debt (not to be confused with karmic lessons). Karma debt is a kind of a debt people accumulate, whether it's a debt of abuse of love or of power. Similarly, numbers 13, 14, 16, and 19 (*karmic debt numbers*) are about selfishness in love, power, work, or freedom in past lives, and indicate a total disregard for others, for consequences, or moral concern. The idea is that if you were self-serving and lazy, or cruel, irresponsible, or greedy in the past life, now, in this lifetime, is your chance to set the record straight.

The number 10 is a different story. It is not a karmic debt number, but it is a karmic number. We will explain the number 10 in a minute.

By the Numbers

The **karmic debt numbers**—10, 13, 14, 16, and 19—represent past life abuses which must be addressed in this lifetime.

Each of the metaphysical sciences have a unique way of identifying your karmic responsibility. In the Tarot, for example, we see the karma story played out in the cards from the Major Arcana: Card numbers 10 through 19 are considered to be karmic cards. Note that the karmic debt numbers are 13, 14, 16, and 19, and the number 10 is a good karma number.

While there are several kinds of karmic indicators in numerology, in this chapter we're concentrating on only two of them: karmic lessons and karmic numbers.

Karmic Lessons

Karmic lessons are indicated by the numbers missing in your birth name. When a number and its vibration are absent from your birth name, it's an indication of an energy that you haven't experienced in a previous life, and so is a vibration missing in your energy field at birth. In this life, you are given the opportunity to experience this energy.

Whether the missing energy was purposely avoided in past lives, or whether circumstances prevented you from including this in your field of experience is open for debate among numerologists. Nonetheless, the missing number(s) will make a significant mark on your life this time. In fact, the experience of the missing number or vibration will show up in your life over and over again, until you finally master the energy of that number.

By the Numbers

Karmic lessons are things you must learn in this life because you haven't experienced them in past lives.

Your Karmic Lessons by the Numbers

Your karmic lesson number or numbers identify the specific action, thought, or understanding you'll want to pay attention to in this lifetime. You can think of karmic lessons as a way to learn what's out of balance in your vibrational pattern or your makeup: Once you know what number or numbers are missing from your name, you'll know what to work on. It's kind of a neat system for bringing balance to your life. Of course, while you're doing the work, it won't seem so spiffy!

But just think, you might get it together this time! When we make the effort, life flows.

Meeting Your Lessons—Not Again!

To find your karmic lesson number(s), find the missing number(s) in your birth name. Note that you can have more than one number missing, and in some cases, there might be as many as five numbers missing. The fact that you're missing numbers in your name means it will be necessary to use these numbers' specific energies to deal with the situations life brings you this time.

> **Numerology Rule #8**
>
> To find your karmic lesson(s), look for the missing numbers in your birth name.

The important thing to remember is that missing numbers represent vibrations missing in your overall essence, kind of like a part of yourself you would want to reclaim so that you might be whole.

Finding the missing numbers in your birth name requires that you lay out your birth name, assign the appropriate numbers to the letters in your name, and then determine which number(s) are missing. You're looking, of course, for numbers 1 through 9 only—no letter will have a number higher than that.

Merlin's Notes

Whether you have to start from scratch and develop the missing qualities indicated by the missing numbers in your name depends on whether any of these karmic lesson numbers show up in your 5 core numbers. If you do have any of your karmic lesson numbers in your core numbers, then the overall effect of the karmic lesson is lessened. This means that you have an innate ability to handle these karmic situations as they arise—unless, of course, you're expressing the negative qualities of the number. Then the karmic lessons will prove to be obstacles.

A Karmic Lesson for Ken Starr

Remember Kenneth Starr, the controversial Independent Counsel who investigated President Bill Clinton in the Monica Lewinsky scandal? Let's see what karmic lessons Ken Starr is working on in this lifetime.

First, let's write out Ken Starr's birth name and each letter's number:

K	e	n	n	e	t	h		W	i	n	s	t	o	n		S	t	a	r	r
2	5	5	5	5	2	8		5	9	5	1	2	6	5		1	2	1	9	9

Next, let's do a missing numbers chart by counting how many times each number appears in the name and writing it into the chart. The following table shows how we would do this for Mr. Starr.

Missing Numbers Chart for Kenneth Winston Starr

Number	How Many Times It Appears
1	3
2	4
3	0
4	0
5	7
6	1
7	0
8	1
9	3

Now we look to see which numbers are missing. In Ken Starr's case, we find three: the 3, 4, and 7. This means that in this lifetime, Kenneth Starr is working on the lessons of

➤ The 3: Learning to say what is true for him emotionally.

➤ The 4: Learning to be practical, reliable, and disciplined without becoming controlling, rigid, or stubborn.

➤ The 7: Learning to look within for wisdom and truth.

How do you think he's doing? Of course, we can't know Mr. Starr's personal, inner work, only what the media shows us—but we'd say he's working on these lessons every day, just as we're all addressing our own karmic issues.

Sixes and Sevens

We can acquire some very personal and private information about a person with numerology. We remind you once again that this information is considered sacred, and all who dip from this well are called to do so with respect and honor.

Getting It Right This Time

Remember, these are karmic lessons, so it's implied that you'll be working on your karma with other people in the picture, very likely karmic souls from another life. In fact, there's speculation in metaphysical circles that Ken Starr and Bill Clinton were doing some kind of a karmic dance. Were they possibly brothers in a past life who betrayed each other? Or, perhaps, competitive warriors? We give more insight about this possibility at the close of this chapter when we discuss karmic debt numbers.

Karmic Debt Numbers

The second karmic aspect we look for in numerology is the presence of karmic debt numbers in a chart. These numbers will show up as your birthday number or one of your 5 core numbers. No matter where they show up, however, it's a signal that you're working with issues from the past. The number itself will tell the nature of the issue you are facing.

Finding Karmic Debt Numbers

As we described in Chapter 4, "Learning to Read Between the Numbers," when you're figuring your birth name or birth date, you reduce first and then add across. It's precisely this process you'll want to check again to see if that final total included any karmic debt numbers (13, 14, 16, or 19) before you reduced them to 4, 5, 7, or 1. Got it? Look to see if you have karmic debt numbers hidden in your name or birth date, or if you have a karmic Birthday Number.

Remember, a karmic debt is owed because of something that occurred in a past life where there was misuse of power or love—and now it's payback time. In other words, some action you took in a past life is now requiring you to set matters right.

183

Merlin's Notes

Karmic lesson numbers and karmic debt numbers are not the same thing! The numbers missing from your birth name represent the karmic lessons—experiences you didn't have or master previously. Karmic debt numbers, however, are found in your 5 core numbers, or your birthday number: Look for numbers 13, 14, 16, or 19. In both cases, you'll be called to consciously address them or unconsciously encounter them. When working with karmic debt numbers you'll want to remember that it is the double-digit number that tells if it is a karmic number or not.

Payback Time

Chances are you're already familiar with this concept, whether because the same people keep showing up, or the same situations keep repeating themselves. Either way, it's clear you're meant to be learning something.

The karmic debt numbers 13, 14, 16, and 19, are defined like this: The number 1 in each number signifies selfish abuse of the number that follows. The number following the 1 indicates the arena in which the selfishness was played out:

Easy as 1-2-3

As you reduce any number, watch for karmic numbers. By the same token, when you find the final reduced number is 1, 4, 5, or 7, look at its double-digit origin, which may reveal a karmic debt number. When a 4 is a reduction of 13, a 5 of 14, a 7 of 16, and a 1 of 19, a karmic debt number is present.

➤ The number 3 in 13: creativity energy and joyfulness turn into frivolity and superficiality.

➤ The number 4 in 14: discipline, hard work, accountability, and stability turn into rebelliousness and indulgence, all in an effort to escape what's required.

➤ The number 6 in 16: love and commitment have been forsaken.

➤ The number 9 in 19: wisdom, spiritual knowledge, and power have been used for personal gain.

Numerologists write these numbers as 13/4, 14/5, 16/7, and 19/1, because the reduced number or the base number tells where the debt lies and what the remedy is for releasing the debt. But we'll discuss each of these in depth in a few pages.

The Burdens of Karma

One thing to keep in mind with these karmic numbers is that it's believed that anyone with one of these numbers has taken on an additional burden in order to learn the necessary lesson. This burden is the karmic debt. These four karmic numbers take on great significance if found in the numbers of the

➤ Life Path.

➤ Destiny.

➤ Soul.

➤ Birthday.

Number 10: The Wheel of Fortune

Let's take a look at a karmic number that's not often listed with the karmic debt numbers because it has a different sort of karma—good karma—and is not really about a debt yet to be paid.

The number 10 means karmic completion, and is the number of rebirth. It suggests that the karmic debt has been paid and now the person is free to begin again, free from past debt. Look to see if this number shows up in your chart. Remember, a 10 might be reduced to a 1 (1 + 0), so be sure to look at your 1s to see if any of them might actually be a 10/1.

No matter where the 10 is found in a chart, it refers to a kind of destiny. This means you'll encounter situations and people in this lifetime that will allow you to complete the karma present in those situations. The 10 gives you the opportunity to stand on your own and to use all of the positive traits of numbers 1 through 9.

Merlin's Notes

In the Tarot deck, the number 10 is the Major Arcana's Wheel of Fortune, which signifies a new cycle of luck is about to begin. In numerology, the 10 signifies all of the energy of the number 1—a new beginning, a time of planting seeds and starting again. But it also carries the energy of the 0, which suggests there's something unknown about the new beginning, which promises potential. As you can see, the karmic number 10 identifies a period of new growth—debt free!

In addition, the 10 usually indicates there has been a past misuse of personal power, and that you're now called to use courage, independence, and leadership to bring about the destined rebirth. It's a time when your life needs to link up with the universal.

The 10 is considered a fortunate number and holds the promise of victory in difficult situations. This rebirth has been a long time coming. Go forth with courage!

Number 13: All Work and No Play

While the number 13 is usually associated with bad luck, when it appears as a karmic debt number, it's not about luck. Instead, expect hard work in all areas of your life. In fact, the 13 is one of the most misunderstood numbers of all.

The purpose and goal of this vibration is to bring a spiritual consciousness into matters of expression and to develop discipline. For example, when you "tell it like it is," you will have to learn how to do it without being abusive in your presentation. The other part of the 13/4 debt is to be disciplined in practical matters, such as not waffling on your commitment to lower your cholesterol. It's not just a matter of you being "good" this time, it's about understanding that what you abuse now will eventually require retribution, either in this lifetime or the next.

The 13 indicates that you are developing a spiritual conscience and beginning to see that all things are linked. With a 13/4 on any of your core numbers or as your Birthday Number, you'll have obstacles that have to be overcome again and again until the lesson is fully learned and the debt completed.

Merlin's Notes

In numerology, the 13 is written 13/4 because if you add the 1 to 3 you get the reduced number 4. It's the number 4 that tells of the hard work, and a person with this number will face tests of discipline, integrity, and hard work. The debt that's been incurred from the past is that of possible laziness, allowing others to carry your share of the work, choosing frivolousness and superficiality as opposed to serious endeavors, and abusing the power you have with words (as in being a gossip, manipulating others with words, or negativity).

Usually people with 13/4 will exhibit the negative traits of the 4, which are

➤ Being rigid.

➤ Needing to control.

➤ Being dogmatic.

➤ Blaming others for limitations they feel.

Living with a 13/4

In this lifetime, the 13/4 will need to accept limitations and restrictions and learn to work constructively through the hard work. If the 13/4 should resort to laziness or negativity (just like the last life), then the problems only magnify. The lesson is to just hang in there, gut it out, and do the hard work.

However, even if you were been born on the 13th of the month or have a 13/4 Life Path, do not despair. Many famous people carry karmic 13 birthdays:

➤ Fidel Castro (born August 13)

➤ Thomas Jefferson (born April 13)

➤ Margaret Thatcher (born October 13)

And even The Queen Mother of England (born 8-4-1900) has a 13/4 Life Path, as does Carolyn Myss (author of *Anatomy of Spirit* and *The Power to Heal*), who was born 12-2-1952.

Wherever the 13 shows up, you'll be given the opportunity to succeed by focusing your energy. Usually there will be temptations in this life to take the shortcut or to go for the quick way out. But because this is the number of discipline and hard work, no shortcuts are allowed.

In order to have success with this number, you must maintain order in your life (the 4 rules order). This means you'll have to keep your appointments, follow through on commitments (yes, you'll have to be the chairman for next year's auction—you promised!), keep your house neat and tidy, and never procrastinate.

With a 13/4 in your chart, you're here to learn this lesson of focus and discipline. But there's good news, too: If you make a steady and consistent effort, you will find reward and success. The key is to concentrate and direct your energies.

What if you don't do it? What if you say, "Forget it, it's too much work"? Well, that's how you got into debt last time! If you choose (and we do mean choose, because we all have free will) to blow off the required focus or discipline, then know that you'll be doing this routine over and over again, in this life or in the next. Remember, this is karma: Debts have to be paid!

Number 14/5: The Temptations

The karmic number 14/5 involves past lifetimes where freedom was abused. The debt is to relearn the value of freedom and the discipline required to earn this freedom. In a past life, those with this number will have found freedom for themselves at the expense of others, and that's where the debt comes in: There was some kind of irresponsibility and lack of accountability in the past.

Now it's your time to set things right. The 14/5 is the number of the rebellious free spirit who knows no limits to his or her desire for adventure, risk, and escape.

As you may remember from our discussion in Chapter 9, "The Number 5: You Shall Adapt!" the number 5 is also the number of sex and sensuality. So it follows that someone with the karmic number 14/5 will take huge risks in the name of sexual, lustful pursuits. At the end of this chapter, we'll let you in on someone with a 14 in her chart who's had her 15—make that 14—minutes of fame.

Sixes and Sevens

In numerology, 14/5 is written as such because it reduces to a 5 (1 + 4 = 5). It's that 5 that calls for change in behavior. Those with a 14 karmic debt (whether as your Life Path, Birthday, Soul, or Destiny Number) will have to spend this lifetime adjusting to ever-changing circumstances and unexpected events.

The number 14/5 in one of the 5 core numbers indicates that you'll tend to exhibit the negative traits of the number 5—jumping from relationship to relationship or job to job, for example—with no sense of accomplishment or goal firmly in mind. There's also a tendency to pleasure oneself through physical sensations, be it food, sugar, sex, drugs, or anything else that meets your fancy.

The 14/5 represents the craving for something new and exciting rather than doing the boring, hard work of discipline or building something by sticking to it and seeing it through (all traits of the 4). Eventually, once you see that this is not the road to freedom, you'll take a more constructive path.

Getting to the Root of the 14/5

Let's look more closely at the root of this number, the 5. The 5, remember, is the number of change and freedom. That means that when the 5 shows up as the karmic debt number 14, the issues will be about having to rein in any escape mechanism tendencies such as drug abuse, alcohol or food addictions, or overindulgence in sensual pleasures. We're talking about past uses of these addictive behaviors as ways to escape (because you crave freedom) from the task at hand.

Now, in this life, you're required to become moderate—not with disregard for tomorrow, but using temperance today. It should come as no surprise that the number 14 card in the Tarot deck is the Major Arcana's Temperance.

The key to this karmic debt number is commitment, something that a person with this number will have found hard to do in previous lives. This means commitments will be hard to make until you've learned the lessons of the 4 in the 14, which says, "You've got to have order to your life in order to maintain clarity and focus."

The 4 also suggests that mental and emotional stability are called for in order to hold a steady course as your life presents you with endless changes. You must commit to order and structure in your life, and being flexible and adaptable are at the very core of this struggle.

What else can you expect when the 14/5 is one of your core numbers?

➤ If you have 14 as your Soul Number, you might expect emotional upsets and delays.

➤ If 14 is your Destiny Number, then you'll possibly learn these lessons through setbacks, disappointments, and reversal of fortune, or, at the very least, be presented with life circumstances where you have to make commitments, stick to your goals, and weather the many ups and downs that come with this number.

➤ If 14 is the number of your Life Path, you are here to learn to let go, resist the temptations of indulgence, allow things to change, and steer a steady course.

Success lies in being able to establish a belief system for yourself that allows you to magnetically draw what you need to maintain order to your life and do all things in moderation. You cannot become fixed, rigid, or controlling under this number, for the law of change will demand that you roll with the punches.

These karmic debt numbers require that we go back and do it over. This time, however, it helps if you know what the lesson is you're trying to learn and be aware of the name of the challenge you're facing. You can do it—just remember Universal Law #5.

Sixes and Sevens

No matter how bad it gets, you can't succeed with 14/5 if you try to gain freedom using destructive methods. This will bring loss, sickness, and, in extreme cases, even death.

Sixes and Sevens

In case we haven't made ourselves clear, the number 14/5 suggests that in some way the person with this number has misused, avoided, or misunderstood freedom in past lives, and now in this life he or she is meant to bring the freedom issue into balance. The 14/5 is basically going to have to learn to love the Universal Law of Change, because it will be a constant in his or her life.

Universal Law #5

You're never given more than you can handle.

The thing to remember with the number 14/5 is *temperance* in all things.

Number 16/7: The Abuse of Love

The karmic debt of the 16/7 arises from past involvement in illicit love affairs that caused suffering to others: In some manner, love was abused. Quite simply, the 16/7 indicates a failure in the past to act responsibly in matters of love.

As with all karmic debt numbers, the 1 in this number indicates self-centeredness. In addition, the 6 in 16 suggests a lack of responsibility and distortion of loving feelings. Past abuses stem from a lack of integrity with regard to the feelings of others involving love, family, or commitment—all components of involvement in the notorious "love affair."

We write this karmic debt number as 16/7, for it's the reduced number 7 where the remedy is for releasing the debt. Until they learn to act otherwise, people with a 16/7 number usually exhibit the negative traits of the number 7:

➤ Indifference

➤ Analytical aloofness

➤ Withdrawal

➤ Difficult to approach

➤ More concern for his or her own needs of privacy than for the feelings of others

➤ Intellectualizing emotions

The influence of the number 7 is that it's the number of the mystic—one who goes within and relies on his or her higher guidance. The 7 requires that a person look to the source of all things as the guiding inspiration. It's only then that a 16/7 person is no longer torn by the outer world. Similarly, the goal with the 16/7 is to link the personal spirit with the universal spirit. Only then does the person's path become tranquil and the repetitive cycle of destruction and rebirth stop.

Sixes and Sevens

Permanent relations are hard to maintain with the 16/7. Remember, the 7 doesn't like to bother with having to relate to others if it appears difficult. People with this number meet with substantial difficulties until they can devote themselves to selfless, loving ways. With this number, it's not unusual (the 7 *is* unusual) to find that sudden, strange circumstances bring loss of friends and relationship.

The karmic number 16/7 is also the Major Arcana Tower card in the Tarot deck, which symbolizes destruction of the old and a rebirth of the new. When unforeseen and sudden events tear down what was established, this card-carrying 16/7 is forced to rebuild yet again. The Tower indicates an awakening to the spiritual truths that lie deep within, and the essence of the number 16/7 carries the same message: A spiritual rebirth is required in order to release the karmic debt. In fact, what happens is that there's usually some kind of fall from the "tower" in one's life.

Destruction and rebirth are two interwoven themes of the number 16/7. Life presents the 16/7 with challenges that will humble the individual, and it's precisely this humility that's the key to future success. An individual with this number will learn to follow a course of higher consciousness that will come from the continual cycle of destruction and rebirth that dominates the 16/7's life.

The number 16/7 indicates that the person with this number has a tendency to use his or her highly intuitive and refined intellect to look down on others. In addition, the 16/7 won't be a stranger to alienation and loneliness in this lifetime.

You Can Run, but You Can't Hide

The number 16/7 is the path of personal development and spiritual growth. It presents the opportunity to transform, but it demands a kind of tearing down and rebuilding of one's life in order to do so. The key word for the number 16/7 is "awaken": The person must awaken to the higher principles of living life on Earth. This number will take you down the path that "rises out of the ashes," reconstructing your life on higher ground.

Remember, this number has great significance if you have a 16/7 Life Path, Soul, Destiny, or Birthday Number. If that's the case, your life will be a series of events that bring you to the bottom, only to rise up again, to fall again, and so on. The pattern will continue until you finally grasp the notion that you must honor the spiritual, higher nature of all things, and that now you must rebuild your life on those principles. That's the debt, the story, and the release of the number 16/7.

The Number 19/1: Abuse of Power—and You Knew Better

The last of the karmic numbers is 19/1. With this number, you might think that the gods are not happy, because the 19/1 is a travesty against all that is sacred, compassionate, and spiritually correct. You can be sure there's been some kind of abuse of power when the 19/1 is present: The karmic debt of this number stems from past abuses of acting in a completely self-centered manner, blind to everything except self-fulfillment of one's own desires. The basis of this number is learning to stand on your own and the proper use of power.

The reduced number 1 of this number indicates that a 19/1 person will often exhibit the negative traits of this number, until the lessons have been understood. The negative traits are

➤ Selfishness.
➤ Intimidation.
➤ Dependence.
➤ Failing to stand up for oneself.
➤ Stubbornly resisting help from others.
➤ Egotism.
➤ Laziness.
➤ Aggression.

Easy as 1-2-3

The central lesson of the 19/1 is that while learning to stand on your own, you must also learn to seek support, assistance, and understanding from others. Of all the karmic numbers, this one will learn in spades that no man is an island.

Merlin's Notes

The 19 is made up of the numbers 1 and 9 and when reduced is written as 19/1. The 1 here indicates past life selfishness, and the 9 represents attainment, particularly of spiritual knowledge. In the old days, 9 was considered the number of God, and in current times, it's still thought to be the number of high cosmic consciousness. The point is, in a past life this person has had the power of the universe at hand. Even with this knowledge and power, the person chose to pursue selfish ends, disregarding the rights of individuals or cosmic consequences.

When you have this number, don't be surprised to find that throughout your life you're forced to stand up for yourself or, worse, are left to stand alone. Difficulties faced in this life will teach independence, consideration of others, and having to assert yourself rather than hang back and appear weak. Because of a tendency to stubbornly resist help from others, you may find yourself in a self-imposed prison.

Paying a Little Karmic Debt

It is thought that the karmic debt of the 19/1 developed from the abuse of power in the past. In some manner, there was a life of selfishness—disregard of anyone else. The 19/1 indicates a past life where you had a position of power in some way, and in that position you chose to live life for yourself instead of for the good of all. In some way, you used your power to gain favors and status or satisfy personal desires.

In this life, 19/1s repeat these patterns until situation after situation arise that call for them to rectify these past abuses. Usually, the 19/1 person will be immersed in his or her own concerns and have difficulty becoming aware of the needs of others. The 19/1s are often surprised by others' negative reactions because they're so used to thinking of themselves that when they finally do see themselves through the eyes of others, they're surprised and often confused. The 19/1s just can't seem to see themselves realistically in relation to others.

Easy as 1-2-3

As with all the karmic numbers, if the 19/1 shows up as your Destiny, Soul, Life Path, or Birthday Number, you're dealing with a karmic debt.

Sometimes 19/1s may appear unable to act on their own. Unhappy with their dependence, yearning to be independent, but unable to take action, they find solace in blaming others or the environment for their own inability to stand on their own two feet.

Success comes from looking past your own needs to the needs of others. When you work toward independence, resisting the urge to be dependent or feel weak, you'll begin to pay off this karmic debt. Of course, just being aware that you have a karmic debt will help you see a path for changing your life and changing your ways. After all, the 1 always promises a new beginning.

A Little Karma in Real Life

One of the most famous and prominent figures in the free world has a 19/1 karmic debt number. President William Jefferson Clinton was born August 19, 1946, so his birthday is the karmic number 19. His fame, aside from having been President of the United States, we think in part originates from this karmic debt number.

Was Clinton's affair with Monica Lewinsky and subsequent encounter with Kenneth Starr a karmic drama played out on the world stage so that Mr. Clinton might begin to pay off his karmic debt? Were these self-serving interludes and Clinton's seeming inability to ask for help a repeat of a very old pattern? Is this not a symbolic, if not actual, abuse of personal power?

One wonders, with the intensity of this story, if in fact Lewinsky and Starr might also be karmic figures reappearing to help Mr. Clinton face this karmic debt. Let's take a look at this karmic play and see what comes up.

A Cast of Karmic Players

Okay—let's take a look closer at the numbers of the three main players in the "Clinton Affair." In this remarkable story of sex, scandal, abuse of power, and search-and-destroy mentality, we find it an equally remarkable coincidence that each of these players has a karmic debt number influencing his or her life. Or is it a coincidence?

Let's start with Monica Lewinsky. She has a 14/5 Life Path Number, which indicates indulgences of the flesh and a karmic debt to be repaid.

Next, there's Kenneth Starr. He has a 16/7 Life Path Number, which represents an abuse of love stemming from an illicit love affair in a past life, and now, in this life, the karmic debt is to be paid (by having to wade through someone else's affair?).

Last, there's President Bill Clinton. He has a 19/1 Birthday Number, which indicates an abuse of power for personal gain. He, too, is required to pay his karmic debt.

Is it any wonder that these three characters came together? We have no doubt that these people have reconvened on the world stage to play out some karmic dance, each with his or her own karmic debt. Remember, "As ye reap, so ye shall sow." That's what karmic debts are all about.

It's believed that those with karmic debt numbers have taken on an additional burden in order to learn their lessons and pay off their debts. We'd say some kind of extra burden is at work in the lives of Monica Lewinsky, Ken Starr, and Bill Clinton.

When a karmic opera such as this one is played out on a world stage, there is a resonant note for all of us. Because the story is played out in a public forum, we are allowed to see the lessons and mistakes of these people and recognize them in ourselves as well. This in turn calls forth our higher consciousness and reminds us to live with honesty and integrity in all of our dealings and decisions.

> ### The Least You Need to Know
>
> ➤ Karmic lessons and karmic debts are not the same thing.
>
> ➤ Karmic lessons are numbers missing in your name.
>
> ➤ Karmic debts are past abuses of love, power, work, or freedom.
>
> ➤ Karmic debts mean extra burdens.

Part 4
Getting Personal with the Numbers

You've learned the meaning of each number. Now it's time to learn to calculate your own numbers and take a closer look at what each of your special numbers means. We'll begin, simply, with your Life Path Number, which is calculated from the numbers of your birth date. Then we'll move on to your Destiny and Soul Numbers, and examine what your name reveals about you, too.

Chapter 16

Your Birthday Number: A Gift for Yourself

In This Chapter

➤ Finding your Birthday Number

➤ A day to call your own

➤ What your birthday says about you

➤ Your birthday number is especially important in the approximate years 28 through 56 of your life

You may remember that in Chapter 1, "Foundations of Numerology," we introduced you to the first of your numbers, your Birthday Number. Quite simply, your Birthday Number is the number of the day you were born.

In this chapter, we're going to take a look at each of the 31 days of the month and see what your Birthday Number reveals about you.

You Say It's Your Birthday

No number is as simple to find as your *Birthday Number*. That's because this number is simply the day you were born, whether it's the 1st or the 31st or any day in between. While it's not the most important number in numerology, it *is* fun and easy to find. All you need to know is the day you were born.

Your Birthday Number influences the middle years of your life. The number under which you were born plays a special role from the approximate years 28 through 56. We discuss the influence of your Birthday Number during those years in Chapter 24, "Your Major Cycles: It's All in the Timing."

One key thing to remember is that your Birthday Number is the day of the month itself, and that day also may be a reduced number as well. If, for example, you've got a 24 birthday, your Birthday Number is 24 (with aspects of both the 2 and the 4 as well as the 24!)—but it's also a reduced 6 (2 + 4). We've grouped each set of Birthday Numbers under their reduced numbers, so that's where you'll find your number.

Here's an index of birthdays, by the numbers.

Birthdays by the Numbers

Number Group Your Birthday Belongs To	Birthday: The Day You Were Born (Look Here for Your Birthday)
Number 1 Birthdays	1st, 10th, 19th, 28th
Number 2 Birthdays	2nd, 11th, 20th, 29th
Number 3 Birthdays	3rd, 12th, 21st, 30th
Number 4 Birthdays	4th, 13th, 22nd, 31st
Number 5 Birthdays	5th, 14th, 23rd
Number 6 Birthdays	6th, 15th, 24th
Number 7 Birthdays	7th, 16th, 25th
Number 8 Birthdays	8th, 17th, 26th
Number 9 Birthdays	9th, 18th, 27th

What's your Birthday Number? Write it in the star at the top of the cake!

What Your Birthday Number Reveals About You

Every day is special and every day is unique, but you share common traits with others born in your number group. If you were born on the 1st, 10th, 19th, or 28th, you share commonalties with others in this number group because all of these birthdays reduce to the number 1. The 1 birthdays, for example, naturally reveal someone who wants to be at the head of the pack.

It's important to remember that, in spiritual numerology, the belief is that your soul chose your birthday because that day reflected what makes you unique. If you were born just before or after midnight, in fact, you could read the descriptions for both days—but it will be your true Birthday Number that is the one to follow.

Number 1 Birthdays

People with number 1 birthdays are born on the 1st, 10th, 19th, or 28th and share an independent spirit, a desire to lead the pack, to be original, and usually are known to have courage. More than anything else, people whose birthdays add up to a 1 are pioneers.

Born on the 1st

You wanted to be first and here you are, leading off the month with your number 1 birthday. Individuality is number one with you, and you are both forceful with your ideas and good at giving orders—but not at receiving them. If your Birthday Number is 1, in fact, you already know that "Innovation" is your middle name.

Born on the 10th

If you've got a number 10 birthday, you'll want to read what we've said about the other number 1 birthdays, too, because you share many of those qualities. In addition, you're enterprising and determined, although you may have to overcome

By the Numbers

Your **Birthday Number** doesn't even need calculating—it's simply the day of the month you were born!

Easy as 1–2–3

When you think about what the Birthday Number means, the words "your special day" take on a whole new dimension, don't they? That's good—because your Birthday Number really is special—as special as you are.

Sixes and Sevens

The principle of the 1 is "I am," so it's sometimes difficult for people with number 1 birthdays to differentiate between ego and enthusiasm. If it seems no one else wants to jump on your bandwagon, maybe you'd better rethink the music you're playing.

some obstacles before getting what you want. More than anything, if you've got a number 10 birthday, you yearn for independence and are here to have some kind of rebirth. The 10 is a karmic number. We discuss this karmic number in Chapter 15, "The Karmic Numbers: 10, 13, 14, 16, and 19: Lessons to Be Learned."

Born on the 19th

A number 19 birthday also resonates to much of what we've said about all of the 1 birthdays. In addition, you're something of a dreamer, and much can make a big impression on you. A 19 birthday indicates ambition and optimism, and, although you're confident, you like to be encouraged. Your potential for achievement and financial reward is great, and you're also strong-willed, but you will have to watch how you use your power. Remember, 19 is a karmic number. We discuss this karmic debt number in Chapter 15.

Born on the 28th

Like the 1 birthday, you're determined and independent, and, with a 28 birthday, you're just rarin' to go. The 28 birthday can indicate that you're often fighting yourself when it comes to playing by the rules, but your sense of determination never allows you to stay down for long. In fact, as a 28, your ability to lead stems from clear thinking, and courage is the way you approach life.

Number 2 Birthdays

People with number 2 birthdays are born on the 2nd, 11th, 20th, or 29th and share the traits of the 2. Number 2 birthdays enjoy any activity that requires more than one person, love to be with others and to belong, and want to make sure there's cooperation and companionship in all they undertake.

Born on the 2nd

This birthday number seeks balance and harmony, and if this is your Birthday Number, you already know that you're the natural mediator in any situation. Adaptable and sensitive to others, your number 2 birthday means you'll always be the peacemaker.

Easy as 1-2-3

Key words for 2 birthdays include partnership, cooperation, agreeable, and amiable. Is it any wonder these birthdays are the numbers of some of your best friends?

Born on the 11th

With your master number birthday, you've got the three capital "I's" to guide you: idealism, inspiration, and innovation. With an 11 birthday, you'll want to read what we've said about the 2 birthday, as well, for 11 reduces to a 2 (1 + 1 = 2). You're both humble and confident. Your 11 birthday indicates that balance is key to a harmonious life, but you probably know that already. This is a master number birthday, so you may want to read more about the 11/2 in Chapter 14, "The Master Numbers: 11, 22, and 33: Potent Potential."

Born on the 20th

A number 20 birthday suggests that, like the 2 birthday, you're adaptable and understanding. In addition, the 0 suggests that you're intuitive as well, and may need to guard against others' taking advantage of your understanding nature. With a 20 birthday, tact is a byword, and you're always considerate of others.

Born on the 29th

A number 29 birthday means you have both personality and potential to spare. In addition, you're intuitive and a dreamer in the real sense of the word, and so should be careful not to let your moods swing too far in one direction or another. With a 29 birthday, inner peace is what you strive for.

Number 3 Birthdays

People with number 3 birthdays are born on the 3rd, 12th, 21st, or 30th and share the traits of creativity, enthusiasm, good senses of humor, and a capacity to spread joy. With their effervescence and confidence, self-expression is key for all of the number 3 birthdays.

Easy as 1–2–3

Many numerologists like to call the number 3 Birthday Numbers the numbers of the cheerleaders. Enthusiastic, bubbly, energetic, and encouraging, 3 birthday people often are the fun ones at the party.

Born on the 3rd

If you've got a number 3 birthday, you aren't just creative—you've got to be creative. In addition, your sense of fun and friendliness is contagious to all those around you. Blessed with a childlike happy spirit, with a 3 birthday, you're a creative joy giver. The 3 is considered the luckiest number of all.

Born on the 12th

Your number 12 birthday indicates that you share the 3's friendliness and enthusiasm, and that you also wish to establish an individuality of your own (that's the influence of the 1 in 12). "Creativity" is the name of the game here, and, in addition, the 12 is emotional, sociable, and affectionate.

Born on the 21st

Like all of the 3 birthdays, you're enthusiastic and friendly, but with a 21 birthday, you can be an absolute dynamo. Because being social is second nature to you, you have many friends—and many interests as well. With a 21 Birthday Number, you have a social gift, and enjoy people immensely, so you're great at entertaining in a creative way. As a 21, you positively radiate life, and, at your best, your creativity is an inspiration to others.

Born on the 30th

A number 30 means that you share similar traits of all of the 3s: You're charismatic, creative, and outgoing. In addition, you're often charismatic, attracting many people from different walks of life. You've probably got a way with words, too, and need to feel appreciated by others. Beware of being lazy or self-indulgent, but lucky as you are with this Birthday Number, your fine sense of art and harmony are positive aspects of this number. In addition, the 0 behind that 3 gives you tremendous power with your words, and self-expression is your emphasis, as well as the ability to inspire others.

Sixes and Sevens

You won't often find the words "sense of humor" associated with any of the number 4 birthdays. What these people do have, however, is a strong work ethic and commitment to seeing things through. Where would we be without them?

Number 4 Birthdays

People with number 4 birthdays are born on the 4th, 13th, 22nd, or 31st and share a desire for stability and order. People with 4 birthdays believe in strong foundations and are both practical and reliable, as well as honest and fair. Self-disciplined is the key word here, and all of the 4 birthdays are known to be hardworking and practical.

Born on the 4th

If you've got a number 4 birthday, you appreciate both form and order, and you'll make sure that everything around you is running like a top—including the tops. Number 4s believe in building strong foundations and then making certain that that order is maintained, and if you're a 4, you're both stable and strong. In addition, security is vitally important to a 4.

Born on the 13th

Like those with 4 birthdays, if you've got a 13 birthday, you understand the value of a good day's work. You're also emotionally sensitive, and the "3" in the 13 means you've got the potential for creative expression, if you're determined. Be aware that this is a karmic Birthday Number. If you're a 13, you may have health problems, and your challenge is to be willing to apply yourself and to not avoid the hard work. The 13s are great lovers of family and tradition and are natural organizers and managers. We discuss this karmic debt number in Chapter 15.

Born on the 22nd

With your master number birthday, your work ethic is matched by your leadership abilities and charisma, and you're practical and honest, without losing sight of the needs of others. People with 22/4 Birthday Numbers are often very successful and have many friends from many walks of life. In fact, we like to call the intuitive 22 birthday the master planner. We discuss this master number in more depth in Chapter 14.

Born on the 31st

A 31 Birthday Number suggests that you are strong-willed and determined, as well as fortunate and blessed with original ideas. You have artistic talent, too, but must search for concrete form to express it. Sometimes too focused on one specific goal, the 31 birthday needs to guard against stubbornness or even selfishness, but at your best, you're both practical and grounded, a builder through and through.

Number 5 Birthdays

People with number 5 birthdays are born on the 5th, 14th, or 23rd and share a sense of adventure and a desire for constant change and stimulation. Versatility is to the 5 birthday what stability is to the 4, and people with number 5 birthdays are both curious and freedom loving.

Merlin's Notes

Risk-taking is second nature to those with number 5 birthdays. In fact, we'd say risk-taking is *first* nature to these folks, so quick are they to take a chance, speculate, gamble, or accept a dare. Quick and clever, number 5 birthdays would sometimes do well to remember that curiosity killed the cat, and beware of get-rich-quick schemes. Paying close attention to such details—or any details—however, is not a number 5 birthday's strong point (leave that to the 2 birthdays). It's more about action—quick action—with a 5.

Born on the 5th

If you've got a number 5 birthday, you're adaptable, daring, progressive, quick-witted, and versatile. Never one to stay in the same place or position for long, with your number 5 birthday you have an active life that offers you many opportunities for change and new things. Patience is not your forte, but having your freedom is. Commitments can be hard to make with a 5 birthday.

Born on the 14th

A number 14 birthday suggests you've got both determination (that's the 1) and pragmatism (that's the 4), as well as many of the qualities of the number 5 birthday. In addition, you're an achiever who's not afraid of hard work or problems. With a number 14 birthday, you may also be a bit of a gambler or risk taker, which goes hand in hand with your restlessness and need for change and travel. This is a karmic birthday number and you may want to turn to Chapter 15 for a more detailed look at the 14/5.

Born on the 23rd

With a 23 birthday, you're likely a person who's emotionally sensitive, creative, and intuitive. Quick thinking and versatile, you learn quickly and are both adventurous and restless. In fact, the 23 is so restless, you may try many different experiences in your life—but you'll always make the best of any situation. With a 23 birthday, you'll want both good communication and lots of excitement.

Number 6 Birthdays

People with number 6 birthdays are born on the 6th, 15th, or 24th, share compassionate and caring natures, and are devoted to creating harmony for their loved ones. Artistic and idealistic, number 6 birthday people strive for balance and are both responsible and family oriented, as well as romantic.

Easy as 1-2-3

We like to think of people with number 6 Birthday Numbers as the moms of the Birthday Numbers. That's because they're nurturing and understanding—and always there for you.

Born on the 6th

Your number 6 birthday suggests that you are devoted to your loved ones and work hard for what you believe in. Creative and artistic, you may well have hand-painted your own furniture or woven your own rugs. When friends come for a visit, in fact, they may find a "Out in the garden," sign on the door, because the 6 birthdays love their gardens. Don't be surprised to find old roses and hollyhocks woven into their gardens, because they're romantic at heart. Domestic and nurturing, that's the 6 birthday.

Born on the 15th

A number 15 Birthday Number reveals that you're instinctive and generous, always willing to cooperate and give to others. Quick and engaging, you can easily apply theory to reality to get things done, and of all Birthday Numbers, may find it easiest to learn on the job. Multi-talented and with a gift for languages, your 15 Birthday Number suggests that you want to settle within the family structure and relationship, but commitment is the struggle, responsibility is the test, and restlessness is part of the bargain.

Born on the 24th

With a 24 Birthday Number, you'll be both hardworking (the 4) and fair (the 2). Because you've got a pragmatic approach to all things, you'll succeed through hard work and determination, as well as your sense of order and honesty. While sometimes stubborn, people with number 24 birthdays are also idealistic and like the other 6 birthdays, they love their home.

Number 7 Birthdays

People with number 7 birthdays are born on the 7th, 16th, or 25th, share a knack for research and analysis, and are often thoughtful and solitary. With a 7 birth number, you may be both psychic and rational (now there's a combination!), but you're also insightful and investigative.

Sixes and Sevens

People with 7 birthdays need to guard against skepticism, as well as a tendency to be secretive. The 7 is not the most trusting of numbers, after all, but 7 birthday people would do well to trust, at the very least, their intuition.

Born on the 7th

With a number 7 birthday, you may be quite the perfectionist, always refining until things are right, and can sometimes be quite self-absorbed. Number 7 birthday people, in fact, learn best when they're self-taught, so these are the great autodidacts (that means self-taught people) of the world. Because you're both inquisitive and secretive, you may appear hard to figure out to others—and there may be times when you don't even trust yourself. People with number 7 birthdays are not inclined to let others know what they're really thinking, because they're very private people. Many 7 birthday people have a scientific, technological preference.

Born on the 16th

With a 16 birthday, you're far more sociable than the reticent 7 birthday, but you still learn by doing. Intuitive and insightful, you're also ambitious and, because you've got both a 1 and a 6, are independent and family oriented. You may be a gifted writer, but you should guard against the mood swings that often plague creative types and learn to balance your dichotomy of overconfidence and doubt. More than anything, integrity is your byword. Because 16 is a karmic number, you might want to turn to Chapter 15 and read more about the karmic debt number 16/7.

Born on the 25th

If you've got a number 25 birthday, you'll seek to express yourself in more than one way. While you'll want everything perfect, your impatience may keep you from seeing things through. People with number 25 birthdays have strong minds, which help them analyze the facts and draw conclusions, and they're both perceptive and good at dealing with people.

Easy as 1-2-3

What makes a leader? Ambition, authority, hard work, and good judgment—all qualities of the 8 Birthday Number.

Number 8 Birthdays

People with number 8 birthdays are born on the 8th, 17th, or 26th, share a strength of character and authority, and may well accomplish great things in this life. If you've got an 8 birthday, chances are you're hardworking and thorough, as well as someone who's a natural when it comes to business and leadership.

Born on the 8th

If you've got a number 8 birthday, you've got a strong character, good judgment, and solid value system—all hallmarks of someone who can accomplish much. In addition, you're ambitious and have a desire for both material success and security, so being in charge goes with the territory.

Born on the 17th

With a number 17 birthday, you are often a specialist of some kind, having developed the expertise through experience or the research that comes so easily to the 7 in your number through the determination of the 1. Introspective and sometimes remote, you may appear quite serious to others, but that also means you can concentrate for long periods of time and learn best through experience. A good phrase for the 17 birthday person is "good business sense," because you'll never take anything at face value.

Born on the 26th

Your 26 Birthday Number suggests that you're practical, responsible, and have a good, solid sense of business. The 26 birthday person feels very strongly about the home (that's the 6) and about supporting and cooperating with those around him (that's the 2). Responsible and caring, with your 26 Birthday Number, you need to learn to be a source of strength to others without taking control of a situation.

Number 9 Birthdays

People with number 9 birthdays are born on the 9th, 18th, or 27th and share the traits of idealism and universal compassion. They're both generous and sensitive, with giving and humanitarianism being of utmost importance.

Born on the 9th

If you've got a number 9 birthday, you're compassionate and sensitive, and you may feel as if your life has already been preordained. You'll need to learn universal understanding, as well as patience and tolerance, all the while developing an impersonal approach that involves detachment and sensitivity.

Born on the 18th

With a number 18 birthday, you've got the assertiveness of the 1 coupled with the dynamism of the 8—rolled into the compassion of the 9. It's not an easy combination, but you are a born leader and an efficient manager. Because you're also a 9, you'll want to use your power to help others, but there's the possibility you could misuse it. Your challenge is to learn forgiveness and acceptance. At your best, you attract money from the service-oriented work you do.

Sixes and Sevens

It's not easy being the universal, detached, idealistic humanitarian, and sometimes people with number 9 birthdays can become frustrated, fragmented, or even selfish. If you've got a number 9 birthday—whether a 9, 18, or 27—beware of fantasizing as a means of escape, living in the dream world, and of others who may try to take advantage of you, for you have a tendency to be gullible and overly generous.

Born on the 27th

A number 27 birthday reveals that you're both intuitive and analytical—never entirely trusting either your imagination or your rational self. Others will find you original and creative, but you may also appear detached or secretive, because you don't like to share your deepest feelings. Learning will be the key to developing patience and self-discipline, and there's an element of sacrifice with this number. With a 27 birthday, you are concerned for the planet, and universal love is paramount to you.

39 Again? Your Birthday Number and You

Your Birthday Number isn't your most important number—but it's easy and fun. As you'll be finding out in the chapters that follow, it's your 5 core numbers that paint the most complete portrait of who you are and what your potentials and talents may be.

Still, your Birthday Number is a good place to begin your study of numerology, and it's a number that it's easy to discover for your friends and family as well. In fact, you may want to include someone's Birthday Number description with their next birthday card.

The Least You Need to Know

➤ Finding your Birthday Number is as easy as the day you were born.

➤ Your Birthday Number reveals your own special talent.

➤ Your Birthday Number especially influences the middle years of your life.

➤ Your Birthday Number shares similar characteristics with other birthdays in your number group.

Chapter 17

Your Life Path Number: Rules for the Road

In This Chapter

➤ Your Life Path Number shows you which road to follow

➤ Your birth date reveals your Life Path Number

➤ Your Life Path Number is one of your 5 core numbers

➤ Finding your own special opportunities

While you can change your name, your birth date will never change (unless your mother got it wrong in the first place!). Your birth date is all yours, so it has a tale to tell about you alone. Your birth date—that is, the month, day, and year you were born—is very important in numerology. It's called your Life Path.

Here's one place to look for your career and vocational options—because your Life Path Number shows your inherent talents and abilities. If you feel as if you're on the wrong path, you'll want to read what your Life Path Number has to say. Even if you know you're on the right path, your Life Path Number can help you understand why.

Learning to Read Your Life Path Map

Some numerologists consider the *Life Path Number* to be the most important number in your chart. That's because it tells of the road you'll follow throughout your life, and it's the number that indicates your talents and abilities that will help you along that road. In fact, it's these very skills that will help you reach your destiny—but we'll get to that in Chapter 18, "Your Destiny Number: It's My Purpose ... and I'll Cry If I Want To," where we discuss your Destiny Number.

Finding Your Life Path Number

You find your Life Path Number by adding together the month, day, and year you were born. To illustrate, let's look at how to figure this number for one of the legendary basketball players of all time, Earvin "Magic" Johnson.

Magic Johnson's birthday is August 14, 1959, so we lay it out like this:

August 14, 1959		
August =	8	
14 (1 + 4) =	5	
1959 (1 + 9 + 5 + 9) =	6	
	19 = 1 = 9 =	10
	10 = 1 = 0 =	1
		1 Life Path

By the Numbers

Your **Life Path Number** reveals your inherent talents and abilities and shows the best career path for you to follow to use those skills. It's calculated by adding together all the numbers of your birth date.

We reduce the 19 by adding the two digits together to get one number, which in this case, is a 1. This means that Magic Johnson has a Life Path of a 1, and his path is one of independence and leadership. To find out more about the meaning of a 1 Life Path Number, read the definition for the number 1 Life Path that follows in this chapter.

Magic has a 19/1 Life Path, which as you may recall is a karmic debt number. So besides having natural abilities in leadership, he will encounter many opportunities in this lifetime to work out the issues of the possible abuses of his position of power. He will meet karmic relationships along the road and have the chance to set things right this time.

Finding Your Life Path

Now, it's your turn. Let's review the steps for calculating the Life Path Number:

1. Find the number of the month. August, for example, is an 8 month. We've provided a chart for you to find the number for your *birth month*.

Months and Their Numbers

Month	Number	Month	Number
January	1	April	4
February	2	May	5
March	3	June	6

Month	Number	Month	Number
July	7	October	(10) or 1
August	8	November	(11) or 2
September	9	December	(12) or 3

2. If your birth day is a double-digit number, reduce it to a single number. If it's 14, for example, 14 is reduced to 1 + 4 = 5. Once you've reduced it to a single number, add that number to the calendar month number. If your birth day is a single number already, just add it to the calendar month number.

3. Now, add the year numbers together to get a single number. Here's an example:

   1959 = 1 + 9 + 5 + 9 = 15

   Then, add 15 together: 1 + 5 = 6

4. Next, add all three reduced numbers together.

   8 + 5 + 6 = 19

5. Last, reduce the final double-digit numbers.

   19 = 1 + 9 = 10 = 1

   10 = 1 = 0 = 1 Life Path

The final single-digit number is the Life Path Number.

The next section has a form for you to calculate your own Life Path Number, or that of your friends, family, and coworkers. Who knows what insights you'll find?

Easy as 1-2-3

Calculate your Life Path Number by adding together all the digits of your birth date, including the month, day, and year.

Easy as 1-2-3

You must always include all 4 digits for calculating the year. For example, don't just add 5 + 9 for the year 1959. You don't want to end up with the wrong number.

Numerology Rule #9

To find your Life Path Number, use this formula:

Birth month + day of birth + year of birth = Life Path Number

Following Your Own Path

Are you ready to calculate your own Life Path Number? We've provided spaces below for you to do just that.

1. Birth month number: _____

2. Birth day number (reduce to a single number, if necessary): _____

3. Add birth year numbers together and reduce: _____

4. Add together your answers to 1, 2, and 3: _____

5. Add the final double-digit together (unless it's a master number) to get your Life Path Number (don't forget to look for karmic debt numbers, too): _____

What's your Life Path Number? Write it in the star!

What Your Life Path Number Reveals About You

Sixes and Sevens

There is an exception! If you get a master number in step 4, write the number as 11/2, 22/4, or 33/6 and don't reduce it. A master number Life Path has special significance! Also, be on the lookout for karmic debt numbers 13, 14, 16, and 19.

Your Life Path Number tells what you can depend upon to find success in the world. This is your own unique path in life. While others may share the same number, it's the combination of all of your numbers that will help to clarify how to proceed down this path of life. Yours can be a path of roses and sunshine, or even the Yellow Brick Road, but this road, with all its bends and turns, will present you with opportunities to use your innate talents.

The Life Path Number can be used to indicate positive vocational/career options. It tells of areas in which you will excel, even without training. You may draw upon this energy as a source of power all throughout your life because it's what you have—inherent skills and talents. Your Life Path Number works hand-in-glove with your Destiny Number, which we'll be discussing in Chapter 18. In short, your Life Path Number indicates what you were born to be!

Life Path Number 1

Your path will take you down the road to independence, and you'll learn the benefits of independence, of standing on your own two feet, standing alone when necessary, and becoming a strong individual. Once these traits have been honed, you move to the next level of the 1 Life Path—leadership.

You're a born leader and your path in life will present you with many opportunities to demonstrate your ability. You have executive and administrative capability, although it may be latent in developing. Your strong pioneering spirit, courage, and determination will serve you well along this road.

What are your career/vocation options if you've got a 1 Life Path? Any situation that allows you to utilize your unique ideas and pioneer spirit will be a career bonanza. Look for a field where you can use your quick mental agility, such as business, health, the entertainment industry, government, or even a bookstore.

For an in-depth discussion of the number 1, be sure to review Chapter 5, "The Number 1: In the Beginning." Remember to double check your number 1 Life Path number; is it possibly a 19/1? If so, you will want to turn to Chapter 15, "The Karmic Numbers: 10, 13, 14, 16, and 19: Lessons to Be Learned," for a look at this karmic debt number.

Sixes and Sevens

People with 1 Life Path Numbers sometimes work for a variety of companies in different positions, all the while feeling vaguely unsatisfied but not quite knowing why. When these same people strike out on their own, however, they suddenly come into their own. That's because a 1 Life Path likes to lead, and taking orders from anyone else just won't work for them.

Easy as 1-2-3

People with 2 Life Paths are extremely sensitive—so sensitive, in fact, that they need to be careful not to become the doormats of the world. Still, these born peacemakers work best behind the scenes and can do much for the rest of the world in the process.

Life Path Number 2

Your path will lead you to seek balance and harmony in all that you do, and you'll learn the benefits of cooperation and compromise, as well as patience and peacekeeping. Once you've incorporated these traits, you'll move on to the next phase of the 2 Life Path Number—drawing others together.

You were born to relate to others—and to make certain that others relate well to each other as well. If there's a fight brewing, a 2 Life Path person will do everything in his or her power to head it off at the pass. In fact, if you have a 2 Life Path, you'll need to remember not to ignore yourself and your own needs while you're making sure everyone else is cooperating.

What are the career/vocation options for a 2 Life Path? You're best at jobs that allow you to mediate, negotiate, take care of details, be in a supportive role, or gather facts. In addition, if you find a job that will allow you to utilize your sensitivity, you'll be using one of your greatest assets, and will naturally thrive.

For an in-depth discussion of the number 2, be sure to review Chapter 6, "The Number 2: Balancing Act."

Life Path Number 3

Your path will entice you to be both creative and spontaneous, to live your life with joy and imagination. You'll learn the benefits of optimism and enthusiasm, and how to express your emotions and your exuberance. Once you've mastered these concepts, you'll move on to the next phase of the 3 Life Path—inspiring others.

Easy as 1-2-3

Your 3 Life Path means you'll walk a path of using your creative gifts (especially the gift of words) to say your truth, which is a compilation of your creative ideas, optimistic view of the world, and unique ability to articulate your own discoveries. Having learned to speak from your heart (a hard-won lesson), as a 3 Life Path person, you'll inspire everyone around you.

You're a born communicator, and your wit and light-heartedness will help others see the joy in any situation. People with 3 Life Path Numbers are artistic, creative, and articulate, painting pictures with their words that spark the imagination and understanding of those lucky enough to hear them. With a 3 Life Path, your inspiration to others lies in the way you speak and frame things, as well as your creative approach to life, because bringing a creative flair to each task is your trademark.

What are your career/vocation options? With your 3 Life Path Number, you'll do well in anything artistic, be it writing, speaking, designing, illustrating, dancing, or acting. You'd make an excellent cheerleading coach (or any kind of a coach), where you can encourage and motivate. You'll also do well in any job where feeling and emotions are valued financially, such as public relations or customer service.

For an in-depth discussion of the number 3, be sure to review Chapter 7, "The Number 3: Keeping It Light."

Life Path Number 4

Your path will lead you to work hard and systematically. You'll learn the benefits of loyalty and following the rules, all the while remaining loyal and steadfast. With a 4 Life Path Number, reliability is the name of the game, and once you've learned this lesson, you'll move on to the next phase—building for the long term.

You're a born builder because security is a big deal to you. Others look to people with 4 Life Path Numbers to manage, control, and make sure that everything falls into place. If you've got a 4 Life Path, you know how important it is to not rock the boat, to move slowly and steadily, and to make sure everything is nailed down and in the right place.

Merlin's Notes

Stick in the mud. All work and no play. The aphorisms that come to mind for a 4 Life Path aren't always the fun ones—especially if a 3 or 5 is the one talking. It's important to remember, however, that someone's got to make sure the road is paved smoothly so those who aren't paying much attention won't encounter unexpected speed bumps. People with 4 Life Path Numbers may be conservative, yes, but they're also the ones who plan ahead—so the rest of us can have a good time.

Here are your career/vocation options: With your 4 Life Path Number, you'd be a natural as a systems or construction manager, or as a bookkeeper or accountant. You'll also do well at any work where organization is valued, be it administration, education, or business, or where documents or a product requires careful management. Your success will be found in work where systems need to be established and maintained, or where you're working to build things of lasting value.

For an in-depth discussion of the number 4, be sure to review Chapter 8, "The Number 4: A Solid Foundation." Remember to check carefully to see if in fact your 4 isn't really a 13/4, a karmic Life Path. In that case, you'll want to review Chapter 15 for a more detailed look at the number 13/4.

Life Path Number 5

You'll have many forks along your path, and you'll welcome each change as a new opportunity with unknown results. With a 5 Life Path Number, in fact, change is the name of the game, and once you've learned this lesson, you'll move on to the next phase—championing freedom.

You're a born progressive—forward thinking, liberal, super-resourceful—and because of those things, you're also a dilettante, equally good at many different trades. If you've got a 5 Life Path Number, you're probably good at sales, marketing, or promotion of any kind, and believe in freedom in all things—whether it's of speech, movement, or moving to the beat of different drummer.

The career/vocation options best for you are working with the public, new-trend companies, communications, advertising, publicity, or sales—any kind of work, in other words, that calls for energizing power rather than routine. You'll also do well as a detective—or as a writer of mysteries! In addition, travel is well suited to you.

For an in-depth discussion of the number 5, be sure to review Chapter 9, "The Number 5: You Shall Adapt!" Once again, you will want to double check for the possible karmic number 14/5. If you discover your 5 Life Path Number is really a 14/5, you will want to turn to Chapter 15 for a more detailed look at this karmic Life Path.

Sixes and Sevens

Other numbers may find those with 5 Life Path Numbers hard to pin down, or worse, unreliable. It's important to remember that 5 Life Path people aren't really unreliable—they just have short attention spans. As soon as something new catches their interest, in fact, they'll forget all about what they were interested in a moment before.

Easy as 1-2-3

Hello, Mr. Chips! Look no further than the teacher who helps as much as he teaches to find someone with a 6 Life Path Number. Think of the role played by Robin Williams as the psychologist in *Good Will Hunting* or as the private boys' school teacher in *Dead Poet's Society,* and you have the idea.

Life Path Number 6

Your path will lead you to live responsibly at home and at work, to achieve balance between giving and receiving. The path of those with a 6 Life Path Number is one of service and aid, and once you've learned this lesson, you'll move on to the next phase—achieving balance between giving and receiving.

You're a born counselor—sympathetic and caring—and you love everyone from the smallest child to the oldest, scroungiest mutt. Others seek out those with 6 Life Path Numbers for advice and wise counsel, and you may well do these things professionally, as a counselor, advisor, teacher, or therapist. With a 6 Life Path, you'll learn to achieve balance between your domestic life and work life, and will seek to beautify the world of all around you.

What are your career/vocation options with a 6 Life Path Number? You'll love any job in the service industry, where you can make life more comfortable, easy, and luxurious for others. Medicine, retail sales in furniture, remodeling, decorating, beauty products, family-run or home-based business, training animals, teaching, and counseling are all naturals for you. Of course, it goes without saying, gardening and any related businesses are your path, too—the garden path!

For an in-depth discussion of the number 6, be sure to review Chapter 10, "The Number 6: We Are Fam-i-ly."

Life Path Number 7

Your path will lead you to study, test, and analyze everything, because with a 7 Life Path Number, you can't be satisfied with anything at face value. You'll seek the meaning of existence, and will always be exploring mysteries and the unexplainable to find meaning for your life. Once you've learned this lesson, you'll move on to the next phase—sharing your wisdom of the spirit with others.

You're a born seeker—spiritual, philosophical, scientific, or technological—and, because of your solitary exploration of the unknown, others will seek you out for your wisdom. People with 7 Life Path Numbers are often teachers or professors, specializing in something quite specific, and this specialization makes them the obvious choice for answers when others need them.

With your 7 Life Path Number your career/vocation options could include computer programmer, technological specialist, or working at any job that calls for analysis, deductive reasoning, scientific knowledge, or technical ability. Bookkeeping and accounting may hold interest as well, although we traditionally would find the 4 or the 2 doing these jobs. In addition, any field where you'll be allowed to study, contemplate, or commune with the higher forces, such as law or teaching, or being a spiritual leader, monk, or nun, will also suit you well.

For an in-depth discussion of the number 7, be sure to review Chapter 11, "The Number 7: Perception and Wisdom." Again, remember to double check to see if your 7 Life Path Number is really a 16/7. If so, you will want to turn to Chapter 15 for a more detailed look at this karmic number.

Easy as 1-2-3

You know how when you're watching the TV news they always have those "experts"? Chances are, the experts have 7 Life Path Numbers, because these people are the specialists, the researchers, those who have explored in depth something that may be a mystery to others, and can now share their findings with others.

Life Path Number 8

Your path will lead you to work out the difference between money and the real value of life. It's a path of mastery, where you must learn what to do with your natural power and authority. This is not an easy path (in fact, it's not considered a lucky one), but once you've learned its lesson, you'll move on to the next phase—being in charge.

You're a born boss, born to be involved in business or a large organization. People with 8 Life Path Numbers know that it's lonely at the top, but their power and authority come naturally to them, so others naturally look to them when a decision needs to be made. The reward for you, if you've got an 8 Life Path Number, won't necessarily be financial but may come in terms of accomplishment and yes, legacy.

What are your career/vocation options? Any field where you can be in charge, be it C.E.O., C.F.O., chief administrator, financial advisor, real estate broker, or even athletic director, is perfect for the 8 Life Path—the person with authority. You'd make an excellent choice for a judge, head of hospital, president of the bank—or any job where you can utilize your superior skill of good judgment. In addition, all business-related work is ideal for this number, because the business environment is a place where you can organize and run things with authority.

For an in-depth discussion of the number 8, be sure to review Chapter 12, "The Number 8: Getting Down to Business."

Merlin's Notes

One of our favorite examples of someone who exemplifies an 8 Life Path Number is Jean Luc Picard, captain of the starship *Enterprise,* in the *Star Trek* series. He's clearly the leader of his crew, making the tough decisions, the person others turn to naturally in times of crisis. Captain Picard is a natural leader who wears his authority easily—but he also knows it's lonely at the top, and accepts that aspect of his role as well. After all, an 8 Life Path is as much about one's legacy as what one is achieving during his life.

Life Path Number 9

Your path will lead you to understand the interconnectedness of all things. It's a path of universal love that learns compassion and tolerance. Once you've learned this lesson, you'll move on to the next phase—tolerance for all, and the importance of caring for each other.

Easy as 1-2-3

Have you ever read a book, seen a film, seen a piece of artwork, or heard a piece of music, that hit you where you lived? If so, you've encountered the connection engendered by those with 9 Life Paths, who not only seek but find ways to truly touch their fellow people.

You're a born healer, and your healing may take the form of writing, composing, painting, or sculpting—reaching others by truly connecting to them, in other words. With a 9 Life Path Number, you'll also be learning how to let go, to surrender the self for the greater good. People with 9 Life Path Numbers truly understand the Golden Rule—and don't understand why others don't.

The career/vocation options suited to the 9 Life Path include international business, the arts (including the stage, literature, filmmaking, dance, sculpting, pottery, painting, writing, and arts administration), education, and health. In addition, any line of work that is designed to help, heal, or humanize belongs to this humanitarian number.

For an in-depth discussion of the number 9, be sure to review Chapter 13, "The Number 9: And, in the End … the World."

Master Life Paths

People with master number Life Path Numbers have unique and special paths to follow. When we get to these numbers, remember, we've moved to a higher plane (the one envisioned by the 9, in fact), that inspires, manifests, and truly gives. For an in-depth discussion of the master numbers be sure to review Chapter 14, "The Master Numbers 11, 22, and 33: Potent Potential."

Life Path Number 11/2

With this Life Path, much is expected of you. Your special path will lead you to illuminate humankind spiritually and inspirationally. You'll sometimes operate at the level of the 2 to attract meaningful associations so that others will find you accessible. Once you've mastered your lessons, you'll move on to the next phase—becoming an inspirational leader.

You're a born charismatic leader, magnetic and electric. The platform is meant for you, and you'll find yourself in the spotlight. Your mission is to be someone others look to for truth and illumination (sometimes spiritual in nature), and the truer you are to universal principles, the happier and more successful you will be on your path.

Merlin's Notes

We've mentioned Bill Clinton, whose 8-19-1946 birthday equals an 11/2 Life Path Number. Others with 11/2 Life Path Numbers are Colin Powell (4-5-1937), Jacqueline Kennedy Onassis (7-28-1929), and Prince Charles (11-14-1948). All of these people are or were charismatic, magnetic leaders who have 11/2 Life Path Numbers who in one form or another have found their way into the spotlight. All are known as charismatic persona and have been leaders in our society.

The career/vocation options for 11/2 include any field that allows you to be the teacher, diplomat, or speaker, because these will utilize your considerable talents at uplifting and inspiring others. This is also the number of the airplane pilot, film director, television personality, charismatic spiritual leader, or philosopher, and you'll do well in any venue that puts you in the spotlight, deals with media or aviation, or allows you to work with large groups.

Life Path Number 22/4

Your special path will lead you to turn dreams into reality. The 22/4 Life Path Number, like the 4, is seen as one who builds and manifests—but with a larger purpose. Once you've mastered this lesson, you'll move on to the next phase—becoming a Master Builder.

You're a born creator of activities that benefit all of humanity, and you're viewed by others as extraordinary. You back up your word with deed, again and again, and others know that your word is as good as gold—or even better. With a 22/4 Life Path Number, good management principles are behind what you do—and what you do is for the lasting good of humankind. Lucky us!

Easy as 1-2-3

The people who planned the United Nations, as well as those who currently lead it, should be considered among those with 22/4 Life Path Numbers. The organization they built continues to believe in peace and goodwill, more than 50 years after its founding.

With a 22/4 your career/vocation options could include a planner, organizer, statesman, diplomat, ambassador, president, business executive for a large organization (national or international), promoter, or organizer, because you'll thrive in any line of work that allows you to utilize your considerable talent for organizing, being efficient, and applying your practical know-how to build a dream. You command respect and are seen as an expert in your field. In fact, you're destined to be a leader who is both practical and inspirational and who understands that success comes not only from cooperation, but from being of service to humankind.

Life Path Number 33/6

Your special path will lead you on a journey of unconditional love. With a 33/6 Life Path Number, you'll be learning about selfless service, altruism, and nurturing of the spirit. Once you've mastered these lessons, you'll move on to the next phase—being the cosmic parent.

You're a born champion of the underdog, empathetic and tenderhearted. With a 33/6 Life Path Number, the self is truly secondary to the needs of others, and people with this Life Path are often known for their humanitarianism and giving. Sacrifice comes easily for you if you've got a 33/6 Life Path—but chances are you don't think of it as sacrifice at all.

Any community service project provides a successful career/vocation option for the 33/6 Life Path Number, whether you work with the homeless, on hunger projects, for refugee assistance, on charities that serve the less fortunate, for children's education, or even as a missionary. In addition, you're suited to any job that will allow you to joyfully bring out the best in people, and to serve with love.

Merlin's Notes

There's a Jewish tradition that comes to us from the Talmud called **tzedakah,** which is all about giving. The first level of giving is giving to someone you know. The second is giving to someone you don't know. The highest is giving anonymously and is considered the level of giving that is closest to God. With a 33/6 Life Path, you practice tzedakah every day.

A Few Pointers for the Road

You're bound to have the same Life Path Number as someone else, but that doesn't mean you'll have the same experience. The difference will be found in the month, day, or year each of you was born. For example, if you have an 8 Life Path Number and your birth date is January 5, 1964, you'll be influenced on your path by a 1 (January), a 5 (birth day), and a 2 (1 + 9 + 6 + 4 = 20 = 2). Your friend (also with an 8 Life Path Number) may have been born February 27, 1959. She'll be influenced by a 2 (February), a 9 (birth day is 27, which is 2 + 7 = 9), and a 6 (1 + 9 + 5 + 9 = 24 = 6). That's just one example of how two people with the same Life Path Number will nonetheless have quite different journeys.

You will have lessons along your path, which are spelled out in the month, day, and year you were born. The lessons of the first 28 years of your life are found in the month you were born. For example, for the person born 1-5-1964, the first set of lessons will be about the number 1—learning to become independent. The second set of lessons for age 28 until age 56 are found in the day you were born. So, using our example, the lesson is in the 5, meaning that this person will be learning the lessons of the 5—to accept change. The last set of lessons from age 56 on—that is, for the rest of your life—are found in the year you were born. Once again using our example, the number 2 tells us that he or she will be learning about the number 2—how to live in relationship with others.

In short, our 8 Life Path person will find his or her path influenced by the lessons of the 1, 5, and 2—just to spice things up!

The Life Path Number works with the Destiny Number, or, to put it another way, the date of your birth works with the name you were born with. We'll be discussing your Destiny Number in the next chapter.

The Least You Need to Know

➤ Your Life Path Number is calculated from the month, day, and year of your birth.

➤ Your Life Path Number shows you your potential paths.

➤ Knowing your Life Path Number helps you live your life to your fullest potential.

➤ It's easy to calculate your Life Path Number and find your own special path.

Chapter 18

Your Destiny Number: It's My Purpose ... and I'll Cry If I Want To

In This Chapter

➤ Your birth name spells your destiny

➤ Your Destiny Number reveals your purpose

➤ Use the full name that appears on your birth certificate

➤ Your Destiny Number tells what you must live up to

Your name has meaning—it tells what you'll be most successful doing in this lifetime. In addition, your name tells of the your best direction and major accomplishment, and points the way to living a fulfilled life. In other words, your name is your destiny.

The Destiny Number describes your purpose in life—your mission—and indicates what you must do, for it's your destined direction. Both opportunities and inner resources will come from this number, and this is the area of your life that must be explored, developed, and embraced in order for your soul to grow to its full potential in this lifetime, and for you to be whole.

Are you ready to meet your destiny? If so, prepare to meet your Destiny Number.

What's Destined for You?

If someone told you that by living a particular way, success was all but guaranteed, wouldn't you want to know how to do it? Now you can, because it's as simple as knowing your *Destiny Number*. Your name is a vibrational energy pattern that spells out the direction for your life, and from your birth name, we can find your Destiny Number. In this way, the numbers of your birth name will give you your own personal cosmic code for success.

Not only does each letter of your name have meaning, each part of your name does as well, and a numerologist will see the individual talents and unique characteristics present in the name you were given at birth. Your name reveals a picture of the real you. In fact, you could think of your birth name as a blueprint and a cosmic code of your potential.

By the Numbers

Another of the 5 core numbers, your **Destiny Number** comes from your name—your birth name.

Sixes and Sevens

Numerologists debate whether our names are accidental, or if our parents subconsciously chose our names from an urge born out of a divine plan for our lives. We believe you were not given your name by mistake. Misspellings and last-minute changes of your name are merely part of the fine-tuning process that takes place to give us the vibration that is truly us.

There's a wealth of information in your name:

➤ Your first name gives you the most personal lessons.

➤ Your middle name reveals hidden abilities that you don't necessarily like.

➤ Your last name tells of the characteristics you've inherited from your family.

What the Destiny Number Reveals About You

As one of your 5 core numbers, the Destiny Number is one of the five most important numbers in your chart. Your Destiny Number reveals

➤ Your life's purpose.

➤ What you must live up to in this lifetime.

➤ Your opportunities for success.

➤ Your spiritual mission.

➤ The qualities and manner of living you must develop.

➤ What you are destined for.

➤ The target you are aiming for in life.

➤ The kind of work that would be a natural expression for your Life Path (for an in-depth discussion of the Life Path Number see Chapter 17, "Your Life Path Number: Rules for the Road").

Finding Your Destiny Number

The Destiny Number is calculated from the name you were given at birth. Traditionally, whatever name appears on your birth certificate is the name that's used to figure the Destiny Number (as well as the Soul Number, which we'll be discussing in Chapter 19, "Your Soul Number: The Heart of the Matter," and the Personality Number, which we'll be discussing in Chapter 20, "Your Personality Number: See Me, See You"). That's your *full* name—even if you never use it, hate it, or have spent years hiding this name from everyone!

Let's go over the most often-asked questions about finding the Destiny Number.

What Name Should I Use?

The name on your birth certificate is generally considered the name to use when figuring your numerology chart and specifically in calculating your Destiny Number. If you don't have a copy of your birth certificate, you may need to contact the office of vital statistics in the county where you were born. Records are also kept in hospitals, although these do not always contain your name as it appears on your birth certificate. Once you've gotten your birth certificate in front of you, keep a few of these tips and warnings in mind!

➤ **Clerical errors:** Yep, mistakes are made on birth certificates. There are lots of stories about somebody goofing up the name on the birth certificate. What to do? Here's the key: If your parents accepted the name goof or allowed the misspelling of the name (or wrong name!) to remain on your birth certificate, then the name on the birth certificate, with errors, is used to find your Destiny Number.

➤ **Spelling errors:** It's always fun to check your birth certificate when you do this calculation because you may find out that the way *you* spell your name is not what's actually on your birth certificate. You may be someone other than who you thought you were!

Merlin's Notes

Here's an example of a spelling error on a birth certificate. Kay has a client who for 50 years spelled her name Carol. Then one fall, when she went to visit her elderly mother, she happened to mention that she was doing her numerology chart. When she showed her mother the layout for her name, her mother said, "That's not how you spell your name. It's spelled with an 'e.'" When Carol went to the county courthouse and got a copy of her birth certificate, sure enough, there was her name in bold print: Carole.

The spelling of your name does make a difference when figuring the numbers for your numerology chart (especially the Destiny Number, Soul Number, and Personality Number), so check carefully before you calculate your name numbers.

225

Adopted Names

If you were adopted and given a new name, and you know your original birth name, use the original name to figure your chart. You will, however, also want to figure a second chart for your adopted name. In this type of situation, no doubt you will have grown up living out the adopted name, and therefore you'll want to figure a chart for your adopted name to see what energy has been influencing your life with this name. Then, with the two charts, you can piece together the story of who you really are.

Merlin's Notes

If you have an adopted name and a different one on your birth certificate, consider the original name the true essence of who you are, and the adopted name the energy you drew to you to work with in this lifetime. Give the most credence to the original birth name chart as your true essence, but consider the impact your adopted name has had on your life and all of your decisions. Think of it this way: You've been given multiple opportunities to achieve your destiny.

If you don't know your original name and have only the adopted name to work with, you won't be working with your true essence, but rather with the influences of your adopted name. If this is the case, your Destiny Number will indicate the type of energy and influence your adopted name has brought you in this life.

It's not unusual for adopted children (as well as adults) to feel unclear about who they are. Numerologists would argue that without knowledge of their original names (which also include the inherited traits of the family name) these individuals may be experiencing a "lost self." If at all possible, learn your original name and integrate it into your current life. In that way, you'll reclaim yourself and your original energy pattern.

I Never Use That Name

Even if you've never used your original name (everyone's always called you "Katie," or "Bubba," for example), it's still the essential data that holds your cosmic code and blueprint for life. When figuring your numerology chart, you must use your original name.

I Had That Name for Only a Few Days

Some babies were given a name at birth and then their parents had a revelation and changed the baby's name within a day or two after their birth. If this is the case, the change must have been made official, that is, the birth certificate must have been changed shortly after birth. This new name is then considered your original name. You will, however, find it interesting to work out the "would-be" name and see who you might have been!

Sacred Names

Many people have been given a name at confirmation. Or perhaps a spiritual teacher or guru gave you a sacred name. Such names are not used to figure your numerology chart and your Destiny Number. Like the earlier example, however, it will be valuable for you to figure this sacred name to see what new energy you've brought into your life. Figure this type of name separately from your original birth name. It represents a new influence in your life.

More Than Three Names

If you were given more than one middle name or last name, use all of the names you were given at birth. Some people from other cultures and many modern American families use a series of family names, and an individual may end up with up to six names. Whatever is on your birth certificate is the name to use. Remember to check the spelling—every letter counts!

Junior, Senior, or The Third

If you have a name that has Jr. or Sr., or uses Roman numerals after your name, disregard all of these addenda. For example, if your name is George Herbert Walker Bush Jr. we figure your numbers only on George Herbert Walker Bush. We drop the Jr. when figuring this numerology chart, and yes, that means you will have the same name (and numbers) as your father or mother ... or grandmother or grandfather. You will walk a different path however, as indicated by your birthday.

Married Names

Married names are not figured in the Destiny Number or the basic numerology chart. Note that we will discuss married names and their significance in Chapter 29, "Names: A Rose by Any Other Name Might Not Smell as Sweet."

In case we haven't made it clear, you will use only your original birth name to do these Destiny calculations!

Calculating the Destiny Number

To figure your Destiny Number, you will lay out your full name and assign the appropriate number to each letter. We've included that handy little number and letter chart from Chapter 2, "What Numerology Can Do for You," for your use.

Letters and Their Numbers

1	2	3	4	5	6	7	8	9
A	B	C	D	E	F	G	H	I
J	K	L	M	N	O	P	Q	R
S	T	U	V	W	X	Y	Z	

To illustrate how to figure the Destiny Number, President Bill Clinton offers a unique example. First off, he was born with another name: His birth name was William Jefferson Blythe, and the name we know him by—William Jefferson Clinton—is his adopted name. In keeping with what we've said about figuring the Destiny Number, we must use Mr. Clinton's original name.

First, figure each name separately, assigning a number to each letter.

```
W  I  L  L  I  A  M      J  E  F  F  E  R  S  O  N      B  L  Y  T  H  E

5  9  3  3  9  1  4      1  5  6  6  5  9  1  6  5      2  3  7  2  8  5

34                       44                            27

3 + 4 = 7                4 + 4 = 8                     2 + 7 = 9
```

Next, add the reduced total of each name. In this case, we'll add:

7 + 8 + 9 = 24

Because this isn't a master number, we reduce it to a single number:

2 + 4 = 6

So, when we look at Bill Clinton's original birth name, we see that he has a 6 Destiny Number. This is the Destiny of one who's to be an advisor, such as a lawyer or counselor of some type, who's sympathetic and understanding, and a hard worker who consciously wants to please and avoid conflict. Sound like anyone we all know?

Now, even though Mr. Clinton doesn't use this name, it is his original energy pattern that is present throughout his life. Just for fun, however let's see what Destiny Number his adopted and current name gives him.

```
W  I  L  L  I  A  M      J  E  F  F  E  R  S  O  N      C  L  I  N  T  O  N

5  9  3  3  9  1  4      1  5  6  6  5  9  1  6  5      3  3  9  5  2  6  5

34                       44                            33

3 + 4 = 7                4 + 4 = 8                     3 + 3 = 6

7 + 8 + 6 = 21 = 2 + 1 = 3
```

When we add together the reduced number for each name (7 + 8 + 6), we find that Bill Clinton has a 21 total, which is reduced to a 3. This means that Mr. Clinton's new Destiny Number is a 3, the number of the optimist who has a gift with words. With a 3 Destiny, success will be found whenever he can use his words to influence people: public speaking, writing, acting, or just communicating with folks. You can read more about the number 3 Destiny Number later in this chapter.

Easy as 1-2-3

Remember to match your letters (and numbers) carefully. One letter left out will make a big difference.

Because his adopted name brings him a 3 Destiny, it's considered to be additional energy that's added to the original Destiny Number 6. Because both of these numbers are emotional numbers, we can expect that an additional element of responding to things emotionally is added, too.

As you looked at our calculations for Mr. Clinton, you might have noticed that the name Jefferson is a 44, a master number, and that Clinton is a 33, another master number. This means that by changing his last name, Bill Clinton has brought a second master number on board. His current name, William Jefferson Clinton, is a more powerful energy than his original name, and the vibration of this new name will bring more demands and challenges, and of course, more potential.

When we consider Destiny pattern 6 along with Mr. Clinton's 11/2 Life Path (remember? we figured it in the previous chapter), it becomes apparent that this is a man with a very powerful and challenging energy. He will be constantly called on to be responsible, to rise to the higher vibration, and will be required to follow the dictates of spiritual principles that are inherent in these master numbers.

As you can see, using the system of numerology to uncover the mysteries in a name reveals fascinating and useful information about a person. Who would you like to know more about? You can figure anybody's numbers if you know their names at birth.

Numerology Rule #10

Use the following formula to find your Destiny Number:

Original first name + second name + third name = Destiny Number

---

Some of us have only two names at birth, some have as many as six. The number of names doesn't matter, only that all of the names you use to find your Destiny are the ones (with the correct spelling) that were given to you at birth.

Reviewing the Steps for Finding Your Destiny Number

Let's review the steps for finding your Destiny Number:

1. Write out your birth name and assign the appropriate numbers to each letter.

2. Add each name separately.

3. Reduce the number of each name separately and then add the reduced numbers together.

4. Reduce the final number to a single number unless it's a master number (11, 22, or 33).

You can read the meaning of your Destiny Number in the section that follows. You might also want to look to see if your Destiny Number is in fact a karmic number. (See Chapter 15, "The Karmic Numbers 10, 13, 14, 16, and 19: Lessons to Be Learned," for an in-depth discussion of karmic numbers.)

Here are the two main things to remember when calculating your Destiny Number:

➤ Add each name separately. Each name in your original birth name has meaning, and it's important to preserve the number of each name.

➤ Once you know each name's number, reduce each name to a single-digit number. Then, when adding these single numbers across your name, you will get a clear idea if a master number is present or not.

Sixes and Sevens

It's easy to make mistakes in adding all of the numbers from your name together (we know—we've made mistakes ourselves!). For this reason, be sure to check your addition—more than once. You don't want to go around thinking you're a 4 when you're really a 3!

Easy as 1-2-3

Watch for master numbers when figuring the Destiny Number!

We've provided spaces here for you to figure your Destiny Number. Be sure to take your time—and to figure each of your names separately before adding them together.

1. Write out your birth name and assign the appropriate numbers to each letter.

First name: _____

Numbers: _____

Second name: _____

Numbers: _____

Third name: _____

Numbers: _____

2. Add each name separately.

   First name: _____ Second name: _____ Third name: _____

3. Reduce the total of each name.

   First name: _____ Second Name: _____ Third name: _____

4. Add the numbers from each name together and reduce the total to a single number unless it is a master number (11, 22, or 33).

What's your Destiny Number? Write it in the star!

A Walk Through the Destiny Numbers

As we told you at the beginning of this chapter, your Destiny Number uses your birth name to find the vibrational energy pattern that spells out the direction for your life. You can think of your Destiny Number as your own personal cosmic code for success. Have you calculated your Destiny Number? If so, then you're ready to find out what your Destiny Number reveals about you.

Number 1 Destiny

With a number 1 Destiny Number, your mission in life is to develop the self and to become a leader. Your purpose in life is to be courageous, take the initiative, be independent, original, innovative, and take charge—all to develop your sense of self, your will, and your determination.

The field of opportunity is where you learn to stand alone, think for yourself, and individualize your character. New ideas, new things, and unique activities give great opportunity for you to move toward your destiny. Even if you lack confidence or are holding back, you are still called to embrace your destiny.

You are destined for leadership. Be it and teach it.

Number 2 Destiny

With a number 2 Destiny Number, your mission in life is to create harmony. Your purpose is to find balance, seek cooperation, and be the patient team player—all to develop your sense of relationship.

The field of opportunity is where you learn gentleness and to be emotionally receptive, and being both adaptable and persuasive will give you greater opportunity to move toward your destiny. Even if you are passive or indecisive, you are still called to embrace your destiny.

You're destined for peacemaking. Go forth and share it.

Number 3 Destiny

With a number 3 Destiny Number, your mission in life is to energize and inspire. Your purpose is to encourage others through your optimism and enthusiasm, using your inspirational creativity to make certain that joy is spread to others.

The field of opportunity is where you learn to express your emotions through your gift of words, and being both lighthearted and witty will give you greater opportunity to move toward your destiny. Even if you are moody or critical, you are still called to embrace your destiny.

You're destined for expressing yourself. Speak up, be positive, and encourage.

Number 4 Destiny

With a number 4 Destiny Number, your mission in life is to build something of lasting value. Your purpose is to be practical and do the hard work, all the while keeping order and convention so that security is assured.

The field of opportunity is where you learn to express traditional values, and being steadfast and stable will give you great opportunity to move toward your destiny. Even if you are stubborn or suspicious, you are still called to embrace your destiny.

You're destined for managing and organizing. Create the foundation and build on it.

Number 5 Destiny

With a number 5 Destiny Number, your mission in life is to adapt, change, and progress. Your purpose is to embrace freedom and follow your curiosity wherever it leads you, all the while using your resources and magnetism to keep you moving.

The field of opportunity is where you learn to express your resourcefulness, and being a free spirit will give you great opportunity to move toward your destiny. Even if you are restless or discontented, you are still called to embrace your destiny.

You're destined for liberation and freedom. Move forward and embrace change.

Number 6 Destiny

With a number 6 Destiny Number, your mission in life is to serve. Your purpose is to nurture family and loved ones, all the while using your love of beauty and community to create harmony in life around you.

The field of opportunity is where you learn to express generosity, and giving comfort to others will give you great opportunity to move toward your destiny. Even if you are codependent or tend to martyr yourself, you are still called to embrace your destiny.

You're destined for nurturing and beautifying. Love with balance.

Number 7 Destiny

With a number 7 Destiny Number, your mission in life is to analyze and seek out. Your purpose is to dig deeply and contemplate all you encounter, using your skill at research and your perfectionist ways to find inner wisdom.

The field of opportunity is where you learn to express your keen observation, and being thoughtful and discerning will give you great opportunity to move toward your destiny. Even if you are cynical or skeptical, you are still called to embrace your destiny.

You're destined for educating the world. Specialize and teach your wisdom.

Sixes and Sevens

Hillary Clinton has the same Destiny Number as Bill Clinton. Yup—a 6. With their 6 Destinies, both are pledged to a lifetime of community service.

Easy as 1-2-3

Did you know that Bill Gates has three names, William Henry Gates? More important, all three names are 7s, which could also be read as an abundance of nerdiness, or as a truly analytical, private guy.

Number 8 Destiny

With a number 8 Destiny Number, your mission in life is to gain mastery of self. Your purpose is to achieve and succeed, using your skill at business and organization.

The field of opportunity is where you learn to express your authenticity and discover your own power, and being visionary will give you great opportunity to move toward your destiny. Even if you are ruthless or overbearing, you are still called to embrace your destiny.

You're destined for material success. Get out there and be the masterful leader you were born to be.

Number 9 Destiny

With a number 9 Destiny Number, your mission in life is to perfect and love unconditionally. Your purpose is to strive for universal brotherhood (and sisterhood), using your selflessness, sensitivity, and healing art.

The field of opportunity is where you learn to transform and heal, and being tolerant and forgiving will give you great opportunity to move toward your destiny. Even if you are gullible or intolerant, you are still called to embrace your destiny.

You're destined for broad horizons. Reach out and help someone.

Number 11 Destiny

With a master number 11 Destiny Number, your special mission in life is to inspire and uplift. As an old soul, your purpose is to live up to and accept your destiny and to recognize that your creativity and intuitive skills are to be used for the good of humanity. Your job is to reform, elevate, and transform others' lives.

The field of opportunity is where you learn to express your teaching ability and rise to the challenge, even though it feels like a test. Stepping into the spotlight will give you great opportunity to move toward your destiny. Even if you are impatient, critical, or high-strung, you are still called to embrace your destiny.

You're destined for inspired leadership. Live up to the demands of spiritual living and you shall be the leader you were born to be.

Number 22 Destiny

With a master number 22 Destiny Number, your mission in life is to build the dream and execute plans and projects that will benefit mankind. Your purpose is to make things happen by working in a practical way in the material world using spiritual principles.

The field of opportunity is where you learn to express your efficiency and competence, and being grounded and true to your nature, which is to never give up, will give you great opportunity to move toward your destiny. Even if you are stubborn—or unable to accept the faults of others, you are still called to embrace your destiny.

You're destined to be a Master Builder. Bring spiritual law into the material world.

Number 33 Destiny

With a master number 33 Destiny Number, your mission in life is to joyfully bring forth the higher consciousness of love. Your purpose is to serve with a loving heart and to teach that life can be fun and full of love.

The field of opportunity is where you learn to accentuate what the 3 represents—joy, light, and creativity—and being a leader in the arena of loving service will give you great opportunity to move toward your destiny. Even if you are overly emotional or demoralized by the poverty you see, you are still called to embrace your destiny.

You are destined to be a master healer. Love and teach love to heal us all.

A Final Note About the Destiny Number

There is no such thing as a bad number. All of the numbers will lead to success and point the way to your purpose in life. So don't be wishing you had somebody else's number—yours is perfect for you.

It takes many years and many cycles for us to become aware of how this Destiny Number fits us. When we don't like a number, it's often because we're working on the negative aspects of the number and don't like that part of ourselves. Hang in there— there's great learning to be realized from these numbers.

The Least You Need to Know

➤ Your Destiny Number shows unique abilities for your life.

➤ Your Destiny Number is determined using your full original name as it appears on your birth certificate.

➤ Your name tells what you are destined for.

➤ Your Destiny is what you are aiming for.

Chapter 19

Your Soul Number: The Heart of the Matter

In This Chapter

➤ Finding your heart's desire

➤ Add up the vowels

➤ A word about the "y"

➤ Finding your inner vibration

Hermann Hesse once said, "Each man's life represents a road toward himself ... and we can understand one another; but each of us is able to interpret himself to himself alone." Not only is this our challenge, it's at the very heart of what the Soul Number is all about.

As one of your 5 core numbers, the Soul Number is one of the most important numbers to be figured and analyzed in a numerology chart—the number of your heart's desire.

Soul-ly About You

Your secret thoughts and wishes are told in the *Soul Number* in a numerology chart. This is the number that says what, in your heart of hearts, is your dearest desire.

Advancing the Soul

In spiritual numerology, it's believed that in each lifetime, your soul has needs and is here to learn and grow. The thinking goes something like this: As an incoming soul, you determined what it is that you need to advance up the spiral path of soul evolution; so you chose a name that would give you the correct energy pattern that would attract certain opportunities to you so you could learn and grow.

It's not uncommon for people to learn of their Soul Number and find that it reveals their heart's desire, because the Soul Number merely confirms what you already know—deep inside. In other words, you know what's in your heart; your Soul Number will give you a framework and language for understanding more about yourself at the very core.

What Your Soul Number Tells You

Among the things your Soul Number can help you discover are

➤ Your heart's desire.

➤ Your true motivation.

➤ What you long for.

➤ What you love best.

➤ What you need to feed you soul.

➤ What you value most.

Merlin's Notes

Each of us is born a free soul, and the times we live in seem to require that we own up to what pulses at the very core of our being. It seems we're being asked to live honestly, both with consciousness and intention, which require that we know our inner selves. As we each come to understand that inner peace, living without stress, and living healthily, demand that we know who we are, knowing our Soul Numbers is enormously useful in helping us to achieve these goals.

The Song of the Soul

There are times when the Soul Number will dominate your energy, subordinating all other traits and characteristics, even those of the Life Path and Destiny Numbers. When this happens, your Soul Number will call you to people and places that resonate with your own energy. For example, it will cause you to feel you must travel to a certain spot or be with certain people, or it may cause you to call out in anguish. These times are asking you to hear the song of the soul, and are times to nurture and feed the very core of your being.

There will be other times when this soul energy will lie dormant, possibly repressed by the current situation. This, then, is the soul energy suppressed. Eventually, however, the energy of the soul will awaken and become active with a startling force, changing the direction of your life. The energy of the Soul Number tells of an inner longing, a yearning for expression. You have a choice, as we all do, to begin to listen to the song of your soul.

Your soul may long to be happy, to live in the energy of enthusiasm and optimism, or it may long to be away from everyone, to experience silence, and to read and study mystical teachings. Or your soul may long to travel, to be thrilled with the newness of the unfamiliar, or to heal people. Whatever your soul desires, you have a tool at your fingertips for finding out what it is that speaks to your heart. All you need is your name at birth.

Sixes and Sevens

It should come has no surprise that those times when your soul seems to call out to you in anguish have been referred to as the "dark night of the soul."

Using Soul Number Information

People use what their Soul Number reveals in a variety of areas, including

➤ Business relations.

➤ Love.

➤ Family relations.

➤ Any time they want to understand someone.

In business partnerships, understanding the Soul Numbers of your partners (as well as their Destiny Numbers) can help you understand what will motivate them and be the driving force behind all of their actions. That's because the Soul Number gives you insight into the inner nature of the person you're dealing with, regardless of how they appear on the outside. In addition, it gives a more complete picture of who a person is, so it rounds out your perceptions.

Even though a person may change with the times, the person will never change his or her heart's desire or Soul Number, because somewhere in the background, a person's

Easy as 1-2-3

If you think about it, the vowel sound of any name or word is the soft inner vibration, and the same can be said of the Soul Number—it's the soft inner vibration of our being.

soul is quietly participating in the affairs of the day. A soul doesn't change—it merely expresses its energy over and over through a multitude of experiences to make itself known to us. Understanding your Soul Number can bring deep insight and greater happiness.

Finding Your Soul Number

Just like the Destiny Number, the Soul Number is calculated from your full name at birth—the original name on your birth certificate. Unlike the Destiny Number, the Soul Number is found from the vowels of your name, which are the letters a, e, i, o, u, and sometimes y. We'll be taking a close look at that "sometimes y" in the following section.

> **Numerology Rule #11**
>
> To find your Soul Number, all you have to do is add together the vowels in your full name.

The Y as a Vowel

When figuring the Soul Number, eventually you'll run into a name with a "y" in it, or in fact, more than one "y." What to do? Here's the trick: The "y" is considered a vowel (not a consonant) when it's the only vowel sound in the syllable. Sound complicated? It's not really.

In the name Lynn it's easy to see that the only vowel sound is the "y," making the sound "i," as in "sit." Similarly, in the name Yvonne, the "y" sound is "e" as in "ether," so this "y" is counted as a vowel, too. To figure the Soul Number for the name Yvonne, you would write it like this:

7		6			5
Y	V	O	N	N	E

When we add Yvonne's vowel numbers, 7 + 6 + 5, together, we get a total of 18, which reduced becomes a 9. This means that the name Yvonne has a Soul Number 9.

Let's look at the name Pythagoras for another example:

	7			1		8		1	
P	Y	T	H	A	G	O	R	A	S

Add the vowel numbers together:

7 + 1 + 8 + 1 = 17

Then reduce the final number. When we add 1 + 7 together, we get an 8. So, the name Pythagoras, the father of the science of names and numbers (and supposedly the father of mathematics), has a Soul Number 8, which is the number of self-mastery, leadership, and achievement.

Now let's look at an example where the "y" is not figured as a vowel sound:

							vowel numbers
5				5			
B	E	N	T	L	E	Y	
2		5	2	3		7	consonant numbers

Why didn't we figure in the "y"? Because the "y" in this case is silent—the "e" is the vowel sound. Because of this, we don't use the "y" to figure this Soul Number.

Here's a list of names in which the "y" is considered a vowel. Use this list when in doubt about how to calculate a Soul Number with a "y":

Names with "Y" as a Vowel		
Amy	Lucy	Sissy
Betsy	Lynda	Stacy
Bobby	Lynn	Sybil
Dusty	Nysa	Tammy
Elly	Patty	Tansy
Henry	Ruby	Toby
Jaclyn	Rusty	Tybalt
Judy	Ryan	Welby
Kyla	Sally	Wyatt
Lily	Sandy	Wyn

When Not to Use the Y as a Vowel

The "y" isn't always used as a vowel in calculating the Soul Number. For instance, in the name May, the vowel sound is "a"—the "y" doesn't have a sound itself. We figure May like this:

			vowel numbers
1			
M	A	Y	
4		7	consonant numbers

Because the "a" is the only vowel considered, the "y" will be used as a consonant. We'll be discussing consonants in Chapter 20, "Your Personality Number: See Me, See You," when we figure the Personality Number.

Easy as 1-2-3

While every name that ever was or will be created isn't listed in this book, the point is that we use the "y" to figure the Soul Number in names in which the "y" is the only vowel sound in the syllable.

Here's a list of names for which you shouldn't use the "y" as a vowel:

Names with "Y" as a Consonant			
Bentley	Jayme	Maya	Tanya
Chearneyi	Jayne	Ramsey	Yale
Day	Kay	Ray	Yates
Jay	May	Ridley	

The point here is that the "y" is not the only vowel sound in the syllable (or it's used as a consonant) in all of the above names and should not be used as a vowel to calculate the Soul Number.

Calculating the Soul Number

To illustrate the calculation of the Soul Number, let's look at the Soul Number of Bill Gates. Remember, you must use your given, original, birth name to find your Soul Number, so we're using Bill Gates's here.

```
      9      9 1        5      7      1   5        vowel numbers
    W I L L I A M     H E N R Y     G A T E S
    5   3 3     4     8   5 9       7   2   1      consonant numbers
```

The "y" in "Henry" is used as a vowel because it's the only vowel sound in the syllable.

Easy as 1-2-3

When figuring a name, the numbers for the vowels go *above* the name and the numbers for the consonants go *below*.

Add the vowel numbers for the names William Henry Gates separately:

```
    9        9 1      = 19 (1 + 9) = 1
  W I L L I  A M

    5        7        = 12 (1 + 2) = 3
  H E N R Y

    1        5        = 6
  G A T E S
```

Next, reduce each name separately. The vowels in "William" equal 19 or 1; the vowels in "Henry" equal 12 reduced to 3; and the vowels in "Gates" equal 6.

Last, add these three numbers together. When we add 1 + 3 + 6, we find the number 1. This means that, according to his Soul Number, Bill Gates is the creative, innovative pioneer whose heart's desire is to be the leader of the pack. If any of your names is a master number, don't reduce the number. Add the master number to the other vowel totals to determine your Soul Number.

242

Synchronizing the Soul Number and the Destiny Number

Where your Destiny Number is outer, your Soul Number is inner. This means that your Soul Number works with your Destiny Number: It tells of the inner path to follow, while the Destiny Number tells of the outer direction to pursue.

Your Soul Number and You

We've provided spaces for you to calculate your Soul Number:

1. Write out your full birth name. Next, above your name, write down the number equivalent for each vowel. (Be sure to determine if any "y"s in your name are vowels or consonants.)

   Vowel numbers: _____

   Birth name: _____

2. Add each name together separately and reduce each to a single digit.

   First name: _____ Second name: _____ Third name: _____

3. Add together all the numbers from #2 and reduce them to one number (unless it's a master number).

   _____

So, what's your Soul Number?

Sixes and Sevens

The Soul Number and the Destiny Number work together for wholeness so that you might achieve success and happiness in this lifetime. Neither number can ignore the other, for you may succeed in the outer world and still feel unfulfilled if you haven't honored what it is that you truly long for.

Once you've found your Soul Number, write it in this star!

What Your Soul Number Reveals About You

Just as you have a responsibility to others, you have a responsibility to yourself to pursue your calling and the inner promptings that come from your very soul. To that end, it's time to examine the meaning of each Soul Number in order to gain insight about following the road to ourselves.

Soul Number 1

A Soul Number 1 wants to lead most of all, and may want control over others as well. People with 1 Soul Numbers don't like taking orders or being subordinate, and they're often headstrong, willful, ambitious, and independent. Not surprisingly, the number 1 Soul Number stays away from teams, committees—and mediocrity.

In matters of the heart, romance is the name of the game—when the object of the 1 Soul Number lives up to his expectations. These people expect their partners to be as charming, clever, and independent as they are, so they won't always want to own up to their romantic sides. In fact, they may sometimes seem cold and distant—but it's only because they're protecting themselves. It is not unusual to find 1 souls seeking singular pursuits; the 1 often prefers to be or work alone rather than suffer "fools."

Soul Number 2

In its heart of hearts, the 2 Soul Number wants harmony at all costs. People with 2 Soul Numbers can't stand conflict, and so don't want to lead—they want peace, and to be supportive. The 2 Soul Number has the unique ability to see both sides of a situation. So we should not be surprised to find them as negotiators and arbitrators. After all, they are sensitive to others and can make them feel good about themselves. In addition, they are tactful and can speak the truth in such a way that one feels supported instead of demoralized. The 2 Soul Number is a warm and loving soul who can bring support when paired with any other number.

In matters of the heart, giving is what a 2 Soul Number does best, and these people can sometimes give so much they forget all about Number 2—that is, themselves. The appreciation of others is paramount to a 2 Soul Number, and criticism can hurt him or her to the very core. Always happier paired than alone, no one makes a more devoted companion than a 2 Soul Number.

Easy as 1-2-3

The 3 Soul Number has all the creativity to be spontaneously romantic—from balloon bouquets, to monogrammed pajamas, to hand-painted invitations—and she'll arrive at the party dressed in a luscious velvet cloak. That's the 3 Soul Number: fun, expressive, and, oh, such a joy.

Soul Number 3

The heart's desire of the 3 is to make people happy, to laugh, to create enthusiasm, and to encourage all to reach for their best. The 3 soul loves life! People with 3 Soul Numbers love to use their creative talents, whether to write, design, dance, decorate, or sing their hearts out.

In matters of the heart, a 3 Soul Number can be a flirt. This person may change his or her mind often, but let's not call it fickle—3 Soul Number just wants to have fun. In fact, you may find the 3 Soul Number tripping over his or her enthusiasm. Trust us, the 3 Soul Number will romance your socks off.

Soul Number 4

In the heart of every 4 Soul Number is the desire to have a plan, to meet life in an organized way, and to be practical about all that it does. A 4 Soul Number loves his or her appointment book, an agenda, setting clear boundaries, and knowing the expectations of all concerned. In short, a 4 Soul Number likes to know the plan and be in control, with no surprises along the way.

In matters of the heart, the 4 Soul Number is practical in emotional attachments, and here, too, likes to keep things under control. The 4 isn't particularly romantic, instead preferring to give and receive practical gifts, or to have a well-planned dinner engagement executed in an efficient manner. As we've said, no surprises for this one.

Soul Number 5

First and foremost in the heart of a 5 Soul Number is the desire to be free from restrictions, followed closely by a passion for change and travel. People with 5 Soul Numbers can't stand to feel trapped—or bored with routine. They love to experience the variety and stimulation that life has to offer.

Merlin's Notes

All of the "bad boys" of TV and cinema—from *ER*'s Doug Ross character played by George Clooney, to the characters played by James Dean, to those of Brad Pitt—come to mind when we think of the 5 Soul Number. These men are the fantasy ideals for women all across the world, because they're sexy, free to feel (and to express) those feelings, to dare, and to take part of that which can't be controlled or committed to. What if the 5 is your sweetheart? Keep him happy, honey, or he won't be around for long. Note that if your sweetie is a woman with a 5 Soul Number, you'd best stock up on bubble bath, champagne, and satin sheets—and hold on to your pants!

In matters of the heart, the 5 Soul Number is ruled by three letters—S-E-X—and is s-ensual, e-xquisite, and x-traordinary. Rebellious and sensual by nature, the 5 Soul

Number is ruled by the sexual drive in matters of the heart (if this energy isn't repressed by other numbers or outside circumstances). The 5 is raunchy, and ready to risk—unless repressed. Most of all, the 5 craves variety.

Soul Number 6

The three things most dear to the heart of the 6 Soul Number are beauty, harmony, and home. Understanding, loyal, devoted, affectionate, and heavy on commitment, you won't find any 5s here. People with 6 Soul Numbers want to protect, nurture, and love their families and homes.

In matters of the heart, these are the idealistic romantics—you'll definitely want to get out the roses and candles. With a 6 Soul Number the love is deep, as in "committed" and "the marrying kind." In fact, this Soul Number wants to be married and to have a family and a home to beautify. Don't even think about just hanging out with this one—it's marriage or forget it.

Soul Number 7

These emotional hermits rarely show their feelings. In fact, many never even marry but prefer their own thoughts and company to those of another. This Soul Number could easily be a priest, a nun, or a wilderness guide, because he or she prefers solitude. It's the lure of silence, quiet, and peace that's seductive and intimate to the 7 soul. People with 7 Soul Numbers really do prefer to be left alone—and read!

In matters of the heart, if a 7 soul should team up with a partner, expect it to be a private affair. In fact, you can bet that the partner is probably a 7 Soul Number, too. The thoughts of people with 7 Soul Numbers will be kept secret, as will their beliefs and their unusual (shall we say eccentric?) lifestyles. These are highly sensitive souls who, with their need to think and analyze, often possess psychic powers and highly developed skills of perception. Don't try to fool a 7 about how you feel—they can sense it a mile away.

Soul Number 8

This Soul Number wants to be the boss, or at the least to have power of some kind in the world. It's hard for people with 8 Soul Numbers to understand the emotions of others, and they prefer to stick to business rather than messy emotional affairs. In their heart of hearts, 8 Soul Numbers want to feel important—not just at home, but more important, in what they perceive to be the real world.

In matters of the heart, don't go getting fancy notions in your head of a romantic little dinner for two in some cozy corner of the restaurant if you're dealing with an 8 Soul Number. More often than not, such a dinner would be interrupted with a business call, which the 8 *will* take, and the closest to intimacy you'll get is to have a detailed conversation about the latest transaction. This Soul Number will look for a strong, capable (and yes, you'd better be organized) mate who's equal to his or her ambitions.

In a rare moment, you may enjoy the warm, loving nature 8 Soul Numbers possess—when they can let their guards down—but for the most part, they're just too busy for romance.

Soul Number 9

This is the very soul of compassion. In its heart of hearts, the 9 Soul Number wants to love the world and all that's in it, and, with its high ideals and power to influence others, it strives for universal perfection and universal love. Deeply intuitive and charitable, people with 9 Soul Numbers are often torn by their own emotional needs and the greater needs of others.

In matters of the heart, the 9 Soul Number is loving, idealistic, and romantic. In fact, we'd bet that this is probably the Soul Number that first started the search for a soul mate. The intensity of a 9 Soul Number's love seems boundless—because it is.

Soul Number 11

The master number 11 soul is extremely sensitive, bordering on psychic. People with 11 Soul Numbers have more emotional ups and downs than the other numbers (no wonder—they're trying to balance all of that incoming psychic information). In addition, they're wise beyond their years, understanding and seeing more than most. In their heart of hearts they want to bring peace to all relations—whether it's partnerships, loved ones, families, neighboring countries, or ethnically diverse groups. People with 11 Soul Numbers have strong hunches and most often these hunches prove to be correct. This is the number of an old soul, one who brings ancient knowledge and spiritual wisdom to all of its undertakings. You may know someone like this—they seem wise beyond their years.

Easy as 1-2-3

Don't be surprised to hear talk of angels and fairy-folk or legends of lore as part of the unusual lifestyle of an 11 Soul Number.

In matters of the heart, like the 2, the 11 can be sweet and gentle, and these people want to please. But watch out for those 1s—two of them to be exact. This Soul Number wants to be the leader and won't settle for playing second, even if its greatest desire is for harmony. This master number will bring a spiritual quality to any relationship, for it knows things—of other worlds and things beyond our realm of imagination.

Soul Number 22

At the heart and soul of all master number 22 Soul Numbers is the desire to build something tangible that will benefit humanity and will live on after them. These souls are capable of bringing about magnificent reforms while at the same time bringing spiritual understanding through their leadership. This is the master number of the futurist who will leave this earth having achieved substantial material security.

In matters of the heart, this soul is cautious like the 4, looking for a partner who's practical, has clear goals, and has achieved security. The 22 Soul Number will want to find a love with whom he or she can build his or her dreams.

Sixes and Sevens

There will be self-sacrifice with a 33, but there's also a strong healing energy with this number. If you're lucky enough to share a relationship with a 33, know that you will be showered with love that heals the heart—that's the 33's heart's desire.

Soul Number 33

The master number 33 Soul Number longs to give freely to all who are in need. Joyful, loving, and energetic, this one touches the hearts of those who ask for its protection, care, and assistance, and this is the Soul Number of one who raises the love vibration to its highest level—compassion for all.

In matters of the heart, with double 3s, this Soul Number will need to master its emotions. Those with this master number have volunteered to come back as returning souls to elevate the race to a higher understanding of the meaning of love. Note that we do not see this number very often.

Putting Your Heart and Soul into It

Now that you've read what we have to say about your Soul Number, consider these questions as well:

➤ How does your Soul Number fit with your Life Path Number and your Destiny Number?

➤ How might you integrate these numbers and allow for them to work harmoniously and supportively together?

The point to remember is that your Soul Number works together with all of the 5 core numbers. For balance and wholeness, it's important to incorporate your Soul Number into the other aspects of your overall energy pattern.

We thought it would be fun to show you one way of understanding how each Soul Number contributes to the whole. What part of a project might each of these Soul Numbers love to do? We're going to take a look at how each would get a job done working from the heart.

Twelve Ways to Get a Project Done

How do you put your heart into a project? Find your Soul Number in the following list:

➤ Number 1 wants to think it up and begin the project.

➤ Number 2 wants to gather things together for the project.

➤ Number 3 wants to design it.

➤ Number 4 wants to plan it.

➤ Number 5 wants to network it—and sell it, of course.

➤ Number 6 wants to help with it.

➤ Number 7 wants to analyze it some more.

➤ Number 8 wants to be the boss of the project.

➤ Number 9 wants to finish it, and then give it to everyone.

➤ Number 11 wants to improve it.

➤ Number 22 wants to make a monument of it so it will last forever.

➤ Number 33 wants to love it to death—and teach it to everyone.

Now you know 3 of your 5 core numbers. In the next two chapters, we'll be looking at the other two—your Personality Number and your Maturity Number.

The Least You Need to Know

➤ Your Soul Number reveals what you desire in your heart of hearts.

➤ The vowels of your full name add up to your Soul Number.

➤ Your Soul Number helps you find the road to yourself.

➤ Your Soul Number is one of your 5 core numbers.

Part 5
Putting Your Numbers to Work for You

Your Personality and Maturity Numbers are the last two of your core numbers, and they'll help ease your travel along your life's road. Beyond those numbers are your Pinnacles and Challenges, which you can think of as forks and intersections, if you like. And we'll also be showing you how to find your own Personal Years, Months, and Days, so that you can put numerology to work.

Chapter 20

Your Personality Number: See Me, See You

In This Chapter

➤ Finding your Personality Number

➤ Adding together the consonants

➤ How others see you

➤ Your Personality Number is one of your 5 core numbers

Your personality is what others remember after a first encounter, and your Personality Number not only helps you make the best possible impression, it invites you to see yourself as others see you.

Finding your Personality Number is as simple as adding together the consonants of your name. Are you surprised others think you come on strong? Could it be you've got a 1 Personality Number? Or do others find you shy and reserved? You could well be a 7 Personality.

Of course, what others see may not really be a true reflection of who you are, which is why we leave that to the Soul Number. But, in this chapter, Personality is what we're after.

'Cause You've Got Personality

The *Personality Number* is one more of the 5 core numbers of your numerology chart. Sometimes called the "outer you" or the "external image" by other numerologists, the Personality Number is what's most obvious to others about you; in other words, it's how others view you.

Figuring the Personality Number

As you may recall from the previous chapter, we used the vowels of your birth name to find your Soul Number. Now we'll use the consonants of your birth name to find your Personality Number.

Calculating the Personality Number

To calculate your Personality Number, you'll once again lay out your birth name (all of your names), just as you did for the Destiny and Soul Numbers. To illustrate how this works, we're going to use the example of Dr. Martin Luther King, whose original birth name was Michael Luther King.

By the Numbers

The **Personality Number** offers clues to habits, mannerisms, and behaviors of the people you know in your life, as well as for your own self discovery. It's found by adding together the consonants of your birth name.

First, we write out the name and then we assign the appropriate numbers to each of the consonants in the name. (Remember to write the consonant numbers *below* the name.)

```
M I C H A E L    L U T H E R    K I N G
4   3 8     3    3   2 8   9    2   5 7
```

Next, we add together all of the consonant numbers for each name separately.

Michael	Luther	King
$4 + 3 + 8 + 3 = 18$	$3 + 2 + 8 + 9 = 22$	$2 + 5 + 7 = 14$
9	4	5

Notice that by adding each name separately, we can see the influence of each name. "Michael" is a 9 number, while "Luther" is a 4, and "King" is a 5.

Easy as 1-2-3

You will find your Personality Number in the consonants of your name—your birth name that is. Like the Destiny and Soul Numbers, the Personality Number is calculated from your original name at birth—the one on your birth certificate.

Last, add the final reduced number for each name together to find the Personality Number. In our example, we add $9 + 4 + 5$ to get a total of 18 and then reduce it to a single digit of 9:

$$9 + 4 + 5 = 18 = 9$$

Remember, if your final digit total is one of the master numbers (11 or 22—we do not find the 33 as a Personality Number very often), do not reduce it further.

What Your Personality Number Reveals About You

We've provided spaces for you to calculate your own Personality Number here.

1. Write out your full birth name. Next, below your name, write down the number equivalent for each vowel. (Be sure to determine if any "y"s in your name are vowels or consonants.)

   Birth name: _____

   Numbers: _____

2. Add each name together separately and reduce each to a single digit.

   First name: _____ Second name: _____ Third name: _____

3. Add together all the numbers from #2 and reduce them to one number (unless it's a master number).

What's your Personality Number?

So, what's your Personality Number? Write it in the star!

Okay. Ready? Personality Number in hand? It's time to look at the typical traits for each number. Just by becoming aware of all of your personality traits as indicated by the Personality Number, you can make better decisions about how you respond, act, and behave.

Personality Number 1

Here are some of the traits of Personality Number 1:

➤ Appears to be dominant, forceful

➤ Creative

➤ Appears confident and self-reliant

➤ Courageous

➤ Comfortable standing out in a crowd

➤ Appears to need no one

➤ Projects a stylish, professional image

➤ Loves to wear designer clothes but prefers to create his or her own fashion statement

➤ Novel attire, novel ideas

➤ Tends to wear bright colors, even loud, bold patterns

Do you want to change? If you're too impeccably dressed, your 1 Personality may be seen as unapproachable and might put others off. In addition, you can be too aggressive and dominant in social situations. If you've got a 1 Personality, you should never be overweight, because you favor straight lines and well-fitted clothing.

Personality Number 2

Here are some of the traits of Personality Number 2:

➤ Can appear mousy and timid

➤ Careful to keep in the background

➤ Shy

➤ Appears clean and neat

➤ Tries to please

➤ Is quiet, peaceful, and diplomatic

➤ Modest and reserved

➤ Cooperative

➤ Appears artistic

➤ Can be critical over details

➤ Considered a good companion by opposite sex

➤ Charming

➤ Will look and be uncomfortable when in the limelight

➤ Can have a fussy appearance, with not a hair out of place

➤ Prefers classic styles that won't stand out in a crowd

➤ Good listener

➤ Does not tend to argue (can't stand conflict or discord)

➤ May look as if he or she needs protection

Do you want to change? With a 2 Personality Number, you can appear too colorless, and so should cultivate a flair by wearing clothing with soft flowing materials and colors that aren't too loud. There's also a danger of being too inconspicuous or a doormat for others.

256

Personality Number 3

Here are some of the traits of Personality Number 3:

➤ Looks like fun—and he or she is

➤ Magnetic personality

➤ Friendly and animated

➤ Life of the party

➤ Great talker—usually has something interesting to say—unless its gossip

➤ Entertaining and charming

➤ Extroverted and sociable

➤ Attractive physical appearance

➤ Optimistic outlook

➤ Contagiously enthusiastic

➤ Witty, and excellent with words

➤ Has a great sense of humor

➤ Looks great in most colors and styles

Do you want to change? If you've got a 3 Personality Number, you can tend toward exaggeration (as we've told you a million times already!), so others may not take you as seriously as you'd like, and may even distrust your judgment at times. It's also possible that your jealously will get you into lots of trouble, so it will be a good idea to get a grip on these feelings.

Easy as 1-2-3

With a 3 Personality Number, you'll be gifted at choosing unique accessories to add sparkle to an otherwise ordinary-looking outfit.

Personality Number 4

Here are some of the traits of Personality Number 4:

➤ Likes the country-outdoor look

➤ Looks like a sober, solid, honest citizen

➤ Does things to the letter of the law

➤ Doesn't takes shortcuts for fear of ruining the end result

➤ Prefers sensible shoes

➤ Chooses clothing that's practical, economical, and lasts

➤ Conservative in most matters and trends

➤ Can be frugal

➤ Hardworking and industrious

➤ Reliable

➤ Trustworthy

➤ Responsible

➤ Shy and reserved

➤ Finds it difficult to enjoy luxurious and frivolous things

Do you want to change? Because the 4 Personality can seem boring and dull, you may want to fun up your life, your wardrobe, or your outlook. Stubbornness and rigidity are two traits that may be contributing to any sense of restriction you might feel in your life. Loosen up and find a new way to do things—it can bring a whole new meaning to your life.

Personality Number 5

Here are some of the traits of Personality Number 5:

➤ Sexually attractive

➤ Sparkling, witty

➤ Likes change and variety

➤ Freedom of choice is the number one priority

➤ Dresses fashionably, in touch with the latest trend

➤ Can wear bright, flashy colors

➤ Outgoing and exuberant

➤ Magnetic personality

➤ Youthful in appearance

➤ Can live completely in the moment

➤ Sensual, enjoys all of the five senses

➤ Likes movement—dance, aerobics, travel, and changing jobs, home, and partners

➤ The consummate networker

➤ Likes to talk

➤ Progressive thinker

Sixes and Sevens

With their innate understanding for promoting, advertising, and selling ideas or products, people with 5 Personalities can sell everything from water filters to slick new diet vitamins to the Brooklyn Bridge—even if you didn't realize you needed it.

Do you want to change? Because you live only for today if you've got a 5 Personality, as you age, you might want to consider the value of planning for the future. Curb those urges to throw in the towel and get on the road—travel is an elixir to a 5 Personality, but it can be merely another way to escape the responsibilities in your life. Try a little stability; it does wonders for having a life to come back to after the journey.

Personality Number 6

Here are some of the traits of Personality Number 6:

➤ Gracious host or hostess

➤ A perfectionist and idealist

➤ Protective

➤ Reliable

➤ Accepts more than his or her share of responsibility

➤ A great problem solver

➤ Counsels and advises others

➤ Has a motherly or fatherly approach to situations

➤ Has an artistic flair and loves to make things pretty

➤ Has an excellent eye for color

➤ Prefers comfortable clothes that are pleasing to the eye

➤ Domestic

➤ Needs to be appreciated

➤ A natural-born teacher—every opportunity is a chance to teach a lesson

➤ Sympathetic and inspires confidence

➤ Romantic

Do you want to change? Some people with 6 Personalities can be slovenly in appearance or live in an untidy, disorganized home. If you're a 6 Personality, in your need to be the center of the family, with all of your nurturing, caring, and problem-solving ability, you might want to be careful not to be perceived as interfering in family matters. Also, you can have idealized notions of romance and marriage, which can make it hard for you to find a mate.

Personality Number 7

Here are some of the traits of Personality Number 7:

➤ Has an air of mystery and secrecy

➤ Seems absorbed in thought

➤ Perceptive

➤ Intelligent

➤ Dignified

➤ Observant

➤ Reserved

➤ Aloof

➤ Dresses with refined taste

➤ Well-dressed, well groomed

➤ Loves antiques—anything from the past, including old movies, old tools, old books

➤ Quiet

➤ Introspective

➤ Introverted

➤ Has unusual tastes, even eccentric

➤ Difficult to get close to, at first

➤ Mystical and philosophical

➤ Can be good conversationalist, when you can get him or her to talk

➤ Good style is important

➤ Very private

Do you want to change? If you've got a 7 Personality, you can be negative, skeptical, and cynical—and so can be hard to live with. You withdraw easily, and then aren't available emotionally. You can also be lonely if you become too aloof and quiet, because people will mistake your withdrawal for a lack of interest.

Personality Number 8

Here are some of the traits of Personality Number 8:

➤ Dresses for success—power suits

➤ Appears influential and powerful

➤ Ambitious

➤ Emanates strength

➤ Can appear larger than life

➤ Appears to be an authority

➤ Wears expensive clothes and accessories—love that Rolex!

➤ Can be controlling

➤ Business minded

➤ Organized

➤ Visionary

➤ Knows how to delegate

➤ Confident

➤ Assertive

➤ Competent

➤ Intelligent

➤ Has natural maturity

➤ Well-balanced

➤ Traditional

➤ Good judge of character

Do you want to change? With your 8 Personality's natural air of authority, you may come across as cold, formal, tactless, and authoritarian—in short, someone who wants to control others. These traits need to be softened so that people will trust you to lead them and to show them the way to success.

Personality Number 9

Here are some of the traits of Personality Number 9:

➤ Generous

➤ Tolerant and compassionate

➤ Philosophical

➤ Warm, kind and caring

➤ Idealistic and romantic

➤ Emotional

➤ Intuitive

➤ Fortunate

➤ Vibrant

➤ Accomplished

➤ Unable to make quick decisions

➤ Vulnerable

➤ Gullible

➤ Abstract and distant

➤ Very wise in the ways of the world

➤ Doesn't judge others on material accomplishments

➤ Sympathetic

Sixes and Sevens

Are you, like Lisa, suddenly saying, "Hey—that's not me!" Don't look to any one number to fully describe you—you are, after all, a composite of 5 core numbers plus a myriad of smaller numbers. You're not ever just one number (even if, like Lisa, you've got three 9s in your core numbers), but a cluster of energies—just like the Pleiades or any cluster of stars.

➤ Problem solver

➤ Greatly loved and respected by others

➤ Clothes are striking, with a flair for the dramatic

➤ No tolerance for injustice

➤ Looks young for a long time

Do you want to change? If you've got a 9 Personality, you can get too involved in other peoples' problems and can become unbalanced by the emotional strain. You may tend to wear black, but it's not recommended for the 9—lighter colors will bring lighter moods.

Personality Number 11

Here are some of the traits of master Personality Number 11:

➤ Visionary

➤ Inspirational

➤ May have genius intelligence

➤ Very bright

➤ Seems to be more spiritual than others

➤ Dresses in an original, artistic, inventive way

➤ Individualistic

➤ Idealistic

➤ Has a real zest for life

➤ Creative and innovative

➤ Has a kind of special aura

➤ Intense

➤ Creates own reality

➤ Has the ability to handle details

➤ Super-sensitive

➤ Intuitive, psychic, or even telepathic

Do you want to change? If you're an 11 Personality, you can be overly dependent on your mate in an unhealthy way. You can also be tense, depressed, or high-strung. Through refinement of your creative expression and leadership skills, you will reach the limelight—something that's dearly sought by an 11 personality.

Personality Number 22

Here are some of the traits of master Personality Number 22:

➤ Has an aura of competence, gives the impression of being superwoman or superman

➤ Purposeful

➤ Determined

➤ Solid and stable

➤ Practical and creative, brings material success

➤ Uses a common-sense approach to problems

➤ Problem solver

➤ Builder

➤ Looks as if he or she could control the world

➤ Appears masterful, efficient, diplomatic

➤ Dresses conservatively in tailor-made clothes

➤ Honest

➤ Productive

➤ Serious

➤ Responsible

➤ Likes to plan things, make lists, and have an agenda

Merlin's Notes

We're not writing for further master number personalities because, while it is possible to have a 33, 44, 55, 66, 77, 88, or 99 personality, we don't see these numbers occur very often. Therefore, the body of knowledge for these numbers hasn't been developed yet. The reason we don't see these numbers is because in our culture birth names are traditionally two to three names long, so the consonant number count just doesn't get that high. Of course, there are exceptions, but not enough so that we have a clear idea of the true characteristics of these master numbers as personalities. However, in other cultures where there are four to six birth names, it is possible to see higher master numbers, but these are usually cultures other than Western cultures and after all, this is a book about Western numerology.

Do you want to change? The word "workaholic" may have been invented to describe the 22 Personality. Need we remind you that there's more to life than just work—even if you're a master at it?

Now that you've read what we have to say about your Personality Number, consider these questions as well:

➤ How does your Personality Number fit with your Life Path Number, Destiny Number, and Soul Number?

➤ How might you integrate these numbers and allow for them to work harmoniously and supportively together?

The point to remember is that your Personality Number works together with all of the 5 core numbers. For balance and wholeness, it's important to incorporate your Personality into the other aspects of your overall energy pattern.

The Least You Need to Know

➤ Your Personality Number reveals the outer you that others see.

➤ Your Personality Number is calculated by adding together the consonants of your name.

➤ Knowing your Personality Number can help you see what you might want to change about the way others see you.

➤ Your Personality Number may not be an adequate reflection of who you are because there's more to you than your personality.

Your Maturity Number: Your Mid-Life Message

Hermann Hesse once said he wanted to live only in accordance with his own true self. If we, like Hesse, wish to do that, we first need to know who our true self really is.

The Maturity Number, also called the Reality Number, Realization Number, Power Number, Ultimate Goal, or True Self Number, attempts to tell of the nature and function of this final core number—the nature of your own true self.

Your Mature Self Is Your Own True Self

Your *Maturity Number,* the last of the 5 core numbers, is the number of the true you. Because it shows how your Soul Number, Destiny Number, and Personality Number work in concert with your Life Path Number, it reveals the true essence of who you are.

By the Numbers

You can think of your **Maturity Number** (also called the True Self Number), the last of the 5 core numbers, as the ultimate harmonic vibration of you. It's found by adding together your birth date and your birth name.

Your Maturity Number becomes fully functional as you approach mid-life, so as you age and mature, the energy of this number will become the dominant force in your life. In other words, the influence of your Maturity Number increases as you grow older.

The underlying force of this number begins to surface at around age 35 to 40, and emerges as you gain a better understanding of yourself. The gift of maturity is that you no longer waste time and energy on things that aren't moving you toward your ultimate goal in life.

It follows that, when we're younger, we're not conscious of the influence or energy of this number. It is, however, present and informs many of your decisions and actions unconsciously. So, whether conscious or unconscious, your life is always affected by your Maturity Number.

Merlin's Notes

As you age and as you move through the mid-life passage, you'll begin to truly sense the pathway of your Maturity Number. You may not have known what to call this sensing, or perhaps you call it something else, but careful study and knowledge of this particular number will point the way to success—the rest, of course, is up to you. Your Maturity Number reveals the ultimate goal of your life.

What the Maturity Number Offers

The success of your Maturity Number must be lived up to and earned. This is the number that tells of

➤ The ultimate goal of your life.

➤ The essence of all your experiences—what they add up to, what they were for.

➤ What's waiting for you when you've reached your peak.

➤ What you should and can develop.

➤ The true you.

➤ The mature you.

The Maturity Number Is Not Active in Early Ages

Even though this number isn't at full throttle until after age 50 or so, its characteristics *are* felt at an early age. That's because there's always going to be some kind of realization about your true inner nature, what we like to think of as an understanding of soul energy.

The Maturity Number always shows itself in the most important experiences of our lives. Another way to say it is that your Maturity Number, or True Self Number, will show its influence in the most important moments of your life, even before you have reached the mid-life point. Because this number is the symbol of the compilation of your birth name and your birth date, it shows your true power, your highest development, and your real goal in life.

> **Numerology Rule #12**
>
> Your Maturity Number is found by adding together the energies of all that you are:
>
> Birth name + birth date = Maturity Number

Finding the Maturity Number

A simple way to think of the formula for the Maturity Number is:

Destiny Number + Life Path Number = Maturity Number

Calculating the Maturity Number

To find your Maturity Number, you add your Destiny Number to your Life Path Number. (Refer to Chapter 17, "Your Life Path Number: Rules for the Road," and Chapter 18, "Your Destiny Number: It's My Purpose … and I'll Cry If I Want To.") It's that simple! The final number is called your Maturity Number and tells of the true goal of your life.

Juno Jordan, the "grandmother" of modern numerology, called this number the lighthouse at the end of the road. The idea goes something like this: We'll all travel our own unique path in life (the Life Path) and as each of us works our way down the path (following our Destiny), there's at first a faint calling of a foghorn somewhere in the distance.

Easy as 1-2-3

Your Maturity Number is the sum total of the vibrational pattern that is you. By adding together your name number (Destiny Number) and birth date number (Life Path Number), you'll find your Maturity Number, which equals your final, ultimate goal.

As we advance farther and farther down the path (as we age), the sound becomes more and more clear, beckoning to us, "This way, this way." Finally, when we've been on our path for more than half of our lives, and the sound of the foghorn is no longer deniable, we begin to see that there is, in fact, something out there—a lighthouse, beaming down on our path, clearly showing us the way. Thus, we find the reality of who we truly are and begin to live upon our path in full awareness of who we are and all that we can be.

This is essentially the journey to the Maturity Number. It's your final attainment—although it just may take you 50 years or more to get there.

A Sample Maturity Number

Let's look at an example of how to calculate the Maturity Number. Mother Teresa's birth name was Gonxha Agnes Bojaxhiu, and she was born on August 26, 1910.

G O N X H A	A G N E S	B O J A X H I U
7 6 5 6 8 1	1 7 5 5 1	2 6 1 1 6 8 9 3
33/6	19/1	36/9

6 + 1 + 9 = 16 = 7 (Destiny Number)

Birth date: 8-26-1910 = 8 + 8 + 11 = 27 = 9 (Life Path Number)

Destiny Number 7 + Life Path Number 9 = 16 = Maturity Number 7

This shows that Mother Teresa had a 7 Maturity Number, the number of spiritual seeking, also called the Christ consciousness number. This suggests that in the latter part of her life she would be looking inward, and would have developed the insight and wisdom to see into people and see them for who they really are. With her 7 Maturity Number, people came to her seeking her wisdom, and in that role, Mother Teresa, and people with 7 Maturity Numbers, become spiritual teachers. Plus, if you add up the numbers of Mother Teresa's birth name without reducing them first, they equal 88—33 + 19 + 36—the Master Number of reconciling the material world with higher spiritual values!

Sixes and Sevens

We remind you that there are no bad numbers—all numbers are good. Forcing the energy of these numbers into conflicting relationships is what creates negative expressions of a number.

Sometimes, a number feels negative or too hard to deal with. If that's the case, check to see if in fact you might not have too many of this same number. An overabundance of any one number will be too much of that energy for anyone. While you can't change your birth date, you can change your name, house number, and even your phone number. (We discuss name changes in Chapter 29, "Names: A Rose by Any Other Name Might Not Smell as Sweet.")

You cannot, however, change your Maturity Number. Like each of your 5 core numbers, it's part of your cosmic code, which is perfect in its design. If an imbalance seems to be present, it's best to examine the full meaning of each number, both the negative and positive attributes, and see if you're exhibiting any of these attributes to an extreme. In addition, remember that this particular number is about maturity—something we all strive for!

Finding Your Maturity Number: Living Your Life to the Fullest

Finding your Maturity Number is simple now that you know your Life Path Number and Destiny Number. In fact, just add them together:

Life Path Number ___ + Destiny Number ___ = Maturity Number ___

What's your Maturity Number? Write it in the star!

So what's your Maturity Number? Is it the same as any of your other numbers? You'll want to go through this chapter carefully to find out what your Maturity Number says about you—and your relationships.

Interpreting the Maturity Number

Remember, your Maturity Number will resonate more and more strongly as you mature, finally reaching its apex in your elder years. Now that you know what your Maturity Number is, it's time to find out what your Maturity Number reveals about you.

Maturity Number 1

With a 1 Maturity Number, you can expect to learn leadership early in life. Your best results will come from beginning new things, and your strong opinions and ambition will lead you to positions of authority, although you should be careful to temper your tendency to be bossy and domineering. With your good memory and excellent power of concentration, you're a natural for taking over what needs to be done, and doing it.

Your true self naturally attracts unusual people and experiences that are different in some way. You have a broad vision and do things in a big way, and, because you like to do what you're thinking, you're seldom without something to do.

The 1 Maturity Number can be set in his or her ways—and we mean that just as we wrote it. That's because the 1 Maturity Numbers are usually a stickler about one thing. Be it their taste in paintings or their approach to raising children, there's usually a good deal of discipline and order evident, because while the 1 Maturity Numbers are not necessarily conventional, they will think that their ways are the best ways—and will expect all others to follow suit.

Sixes and Sevens

With a 1 Maturity Number, you're so single-minded once you're focused that, if you haven't got a plan, you may feel uncertain about how to proceed. As long as you've got a plan, though, you'll forge ahead—often in your own unique way.

Maturity Number 1s are not always as strong as they think when it comes to their health, but they do recover quickly, because being active is what they live for. Anywhere originality and dynamism are required are places you'll find 1 Maturity Number people living up to their potential.

Your elder years will give you an opportunity to be truly independent and self-reliant.

Maturity Number 2

With a 2 Maturity Number, you can expect to get others to help you, because you'll naturally attract those who will want to support you. You may have trouble with relationships early in life until you learn that helpfulness is the name of the game, both in giving and receiving.

Easy as 1-2-3

The Number 2 Maturity Number will excel anywhere diplomacy is required, and will also shine in groups and organizations where cooperation is key.

Your true self is a peacemaker to the core, and you will do whatever is necessary to ensure harmony in both your surroundings and relationships, although you will fight for your peace if you're pushed too far. Naturally sensitive, you have inherent artistic ability, be it in music, painting, writing, or dancing, which, if ignored, may cause you regret as you get older.

Maturity Number 2s find happiness through ensuring harmony all around them, which they accomplish by expressing the beauty, tenderness, sincerity, and spirituality of their nature. Often psychic, always intuitive, Maturity Number 2s must guard against self-consciousness, which comes as a result of intuiting (sometimes incorrectly) the opinions of others. Cooperation is the byword of the 2 Maturity Numbers, and they long for the same sincerity and sympathy of others that they gives to them.

Your elder years will find you in a relationship, not alone, and very possibly living from a place of true inner peace.

Maturity Number 3

With a 3 Maturity Number, you can expect a vibrant imagination and a notable artistic talent to be yours, although this may be repressed early in your life. Because a 3 Maturity Number means your creativity comes naturally, the more you use it, the happier you'll be.

Your true self is both sensitive and expressive, and if either of these is not allowed to flourish, you can become depressed, touchy, or even childishly insolent. At the same time, you have a true gift for words (among your many other talents), you're fun and humorous, and you're a master of the quick retort. Most notable is your zest and enthusiasm for life.

Sixes and Sevens

Like children, people with 3 Maturity Numbers can get very stubborn if they don't get their own way. But, also like children, they bring so much joy to those around them that their little snits seem minor by comparison.

The Maturity Number 3 does best when allowed to create and accomplish great things. As Juno Jordan said, "It is the 3s who give color to life, who amuse, thrill, and inspire." Friendship is of utmost importance, and the 3 Maturity Number's ability to enjoy everything draws others to them. In fact, people with 3 Maturity Numbers can do very well financially when they're working in harmony with their world.

Your elder years should be filled with the joy of friends and time for creative pursuits.

Maturity Number 4

With a 4 Maturity Number, you can expect the desire to make dreams practical, and in your younger years, you'll learn the value of discipline and hard work. As you mature, you'll make sure to create opportunities for yourself to contribute to something lasting. Your 4 Maturity Number indicates that you're a natural organizer, able to build, plan, and order things, and bring ideas into form—always with a backup plan, of course.

Sixes and Sevens

Maturity Number 4s are often certain their ways are the best ways (and they often are). Because being "right" is very important, they can become domineering or dogged in their efforts to get things done their way. Management is their forte, micromanagement their downfall.

Your true self has a talent for organizing, and you're steadfast, honorable, straight, and true (just like a Boy Scout!). Permanency is your byword, and you have both high standards and expectations, as well as the responsibility and fortitude to see things through to their conclusion.

In addition, there can be a tendency toward self-righteousness, or worse, to not take responsibility for their mistakes; but if a 4 Maturity Number holds true to his or her strong principles, he or she is bound to succeed. Hard working, never idle, and never one to waste time or money, a 4 Maturity Number person is reliable and down-to-earth.

In your elder years you can expect to build something of lasting value. Your health will be of great interest, and you will find practical, economical ways to organize around your health needs.

Maturity Number 5

With a 5 Maturity Number, you can expect your life to be exciting and full of changes—because if it's not, you'll see to making a change. Interested in many things and curious about everything, you may have the tendency early in your life to be confused about what direction your life should take.

Your true self is resourceful, many talented, and independent, and you may truly believe that "freedom" is what it's all about. People with 5 Maturity Numbers thrive on the new and consider life to be full of opportunities for stimulation and adventure. You are attractive to the opposite sex, a quick thinker, bold, and probably unconventional.

Maturity Number 5s understand the value of change and new opportunities, but also have learned to get everything they can from each experience before moving on. People with 5 Maturity Numbers can be great leaders because they make working with them fun and exciting mainly because they want to try new, progressive ways, and are willing to take risks. Your biggest life-long struggle is to find stability, stick-with-it-ness, and commitment.

As an elder, you can expect to travel the world over, meet people from a variety of cultures and backgrounds, and be on the go, taking risks and exploring new things. This is the number of someone who is said to be "forever young."

Sixes and Sevens

There is a destructive side to the 5 Maturity Number—a desire to tear things down or just plain cause trouble brought about by this number's inner restlessness, rebellious nature, and sense of invincibility. With this Maturity Number it's best to channel your energy into worthwhile activities.

Maturity Number 6

With a 6 Maturity Number, you can expect the welfare of others—all others—to be of utmost importance. This is the number of the humanitarian and the giver, and with your strong principles about fairness, goodness, and family values, you'll shine when you learn the balance between giving and receiving.

Your true self loves both things of beauty and the home, so your home is quite literally your haven, your nest. You're a nurturer and a giver, and your kitchen is often the center of activity. You need to beware of giving too much, as well of as clinging to your ideals, especially when it comes to your idea of the perfect mate. Generous and helpful, though, you'll never stop giving no matter how many problems are put on your plate.

Maturity Number 6s are often wealthy through marriage or inheritance and love to surround themselves with beautiful and comfortable things. Often devotees, they must take care to not become a zealots; but at the same time they are unhappy if they're not serving others. At their best, they'll share what they have with the world, because when they're helping humanity, they're truly happy. With a Maturity Number 6, you can expect to have a good earning capacity because you have a natural financial attraction.

In your elder years you will find yourself surrounded by your family, children, grand-children, and great-grandchildren. Contentment and harmony should be yours all the days of your life.

Maturity Number 7

With a 7 Maturity Number, you can expect to live your life in your own unique way. Solitary and analytical, you truly do travel to the beat of a different drummer and are at your best when left to your own devices.

Your true self values solitude and specialization, and if you're left to your own devices, you'll find an area in which you can shine. Getting to the truth of a matter is what excites you—although you won't seem excited to others. Wasting time is a waste of time to you, and you won't be caught doing anything frivolous or—God forbid—fun. Seeking the truth, be it spiritual, scientific, or philosophical, is what suits you best.

Maturity Number 7s are often solitary, and may seem aloof or reserved to others. Sometimes unmarried, because expressing love isn't what they're good at, people with 7 Maturity Numbers nonetheless demand and appreciate the best life has to offer. These people enjoy the finer things in life, often preferring antiques (things from the past) and quality. At the same time, when working at their best, 7 Maturity Number people may become well-known for their discovery of something new, because following their hunches is what this number's all about.

Easy as 1-2-3

If you've got a 7 Maturity Number, while you're young you may have trouble understanding why others need other people so much; but as you mature, you'll learn that they're not like you—the person who understands the value of introspection and silence.

In your elder years, you can expect to pursue spiritual and philosophical interests, moving farther into the interior landscape of your own world. Long hours of contemplation, writing, and reading will be the normal lifestyle for this Maturity Number. Solitary, though not alone, 7 Maturity Numbers will find people seeking them out for their insightful wisdom.

Maturity Number 8

With an 8 Maturity Number, you can expect reward through accomplishment, because as you reap, so you shall sow. Your 8 Maturity Number suggests you have the potential for mastery, but you must learn to find a balance between the material and the spiritual to achieve it. Your ability to see the big picture means you have the ability to lead others, but you must always work toward a clear purpose to achieve success.

Your true self will have to work hard to achieve anything, but this is part of what makes you strong. Directing and organizing is what you do best, because you're efficient, organized, capable, and most of all strong. You have to be strong to achieve balance between the two levels of life represented by the two loops of the 8—the material world and the spiritual world. Your life will be marked by ups and downs as one or the other of these loops gains ascendance; but striving for mental strength will help you to achieve the inner power to see things universally and metaphysically.

Maturity Number 8s will work for the cause of humanity because they love the work, not for personal gain or recognition. At their best, they'll make easy connections between facts and feelings, and will be able to use their abilities to see things clearly to help others see them, too. Because 8 Maturity Numbers are self-reliant—and often the people in charge—they aren't always the best companions. They can, however, become great leaders and teachers of others, even great masters or mystics who others seek out for their wisdom.

Easy as 1-2-3

Working for money or power alone won't do the trick with an 8 Maturity Number, because personal success is ultimately more important than financial reward.

In your later years you can expect to be called upon to direct or lead in some capacity right up to the end—for others see you as an authority. You will organize and be involved in business matters until the last nail is in the coffin.

If you've lived from a place of serving the greater good rather than from a place of ego gratification, you will be remembered as one of the great ones!

Maturity Number 9

With a 9 Maturity Number, you can expect that life won't always be easy. That's because you're learning to give up the physical world for the spiritual one, and you'll have to learn to let go of loving people in order to love humanity. At the same time, things will come easily to you, so you may mistakenly believe your gifts are meant to be used to attain the easy life, when in reality, they're given so that you can master this plane and move on.

Your true self is both compassionate and humanitarian, but for you to be at your best, you must practice these qualities on an impersonal level. Your love of humanity can be a light for the world, but there is the danger of using it for personal gain, which can truly bring destruction to your own life—and the lives of those around you. The other danger is to ignore your sense of service. Your greatest joy is found in true universal love, because with this number of reward, the greatest good will come from the greatest giving.

Sixes and Sevens

It's not easy achieving perfection, and early in life, the 9 Maturity Numbers may appear inconsistent as they move from tolerance to detachment. Over time, people with this Maturity Number will learn to balance the needs of others with their own needs, and so move toward the perfection they're constantly seeking.

The Maturity Number 9 will learn to let go of self in order to serve others, as well as to let go of attachments to outcome. You will learn to live in the flow. Surrender and release are the operative words at this time of life. Kind and generous, you'll need to beware of taking on too much responsibility, or trying to be all things to all people. Through your disappointments, you'll learn to help others without losing yourself. As a wise man recently told Lisa, "The goal of every baseball game is to return home." Think about that: It's the lesson of the 9 Maturity Number.

In your elder years, you can expect to be more involved in the pursuit of the healing arts, metaphysics, the performing arts, writing, teaching, or philanthropic activities, if not in humanistic organizations that benefit large numbers of people. You have a compassionate heart and are willing to give your love to the sensitive, healing foundations of humanity.

Master Maturity Numbers

When a person has a master number as a Maturity Number, it gives possibility for mastership in handling human affairs. Remember to check your numbers before reducing them to see if you've got a master Maturity Number. The master numbers are intense, highly intuitive vibrations. This means your energy is more vibrant, but that at the same time many people will pull back from the intensity of your energy when you have it on full force.

Maturity Number 11

This Maturity Number occurs when you have a combination Life Path and Destiny Numbers of 7 + 4, 8 + 3, 5 + 6, or 9 + 2. Each combination adds up to 11.

At an early age, you'll have an unusual amount of self-understanding as well as the ability to see through emotional experiences to the truth within. With your higher knowledge, you demonstrate a wisdom beyond your years.

Merlin's Notes

The 11 represents a high intensity energy, which can lead to moving into the realms of psychic phenomenon. With an 11 Maturity Number, you can get involved in other peoples' problems, and you may also tend to get involved with a nontraditional spiritual system. You're extremely sensitive to others' feelings, environmental conditions, various products, and even certain foods. This means that your lifestyle must be balanced, because you're a much higher vibration—pulsating at a more rapid frequency than most. To learn the depth and scope of your outstanding gift of intuition, you'll need to protect your immune system by following cleansing and detoxifying routines and by resting often.

You'll need a good diet and rest with this highly nervous, intense number, and nervous system health issues are possible. In addition, you'll need companionship with built-in independence, and you may attain fame or move into the spotlight somehow.

Easy as 1-2-3

As Juno Jordan points out, "Blessed are the peacemakers, for they shall be called the children of God," and for no Maturity Number is this more true than the 11/2. Your work is to inspire in whatever field you choose.

If you're female, chances are you're strikingly beautiful and feminine, while if you're male, you're likely charismatic and refined, with exceptionally good manners. These are such extraordinary qualities in combination with a high level of intensity that it may be too intense for everyday life. In that case, you'll revert to the 2 and all that that number entails.

In your elder years, you can expect to pursue spiritual interests (such as intuition development, clairvoyance, or a healing touch), and health and nutrition interests for purification. You'll have select relationships with those who share your psychic and intuitive wisdom, and you may find yourself in the role of mediator, arbitrator, or peacemaker. But more than that, you'll be called to inspire and uplift humanity, whether close to home or in the broad reaches of public service.

Maturity Number 22

This Maturity Number means you have a combination of an 11/2 Destiny as well as an 11/2 Life Path.

With a 22 Maturity Number, you can expect to make things happen. While you'll encounter more obstacles than most, your masterful competency will allow you to overcome any barriers you might encounter in life. You'll be very, very successful, because you're the Master Builder.

Your true self is both a manager and a leader. You have an inner stability and inner power that stem from a firm rooting in universal principles, spiritual truths, and management know-how, and this power is what you draw upon when you encounter challenges. You're not as high-strung as the master number 11, most likely because you're grounded in practicality, competence, and know-how (the energy of the 4). Nonetheless, like all master numbers, you're bound to feel you're being tested many times in this life.

You may have some physical defect or health challenge that only strengthens your belief in higher principles and self-discipline. In your mid-life, you'll go through a reexamination process:

Easy as 1-2-3

As a Maturity Number 22, you'll find yourself in situations or jobs that demand multifaceted ability, and through these experiences you'll begin to see all that you've gained and accomplished over the years. You'll become an expert, because in spite of the restrictions, red tape, and negative thinking, you'll find a way to hold to your ideals and standards and to honor universal law.

1. To determine if living with such high ideals is truly allowing you to attain your goals. You may choose to give up your pursuit of these lofty goals because of a seeming lack of satisfaction, or because the "test" seems too hard.

2. To learn new mastery combining spiritual beliefs with material goals.

3. To allow for a new awareness of your true potential as a 22, a spark that emerges as the result of feeling the urge to work for the benefit of mankind, or, at the personal level, the feeling that you've got what it takes to achieve more.

In your elder years you won't slow down much, and you'll always have a goal and a mission. You will require security, though, because the 4 aspect of this number says that stability and security are foremost priorities. You'll have to learn balance in all things—relationship, work, health, and a happy heart.

Maturity Number 33

This is an extremely rare combination of an 11/2 and 22/4 Life Path or Destiny for a combined total of 33/6.

This rare 33 Maturity Number can expect to benefit from long years of responsibility and service. Usually, the direction of a 33/6 in mid-life will move to one of affection,

Easy as 1-2-3

Maturity Number 33 is a gift from heaven. You'll understand the balance between being responsible and taking responsibility for everyone else, between honoring your own needs and the needs of others, and between giving and receiving. You'll give your love openly, willingly, and intensely to those in need.

joy, love, and the careful nurturing of these three. You can expect to serve mankind in some way through your highly developed skills of sympathetic understanding and problem solving.

Your true self lives from the heart and can know no limits when it comes to caring for others. Your abundant creative energy, coupled with your heart-felt care and nurturing of all those around you, is an extraordinarily healing combination. Like all of the master numbers, you'll face many tests and obstacles unique to the numbers 3 and 6, yet you'll meet the challenge again and again. Also like the other master numbers, you'll be naturally drawn to higher principles, universal consciousness, and spiritual understanding.

Your extreme emotionalism will cause you to find a way to live in balance. This is the number that will struggle with reconciling what's right in your own heart with the needs of others. Codependence and failed marriage may be among your many tests.

Universal Law #6

When it's right for you, it's right all the way around—trust this.

In your mid-life years, you'll come to know love on a larger scale, where the strong emotional energy you feel so adamantly in your heart can be channeled into effective and appropriate outlets that benefit large numbers of people and heal mankind.

In your elder years, you can expect to be sought after for your friendship, your creative energy, your sympathetic manner, and the healing energy of your love. You will learn how to protect your energy and your heart.

Looking for the Maturity Number in All the Right Places

Look for your Maturity Number in both the numbers in your chart and in others' charts as well. This means that if you have a 6 Maturity Number, you'll look to see if that 6 shows up again as one of your other numbers in your chart or in the charts of those with whom you have relationships. There are eight other important places in the numerology chart where your Maturity Number might appear. In this case, the position itself, rather than the number, tells of the possible harmony or discord.

➤ Soul Number (sum of vowels in a name)

➤ Personality Number (sum of consonants in a name)

➤ Destiny Number (sum of all the letters in a name)

➤ Life Path Number (sum of birth month + birth day + birth year)

➤ Maturity Number (Destiny + Life Path Numbers)

➤ Personal Year Number (sum of birth month + birth day + current calendar year) (see Chapter 23, "Climb Every Pinnacle, Ford Every Challenge")

➤ Pinnacle Number (see Chapter 22, "Predictive Numerology: Future Forecasts")

➤ Challenge Number (see Chapter 22)

Some of your deepest experiences will come through those people who have your own Maturity Number in their names. When this happens, there will be either an instant attraction or a strong sense of repulsion. That's because you're experiencing either the positive or negative energy of your Maturity Number when you meet these people.

Because your Maturity Number is such an important aspect of who you are, we're going to show you how your own number works with others who have your same number—from Soul to Pinnacles and Challenges.

Your Maturity Number and Another's Soul Number

The deepest and most personal relationship will be when your Maturity Number matches the Soul Number of another person. When this occurs, there will be a deep and binding attraction felt by each of you, and from the beginning there will be a warmth and sense of understanding each other that will last even after there's been a separation. That's because this is a matching of heart energy (Soul Number) and true self (Maturity Number).

Usually, the situation or way in which the attraction occurs is unusual or peculiar, possibly even having a romantic flavor to it, although it's also possible to have an immediate antipathy for each other at first, because underneath all that, there's a deep attraction. Like attracts like, in this case.

It's much more than an ordinary acquaintance in this kind of relationship. That's because this relationship isn't meant for the material world or superficial matters, because it's a relationship that's the pathway to the soul.

Your Maturity Number and Another's Personality Number

If your Maturity Number is the same as another's Personality Number, the relationship won't be as deep or lasting as a pairing with the Soul Number. That's because these two people will be drawn to each other because of something in their manner or appearance which appeals through similar tastes. When a close association is formed with this combination of numbers, there's apt to be unhappiness or disappointment. That's because there's no real foundation on which to base the relationship.

279

Merlin's Notes

It may be looks, or style of dress, or how someone comes across in a social situation that is attractive, but don't get carried away—it's not based on the solid stuff. For example, a man may see something attractive in the personality of a woman and fall in love with her, but what's really happening is that he's seeing in her the qualities that he's developing in himself—the qualities of his Maturity Number. But if it's just her Personality, it may all be an illusion.

This type of relationship teaches us that it's not wise to judge the book by its cover. Appearances don't go deep enough when we're dealing with the Maturity Number. Remember, this number is the essence of who you are, not just what you show to the outer world.

Your Maturity Number and Another's Destiny Number

When someone has your Maturity Number as a Destiny Number, the association may not be long lasting, because the *relationship* may have more to do with a particular experience you're having than a true heart connection.

By the Numbers

Relationship is a broadly defined term. It can mean friend, lover, marriage partner, business partner, mother-in-law, or child, to name but a few. Think in inclusive terms, with broad application, when you read these descriptions.

Often the Maturity-Destiny combination may not go beyond a social or business contact. The person with the same Destiny Number as your Maturity Number may find you interesting or inspiring—or some other quality he or she can use as a stepping stone along the road to his or her own destiny. Because of that, when it's time, that person will be able to break the tie easily with no regret. This isn't a binding relationship!

In this case, it's the Maturity Number person who must make the effort, because that's the person with the lesson to learn and work out, and he or she must have the self-control. After all, this experience with a matching Destiny person is happening to help you move toward that ever-present calling, to move you in the direction toward which you are being called.

Your Maturity Number and Another's Life Path Number

When there's an attraction and subsequent relationship between someone whose Life Path Number is the same as your Maturity Number, it's a deep link because it has to do with a past life connection. It may not, however, be the "land of milk and honey." Even though you may do some kind of important work together, the tie may not be harmonious. Oh, there will be love, but it's best not get gooey over this connection.

The person with the Life Path Number that matches your Maturity Number will find that things aren't quite balanced. In fact, the Life Path person will find this relationship a kind of test, because that person will be more fixed in his or her characteristics. (And why not? These are traits and skills brought in from past lives.) On the other hand, you, the Maturity Number, are just unfolding your character and are therefore not beholden to a certain path.

Shall that deter these two? Oh, no—this tie can be very hard to break. A real effort will have to be made on both sides and compromise for the good of both will be required.

Sixes and Sevens

The Life Path-Maturity Number relationship isn't a marriage made in heaven, because the Maturity Number person meets a strict teacher in the Life Path person and will have to conform to that person's requirements, while the Life Path person finds a difficult student in the Maturity person.

Your Maturity Number and Another's Maturity Number

How about when you meet someone who has your exact same Maturity Number? What kind of relationship can you expect?

This relationship can be very supportive, and the attraction to each other may result in much good, leaving a lasting mark upon the character of each. The tie here may be unusual, odd, out of the ordinary, or no tie at all in the normal sense, just a mutual sharing and pleasure in finding someone of one's own type with one's own interests.

If each unfolds at the same rate of development, then the tie may last a lifetime. However, if the spiritual development isn't equal, then the relationship is doomed. If you can work in common, it can lead to the most satisfying and meaningful relationship one can have.

Your Maturity Number and the Personal Year

A special situation occurs when you meet someone who is in a Personal Year that is the same number as your Maturity Number (see Chapter 23). When this happens note it, because whatever takes place under these conditions will have more influence on your future than at any other time, or more than any other event in a nine-year cycle. Therefore, make the most of it. Take advantage of the opportunity to grow toward your Maturity Number.

Your Maturity Number and Your Pinnacles

If your Maturity Number appears on one of your Pinnacles (see Chapter 22), the time of that cycle is a potent one, because it will be a time of advancing your future by working along the lines of the characteristics of the Maturity Number. You'll experience your maturation process profoundly during this time, when you come to know your true self.

If your Maturity Number doesn't appear on any Pinnacle, your development of the Maturity Number will take place more generally, usually showing its full force late in life.

Your Maturity Number and Your Challenges

When your Challenge Number (see Chapter 22) is the same as your Maturity Number, it's a time of intense challenge. You'll be challenged to grow into all that this number demands—it's rather like being forced through the eye of a needle! While your natural instinct will be to resist and run—forget it—it's time to turn and face it. The Challenge Number is what you are to become—not something to overcome—and so is the Maturity Number.

> **Universal Law #7**
>
> Life is what you make it—lemonade or finely aged wine.

If you meet or have a relationship with a person who has your Maturity Number as his or her Challenge Number, trust us, that person will put you to the test. His or her character, manner, and expression will be the source of your dismay. Remember, this person is a mirror for you, so while he or she may be exhibiting the negative energies of your number, know that you must work through this energy to be free from its negative influence. Your life's goal is to understand and develop the positive aspects of your Maturity Number—no matter what.

It's your life, of course, and you have free will and free choice. But even if you run—you can't hide. You're challenged to become the highest form of human expression possible—and your challenge numbers tell you how!

A Few Words About Your Maturity Number and Mid-Life

Remember, the Maturity Number begins at approximately 40 years of age and becomes a stronger influence as you get older. By 50 years old or so, you should have your Maturity Number fully functioning. After you move through a mid-life transformation, or slip past the mid-life marker, you begin to reevaluate and, as anthropologist/

psychologist Angeles Arrien says, to "revision your dreams." Your Maturity Number is an invaluable tool for helping you understand the direction for your later years in life.

It's important to remember that in order to have a fulfilled and fully lived experience in life, you mustn't ignore the Maturity Number. Its influence is felt throughout life, but won't take the front seat until the second half of your life. This, then, will be the time when you can best live in harmony with your true self—your mature self. Look forward to it—it's the best!

The Least You Need to Know

➤ Your Maturity Number reveals your true self and manifests as you grow older.

➤ Your Maturity Number is found by adding together your Life Path Number and your Destiny Number.

➤ When you meet others whose numbers are the same as your Maturity Number, there will be a strong attraction or strong test.

➤ When your Maturity Number is the same as another of your numbers, there will be special challenges and rewards.

I PREDICT... RAIN.

Chapter 22

Predictive Numerology: Future Forecasts

> ### In This Chapter
>
> ➤ Predictive numerology looks to the future
>
> ➤ Your Pinnacle Numbers reveal your potential for achievement
>
> ➤ Your Challenge Numbers pinpoint your potential difficulties
>
> ➤ All of us have 4 Pinnacle Numbers and 4 Challenge Numbers

Finding our way in life is one of our biggest challenges—we want to do it right and we want it to be successful. In the next two chapters, we have a set of numbers to tell you about that will help you navigate the course of life—in this chapter, the Pinnacle and the Challenge Numbers, and in the next chapter, the Major Cycle.

All three of these sets of numbers, when executed fully, will yield a fully lived, fully engaged life. So come along and find out what your future holds, using predictive numerology.

Knowing the Way

We now come to the phase of numerology that predicts when to do what. In this chapter, we look at two of the three *predictive* indicators in your chart: the Pinnacles and the Challenges.

Your Personal Best

One set of numbers can guide you to your highest attainment, because they point the way for knowing what it is that can be achieved in a particular period of time. We're talking about the *Pinnacle Numbers*.

By the Numbers

Predictive numerology uses numbers to look at the future.

By the Numbers

Your **Pinnacle Numbers** reveal your potential for achievement and success. These numbers show what is possible to attain at a given period in life.

Easy as 1-2-3

Changing conditions may bring new horizons, but if you're in the middle of a change, the promise of something new is often no comfort. What you want to know then is what's happening and why. Now, you can look no further, because your Pinnacle Number (and your Challenge Number, which we'll discuss later in this chapter) alert you to your future, your present, and your past.

Pinnacles tell of the road ahead, as well as the name of the road you're on right now. It can be hard for any of us to understand a sudden, unexpected change in our lives, such as a time of uncertain finances, or a time when, no matter how you slice it, the marriage just seems to be falling apart. Each of these is part of the story of our lives, and knowing your Pinnacle Number can explain many a mystery.

The Pinnacle Number is one of the forecasting numbers in your chart. From it, you'll learn what to expect on the road ahead. Then, you can look ahead to what's coming for your life, as well as look back to see where you've been.

Pinnacles Equal Attainments

Each of us has four Pinnacle Numbers, each representing a distinct period in your life that's governed by a singular theme. Each number shows the attitude and effort needed during the specified period, and all four of these numbers work together to help you work out your destiny. We'd suggest, in fact, that you might want to view these Pinnacles in relationship to your Destiny Number.

Here are some important points to remember about your Pinnacle Numbers:

➤ Pinnacles are instructive on how to live with the least amount of resistance. They point the way toward manifesting your best.

➤ Each Pinnacle demands that you live up to the qualities indicated by the number on that Pinnacle. Circumstances will present themselves that will force you to live up to the elements of your Pinnacle Number.

Because they're based on nine-year cycles, Pinnacles can help you learn at exactly what age you should be doing what. Each of the four Pinnacles has a distinct meaning and a distinct length. The first and last Pinnacles are the longest, with the two middle ones being nine years each. Remember the concept of nine-year cycles, because they will come into play when you start to figure your Pinnacles.

1. The **First Pinnacle** represents the spring of life, a time of newness. It's very personal, and it's one of the longest periods. It covers approximately ages 0 through 27 (three nine-year cycles) at the least and can be up to 35 for some. The First Pinnacle varies in length for each person.

2. The **Second Pinnacle** covers the summer of life, a period of blossoming and ripening. It's the period of responsibility and family. It's nine years in length.

3. The **Third Pinnacle** covers middle age and maturity, and is also nine years in length. It represents the autumn of your life, a time of manifestation and reward.

4. The **Fourth Pinnacle** represents the winter of life, a time of aging and wizening, of retirement and reflection, and spiritual wisdom. It's the harvest cycle and lasts at least three cycles of nine years (roughly from age 50 to end of life). With new technology, however, some of us will have up to six cycles under this Pinnacle Number, up to age 104 or so.

Each Pinnacle is a time of development, each is accurately timed, and each is part of the blueprint of your life. It's all part of the master plan. Each pinnacle represents major growth for you that occurs along the lines of the designated number.

Finding Your Pinnacle Numbers

To find your Pinnacle Numbers you will simply use your birth date—but have your Life Path Number ready, too, because we'll be using it later. Finding your Pinnacles is easy—you just have to follow the directions carefully.

> **Numerology Rule #13**
>
> Here are the formulas for finding your four Pinnacle Numbers:
>
> First Pinnacle = month of birth + day of birth
>
> Second Pinnacle = day of birth + year of birth
>
> Third Pinnacle = First Pinnacle + Second Pinnacle
>
> Fourth Pinnacle = month of birth + year of birth

A Walk Through a Sample Pinnacle Chart

Now, let's take it one step at a time. Using Whoopi Goldberg as a sample, we're going to walk you through finding each of her four Pinnacle Numbers. As you read through the instructions and follow the steps, we'd like you to fill in the blanks for practice.

Sample Chart for Whoopi Goldberg's Pinnacles

1. Whoopi Goldberg has a birth date of November 13, 1949. First, we'll reduce all of the numbers in her birthday to single-digit numbers.

   Birth date: 11   13   1949

   Reduced to: 2   4   5 (2 + 3)

   Note that each segment of the birth date has been reduced to a single-digit number.

2. Now, to find the First Pinnacle Number, simply add the month and day of birth together, arriving at a single-digit number. For example:

   Month of birth + day of birth = First Pinnacle Number

   2 + 4 = 6

   So Whoopi's First Pinnacle is a 6. Write this number here:

   First Pinnacle Number _____.

   Got the idea? Now let's try the second one.

3. To find the Second Pinnacle, add the day of birth to the year of birth.

   Day of birth + year of birth = Second Pinnacle Number

   4 + 5 = 9

   So Whoopi has a 9 as her Second Pinnacle Number. Write this number here:

   Second Pinnacle Number _____.

4. To find the Third Pinnacle Number, add the number of the First Pinnacle to the number of the Second Pinnacle.

   First Pinnacle + Second Pinnacle = Third Pinnacle

   6 + 9 = 15 (1 + 5) = 6

   So Whoopi's Third Pinnacle Number is like her first, a 6. Write this number here:

   Third Pinnacle Number _____.

5. To find the Fourth Pinnacle, add the month of birth to the year of birth.

   Month of birth + year of birth = Fourth Pinnacle

   2 + 5 = 7

   So Whoopi's Fourth and final Pinnacle is a 7. Write this number here:

   Fourth Pinnacle Number _____.

Finding Your Own Pinnacles

We've provided space for you to figure your own Pinnacles. Take your time, following the steps carefully.

Merlin's Notes

A word about master number Pinnacles: You can have a master number Pinnacle. Dealing with these master numbers in the Pinnacle position is considered more advanced numerology. If you're confused by the master number calculations, simply reduce the numbers 11, 22, or 33 to their lower number 2, 4, and 6 respectively.

1. Reduce each number in your birth date to one digit.

   Month of Birth   Day of Birth   Year of Birth

   _____   _____   _____

2. Now, to find your First Pinnacle, simply add the month and day of your birth together, being sure to reduce the numbers to single digits—unless of course, you run across a master number (in this case, it's only possible to get an 11, 22, or a 33). For master number sums, simply write the master number in the appropriate slot.

   Month of birth + day of birth = First Pinnacle Number

   _____ + _____ = _____ = _____ (single-digit or master number)

   Write this number here:

   First Pinnacle Number _____.

   Got the idea? Now let's try the second one.

3. To find your Second Pinnacle, add your day of birth to your year of birth. Once again, remember to reduce your final sum to a single digit—unless you find a master number. If, however, you're adding a master number here, reduce it to its lowest number first (11 = 2, 22 = 4, 33 = 6) and add the *reduced* number. If you end up with a master number as the total for this Pinnacle you'll keep it and record that number (for example, 11/2, 22/4, 33/6).

   Day of birth + year of birth = Second Pinnacle Number

   _____ + _____ = _____ = _____ (single-digit or master number)

   Write this number here:

   Second Pinnacle Number _____.

4. To find your Third Pinnacle, add your First Pinnacle Number to your Second Pinnacle Number. You'll want to reduce this number to a single digit, too—except if it's a master number. If you're adding only one master number to a single number, then use the reduced master number to add to the single number. There is one exception: If you're using two master number Pinnacles, such as 11 + 11, then you won't reduce, but will instead simply add them together to get 22 as the number of the Third Pinnacle.

   First Pinnacle + Second Pinnacle = Third Pinnacle

   _____ +_____ = _____ = _____ (single-digit or master number)

   Write this number here:

   Third Pinnacle Number: _____.

5. To find your Fourth Pinnacle, add your month of birth to your year of birth. This number, too, will be reduced to a single digit. If your birthday is in November, the master number 11, reduce this number to a 2. If your year of birth adds up to 22, another master number, simply reduce this number to a 4. Both of these master numbers, then, are reduced to single digits in this position. This is the *only position* where you will reduce master numbers to a single-digit number. You can, however, end up with a master number total.

   Month of birth + year of birth = Fourth Pinnacle Number

   _____ +_____ = _____ = _____ (single-digit or master number)

   Write this number here:

   Fourth Pinnacle Number _____.

Once you know all four of your Pinnacle Numbers, the next step is to figure the length of each pinnacle. Each Pinnacle will run for a specific length of time, so you can figure how old you'll be under each of these four numbers.

Figuring the Length of the Pinnacle

Here's where your Life Path Number comes in. The First Pinnacle lasts from birth to age 36, minus your Life Path Number. Hold on—we'll show you. It's easy, actually.

Let's use our same example to practice. Whoopi Goldberg's Life Path Number is 11/2 (another master number!), but we'll use the reduced number 2 here instead of the 11 to determine how old she is when each Pinnacle Number is active. To find the length of each Pinnacle, we take her Life Path Number and subtract it from 36 (36 is the standard number used to figure the length of the First Pinnacle Number). The number 36 is not about your age, it is a number determined in the original ancient tradition of numerology to be used to calculate the length of the first Pinnacle.

   36 − 2 (Whoopi's Life Path Number) = 34 (Whoopi's First Pinnacle Length)

Therefore, for Whoopi, age 34 is the end of the First Pinnacle, which means her First Pinnacle lasted from birth through age 34. We've started the following chart and filled in the first blank as 0–34. You can fill in the rest as we go along.

Pinnacles for Whoopi Goldberg

Pinnacle	Ages	Number to Add or Subtract to Find the Pinnacle Ages
First	0–34	36 – Life Path
Second	_____	Age at end of First Pinnacle + 9
Third	_____	Age at end of Second Pinnacle + 9
Fourth	_____	Age at end of Third Pinnacle, no addition or subtraction

To figure the age span for the Second Pinnacle, we add 9 (remember, the Second Pinnacle lasts one cycle of nine) to the number of Whoopi's First Pinnacle, in this case, 34. For Whoopi, we find that the Second Pinnacle is a nine-year span from age 34 through 43. Write these ages in the blank for Whoopi's Second Pinnacle.

The Third Pinnacle is like the second, in that it, too, covers a nine-year span. Therefore, we'll simply add 9 to 43. Whoopi's Third Pinnacle will take place between the ages 43 through 52, so write these ages in the blank for Whoopi's Third Pinnacle.

The last Pinnacle age span is possibly the longest one we have. The Fourth Pinnacle age span is found by looking at the last year of the previous pinnacle. For Whoopi, this is age 52. We would then say that Whoopi's Fourth Pinnacle is from ages 52 to the rest of her life. We write it as 52 with a dash showing that the Fourth Pinnacle goes from age 52 on.

Putting it all together, Whoopi Goldberg's Pinnacle chart looks like this:

Whoopi's Pinnacle Chart

Ages	Pinnacle Number
0–34	6
34–43	9
43–52	6
52–	7

Note that we have included Whoopi's Pinnacle number for each age in this chart.

Some Pinnacles of Your Own

Okay, now it's your turn. We've provided the following spaces for you to calculate your Pinnacles, as well as a chart in which to write them down.

1. The First Pinnacle lasts from birth to age 36, minus your Life Path Number. This means you'll subtract your Life Path Number from the number 36.

   36 – ____ (your Life Path Number) = ____ (end of your First Pinnacle)

2. To figure the age span for your Second Pinnacle, add 9 to the age ending your First Pinnacle.

   ____ (end of your First Pinnacle) + 9 = ____ (end of your Second Pinnacle)

   Your Second Pinnacle runs nine years from the end of your First Pinnacle.

3. Your Third Pinnacle is like your Second in that it, too, covers a nine-year span. This time, add 9 to the end of the Second Pinnacle.

   ____ (end of your Second Pinnacle) + 9 = ____ (end of your Third Pinnacle)

   Your Third Pinnacle runs nine years from the end of your Second Pinnacle.

4. Your Fourth Pinnacle age span is possibly the longest one you have. The Fourth Pinnacle age span is found by using the last year of the Third Pinnacle pinnacle.

   ____ (end of your Third Pinnacle) + ? = ____ (the span of your Fourth Pinnacle)

   Write this as the year ending your Third Pinnacle with a dash. Remember, Whoopi's last Pinnacle was written 52–.

5. Fill in your 4 Pinnacle Numbers after each age.

Now that you've figured the length of your Pinnacles, fill in the following chart.

Your Pinnacles

	Pinnacle Ages	Number to Add or Subtract to Find Your Pinnacle Ages	Your Pinnacle Number
First	_____	36 – Life Path	_____
Second	_____	Age at end of First Pinnacle + 9	_____
Third	_____	Age at end of Second Pinnacle + 9	_____
Fourth	_____	Age at end of Third Pinnacle, no addition or subtraction	_____

Of course you'll probably want to turn to the chapter that interprets the meaning of each Pinnacle Number. But hold on, the picture isn't complete until we've the figured the Challenges Whoopi (and you!) will face in each of these Pinnacles. We discuss Challenges and how to figure them next.

Merlin's Notes

Let's do a quick review of some Pinnacle facts:

➤ The First and Fourth Pinnacles are the longest, spanning more than nine years each.

➤ The Second and Third Pinnacles are just nine years each.

➤ The age and length of the First Pinnacle are determined by your Life Path Number subtracted from the number 36.

Go slowly, double check your addition, and you'll do just fine!

The Challenge Number

Another predictive tool in the numerology chart is the *Challenge Number*. The job of becoming whole in this lifetime means we have to face and conquer our weaknesses, and there are four challenges we must meet in our lifetime.

Merlin's Notes

Knowing your Challenge Number and understanding its meaning can make all the difference in your life. Instead of beating your head against the wall repeatedly, or to continuing to bring grief into your life, if you know and face your Challenge Number, you'll find life flowing in a natural rhythm, rather than in jerking fits and failures. This is your opportunity to understand the major lessons you've come here to learn, and by so doing, you'll uncover the unique plan for your life, set in motion by your birth date—your own cosmic code for living this life well.

Challenge Numbers are not meant to be *overcome,* but rather indicate what you must *become.* As in most challenging circumstances, we all would rather avoid the situation or resist what's presented to us in this challenge. However, resisting won't help, because this number demands that you pay attention and learn the lesson—even if you don't want to.

Your four Challenge Numbers go right along with your Pinnacle Numbers, and cover the same years you calculated for your Pinnacles as well.

By the Numbers

The four **Challenge Numbers** in your chart outline for you what it is that you must face in order to reach the highest peak of your Pinnacle. You might think of your Challenge Numbers as doors you must go through in order to advance up the spiral staircase of your personal development.

Calculating Your Challenge Number

The Challenge Numbers are found in your date of birth, and we use the month, day, and year of your birth. The difference here is, where the Pinnacles are found by adding up the numbers in your date of birth, the Challenges are found by subtracting them.

Here's how you do it.

Numerology Rule #14

Here are the four formulas for finding your Challenge Numbers:

First Challenge Number = day of birth – month of birth

Second Challenge Number = year of birth – day of birth

Third Challenge Number = Second Challenge Number – First Challenge Number

Fourth Challenge Number = year of birth – month of birth

A Walk Through a Sample Challenge

As with the Pinnacles, to find the Challenge Numbers, we'll reduce all of the numbers first, then subtract.

Let's stay with our same example: Whoopi Goldberg's birth date of November 13, 1949.

1. First we reduce all of the double-digit numbers:

11	13	1949
2	4	5 (2 + 3)

2. To find the First Challenge Number, subtract the month of birth from the day of birth.

Month of birth – day of birth = First Challenge Number

2 – 4 = 2

Whoopi's First Challenge is a 2, getting along with others. Write this number here:

First Challenge Number: _____.

Note that when you are subtracting these numbers, it's okay to subtract a larger number from a smaller one. Remember, there are no negative numbers in numerology.

3. The Second Challenge Number is found by subtracting the day of birth from the year of birth. Again, it doesn't matter which number is bigger, because we'll simply convert a negative number to a positive one.

Day of birth – year of birth = Second Challenge Number

4 – 5 = 1

This means that Whoopi's Second Challenge is a 1, to learn to stand on her own and be independent. Write this number here:

Second Challenge Number: _____.

4. To find the Third Challenge Number, subtract the First Challenge Number from the Second Challenge Number.

Second Challenge – First Challenge = Third Challenge Number

1 – 2 = 1

Remember, there are *no negative numbers* in numerology! You can subtract a big number from a smaller one.

Whoopi's Third Challenge is also a 1. Write this number here:

Third Challenge Number _____.

5. The Fourth Challenge Number is found by subtracting the month of birth from the year of birth.

Month of birth – year of birth = Fourth Challenge Number

2 – 5 = 3

So Whoopi's Fourth Challenge is a 3. This Challenge Number is all about seeing what's truly in her heart, and finding the words to say what she truly feel. Write this number here:

Fourth Challenge Number: _____.

Sixes and Sevens

It's not uncommon to have two Challenge Numbers the same—it just means it takes some of us longer than others to learn the lesson.

Now that you've figured all of Whoopi's Challenge Numbers, fill in the following chart.

Whoopi Goldberg's Challenge Chart

Age	Pinnacle Number	Challenge Number
0–34	6	_____
34–43	9	_____
43–52	6	_____
52–	7	_____

It's interesting to note that Whoopi will have two Challenges of the number 1, but they'll be experienced under two different Pinnacle Numbers. Both 1 Challenges mean she'll have to learn to be independent, self-reliant, and, in the later Pinnacle, to become a leader as well.

> **Numerology Rule #15**
>
> When subtracting the Challenge Number, it doesn't matter if the result is a negative number. In numerology, we ignore negatives and convert them to positives.
>
> Example: If your First Challenge Number is 3 and your Second Challenge Number is 8, you'll subtract the 8 from the 3 or the 3 from the 8, it doesn't matter which is bigger. There is no negative number.

Some Challenges of Your Own

Now, we're going to give you the opportunity to figure out your own Challenge Numbers. Don't worry—we'll take it one step at a time, just as we did with your Pinnacles.

1. Reduce each number in your birth date to one digit.

   Month of Birth　　　　　Day of Birth　　　　　Year of Birth

   _____　　　_____　　　_____

2. Now, to find your First Challenge Number, subtract your month of birth from your day of birth.

   Month of birth – day of birth = First Challenge Number

   _____ + _____ = _____ = _____ (single-digit or master number)

   Write this number here:

   First Challenge Number: _____.

3. The Second Challenge Number is found by subtracting your day of birth from your year of birth. Remember to convert any negative numbers to a positive.

   Day of birth – Year of birth = Second Challenge Number

   _____ – _____ = _____ = _____ (single-digit or Master Number)

   Write this number here:

Second Challenge Number: _____.

4. To find the Third Challenge Number, we subtract the First Challenge Number from the Second Challenge Number.

   Second Challenge Number – First Challenge Number = Third Challenge Number

   _____ – _____ = _____ = _____ (single-digit or Master Number)

   Write this number here:

   Third Challenge Number: _____.

5. Your Fourth Challenge Number is found by subtracting your month of birth from your year of birth.

   Month of birth – Year of birth = Fourth Challenge Number

   _____ – _____ = _____ = _____ (single-digit or Master Number)

   Write this number here:

   Fourth Challenge Number _____..

Now that you've found all your Challenge Numbers, you're ready to complete the following chart. Remember, you've already found the ages and Pinnacles earlier in this chapter. You'll want to fill those in along with each of your four Challenge Numbers.

Your Challenge Chart

Challenge	Age	Pinnacle Number	Challenge Number
First	0– ___	_____	_____
Second	_____	_____	_____
Third	_____	_____	_____
Fourth	_____	_____	_____

The Cipher: The Zero

Note that it is possible to have a 0 Challenge Number. Some numerologists believe that this indicates the person is an *old soul*. We would say that if one of your 5 core numbers is a master number and you have a 0 challenge as well, then it is indeed an indication that you're an old soul.

A 0 Challenge Number would indicate that the person will bring spiritual knowledge and universal law to assist him- or herself in working out of this 0 challenge. A 0 Challenge Number also means that you can have all of the challenges and none of the challenges. That is to say, you can have all of the Challenges of the numbers 1 through 9 and have to work through each and every aspect of these numbers' negative and positive qualities, or it can mean that you have none of these Challenges. In other words, it's your choice—you can live challenge free.

By the Numbers

Old souls are souls who have returned through many lifetimes. They're thought to be wizened in the ways of spiritual matters.

The main thing to keep in mind is, as always, you have free will—and it's up to you what you make of this Challenge Number: You can make things a challenge or not. This is a very heavy responsibility and obligation for a soul and not to be taken lightly.

With a 0 Challenge, it'll seem as though somebody threw away the guidebook, so you'll have to make it up on your own. Should I let money be my challenge? Power? Relationship? Integrity? Love? If you have 0 in any one of the Challenge positions, the choice is yours—you have it in you to live life free from complexities and struggles that challenge others. You've already mastered all of this stuff in the last life, now all you have to do is remember what you learned!

Putting It All Together

Pinnacles and Challenges in hand, it's time to learn what it all means. The next chapter is the place for that, so gather your numbers and turn the page.

The Least You Need to Know

➤ Predictive numerology looks to the future, using your Pinnacles and Challenges.

➤ Your Pinnacle Numbers reveal your potential for achievement through four different phases of your life.

➤ Your Challenge Numbers pinpoint your potential difficulties and problems along the path of your life.

➤ You have 4 Pinnacle Numbers and 4 Challenge Numbers.

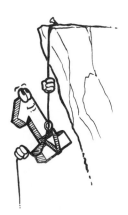

Chapter 23

Climb Every Pinnacle, Ford Every Challenge

In This Chapter

➤ The meaning of Pinnacle and Challenges 1 through 9

➤ Your Pinnacles—from independence to universality

➤ Your Challenge—from standing up for yourself to sharing with everyone

➤ Some 0 Challenge lessons

Your Pinnacle Numbers represent the goals, attainments, and lessons possible in a given period of time at a specific age. Challenge Numbers represent your specific, weak spots in attaining your Pinnacles. Knowing what's happening (or going to happen) in your life can make the difference between smooth sailing or canoeing without a paddle!

Either way, be sure to have your Pinnacle and Challenge Numbers from the previous chapter in hand as you navigate these waters.

The Meanings of Pinnacle and Challenge Numbers

Now that you've got your own Pinnacle and Challenge Numbers in hand, it's time to take a look at what they mean for your life. Note that we've grouped each number's Pinnacle and Challenge together, so if you're looking for the number 6 Challenge, you'll find it right after the number 6 Pinnacle.

Number 1 Pinnacle

A number 1 Pinnacle means that during this time in your life, you're striving to attain independence, self-reliance, and individuality. This is the main goal during this phase of your life, so all circumstances and people who cross your path in a significant way are teachers, who will help you move toward being independent.

If the 1 is the third or fourth Pinnacle, you're being groomed for leadership. Your greatest attainment will be to lead and understand all that it means to be thought of as a leader: integrity, vision, courage, drive, and determination.

Number 1 Challenge

When 1 is your Challenge, you're learning to stand up for yourself, be true to your own beliefs and ideas, be self-reliant, and, finally, find the courage to lead. You'll have test after test to see if you've finally learned to stand firm and not compromise yourself.

When the 1 is the First Challenge, you're learning to recognize that you have a self, while in the other Challenge positions, it means that you're learning to remain true to this self and have self-confidence.

Sixes and Sevens

There are extremely sensitive forces at work in the 2 Pinnacle. If you fail to identify and work with the complexities of relationships and partnerships, you will experience a good deal of pain as well as a devaluing your own self-esteem in the process. The 2 Pinnacle causes a person to turn to spiritual principles and to learn to trust his or her own instincts. It's a time to achieve harmonious relations within and without.

Number 2 Pinnacle

If 2 is your Pinnacle Number, your greatest attainment will be to learn how to have harmonious relationships without sacrificing yourself. This is the number of unions, partnerships, patience, and keeping things fair. It's not a period of independence—the focus is on working as a team. You may be learning to cooperate, share, and be considerate of others.

Because the 2 has a natural talent for relating facts, gathering and perfecting details, and knowing what's correct and right, the 2 Pinnacle may well be a time where you will find attainment in fields of work where precision and detail are valued. With these same talents, you'll have an abundance of opportunities to use these attributes in perfecting the art of relating.

Number 2 Challenge

The number 2 Challenge is one of the most common ones, for it emphasizes sensitivity to all human relations. In its negative form, the 2 Challenge can be about fear, timidity, or lack of self-confidence, and, needless to say, it can be very painful. There might be a struggle with subordination or undue attention paid to what others think. The value of this Challenge is that you become sensitive to the feelings and nuances of others—their needs—but do not suppress your own needs at the same time.

Another aspect of the 2 Challenge is that it requires a constant vigilance to stay balanced, for, remember, the 2 is the symbol for duality. This Challenge says you're trying to juggle two seemingly opposing forces. Eventually, you'll learn where the balance point is, and then it's up to you to maintain that evenness. What you must become is balanced and sensitive, and learn to live in harmony—both with yourself and with others.

Number 3 Pinnacle

Here's a Pinnacle that opens the door for personal expression—more than any other Pinnacle. This period of life deals with the emotions, the imagination, and the creative spirit. In early life, this Pinnacle is about pursuing a creative career, and in later life, a 3 Pinnacle is about friends, joy, the pleasures of life, and creative expression. In the middle Pinnacles, this is a time to deal with your emotions and to learn to say what's in your heart.

The 3 Pinnacle has a natural attraction for money and the easy life. It's also a highly creative period, when you're meant to encourage and inspire others. You'll learn that your energy can be easily scattered with this vibration, so discipline will become an issue under this number.

Easy as 1-2-3

Overall, the energy of the number 3 Pinnacle is of joy and happiness. It positively invites you to live with a positive, optimistic outlook on life.

Number 3 Challenge

When 3 is your Challenge Number, you're learning to identify your feelings and to speak from the heart. You may be critical with your words—especially critical of yourself—and this is one of the things the 3 teaches: Your words have a profound impact on your life. Instead of addressing the truth of what's in your heart, you may tend to use humor (or criticism) to cover your feelings. This is because when the 3 is in the Challenge position, it's the negative uses of the 3 that must be overcome: superficiality, exaggeration, gossip, scattered energy, self-centeredness, moodiness, and talking just to hear yourself talk.

What you're invited to achieve under the 3 Challenge is to use your creative energy to create a loving, encouraging, positive, and joyful spirit. It's particularly sad to waste the 3 energy, because it's what we all long for: pure, unadulterated happiness.

Number 4 Pinnacle

The 4 Pinnacle is the time for building your life with solid, stable foundations that will last. Usually this means it's a time of building a home, career, and family. Endurance, hard work, and patience are all part of what you're learning in this Pinnacle, and planning, organizing, setting up systems, orderliness, and moving ahead methodically are all part of this 4 energy as well. It's a time of practical application, of putting ideas into form, and of crafting a place for yourself in the material world. It's also a demanding time, requiring discipline, recognition of limitations, and a serious attitude. It's definitely not a time of leisure.

Easy as 1–2–3

The 4 Pinnacle is an especially important learning period if you have prominent 5s and 1s in your chart, because you're learning to ground your energy, build something of lasting value, and stick with it. Money, timelines, and things that limit you are your teachers under this Pinnacle.

The 4 Pinnacle teaches that it's the effort one makes that counts. You'll find reward, lasting throughout your life, for the effort that's made during this period. When children have this as their First Pinnacle, they tend to be serious and are often influenced by their parents' financial limitations.

Number 4 Challenge

When the 4 is your Challenge Number, you're learning the value of discipline, organization, thrift, practicality, and hard work. This is a difficult challenge, and restriction and limitations are usually present in this period. The Challenge is to learn how to work within these boundaries. It's a time for learning to curb impatience, stubbornness, narrow-mindedness, and self-righteousness.

Number 5 Pinnacle

If you have a 5 Pinnacle, get ready for change and uncertainty. Ultimately, this period is about loosening up restricted patterns of the past to bring you freedom and liberation. However, because it's a time of the unexpected, and change is not everybody's favorite, it can be an unsettling time. This can be a period of restlessness, activity, public life; but it also favors sales and promotion.

Change is the constant in this pinnacle. Attitudes, career directions, and business decisions that are forward thinking and progressive do well under this 5 energy. This isn't a domestic or homey sort of Pinnacle, because you'll find yourself being drawn into the public world. You'll be learning to avoid impulsive, hasty decisions, especially the urge to pack it in and run. The main lesson here, and the major attainment, is to learn to be adaptable and flexible, and to trust that everything always works out in the end. And it does—as you'll learn under this Pinnacle.

Sixes and Sevens

During a number 5 Challenge, there may be a tendency to quit something before it's completed, to choose love affairs that don't last (usually because they were based on sex, not love), and to overindulge in food, drugs, drinking, gambling, or sex. Don't forget—this is the number of the one-night stand!

Number 5 Challenge

During a 5 Challenge, you'll discover that the love of changing rules can bring impatience and restlessness and a desire for freedom in some way. If you've been stuck in a rut (usually the 4 energy), it's a great time to loosen up.

Change and all that it brings may cause fear, holding back, or confusion. But taking a risk and being flexible are encouraged under this Challenge Number. You're learning to free yourself from limiting behaviors that are restricting your creative energy. Change, baby, that's the name of game with this one—but it's change for the better that is the true Challenge.

Number 6 Pinnacle

When you have a 6 Pinnacle in any of the four positions, it's a time for love, duty, and responsibility to family. These are the years of responsibility, when you're to care for others, and the usual dominant choices for this period are teaching, counseling, and marriage. Your lesson is to learn to think of the needs of others and to work with balancing your life. If you do all the giving, are responsible for everyone else, and do all the work, you'll learn the difficult lesson of having to love not only others but yourself as well. You'll learn to give to and care for yourself. This number demands that balance be restored at home and within the family.

This is very much the Pinnacle of home, children, and beautifying your surroundings. The 6 also carries with it the energy of community and humanitarian service, so in your 6 Pinnacle, you may find that your work centers on giving to the community, children, and animals. There is money to be made and happiness to be had when you focus your energy on some kind of service, although some of your money may need to be spent on family or loved ones under this Pinnacle. Under a First 6 Pinnacle, young people will tend to marry too early and feel a tremendous responsibility to the family.

This is the love and marriage Pinnacle, the Pinnacle of babies and home. It can also be a period of divorce when commitment and responsibility to the marriage can no longer be sustained. You're ultimately learning about responsibility—when it's required and when enough is enough. This is a time for honoring what's in your heart—because it's there that you must be truly responsible.

Number 6 Challenge

When 6 is your Challenge, the lessons are about responsibility for others or feeling burdened by family obligations. You're learning to serve others and to find the balance between honoring your commitments to family and honoring those you make to yourself. You can't avoid giving and caring for others with this Challenge, however.

Merlin's Notes

If you have a number 6 Challenge and idealize beyond reasonable limits, you'll find unhappiness and the loss of family and marriage. In fact, there's a tendency with this Challenge to be too stubborn and set in your opinions—especially on parenting issues. The lesson you're learning is to move the energy from the negative qualities of the 6 to the positive: to create warmth, beauty, nurturing, and love in your environment and home.

The number 6 Challenge is also about codependency and giving for the wrong reasons. Under this Challenge Number, you'll learn when you're taking care of others in an unhealthy way. But no matter what, this Challenge is a domestic one. Because 6 idealizes things, you may be challenged to discover when loyalty, obedience, the desire to be the head of household, and even love, have gone too far.

Number 7 Pinnacle

With a 7 Pinnacle, you're in a time of study, research, introspection, or soul development. Under this Pinnacle, education, scientific interests, study, and specialization are not only favored but strongly recommended. There's a quality of the individualist, separatist, and the loner present under this number, and it's a time to be reclusive, and focus on the inner landscape.

Country living is excellent during this period—or anywhere you'll have time to learn to be alone, learn about yourself, do research for areas of specialization, learn about mystical thinking, and understand the principles of right living. This Pinnacle brings much wisdom, and people come to you for your wisdom, because you develop a talent for explaining the unexplainable. In addition, specialization in a field brings good money.

Sixes and Sevens

During a 7 Pinnacle you most likely will feel the urge to withdraw, be left alone, and have privacy, so it can be a difficult time for marriage because of your high need to be alone, think, and contemplate. Unless, of course, your sweetie has 7 in a prominent place in his or her chart!

As a First Pinnacle, the 7 can be difficult, because it usually means you feel alone or isolated. Unusual circumstances bring you to a deeper understanding of life's mysteries, and you may have talent or special ability in technical or scientific fields. (The stereotype of computer nerds comes to mind with this Pinnacle.) In addition, you'll be very selective about friends.

As a Second and Third Pinnacle, this 7 offers a chance to refine or specialize your skills—to move deeper in your chosen direction while, at the same time exploring the meaning of life on the inner planes. As a last Pinnacle, the 7 brings spiritual development. This is a quiet, reserved time of inner analysis and gaining of knowledge, which eventually you teach to others.

Number 7 Challenge

The 7 Challenge, like the 4 Challenge, is one of the most serious times in your life. Feelings of aloneness and isolation must be overcome by turning the energy inward to the rich, vast interior world of meditation, soul development, spiritual awakening, and the contemplation of the meaning of life. The lesson you're learning is to recognize that your inner self is searching for experiences that will allow you to grow.

Often there can be a big test or serious repression under this Challenge Number. Holding yourself in reserve, hiding feelings, or acting in secrecy only further isolates and separates you. There can be some kind of a secret, or something that happened within the family life, which is kept hidden or considered an embarrassment.

The Challenge is to learn to discern reality from false notions. By being more real yourself, connecting to others, and learning to listen within for inner guidance, you'll cultivate those keen powers of analysis and observation that are particular to the number 7. The 7 Challenge promotes inner awareness through enhancing your intuitive skills, examining philosophical and metaphysical material, and learning the universal laws of nature.

Sixes and Sevens

Withdrawing, whether through drugs, alcohol, or by spending your life on the Internet, will not allow you to meet the Challenge of the 7. You are to become safe in being alone, to find meaning in your analysis of the mysteries of life, and to understand that all things in life are connected and in relationship.

Number 8 Pinnacle

This is the Pinnacle where you learn to deal with the business world and authority of any kind, and to find your own sense of personal power. It's the Pinnacle of authenticity and mastery, and you learn about money, power, and authority. Organization, responsibility, leadership, management of financial affairs, and efficiency are the essential elements of this number 8.

Under an 8 Pinnacle, your judgment is tested repeatedly, and the activities of this period of life bring you the opportunity to manage property and business and to advance your career. Achievement and recognition for your efforts are significant under this number.

Home life may be of less importance under this Pinnacle, because career and success are usually your top priorities. This is not an easy Pinnacle—it requires a constant shoulder to the wheel, and you're required to demonstrate strength and courage, with no time for weakness.

Often, there's a big expense to pay under this Pinnacle, but careful management of financial affairs, coupled with hard work, should bring reward—both monetarily and in satisfaction of a job well done. This is not a time to trust luck or to be misguided in placing your trust. The lesson you're learning under the 8 Pinnacle is to become your own authority, and to understand your true power and how best to use it for the good of all.

Number 8 Challenge

When the 8 is in the Challenge position, you're clearly being called to step up to the plate and achieve. You'll be challenged on material issues, either to have more or to get some—money is what we're talking about. Striving for material gain alone will not reap the rewards you're hoping for. Instead, the 8 Challenge Number says that you're learning to look beyond the dollars to the true meaning of life. Integrity, right living, and moral motives are some of the qualities you're called to incorporate in your manner of doing business in the world.

This is not an easy Challenge. Any attempts to misuse your power, to falsely claim authority, or to abdicate your power will only delay success and advancement. When the 8 shows up in the Challenge position, it often signals that this individual needs to stop giving away his or her power. It's a period of development where you're meant to take back your power and to learn to empower others, rather than defer to authority or dominate others.

Number 9 Pinnacle

When you have a 9 Pinnacle, you'll be expected to show a great deal of tolerance, compassion, and love, and you're meant to inspire and uplift others with your wisdom and deep loving nature. The 9 Pinnacle is known for emotional crises, partly because you'll have to end and release any matters in your life that have no further energy for you—no matter how scared you are. This Pinnacle is the time for maturation—and working through your emotions seems to be a part of this growth process.

This is not considered an easy Pinnacle, partly because of the inherent endings, but also because it's not easy to have to be loving and tolerant all the time. However, tolerance and compassion will have to be learned or this Pinnacle becomes one of great disappointment. You're meant to develop a philosophical attitude—grounded in global consciousness, universal principle, intuitive knowing, and a great love for your fellow human.

Merlin's Notes

With the 9 Pinnacle there are many rewards, even the potential for money and fortune; but the lesson you're learning is to yield and surrender to the universal order of all things, and in so doing you begin to receive rewards beyond your most imagined expectations. In short, you're learning that you'll have to give and expect nothing in return in order to receive, and that includes the love you so dearly desire.

The 9 is not a personal number, and this is a period when you'll be called to think big—beyond your own comfortable little world. You're in a period of understanding and working with the human condition, and the following areas are where you might find your best success: the arts, drama, writing, higher education, healing work, spiritual pursuits, philanthropic projects, international travel and business, and anything that advances global awareness and giving.

As a First Pinnacle, this may be a time of early losses that bring early maturity. In the middle Pinnacles, it's a time of integration and giving back to the world. As a last Pinnacle, the 9 brings completion and material and spiritual wealth. But on all of the Pinnacle positions, the number 9 requires that you forget the self and grow into a true humanist.

Number 9 Challenge

There is no 9 challenge possible using the simple numerology system we've described in this book. Instead, you'll find the 0 Challenge Number, which we'll discuss next.

The 0 Challenge

This number is also called the *Cipher Challenge;* it stands for all or nothing. As a symbol for the circle, the 0 Challenge contains all things: It can be full and empty at the same time. With this number, you have full free will—you have the right of choice—to drift in life or to rise above the problems of life to achieve greatness. You have the choice to create your own world as one filled with love, compassion, integrity, responsibility, and vision.

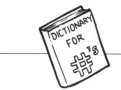

By the Numbers

The **Cipher Challenge** is another name for a zero (0) Challenge Number. It contains all or none of the other Challenges, depending on how you look at it—and how you live it!

When a period of your life is governed by the 0 Challenge, it should not be taken lightly, for some kind of selection must be made, and it should be done with clear consideration for your Destiny Number and for the higher laws of universal order. Your test and Challenge, like the number 9, is to nurture a desire to make the world a better place. There's a great deal of responsibility with the 0 Challenge Number.

Easy as 1-2-3

There's nothing holding you back with a 0 Challenge Number, except yourself. It's up to you—the possibilities are limitless. Meditation, prayer, and positive visualization will assist you in creating your ideal world.

Metaphysics teaches that the soul migrates from past life to present life, and it's thought that a person who has a 0 Challenge is an old soul, especially if this same person is carrying a master number as his or her Soul Number. As an old soul, this person is thought to have lived many lifetimes and is open to utilizing soul knowledge in this lifetime. Under this 0 Challenge, a person is expected to make choices that honor this higher awareness and that foster spiritual growth on the material plane. There's a much greater chance for profound growth with this Challenge Number. The various tests and lessons encountered in this life are meant to advance your understanding of the meaning of life.

Number 11/2 Pinnacle

This master number Pinnacle may also be reduced to its lower vibration, the 2, and for many, this Pinnacle will be experienced and lived as a 2. It's only when you're working at the level of the 11 (which emphasizes the metaphysical, spiritual, and philosophical, rather than the material) that you'll be addressing the unique qualities of this number.

Easy as 1-2-3

With an 11/2 Pinnacle, there's a great possibility you'll become famous or be thrust into the spotlight. Sudden changes often occur under this vibration as well, and marriage is possible now—as long as you aren't so famous that you have no need for a partner. Work that's favored under this number includes art, psychology, poetry, public speaking, media work like film and television, or work that entails visionary, futuristic focus.

As an 11 Pinnacle, this is a challenging time because you will be at the high point of your intuition and sensitivity. Because this is a time of extraordinary sensitivity, you'll have to take measures to ensure balance under this volatile number. There's a wide-open channel with the number 11, and it stretches between your personal consciousness and the realms of higher consciousness. This means that there will be intense revelations, enormous personal and spiritual growth, and a compelling sense of being different, and you'll develop an uncanny ability to see into the soul of things. In fact, in an 11/2 Pinnacle you have a message to deliver to people, and you'll have the desire to inspire, uplift, and share your revelations with those in your sphere.

If the 11 is too intense a vibration for you, then you'll revert to the energy of the 2 and the issues that will dominate this pinnacle are those of the 2. But either way, sensitivity is one of your major tests, and a radical change in consciousness is at hand.

Number 11/2 Challenge

The Challenge of the 11/2 is to honor the demands of both the 11 and the 2. A constant vigilance is required to stay in balance physically and emotionally. Under this Challenge, a person is called to step up to the leadership role of the 11 using spiritual principles, and in some way this presents a challenge. At the same time, the 11/2 Challenge presents all of the challenges of the 2: lessons of partnership and relationship.

Number 22/4 Pinnacle

The 22/4 Pinnacle is fairly rare and can occur only after having two preceding pinnacles of 11/2. Because of these preceding Pinnacles, you'll most likely have undergone a radical change in consciousness and may have even experienced some kind of handicap or health issue. But now, with a 22/4 Pinnacle, you're given the chance to do something truly great that will affect the masses on a national and even international scale.

This is a time of building something of lasting value that will benefit humankind. Your keen organizational and managerial skills will be fully utilized under this number. All that you've done in your life prior to this 22/4 period will be realized as experiences you've accumulated, so that now you can execute these masterful plans. This is a highly productive time; it's also a testing time, but you have the necessary endurance and vision to see yourself through any challenging periods.

Because the 22 is also the vibration of two 2s, you'll want to take time to live fully balanced in your personal life, because, like the 11/2, you're subject to extreme sensitivities. One of your tests will involve learning to limit your workaholic capacity and to find the balance between your visions for making the world a better place and your need to manage boundaries for your own health. People look to you as an example under this master number vibration.

Number 22/4 Challenge

At this time, numerologists do not recognize the 22/4 as a Challenge Number. Instead, the 22 is reduced to the 4 and read as a 4 Challenge.

Number 33/6 Challenge

While numerologists do not recognize this number in the Challenge position, we would offer to those of you who might find this number as a Challenge that the 33/6 is the vibration of healing oneself and others using spiritual principles. It is through teaching love and understanding the responsibility of love that you will move through any challenge this number brings.

Pinnacles and Challenges Worksheet

We thought you'd like to see the Pinnacles and Challenges worksheet a professional numerologist like Kay uses. If you'd like, you can use this form to calculate your own Pinnacles and Challenges instead of the step-by-step instructions within the chapter. For some, having a graphic picture of how the Pinnacles and Challenges are figured is easier.

The last part of the predictive numerology triad is the major cycles. We'll be devoting the entire next chapter to them.

PINNACLES & CHALLENGES WORKSPACE

_____ 1st + 2nd Pinnacle
3rd Pinnacle

_____ Month + Year*
4th Pinnacle

_____ Month + Day
1st Pinnacle

_____ Day + Year*
2nd Pinnacle

START HERE ➤

ADD

Date of Birth _____ + _____ + _____ = _____ **Life Path**
        Month   Day   Year*

SUBTRACT

_____ Month – Day
1st Challenge

_____ Day – Year*
2nd Challenge

_____ 1st – 2nd Challenge
3rd Challenge

_____ Month – Year*
4th Challenge

NOTE: when calculating PINNACLES & CHALLENGES reduce all master numbers

Age of Pinnacles and Challenges

To find Age of 1st Pinnacle: use 36 - Life Path Number = Age at end of 1st Pinnacle _____

To find Age of 2nd Pinnacle: use Age at end of 1st Pinnacle + 9 = Age at end of 2nd Pinnacle _____

To find Age of 3rd Pinnacle: use Age at end of 2nd Pinnacle + 9 = Age at end of 3rd Pinnacle _____

To find Age of 4th Pinnacle : use Age at end of 3rd Pinnacle for rest of life _____

Personal Year and Months

Personal Year for _____ (current year* of calculation) = __ total = __ (reduce it)

Add _____ + _____ + _____ = __ total = __ (reduce it) **Personal Year**
      Birth Month   Day   Calendar Year*

Personal Months:

Add the Personal Year number to the number of each month.

Jan (1) ___ Feb (2) ___ Mar (3) ___ Apr (4) ___ May (5) ___ Jun (6) ___

Jul (7) ___ Aug (8) ___ Sep (9) ___ Oct (1) ___ Nov (2) ___ Dec (3) ___

*REMEMBER TO USE ALL YEAR NUMBERS TO CALCULATE THE YEAR NUMBER (e.g.1953, 1997, 2001)

YOUR NUMEROLOGY CHART

The Least You Need to Know

➤ Your Pinnacles show you how to achieve your destiny.

➤ Understanding your Challenges can help you stop being your own worst enemy.

➤ The 0 is called the Cipher Challenge.

➤ Pinnacle and Challenge themes are told in the numbers.

Chapter 24

Your Major Cycles: It's All in the Timing

Another aspect of predictive numerology is your Major Cycles, which, like your Pinnacles and Challenges, are found within your date of birth. From your formative beginning, through your productive mid-life, to your completion in your harvest cycle, your Major Cycles can help you understand the particular rhythms of your own life.

In this chapter, we'll be looking at three of numerology's Major Cycles, as well as the interpretation of each number as a Major Cycle. Once you learn your own rhythm, you will better understand and be able to interpret the major events and transitions of your life. The fourth Major Cycle is your Personal Year, which will be covered in the next chapter.

Major Cycles

Another predictive element in your numerology chart, the *Major Cycles,* also comes from your date of birth.

Here's how it works: We work our way through our birthday—the month, day, and year of our birth—and find three distinct cycles with approximately 28-year chunks in each. The *number* of the month of your birthday is the First Cycle, the *number* of the day you were born is the Second Cycle, and the *number* of the year you were born is the Third Cycle. It's as simple as that.

By the Numbers

Your **Major Cycles** show the major lessons you are learning at specific times in your life. They're found in the date of your birth.

The Major Cycles have great influence on our lives and our approach to life, and they also have a great deal to do with our destiny. Each cycle has its own distinct theme. The number of your cycle tells of the conditions and lessons you'll need to meet that will advance you down your path (Life Path Number), and assist you in meeting your destiny (Destiny Number).

Getting the Timing Right

Like all good stories, your story has a beginning, a middle, and an end. Your story is told in the three cycles of your birth date, and each cycle governs a distinct period of time in your life.

➤ **First Cycle:** This is your formative cycle. It governs approximately the first 28 years of your life, and its theme is found in the number of the *month* you were born.

➤ **Second Cycle:** This is your productive cycle. It governs approximately the middle years of your life, and its theme is found in the number of the *day* you were born.

➤ **Third Cycle:** This is your harvest cycle. It governs the later years of your life, and its theme is found in the reduced number of the *year* you were born.

We'll be figuring the exact ages of these three cycles in this section. But first, there are a few things you should know about the Major Cycles.

Here's where numerology and astrology work together. (You can also read more about numerology and astrology in Chapter 27, "Numbering by the Stars: Numerology and Astrology.") Your Major Cycles are in approximate conjunction with your progressed moon, which happens every 28+ years. It's at this juncture that you move from one Major Cycle to the next. However, it's not as neat and clean as every 28 years.

The rule of thumb in figuring the length of the Major Cycles is that your First Major Cycle starts at birth and lasts for approximately 28 years. The Second Major Cycle runs for approximately the next 28 years, and the Third Major Cycle lasts from the end of the Second Major Cycle for the rest of your life. Lost? The following chart may help, because the Major Cycle is calculated using your Life Path Number.

Timing of Major Cycles Chart

First Cycle Duration	Start of Second Cycle	Start of Third Cycle
0–26	27	54

Life Path Number	First Cycle Start	End of First Cycle, Start of Second Cycle	End of Second Cycle, Start of Third Cycle
1	0–26	26–27	53–54
2 and 11	0–25	25–26	52–53
3	0–33	33–34	60–61
4 and 22	0–32	32–33	59–60
5	0–31	31–32	58–59
6 and 33	0–30	30–31	57–58
7	0–29	29–30	56–57
8	0–28	28–29	55–56
9	0–27	27–28	54–55

Note: You will always begin a new major cycle in your 1 Personal Year.

The change from one cycle to the next can be almost unnoticeable and easy, or it can be very dramatic and life-changing. Big changes can occur as you move from one Major Cycle influence to another, especially if the numbers of those cycles are not harmonious, such as moving from a 3 to a 4.

Major Cycles are like grand themes in you life. You might want to think of these three major periods of your life as three books, and within each book (Major Cycle), there are distinct chapters (Pinnacles and Challenges) which show you how to get the most out of each period of your life. Each book or Major Cycle has a different number of chapters—or a different number of Pinnacles and Challenges to learn about. While the Pinnacles and Challenges have their own unique themes, the Major Cycle's theme encompasses the smaller themes of the Pinnacles and Challenges.

This is where we can see how all of these predictive numbers fit together. The Major Cycle is the major theme and major lesson for a given period of time in your life (in 28-year chunks), and the Pinnacle and Challenge Numbers, which happen during a Major Cycle, are sub-themes to the major

Easy as 1-2-3

The advantage of knowing about the three Major Cycles and their influence is that we can prepare for them in advance, make sense of what's happening presently in our lives, and finally, piece together the story of our life with its many lessons.

theme. Underneath the Pinnacle and Challenge theme is the Personal Year theme, which tells you on a year-by-year basis what the focus is. It all weaves together to guide you to an expression of your higher and best self. Read more about your Personal Year, numerology's Fourth Major Cycle, in Chapter 25.

Karmic Periods as Major Cycles

If your day of birth or year of birth (reduced number) is a karmic number, this Major Cycle is influenced by the karmic aspects of these numbers. If you have a number 13/4, 14/5, 16/7, or 19/1, then this Major Cycle is influenced by karmic patterns, and can have a strong negative impact until you become aware of the karmic influence and begin to work with this energy. (See Chapter 15, "The Karmic Numbers 10, 13, 14, 16, and 19: Lesson to Be Learned," for an in-depth discussion of karmic numbers.)

Calculating the Major Cycles

This one is easy: To find the number of your Major Cycles, look no further than the month, day, and year you were born.

The First Major Cycle is the number of the month you were born. For example, if you were born in July, your First Major Cycle Number is 7. If you were born in December, your First Major Cycle Number is 3 (1 + 2 = 3).

> **Numerology Rule #16**
>
> The First Major Cycle Number is found in the reduced number of the month you were born.

Here's a chart for quick reference in finding your *First* Major Cycle, a major growth cycle and the time of formation as you begin to form who you are.

First Major Cycle Reference Chart

Month	First Major Cycle Number
January	1
February	2
March	3
April	4
May	5
June	6
July	7
August	8

Month	First Major Cycle Number
September	9
October	1
November	2
December	3

The number of your birth month tells the theme of your first 28 years (approximately) of life.

The Second Major Cycle—the *productive* years or achievement years—is found in the number of the day you were born. If, for example, you were born on the 8th day of the month, then your Second Major Cycle Number is an 8, which tells us that this period of time in your life is all about the issues of money, power, and success. You will learn your lessons in the business arena during an 8 Major Cycle.

Numerology Rule #17

The Second Major Cycle Number is found in the day you were born. If you were born on the 17th, 23rd, or 30th of the month, for example, reduce these double-digit numbers to a single number. All double-digit numbers are reduced unless you have a master number or karmic number. If you were born on the 11th or 22nd of the month, then don't reduce these numbers. As master numbers, they have special significance. If you were born on the 13th, 14th, 16th, or 19th, you have a karmic debt cycle as your second Major Cycle.

The number of your day of birth tells of your Second Major Cycle theme.

The Third Major Cycle Number—the *harvest* years—is found in the year you were born. If you were born in 1964, you will add these numbers together to get the single reduced number of 2, which is the vibration and theme of your last Major Cycle.

Numerology Rule #18

The Third Major Cycle Number is found in the reduced number of the year you were born.

The reduced number of your year birth tells of the theme for your last Major Cycle.

Some Predictions of Your Own

It's time to calculate your own Major Cycle Numbers. The steps are as easy as 1-2-3.

1. The First Major Cycle Number is the reduced number of the month you were born. (You can look up your number in the First Major Cycle Reference Chart we gave you a few pages earlier.) Write your number here:

   Your First Major Cycle Number: _____.

2. The Second Major Cycle Number is found in the reduced number of the day you were born. Remember, if you were born on the 11th or 22nd of the month or on the 13th, 14th, 16th, or 19th of the month, then don't reduce the number, because it's a master number or a karmic number, and it has special significance. Write your number here:

   Your Second Major Cycle Number: _____.

3. The Third Major Cycle Number is found in the reduced number of the year you were born. Write your number here:

   Your Third Major Cycle Number: _____.

4. Now, look up the timing of your Major Cycles in the Timing of Major Cycles Chart we showed you earlier in this chapter. Find out when your Major Cycles begin and end and then start filling in your Major Cycles chart that follows. Transfer the numbers you found in steps 1 through 3 and you've got yourself a complete Major Cycle chart.

Your Major Cycle Chart

First Major Cycle	Second Major Cycle	Third Major Cycle
Age at the end ____	Age it begins ____	Age it begins ____
Cycle number ____	Cycle number ____	Cycle number ____

Easy as 1-2-3

Your Personal Year number dictates the end and the beginning of the new Major Cycle.

The Meanings of the Major Cycles

So what do these numbers mean? Each of the three Major Cycles coincides to a period of life: the beginning, the middle, and the end of your life. Which Major Cycle Number you have during each one can help you understand the lessons to be learned and the heights to which you may rise during that period of time. The three Major Cycle themes together point the way for you to live your life to its fullest potential.

Major Cycle Number 1: An Active Cycle

When the 1 is your First Major Cycle, you'll gain independence and build self-confidence, although you may feel lonely or different. You'll need to stand for what you believe in. If you have 1 as a Second Cycle number, however, you'll find increased confidence, leadership, or entrepreneurial enterprise, but will also learn to deal with loneliness, and proving that one person can make a difference. You'll demonstrate resilience and strength and may even start a new business.

If the 1 is your last cycle, you'll be assertive and proud. You'll discover new ways of doing things, maintain your independence, and work on issues of integrity and self-discovery.

Major Cycle Number 2: A Slow Cycle

This is a period of slow, patient development. Your natural gifts of gentle persuasion and peacemaking will be utilized often. You're learning how to cooperate with others, how to be part of the team. Under this cycle, partnerships of any kind are important, and the lessons will be around learning the skills of tact, diplomacy, and compromise, while gaining a clear understanding of how relationships work.

This is a gentle vibration and teaches gentleness, support, and harmony, and encourages you to seek out beauty and harmonious environments. Discord and disruption are not tolerated well under this number's energy. As a third cycle, the 2 means that patience and cooperation will be the hallmarks of your mature years.

Major Cycle Number 3: A Time of Self-Expression and Joyful Living

Under this period, any ability you possess in the performing arts, and especially writing, will be met with great reward. The emphasis is on creativity and the expression of that creative self. As a young adult under this cycle, you may choose to use your creative expression to entertain friends and live the party life.

In the later cycles, the emphasis encourages the delight of living and warmth of many friends. This cycle requires discipline and focus to harness the considerable creative energy pulsing through your life at this time. As a third cycle, the 3 means your later years will be both creative and rewarding, and you'll enjoy the pleasures of life.

Easy as 1-2-3

In all three Major Cycles, the 2 means cooperation and partnership.

Easy as 1-2-3

A 4 Major Cycle is a time for learning how to set boundaries and to maintain good health.

319

Major Cycle Number 4: A Time of Putting Things in Order

In all cycles, this is a time of hard work and building foundations for your life. It's the practical things of life that will dominate this period of time: work, career, family, buying a home, building a solid community. Money matters are of top priority now, as you build a sound financial plan for your life.

The 4 Major Cycle is a time of discipline, order, economy, and self-motivation, and as a third cycle, it means that your mature years will be both stable and secure.

Major Cycle Number 5: A Freeing Cycle

Rapid progress and change characterize the 5 Major Cycle, and travel, moving your residence, and changing jobs are all part of this cycle's energy. During this period, you'll be free of the burdens of responsibility seen in some of the other cycles, such as the 4 and the 6, because it's a time for promoting yourself, seeking new opportunities, and there's the prospect of visiting foreign lands, discovering other cultures, and having exciting new adventures.

Seeking change, taking risks, and facing new adventures will bring great satisfaction. You're learning the lessons of freedom, which, if managed well, will show you the excitement of life, and, if managed poorly, will teach, as Janis Joplin sang (and Kris Kristofferson wrote), "Freedom's just another word for nothin' left to lose."

Easy as 1-2-3

A 5 Major Cycle means your major lesson is to learn to change and adapt.

Easy as 1-2-3

A 6 Major Cycle is a time for learning the lesson of co-dependence, that is, to not subjugate your needs for another's.

Major Cycle Number 6: A Cycle for Marriage, Family, and Responsibility

Under this Major Cycle, the issues of commitment, marriage, family, and responsibility all dominate, so this is the best cycle for marriage, because when one is committed and can live with acceptance and respond lovingly, this is the cycle of happy heart and happy home. However, if commitment cannot be made deeply or is broken, then divorce and separation will punctuate this cycle.

This is also a time that favors starting a business—especially one that is service oriented—in the home or a family-run business. Under this cycle new opportunities for self-expression are found as well—gardening, painting, music, especially singing, decorating, or writing.

Family, or the lack of family, home, and children also play a large role in this Major Cycle. You're learning the power and problem of responsibility, and, when it's your third cycle you can expect to be surrounded by family, content with your home and garden, and active in community service. It's a perfect time for all those Cancer sun signs out there—or for anyone who's ready to become a homebody!

Major Cycle Number 7: A Cycle for Understanding

The 7 Major Cycle emphasizes study, learning, investigation, and gaining skills, and generally centers on scientific, technical, intellectual, religious, or metaphysical fields. This is the time for analysis and contemplative thinking—reflecting upon the deeper questions of life, and it's also the time of specialization. Here, intuitive skills are enhanced, the inner life becomes compelling, and wisdom is developed.

Relationships require understanding partnership during a 7 Major Cycle, because a great sum of your energy will be spent in time alone or in introspection. You're called upon to share your knowledge and wisdom with others through teaching, counseling, writing, or conversation. As a third cycle, the 7 brings spiritual development, and a quiet, reserved time of inner analysis and the gaining of knowledge—people will come to you for your wisdom.

Easy as 1-2-3

A 7 Major Cycle is a time for study, specialization, and sharing your wisdom.

Major Cycle Number 8: A Cycle of Money and Recognition

The 8 Major Cycle is an excellent time for work, career, success, and financial reward. It's the hard work and ability to overcome obstacles and setbacks that bring your true success. This is a time of competent management, good planning, and acute organization, because you develop the gift for seeing the broader picture and boldly carrying out that vision.

It's not uncommon under this cycle to gain financial freedom, and business and career dominate this cycle, because there's a compelling drive to take control of your work and bring it to new heights of achievement. You're viewed as an authority during the later stages of this cycle, and others deem you powerful. If it's your third cycle, you'll know monetary reward, with the possibility of inherited money. You won't really retire; instead, in some way, you'll utilize your skills as "the boss" to the last breath you take!

Easy as 1-2-3

An 8 Major Cycle is a time for learning about power, money, and success in the business world.

Easy as 1-2-3

A 9 Major Cycle is a time to learn the lesson of letting go and trusting in the universal order of all things.

Merlin's Notes

Under Major Cycle 9, there's an element of sacrifice, of letting go, of forgiveness, and of surrender to the mystery of life. It's here that you finally make the connection between human existence and the spiritual energy of all that is. Intuition is enhanced and much personal and spiritual enrichment is found. It's a rewarding cycle for those who live selflessly and altruistically. You're learning the lessons of giving and loving in this cycle, as well as the lesson of completion. This can be an emotional time until you understand that all things are a part of the great cosmic plan, and that when something ends, it makes room for something new to move in. You will learn to let go.

Easy as 1–2–3

In an 11/2 Major Cycle, you may have to relearn the lessons of the 2: partnership and cooperation.

As an 11, if you accept the path of the "spiritual messenger," you will find great reward, including financial support, even fame. If the energy of the 11 is too intense or too demanding, then you will revert to the energy of the 2 (1 + 1 = 2), where the issues of sensitivity, cooperation, and relationship will dominate your days. Either way, this is a period in your life where you will have to learn to find harmony within yourself while you learn to lead.

Major Cycle Number 9: A Cycle of Selfless Service and Reward

Under this cycle, you develop compassion and tolerance, a broad view of humanity, and a sincere concern for the welfare of your fellow human. Obviously, it means you'll have to bring the lessons of all the other numbers to bear upon this humanitarian cycle.

You grow toward your ideals of perfection, an expanded view of love, and selfless service. Your work is directed toward the improvement of the world, the planet, the unfortunate, and the healing of others. Creative talent is enhanced under this cycle, especially if your efforts encompass a larger social purpose or message.

Major Cycle Number 11/2: A Cycle of Illumination

If you have this master number as one of your Major Cycles, it means you were born either in November or on the 11th of the month. The 11 is a cycle of growth and understanding of higher human ideals, and it's a time of inspiration, self-improvement, and hard-won revelations about how life truly works.

322

But it's only through a deep personal transformation and improvement of self-expression that you'll be able to bring forth these revelations, because you were born to illuminate others and share with your community. The more willing you are to work on yourself, the more good you will do the larger world. This cycle requires courage, determination, and strength to delve deeply into a higher consciousness of universal principle and spiritual interconnectedness.

Major Cycle Number 22/4: A Cycle of Enormous Potential

A cycle with this master number can occur only if you were born on the 22nd of the month or in a year which reduces to 22/4. The 22/4 Major Cycle is a time of tremendous potential for establishing lasting institutions, monuments, and/or teachings that will benefit others.

During this time, your level of mastery as a builder, organizer, and visionary is at its peak; you're filling a great human need. It's an all-consuming role that you must play, requiring great sums of energy and focus. In return, you're rewarded with the satisfaction of knowing you've made a lasting contribution to the betterment of the earth and humanity, and have left a legacy for generations to come.

Easy as 1-2-3

The 22/4 Major Cycle is learning the lessons of integrity, balance, and responsibility to a larger purpose.

Easy as 1-2-3

Generally, the 22/4 Major Cycle is rewarding financially and spiritually, for you will be called to build things for your society that reflect your understanding of spiritual principles and the material world. It's the weaving of these two together that is your true mastery.

Major Cycle Number 33/6: A Cycle of Healing Love

The number 33/6 can only occur if you were born in a year which reduces to a 33, and we have not seen this number in the 20th century. The first time this number will occur is over 100 years away—in the years 2103, 2112, 2121, and 2130. What does this tell us? Perhaps that we have a ways to go before we are ready to have a 25 + year cycle on the personal level where love is the dominant theme.

As we enter the new millennium and the vibration of the 2 (as in 2000), we will begin to work and live in partnership and harmony. This is the groundwork that will have to be done to prepare the way for a 33/6 cycle.

The Least You Need to Know

➤ Your Major Cycles show you the timing for your life.

➤ Your First Major Cycle is the formative cycle.

➤ Your Second Major Cycle is the productive cycle.

➤ Your Third Major Cycle is the harvest cycle.

Chapter 25

Your Personal Year: For Every Time There Is a Season

In This Chapter

➤ Every year has a theme and lesson

➤ You can have a Personal Year from 1 to 9

➤ Finding your Personal Year Number

➤ The nine-year cycle and you

➤ Finding your age vibration

Now that you've learned how to find your core numbers, Pinnacles, Challenges, and Major Cycles, it's time to take a look at the Personal Year and how you move through the cycles of your life. Each of the nine numbers represents a year in a nine-year cycle, and each year carries its own unique identity and demands.

In addition, each month and even each day have their own special numerological vibration as well. We'll be adding those in the next chapter. But first, let's take a look at your Personal Years.

What Is Your Personal Year?

Your *Personal Year Number* is a number that tells you what's happening for you, personally, this year. Every year has a number and carries with it an energy that vibrates to that number. If you know how to read this energy—that is, if you know the number of your year—then you can direct your affairs for the best possible result!

By the Numbers

Your **Personal Year Number** represents where you are in a nine-year cycle of personal growth. It's found by adding your month and day of birth to the current year.

Easy as 1-2-3

The Personal Year starts on January of any year, and runs through the entire 12 months. Each Personal Year has a theme, so you'll have nine Personal Year themes in a cycle (because Personal Years run in nine-year cycles. Some people feel the thrust and purpose of their Personal Years more toward their birthdays, especially if their birthdays are in the summer or fall, rather than at the beginning of the year.

Your Personal Year can show you how to avoid difficulties, position yourself for what's coming, and, in addition, what you can expect during this 12-month cycle. As one of the predictive numbers in numerology, your Personal Year is one of the most easily recognized numbers at work in your life.

By knowing your Personal Year Number, you can know in advance what to expect, what obligations might lie ahead, and how best to prepare for this year. In fact, once you know your Personal Year Number (or someone else's), events and situations make more sense, because you can put them in the context of the predicted pattern for the year.

Each year has both an identity of its own and certain demands. We're told there's a time for everything under the sun, and wise men and women will succeed (where others may fail) by reading their Personal Year Numbers and planning accordingly. In fact, your Personal Year Number is one of the most significant numbers in your life, so it's worthwhile to spend some time getting to know your Personal Year Number and what it means.

Figuring Your Personal Year Number

It's quite simple to figure your Personal Year Number. Just remember one tip: You'll be using the *current calendar year* when you figure the Personal Year Number. Plus, you'll want to be sure to use all four digits of the year to get the right reduced number—no shortcuts allowed! You'll want to use 2000, not 00, or 1999, not just 99.

Numerology Rule #19

This is the formula for finding your Personal Year Number:

Month of birth + day of birth + current calendar year = Personal Year Number

---

Let's say you were born July 8th, and that you want to know what this year's Personal Year Number is. Just add 7 (July) + 8 + the calendar year.

If you were figuring the Personal Year Number for the calendar year 2000, then you would simply add:

> 7 + 8 + 2 (2000 reduced) = 17 = 8 (17 reduced)

This means that anyone born on July 8 in the year 2000 is an 8 Personal Year. Get it? Let's try another example.

If you want to know what year you were in for 1999, you would add 1999 together (1 + 9 + 9 + 9 = 1) to get the single-digit number 1 and then add that number to your month and day of birth (leave out your birth year). If you were born December 10, for example, it would look like this:

Sixes and Sevens

One mistake frequently made when calculating the Personal Year Number is to use your *year of birth* instead of the current *calendar year*. No, no—it's the *current* calendar year that you need to figure your Personal Year Number. You drop the year you were born when figuring the Personal Year number— and replace it with the current calendar year.

Month of birth	12 (reduced to 1 + 2) = 3
Day of birth	10 (reduced to 1 + 0) = 1
Calendar year	1999 (reduced to 1 + 9 + 9 + 9) = 28 = 10 = 1

Now add the reduced numbers together:

| Personal Year | 3 + 1 + 1 = 5 |

So, this person would be in a 5 Personal Year.

Days of Your Life

Now it's time to figure your own Personal Year Number. Fill in the number in steps 1 through 4 and see what you find.

1. Your month of birth: _____ (reduce if necessary) = _____ = _____

2. Your day of birth: _____ (reduce if necessary) = _____ = _____

3. The current year: _____ (reduce this number) = _____ = _____

(Be sure to use the *whole year*. For example, use 1999, not 99.)

4. Add together the numbers from steps 1 through 3, and this is your Personal Year Number: _____

    My Personal Year is for _____ (current calendar year)

Now circle the number of your Personal Year in the following table. That's where you are in the nine-year cycle.

Table for Personal Year Cycle									
Personal Year Numbers:	1	2	3	4	5	6	7	8	9

How the Personal Year Fits into the Nine-Year Cycle

We're all living under nine-year cycles, from a numerology standpoint. Somewhere in that cycle of nine is where you are.

Once you've found your own Personal Year Number, circle the number in the preceding chart that shows where you are now in this nine-year cycle. This will also allow you to see what year you were in last year and what next year will bring as well. You may want to tab this page for future reference, so that you can find all your Personal Years.

The Rhythm of the Years

Each year has its own natural rhythm and flow, and fits into a larger flow of the nine-year cycle. Here's the pattern of flow for each Personal Year:

The Flow of the Nine-Year Cycle

Personal Year Number	What It Means
1 Personal Year	A time of new beginnings, planting seeds; an active year
2 Personal Year	A year of cooperation, sensitivity, and relationship; a slow year
3 Personal Year	A year of creative ideas, having to say your truth, expressing yourself; an active year
4 Personal Year	A year of putting down roots, hard work, discipline, health, and putting into form the ideas of the 3 Personal Year; a productive year—must persevere
5 Personal Year	A year of change, unpredictability, risk taking, and freedom, getting unstuck from the 4 Personal Year; an active year
6 Personal Year	A year of tending to domestic affairs, family obligations, nurturing others; constant effort is required
7 Personal Year	A year of turning inward, rest and rejuvenation, contemplation and pursuit of spiritual quest; will spend time alone, can study and read this year
8 Personal Year	A year of respect, achievement, recognition; business matters dominate, especially financial management; an active, busy year where you must administrate

Personal Year Number	What It Means
9 Personal Year	A year of completion, release, forgiveness, and transformation; a quieter year, a time to rest, but can be busy in the first half

You can trust these Personal Year Numbers; they're uncanny in their accuracy in terms of describing the events that show up under each number, and how the year will play out.

Merlin's Notes

As an example of how accurate Personal Year Numbers are, Kay cites a client who knew nothing about numerology. One November, it was explained to her that the next year she would be in a 6 Personal Year, known to be the year of duty and responsibility to family. The client informed Kay that she had broken away from her family and couldn't see how the year could possibly be about family. (She has no children or family in marriage.) Then, in about March of her 6 Personal Year, she called to say, "I can't believe it, you were right. I am having to help my family deal with my brother who is troubled and has had a near-death experience."

Each Personal Year Number has its own characteristics. The number tells the tale.

Personal Year Numbers

So, what year's best for having a baby? For buying a house, or moving to another apartment? Do you want to go into business? Get married? Ditch it all and hitchhike across Europe (or Nepal)? Your Personal Year Numbers can help you determine all of these things—and more. You'll also want to check out Chapter 30, "Numbers for Daily Living," where we discuss how to use your Personal Year Numbers for everything from researching to planning for the future.

If you miss out on a Personal Year number because you didn't know about it, weren't able to focus on it, or whatever, don't despair—out of the 12 months of each year, you will have at least one more chance to deal with the number (and theme) you have missed. That's because each month of the year has a personal theme and personal number. We get to the Personal Months in the next chapter.

Personal Year Number 1

This is the year to begin any project. Begin it now because the flow is with you, and anything begun in a 1 year is favored and in synch with your natural rhythm. It's also a time for independence, courage, taking charge, and applying yourself. Unlike last year (which was a 9 year, a time of letting go), now is the time to start anew. Everything you do now will affect your future: You're planting seeds this year for your whole nine-year cycle.

The 1 year means it's time for you to focus on yourself. Use this year to take self-improvement classes, change your image, and/or focus on your personal goals. More than any other year, this is the time to become acquainted with the needs of your self. Here's the seed for all of the new beginnings that might be planted this year. It's time for a new you, and if you don't take time for yourself this year, you won't really get the chance again for nine more years, when you'll have another 1 Personal Year.

Personal Year Number 2

This is the year to back up and regroup. It's a time to listen to others, and perhaps even defer to them. A time of waiting and delays, this isn't a year for getting things done, but you will be more sensitive to the nuances of relationship and the needs of others. Unlike last year, this year your own needs will be secondary now. In addition, people often move in a 2 year, because this is a year of adaptability and balance.

The 2 year means it's time for you to relate to others. Cooperation is the lesson. Use this year to listen, be sensitive, and take the time for others. More than any other year, this is the time to compromise and seek harmony in all that you do. It's time for taking things slowly, and if you don't take your time this year, it will be another nine years before you can. In a 2 Personal Year, you often find a quiet, soothing rhythm to life, and may even truly experience a sense of peacefulness.

Easy as 1-2-3

The 3 Personal Year is the year for projects that involve writing, artistic flair, inspiration, public speaking, or a dramatic flair. In a 3 year, in fact, the creative juices just flow more freely—provided you're not an emotional basket case from struggling with having spoken your truth!

Personal Year Number 3

A 3 year is one of the hardest to understand, but no matter what, it won't be like your 2 year. Because the number 3 is supposed to be about joy, fun, and socializing, it may be hard to understand the agony experienced during this year. So many times Kay has heard students say, "What's fun about this 3 year?" The truth is, you may be working the emotional aspect of the 3: learning to say what's in your heart; finding words for what you feel; and having to go out into the world and speak your truth. This can be a very painful part of the 3 year; however, once you've conquered this milestone, the creative juices just seem to flow. Then it's time for fun, creative endeavors, and playing with friends.

The 3 year means it's time for you to express yourself. This is the year to write, keep a journal, paint, sing, dance, or have that heart-to-heart discussion—anything that allows you to speak and express your truth creatively. More than any other year, this is the time to use your imagination. It's time for playing and being with others, and if you don't take time to express yourself and your emotions this year, it will be waiting for you in your next 3 year—nine years away.

Personal Year Number 4

This can be a year to manage things, especially your health. It's a time to set things in order, set up systems, and lay down solid foundations for your future. Getting a home, having a family, getting insurance—all of these are the foundation pieces for our life. Needless to say, a 4 year takes a lot of hard work.

Merlin's Notes

Another facet of the 4 Personal Year that you may be working on is going back into the roots of the family dynamic in order to sort out your relationship to the early childhood drama. This work is usually called "family of origin" work, and (so fitting for the 4) it's about getting to the root of the problem. For this reason, this year may feel like the year from hell; it's very hard work to dig deep and reset the foundation pieces of your adult life.

The 4 year means it's time for you to build for the future, lay a foundation, or put down roots. Use this year to make lasting decisions and put these into action. More than any other year, this is the time to make things secure. It's time for stability and reliability, and if you don't take time to build your life this year, it will be another nine years before the energy will be available to do this work.

Personal Year Number 5

This is the year of personal transition, as opposed to the 9 year, when you'll be working on transformation. The 5 is a time of change—change in attitude, change of work, residence, change of direction. Travel is good during this year, and you may do a lot of it. In addition, because the 5 is curious, you may find yourself delving into metaphysics, taking classes, or investigating some new subject.

The 5 year means it's time for you to take some risks. Use this year to make big changes in your life. More than any other year, this is the time to move, change jobs or careers, or even try unconventional things you haven't tried before. It's time to be curious, and if you don't take time to investigate new things that interest you this year, it will be another nine years before you can.

Sixes and Sevens

Marital issues move to the forefront in a 6 Personal Year, too, and you'll either re-commit to your relationship or decide not to, thereby putting in motion an end to the marriage. It may take you until your 9 year, when the energy is about truly ending something, to finalize the divorce, however.

Personal Year Number 6

If you have elderly parents, this is the year for them. In an uncanny way, you'll become needed by your family this year more than any of the other years. It's also a year that demands that you balance your domestic life with your work life, and you'll be shown many opportunities to get your work life in balance—even if it means getting another job.

The 6 year means it's time for you to pay attention to your family duties and responsibilities. Use this year to nurture and serve those your care about. More than any other year, this is the time to balance the needs of others with your own needs. It's time for generosity and sympathy, and if you don't take time to give to your family, or to nurture your own needs, it will be another nine years before you get back to this.

Personal Year Number 7

This is a time to move inside yourself. You'll need alone time and rest as you reexamine your goals, relationships, and the very direction for your life. Often, during a 7 year, you're drawn to the study of spiritual, mystical, or metaphysical subjects, and it's not unusual to find you need spiritual direction, and so look to a counselor or healer who can help further your quest.

This year is also a time of body purification, so diets, cleansing, and detoxifying programs may become of interest now. In addition, the 7 rules legal affairs, so it may also be the year you get that insurance settlement finished, or any matter where legal papers are involved. But no matter what, you'll need and seek solitude, because this is the time to be alone and quiet.

The 7 year means the time is favorable for you to take a sabbatical, or do a vision quest. More than any other year, this is the time to be quiet and listen to your inner guidance. It's a time for seeking counsel from both yourself and others, as well as learning about what will help you find your own particular peace. Don't miss your chance for this introspective time, because you don't get another 7 year for nine more years!

Personal Year Number 8

This is a year to learn about your own power, to deal with authority issues, and to become the boss, because people will look to you this year for your executive ability or to act as an authority in some respect. This is the year where you'll be challenged to take the lead, to stand up as an authority, and in that way to begin to empower yourself with your full sense of power.

The 8 year means it's time for you to be thrust into the role of the leader, boss, or authority and to tend to business. Use this year to administrate something—the family estate, the school auction, or the company's overseas spring tour. More than any other year, this is the time to deal with the energy of power, money, and success, and to achieve something. If you don't make the most of this year, it will be another nine years before you get an 8 year again.

Personal Year Number 9

The tide is out in a 9 year, but the harvest is in! This is the year of rewards for all the effort you've made in the past eight years. This is the end, the conclusion of your nine-year cycle, so the seeds you planted in your 1 year are now harvested.

When the tide goes out, it means that the ending of a cycle is at hand, and the energy of this year is more about letting things go, finishing, and dreaming about the next nine years. It's time to re-vision, dream, and envision once again how you would like your life to proceed, to allow things to conclude, and wait, because the beginning that you sense is coming is for next year. This is also a time for healing and dreaming on both a figurative and literal level. Have a massage, and pay attention to your dreams.

On another note, this is a good money year, because efforts of selfless giving and loving are favored and rewarded this year. Of course the inverse can be true as well. If you're behaving selfishly and needing to revamp your money picture, with this number of endings, it may be a trying time for money. Don't despair; next year is a 1 year and starting anew is always favored under a 1.

Sixes and Sevens

In an 8 Personal Year you can have some kind of big expense, but money will be good this year. In fact, money flows toward you in an 8 year—as long as you're working for the good of all, and not just for personal profit. Still, as the money flows in, it flows out at almost the same rate. You must keep your head on and manage your financial affairs well this year. It is not time for extravagance or to get carried away with your emotions.

Sixes and Sevens

Sometimes, the 9 Personal Year can be emotional, because you're letting go of the old so the new can come in. For others, the 9 year is a transformational year: A large piece of their life stories is healed or released, and with it, an end occurs.

The 9 year means it's time for you to forgive and forget. Use this year to complete things and bring things to closure on every level. More than any other year, this is the time to follow your intuition and seek to perfect what was begun eight years before.

It's time for tying everything together, and if you don't take time for finishing things this year, you will most likely find your unfinished business lurking about and needing to be faced, again—in nine years.

Looking Back

Now that you know your Personal Year Number, you'll find it fun to look back and see what was happening for you nine years ago, when you were in the same Personal Year as you are now. In fact, you may want to look at the entire nine years of the past with this new tool—or you may even want to look back at your whole life! You'll be surprised at how true to your life each Personal Year's vibration is, and once you do see it, you'll want to calculate the future, of course.

Nine Years Ago

Personal Year Numbers move in nine-year cycles as we have said; however, nine years ago you may have been in a different Pinnacle than the one you're in now—and had a different Challenge Number, too. Check your Pinnacle Number (in Chapter 22, "Predictive Numerology: Future Forecasts") to see what you were trying to attain when you last had this Personal Year Number. You'll also want to check your Challenge Number from nine years ago, to see what lesson you were working on during this Personal Year.

Even though you repeat the Personal Year every nine years, the experience is not exactly the same. That's because you were working on a different facet of this personal number last time around. Still, upon close examination—and with a good memory (or good journal)—you'll see that it was, to cite a few examples, a time of new beginnings if you were in a 1 year, a time of duty and responsibility to the family if you were in a 6 year, or a time of study and wanting to withdraw if you were in a 7 year.

Numbers Are Like Crystals

Each number is like a multifaceted crystal. When you look at each number as a crystal, you're actually viewing only one facet of the crystal at a time. When you've finished with one aspect of a number, you'll move to the next facet of the number. Someone else may be looking at the same number (or crystal), but will be viewing a different facet.

We're not all the same; each of us is working our way through our own blueprint for life, but all of us will go through nine-year cycles, one Personal Year at a time. That's why, when you and your friend are both in an 8 year, you may not be working on the same thing. While each of you will be learning about the basic characteristics of the 8, you'll experience it differently, because whatever Pinnacle or Challenge you're in during your 8 year will influence and color that year.

Easy as 1-2-3

Your Personal Year is influenced by your Pinnacle and Challenge Numbers.

Study the basic meaning of each number, and you'll begin to see that each number has many facets. You're currently working on some facet of a particular number right now. For example, the number 6 is about nurturing and caring for others, service, romance, marriage and divorce, duty and responsibility, and balance. If you're currently in a 6 Personal Year, you may be working on caring for family members, while when you were in a 6 Personal Year nine years ago, you may have been working on marriage and/ or divorce, or attracting a new love interest.

This is what we mean by facets of the number: When a certain number comes up, you'll naturally be involved with issues of that number. We work our way around the facets of the crystal—the number crystal.

Don't Miss Your Chance

What happens if you pay no attention whatsoever to your Personal Year Number? Well if you didn't know about your Personal Year before reading this chapter you already know that things will happen anyway! Whether you're aware of it or not, whether you choose to pay attention or not, your life is proceeding in a distinct pattern, and moving through these cycles of personal growth. It's when you pay attention that you can make the most progress and gain a sense of mastery.

Now that you've got this key, however, there are certain things about certain Personal Years you won't want to miss. You won't want to miss the 1 year, for example, because it's the time to put yourself into a new start. A new time is forming.

Merlin's Notes

Things *begun* in a 9 Personal Year don't tend to last; they're not supported by the energy flow that's naturally to that number. Instead, if you start something in a 9 year, you are beginning when the tide is going out. Of course, there is another way to look at this: If you get married, or finally begin that novel, it may be a time of rewards—what's long been waited for. Then the new beginning is really more of an end to a long cycle of events.

You'll know a new start when it shows up—if you're paying attention. You'll feel the highly active energy of the 1, as opposed to the more subdued energy of the 9, which feels like a big sigh of relief.

Another year you won't want to miss is the 5 year. In a 5 Personal Year, change is afoot. This is a very significant time for personal transition, and setting yourself on a course of action that will affect the next four years (the rest of the nine-year cycle).

Still another year you don't want to miss is the 7 year—it's the only year you'll have in nine years to turn inward and re-evaluate. At the very least, you'll want to devote a good portion of this year to re-evaluating where you're headed with your life. The 7 year requires that you pull back from others and have time alone. Solitude, nature, the woods, and the mountains all provide sacred places and quiet energy to restore you and allow you to listen within. Of course, you'll have a 7 month every year, so if you miss the boat in this 7 year, at least you'll have a chance to do the 7 thing once or twice each year. (We'll tell you all about your Personal Months in the next chapter.)

The Age Vibration: Harmonic Resonance

A sub-theme to your Personal Year is found in the age you'll be during a particular Personal Year that is called your *age vibration*. Simply stated, how old you are during a Personal Year has a subtle influence on your year.

To figure your age vibration number, just determine how old you'll be in the given year. Most of us are two ages in a given year. If, for example, your birthday is March 30, 1948, and you're figuring your Personal Year age vibration for the year 1999, then simply subtract 1948 (year of birth) from the current year, 1999: 1999 – 1948 = 51.

By the Numbers

Your **age vibration** is the way your age influences your Personal Year.

Sixes and Sevens

Don't forget—whenever you're figuring the year, you must use and reduce *all four digits* to come up with the right number. So use 2000, not 00, and 1999, not 99!

Now, if you were born in March, we know that you'll live almost four months of this year as 50 years old, and then on your birthday (March 30), you'll be 51. So we then say that in 1999 you were both 50 and 51.

We find your age vibration by taking these ages and adding them together. In other words, for this example, we add 50 + 51 to get 101, which we reduce to a single digit, or 1 + 0 + 1 = 2. During the year 1999, you would have an age vibration of a 2.

It's important to look at the age vibration in relation to your Personal Year theme. Let's say you're in a 5 Personal Year and you have a 2 age vibration. The 5 means change and the 2 means relationship, so we might conclude that this person will experience change along the line of relationship during the year. It also means that partnerships of all kinds are up for change. See how it works? All of the numbers work in relationship to one another.

What if your birthday's in January? Well, you won't have many days of being two different ages so if you have a January birthday, just calculate the one age you'll be. For example, if you're turning 34 in January, just add 3 + 4 = 7, which means that you'll have a 7 age vibration that year.

The Least You Need to Know

➤ Every Personal Year—from 1 to 9—has its own special message and demands.

➤ Finding your Personal Year Number is as easy as adding your month and day of birth to the current year.

➤ Knowing where you are in your own nine-year cycle can help you plan for the future—and understand the past.

➤ Your age vibration adds a secondary influence to your Personal Year's vibration.

Chapter 26

Your Personal Month: The Year at a Glance

In This Chapter

➤ The natural rhythm of the months of the year

➤ Finding your Personal Month Numbers

➤ Laying out your year

➤ A word about Personal Days

In addition to finding Personal Years, you can also find your Personal Months—even your Personal Days! Personal Years have the strongest influence, but laying out your year month by month can help you understand the natural rhythm of your year.

According to its number, each month's theme has a rhythm of its own, and, once you know the meaning of your Personal Month Number, you can use it to know which tasks will go best in which months. In this chapter, we'll show you how to do just that.

You've Got Personal Months, Too

So what exactly is a *Personal Month Number?* Personal Month Numbers are found by adding the number of the calendar month to the number of your Personal Year.

In terms of emphasis, the Personal Year is the most significant number. You can think of it as the main ingredient in a recipe. The Personal Month Number is what's added for flavor—the herbs and spices, if you like. Every Personal Month Number has its own special spice, which flavors that month in a certain way.

By the Numbers

Each **Personal Month Number** has a theme which is part of the rhythm of your Personal Year. The Personal Month Number is found by adding the number of your Personal Year to the number of the calendar month. You have 12 Personal Month Numbers for each Personal Year.

Personal Day Numbers have the least amount of emphasis. In fact, some people won't even feel the influence of a Personal Day Number at all—unless it's the same number as their Soul Number. We'll take a closer look at Personal Days toward the end of this chapter.

Figuring Your Personal Month Number

Figuring your Personal Month Number is easy, once you know your Personal Year. (To review the calculation of the Personal Year, see the previous chapter.) You'll simply add the number of your Personal Year to the number of each month. Here's a chart of the numerical equivalent of each month to get you started.

The Numbers of the Months

Month	Number
January	1
February	2
March	3
April	4
May	5
June	6
July	7
August	8
September	9
October	1 (1 + 0)
November	2 (1 + 1)
December	3 (1 + 2)

As an example, let's say 2001 is a 5 Personal Year for you. Look at the following table to see how each Personal Month for that year is calculated.

Personal Months for the Year 2001 and a 5 Personal Year

Month	Month Number	+	Personal Year Number	=	Personal Month Number
January	1	+	5	=	6
February	2	+	5	=	7

340

Personal Months for the Year 2001 and a 5 Personal Year

Month	Month Number	+	Personal Year Number	=	Personal Month Number
March	3	+	5	=	8
April	4	+	5	=	9
May	5	+	5	=	10 = 1
June	6	+	5	=	11 = 2
July	7	+	5	=	12 = 3
August	8	+	5	=	13 = 4
September	9	+	5	=	14 = 5
October	1	+	5	=	6
November	2	+	5	=	7
December	3	+	5	=	8

Numerology Rule #20

This is the formula for finding your Personal Month:

Personal Year Number + calendar month number = Personal Month Number

---

Personal Month Meanings

When we do a person's numerology chart, we like to lay out their Personal Months for them, using a template that we fill in. We've created just such a template for you to calculate your Personal Month Numbers.

Your Personal Month Numbers

To find the numbers of your Personal Months, add the number of your current Personal Year to the number of the month. Do your calculations and fill in your numbers in the following spaces.

Easy as 1-2-3

Finding your Personal Month Numbers for any given year is really simple. Remember, just add your Personal Year Number to the number of the calendar month!

For the calendar year ____, which is my Personal Year Number ____, my Personal Month Numbers are:

Jan. ____   Feb. ____   Mar. ____   Apr. ____   May ____   June ____

July ____   Aug. ____   Sept. ____   Oct. ____   Nov. ____   Dec. ____

So what month are you in right now? You'll find that each Personal Month Number has its own particular spice.

Easy as 1-2-3

As we were finishing this chapter, someone we know well started a job with a new company—after 15 years with another. He was in a 1 Personal Month—and a 5 Personal Year. He couldn't have timed it better if he'd tried!

If you have a master number for your Personal Year Number, simply reduce it to its lowest number and add the reduced number to the current calendar month. For example, if you are in an 11/2 Personal Year, use the reduced number 2 to add to the calendar month number under consideration.

Personal Month Number 1

A 1 Personal Month is a lot like chili pepper—it will make you sit up and take notice. That's because a 1 Personal Month is the month of beginnings, when you'll tackle new projects, take charge, take over, and just plain get things rolling. This month comes on the heels of a 9 Personal Month, which was good for tying up loose ends and finishing things up, so it will be only natural during this Personal Month to have the time and energy to want to start new projects.

Personal Month Number 2

A 2 Personal Month has the nice complementary spice of a bouquet garni; it works with the rest of the Personal Year to subtly bring everything together. This is the Personal Month when the seeds you planted during the 1 Personal Month will begin to take root. You'll seek the help and advice of others, and work with them cooperatively on their projects as well. That's because this is a month for relationships, for paying attention to others after the "me-first" spirit of the 1 month.

Personal Month Number 3

A 3 Personal Month adds a touch of ginger to the recipe: It's a lot of fun and adds a nice creative touch as well. This is the month where you get to add those creative touches to your project, too, and you may find that you are expressing yourself verbally, emotionally, and artistically during this Personal Month.

A 3 Personal Month can be playtime, but it's personal playtime as much as playing with others. This means it's a great time to go shopping, buy gifts, go out to lunch, or buy yourself that sterling silver pin you've wanted since last Christmas. It's also time to play with color and design—so redesign your bedroom, put up new wallpaper in the bathroom—whatever gets your creative juices flowing.

Merlin's Notes

The 3 is considered the lucky number, so when you're in a 3 Personal Month, things may just be easier for you. The 3 month can also be an opportunity to express yourself—you know, speak up about that issue you've been reluctant to mention.

Personal Month Number 4

A 4 Personal Month is where you'll find the salt—the salt of the earth, that is. This is a good month to make sure that your project is on track, building for the future, and creating a solid foundation. You'll work hard in a 4 month, but you'll be doing that work to ensure that your project's security and stability are assured. You may also work hard on family issues this month in order to make sure that your life is standing on solid footing—with no dry rot.

The 4 Personal Month is also a time to attend to health matters—go get that check-up, see that therapist, get a massage, get that juice maker, or investigate the proper vitamins/minerals for yourself and your family. In some manner, create a solid foundation for your health program this month—and that includes getting the right insurance program. This is the month to attend to these tasks, because this is the natural rhythm of the 4 month—to put down roots, secure things, get a plan, or build a foundation of stability for the rest of your Personal Year.

Personal Month Number 5

A 5 Personal Month has the spice of cumin, which dramatically changes the flavor of your Personal Year. In fact, everything can change this month—your life may take off in a new direction or you may decide to abandon it entirely. "Variety is the spice of life" may well be your 5 Personal Month motto, and you may decide to take a new class, travel somewhere you've never been, or do something different so you can meet new people and

Sixes and Sevens

It's natural to want a change during a 5 month—after all, you've been following the same path step by step since you began in the 1 month. Just be careful not to throw out the baby with the bath water—you wouldn't have started that project in the first place if it wasn't something you wanted to see through to its finish.

have new experiences. In a 5 Personal Month, you can expect change—including sudden, unexpected change.

A 5 Personal Month is also a good time to network, promote yourself, or sell, because you'll be more apt to communicate with others with enthusiasm, excitement, and magnetism in this month. The change you may feel in a 5 month is that of being willing to finally take a risk—that certainly will change things!

Personal Month Number 6

A 6 Personal Month adds some honey to your recipe for this year. We know it's not a spice, but its sweetness adds that distinctive 6 touch. In fact, you may be doing a lot of cooking this month—after the get-out-and-go that characterized your 5 Personal Month, you'll probably want to stay home and be with your family. In addition, in a 6 Personal Month, you'll be feeling dutiful and responsible, and will make sure that all those loose ends that you dropped during the 5 month get picked up again—and put back in the pot!

A 6 Personal Month is a great time to tend to matters at home: Repot those plants, trim out the yard, add a little paint to the front door—it's the natural time to beautify the home. Of course, you may find it beautifying to just clean the house! It's a great time to just be family oriented: Go to that soccer game, make the trip to the zoo, go visit your parents this month.

Personal Month Number 7

A 7 Personal Month adds saffron, an exotic spice that accents your interest in looking within yourself this month. A 7 Personal Month is a month for R&R, for studying the esoteric aspects of your life that you may not have previously pondered. You may want to schedule a retreat this month, because you'll feel the need to be alone to reflect and consider how things are going. It's natural during a 7 month to seek solitude, because you'll feel introspective and will want to re-evaluate where you've been—and where you going.

The 7 month is a great time to go to the woods, to the mountains, or to the ocean to be restored by nature. Curling up with a good book or investigating a Web site or two are also activities for a 7 month. It's the one time in the year where you'll want to pay attention to the need to be by yourself and have time to think.

Personal Month Number 8

No nonsense in an 8 Personal Month—just a good dash of pepper to make sure it's a successful brew! It's time to take it by the reins and lead with your sure power and strong authority. At this point, you're certain of your direction and you're certain of success, and you'll want to assume command so that everything goes the way it should. You'll want to make sure that everything's taken care of in an 8 Personal Month—and you will.

An 8 month is a time to get down to business—all manner of business. Whether it's about speaking to the neighbors about their barking dog, calling the phone company about a new fax line, paying the taxes, handling those divorce papers, or making an investment; this is the month for taking charge of your life and manage things.

It's also a good time to organize your financial affairs, and this month also favors business deals and making arrangements for expanding into new markets. It's about money, power, and management this month!

Personal Month Number 9

In a number 9 Personal Month, you get to add the garnish: Is it parsley? Shredded cheese? A perfect swirl of chocolate drizzled across the top? This is the month when you get to reap what you sowed—and you get to harvest all that you have done in previous months. You've earned the reward for all your hard work, and, whether it's monetary or spiritual, you'll know it was worth the effort.

A 9 Personal Month is a time to clean out, let go, and release. This is the month of endings. Something wants to draw to a close in this month, so you may feel like cleaning out file drawers, closets, or old boyfriends, or putting an end to your credit card. This month's energy is inviting you to finish up, let it go, and make room for the new that is coming in next month.

Easy as 1–2–3

During a 9 Personal Month, you'll get to close the book on this recipe and put away all the ingredients, because next month, you'll begin cooking up a new stew!

Putting the Month in Context with the Personal Year

It's important to remember that the Personal Year has the strongest influence—it's the main ingredient, the main theme for the whole year. The Personal Month adds its own particular flavor. For example, a 3 Personal Month in a 4 Personal Year won't be as much fun as a 3 Personal Month in a 5 Personal Year.

If we were to list the subtle Personal Month influence on every Personal Year, we'd have 144 things to show you! Instead, to make things easy, we thought we'd set up a table that lists an accent for each month. Each accent characterizes the mood or activity of a particular month, and you can add its unique flavor to any Personal Year.

In order to use this table, you'll need to have a good understanding of what each Personal Year's emphasis is. (You'll find what you need to know in Chapter 25, "Your Personal Year: For Every Time There Is a Season.") Now have a look at the key accents for each of your Personal Month Numbers and see how they can modify or enhance your Personal Year.

What Those Months Mean, Every Year

Personal Month Number	Accent
1	Seed something, begin it
2	Cooperate, be patient
3	Have fun
4	Work hard
5	Make a change
6	Nurture
7	Take some R&R
8	Take charge
9	End it, get your reward

By the Numbers

Biorhythm is the name for any biological cycle that involves periodic change. Because biorhythms are cyclical, like numerological cycles, they can be predicted.

By the Numbers

Your **Personal Day Number** adds a certain number's subtle energy to every day of your life. It's found by adding the number of the calendar day to the number of your Personal Month.

Learning to Work with Your Own Natural Rhythms

You've probably heard of *biorhythms*, which are your own natural physical cycles. Personal Years, Months, and Days act a lot like biorhythms, moving you through your own particular metaphysical cycles, and helping you to understand them and how to use them to work, play, or rest, at the times when these activities are best for you.

This is not to say that you can't begin something in a 5 month, or even a 9 month—but it does suggest that things begun in a 1 month will more closely follow your own natural rhythm and therefore have a greater chance for success. If you must be social during a 7 month, something will probably feel "off"—just as if you try to have fun during a 4 month—or work hard during a 3 month.

Knowing your Personal Months can help you time when to begin things and when to end them, and it can also help you understand why sometimes, something just doesn't feel right, or seems harder than it should.

Matching Your Day with Your Number

The *Personal Day Number* is the least emphasized of the three numbers: Remember, the Personal Year has the strongest influence, while the Personal Month adds flavor. In fact, some people don't feel their Personal Days at all—but there are places where you should pay attention.

When your Personal Day Number matches your Life Path Number or your Soul Number, however, you'll want to pay attention, because its subtle influence is added to what's already a strong influence in your life. These days will resonate more closely for you than other Personal Days.

The important thing to remember about Personal Days is that every Personal Day Number does have a subtle energy that it adds to the mix. These energies are more like little charged ions that add a certain spark to any given day. We've listed those sparks for you in the next table.

What Your Personal Day Number Means

Personal Day Number	A Day to:
1	Begin things, be independent
2	Be patient, attend to details
3	Be creative, be with friends, communicate
4	Get organized, attend to your health
5	Make a change, network and promote
6	Pay attention to family or home
7	Rest and re-evaluate, time for quiet solitude
8	Handle money, take charge
9	Finish up, use your intuition

Merlin's Notes

One other thing you can do with your Personal Day Number is match it up to the calendar. If you have a 3 day on the 3rd day of a month, for example, another extra little spark will be added to the mix. Or, on a 6 day in a 6 month in a 6 year that occurs on the 6th day of the month, you can plan on paying close attention to family issues for sure.

You can create an easy guide for finding your Personal Days. Write the number for each day directly on your regular calendar, once you've got them calculated. Simply add your Personal Month Number to the calendar day and write in your Personal Day Number. You might want to use a pocket month-at-a-glance calendar just for this purpose, keeping it as a handy reference for your Personal Days year round.

For example, if you are in a 7 Personal Month, using your calendar, the first day of the month will be an 8 day for you (7 + 1 = 8). Write the number 8 on the calendar for the 1st of the month, then write in your Personal Day Numbers for each day. Remember, this 7 month and 8 day belong to your Personal Year theme. Look to see how they fit together. What are you learning this month?

The Personal Months are indicators of the natural flow of your Personal Year theme. And like we've said before in this chapter, your Personal Month and Personal Day Numbers are guideposts for your journey through the year.

The Least You Need to Know

➤ Each Personal Month Number has a theme, or "spice" which is part of the rhythm of your whole Personal Year.

➤ The Personal Month Number = the number of the calendar month + the number of your Personal Year.

➤ Laying out the Personal Months in your year can help you understand the natural flow for the year.

➤ The Personal Day = the number of the Personal Month + the calendar day.

Part 6
Living by the Numbers

Now that you've learned the basics of numerology, it's time to apply it to your own life. We'll take you on a tour of how numerology works hand-in-hand with astrology, and then we'll show you how you can map your relationships by the numbers as well. Last, we'll take a look at other names and numbers in your life—from your bank account to your dreams—and show you how you can use numbers every day.

Chapter 27

Numbering by the Stars: Numerology and Astrology

In This Chapter

➤ Astrology and numerology: systems to examine the mysteries of life

➤ Planets and signs are symbols, like numbers

➤ Every planet and sign corresponds to one or more numbers

➤ Astrology's cycles and numerology's cycles

Astrology and numerology are both profound spiritual tools to finding the mysteries of life, and both are also highly intricate systems based on mathematical truths that reveal the deeper universal order that weaves together everything in life. In this chapter, we explore similarities between these two spiritual systems and how they mutually support one another's essential truths.

What Is Astrology?

Astrology is an ancient metaphysical system that explores the spiritual connection between humans on Earth and the planets and constellations in the heavens. The primary metaphysical truth that lies at the heart of astrology is that everything (humans, planets, and stars) is interconnected in a dynamic, spiritual, and energetic relationship.

Planets and Signs Are Symbols

Two main components of astrology are *planets* and *signs*. In astrology, the planets in our solar system symbolize key universal characters that live within everybody. For example, Venus symbolizes the lover; Mars symbolizes the warrior; and Jupiter symbolizes the teacher. The following table lists the 10 planets, their corresponding astrological symbols, and the characters that personify each planet as used in astrology.

Astrological Planets: Their Symbols and Meanings

Planet	Symbol	Character
Sun	☉	Hero/heroine
Moon	☽	Nurturer/feeler
Mercury	☿	Communicator/free spirit
Venus	♀	Lover/negotiator
Mars	♂	Scout/warrior
Jupiter	♃	Philosopher/teacher
Saturn	♄	Administrator/authority
Uranus	♅	Liberator/revolutionary
Neptune	♆	Mystic/dreamer
Pluto	♇	Transformer/teacher of power

The signs in astrology are named after the zodiac star constellations that appear to form a circular belt around the earth. From our perspective on Earth, the planets appear to move against that imaginary belt as they orbit around the Sun.

Astrological signs are descriptions of how the planetary characters express their energies. For example, when a planet is in the place of the sky designated Taurus, that planetary "character" expresses itself as grounded, stable, and somewhat stubborn. The next table lists the 12 astrological signs, their corresponding astrological symbols, and the meaning of each sign as used in astrology.

Astrological Signs: Their Symbols and Meanings

Sign	Symbol	Meanings
Aries	♈	Take risks; pioneer; be independent
Taurus	♉	Create physical security; stabilize
Gemini	♊	Explore options; dialogue; be free
Cancer	♋	Create emotional security; nurture
Leo	♌	Express creativity; enjoy life; shine
Virgo	♍	Heal; serve; apply spiritual truths
Libra	♎	Create fair relationships; balance
Scorpio	♏	Seek emotional depths; catalyze endings
Sagittarius	♐	Seek higher truths; work for justice
Capricorn	♑	Organize; manage; use power wisely
Aquarius	♒	Honor humanitarianism; trust intuition
Pisces	♓	Contemplate; seek spiritual oneness

Astrology uses a symbolic map of the heavens, called a *natal chart,* as a tool to understand your life journey and your soul's purpose.

If you want to know more about astrology, we recommend *The Complete Idiot's Guide to Astrology*, by Madeline Gerwick-Brodeur and Lisa Lenard, or, if you are interested in the astrological influences for the new millennium, we recommend Sheila's chapters in *The Complete Idiot's Guide to New Millennium Predictions*.

Correspondences: Numbers, Signs, and Planets

In this chapter, we explore the correspondences between the numbers of numerology and the signs and planets of astrology. By exploring the link between them, you will get a glimpse of the intricate unity of spiritual truths. Just as all human religions speak the same universal truth about our unity with the Divine, the two systems of numerology and astrology speak the same metaphysical truth that there is a higher spiritual order that organizes human life on Earth.

What Sign Is My Number?: Zodiac Signs and Their Numbers

The numbers 1 through 9, plus the three master numbers of 11/2, 22/4, and 33/6, each have a unique energetic vibration that corresponds to one or more zodiac signs. In addition, each zodiac sign has a mythical association to an animal, person, or object that exemplifies the essence of the sign. For example, like the lion, Leo can express itself majestically and forcefully.

Remember that your Sun sign describes where in the zodiac the Sun appeared to be traveling when you were born. Your Sun sign symbolizes your conscious identity in the world. For example, someone whose Sun sign is Libra enjoys relating to others and supporting fair and equal partnerships. To determine your Sun sign, look up your birthday in the table that follows.

By the Numbers

Astrology studies the interconnectedness of humans, planets, and stars by studying their interrelationship with each other.

By the Numbers

Let's use an analogy from the theater. The **planets** are like actors in the great play that is your life. Each planet is a performer playing a role that gives voice to a part of your personality. The **signs** are the costumes the actors wear in their role.

By the Numbers

Your **natal chart** describes symbolically in which zodiac sign each of the 10 planets were located at the moment you were born. For example, if your Sun sign is Pisces, it means at the time you were born, the Sun appeared to be moving in the sky against the backdrop of the Pisces sign.

Sun Signs and Birth Dates

Sun Sign	Birth Dates
Aries	March 21st–April 20th
Taurus	April 20th–May 21st
Gemini	May 21st–June 22nd
Cancer	June 22nd–July 23rd
Leo	July 23rd–August 22nd
Virgo	August 22nd–September 22nd
Libra	September 22nd–October 23rd
Scorpio	October 23rd–November 22nd
Sagittarius	November 22nd–December 22nd
Capricorn	December 22nd–January 21st
Aquarius	January 21st–February 19th
Pisces	February 19th–March 21st

If you know your Sun sign, you can look up its associated number(s) to gain a greater understanding of that part of your nature. Because of the depths and nuances of astrology and numerology as spiritual tools, there is not always an exact equation between a number and a sign. The following table lists the numbers and their corresponding signs and planets. We'll discuss these associations in more depth in the section that follows.

The Numbers and Their Astrological Signs and Planets

Number	Sign	Planet
1	Aries	Mars
2	Libra	Venus
3	Leo	Sun
4	Taurus	Earth
5	Gemini	Mercury
6	Cancer/Libra	Moon
7	Pisces/Virgo/Scorpio	Pluto
8	Capricorn	Saturn
9	Scorpio/Pisces/Aquarius	Uranus
11/2	Aquarius/Sagittarius	Jupiter
22/4	Virgo/Libra/Capricorn	Earth
33/6	Sagittarius/Cancer/Pisces	Neptune

Aries: The Ram Leads the Way to 1

Aries is the mythical ram who carries the energy of a courageous pioneer and independent leader. The ram wants to express itself in a direct and self-reliant way. Like the 1, its challenge is not to be impulsive, isolated, and overly aggressive.

Taurus: The Bull Stands in the Solid Pasture of 4

Taurus is the mythical bull who typifies the energy of solid physical security. The Bull doesn't move quickly unless it is really pushed. It prefers to create a stable foundation and rest on it. Like the 4, its challenge is to avoid being inflexible and stubborn in a destructive way.

Gemini: The Twins Explore the Freedom of 5

Gemini is the mythical twins who symbolically invite you to see the other side of the coin. The twins like to travel all over the map in their exploration of diversity and options. The pursuit of freedom to talk about different points of view and enjoy the extremes of life can get the twins into trouble. Like the 5, the challenge is to not get superficial and scattered by all of life's myriad choices.

Cancer: The Crab Creates a Safe Haven with 6 and 33/6

Cancer is the mythical crab who carries its hard-shell home on its back as protection for its soft under belly. The crab seeks to have emotional security and to nurture. In its desire to be part of a family, the crab is loyal and dutiful to its clan. Like the 6, the crab needs to avoid sacrificing its own emotional needs in order to nurture the needs of others. Like the 33/6, the crab also desires deep heart connection.

Leo: The Lion Expresses the Creative Joy of 3

Leo is the mythical lion who majestically expresses its potent creativity. The lion is fun loving and playful as it shines its charismatic charms for the world to appreciate. Like the 3, the lion needs to resist being arrogant and narcissistic and always come from the heart.

Virgo: The Virgin Integrates Body, Mind, and Soul with 7 and 22/4

Virgo is the mythical virgin who contains wholeness within itself. The virgin has the ability to discern where unity and wholeness are lacking and, from that insight, effect change to heal and restore wholeness. The virgin seeks to serve the greater good for all. Like the 7, the virgin carries analytical abilities to determine how best to effect healing changes. Like all 22/4s, the hardworking virgin must guard against workaholism and self-sacrifice and seek to serve itself as well as others.

Libra: The Scales Keep the Balance of 2, 6, and 22/4

Libra is the mythical scales, which seek to maintain beauty and balance. The scales help to determine what constitutes fair and equal relationships. They are constantly weighing issues with negotiation and cooperation. Like the 2, the scales can go on forever weighing and balancing both sides of an issue so that no clear choices and direction can be decided upon. Like the 6, they love beauty and balance for their own sake. Like the 22/4, the scales are deeply sensitive to harmony in relationships.

Scorpio: The Scorpion Strikes to Completion with 7 and 9

Scorpio is the scorpion with the sharp tail that seeks to get to the heart of the matter. The scorpion carries a hard shell to protect its vulnerable side. It seeks emotional depths and wants to catalyze endings and completion. The scorpion can sting if it senses falsehoods and game-playing behavior. Like the 7, it craves privacy and authenticity. Like the 9, the scorpion can be overwhelmed by passionate emotions and strike in reaction to them. Its challenge is to develop compassion and discernment to know how to support appropriate transformation for self and others.

Sagittarius: The Archer Aims for the Unity of 11/2

Sagittarius is the mythical archer who aims its arrow into the heavens, seeking higher metaphysical awareness. The archer wants to understand universal truths and teach others about them. It wants justice based on higher principles for all. Like the 11/2, the archer must learn detachment and resist being emotionally dogmatic in its search to find the Truth with a capital "T."

Capricorn: The Sea-Goat Climbs the Mountain of 8 and 22/4

Capricorn is the mythical sea-goat, a mountain goat with a dolphin's tail. The sea-goat seeks to organize and manage physical reality. The sea-goat loves its world to be efficient and functional so that it can climb the mountain of achievement. Like the 8, the sea-goat must learn to use power wisely and not dominate or over control. It can call on the feminine side of its dolphin nature to learn to "go with the flow." Like the 22/4, the sea-goat creates solid form and structure.

Aquarius: The Water Bearer Seeks the Truth of 9 and 11/2

Aquarius is the mythical water bearer who brings the gift of illumination and spiritual insight to others. The water bearer is at heart a humanitarian who wants to support the uniqueness of others while staying true to its own individual nature. Like the 9, the water bearer is an idealistic reformer. Like the 11/2, it carries deep idealism and electrifying energy and is challenged to not be insecure and self-alienated.

Pisces: The Fish Swim in the Mystic Currents of 7, 9, and 33/6

Pisces is the mythical pair of fish joined together, yet swimming in opposite directions. The fish recognize that two worlds can coexist beside one another and at times can confuse which reality is which. The fish are dreamers and seek to contemplate the spiritual mysteries of the great ocean in which they swim. Like the 7, their challenge is not to get lost and isolated in their own little dream world but to remember that they are always in oneness with life. Like the 9, they are compassionate and can express universal love. Like the 33/6, the fish are creative and willing to serve others.

What Planet Guides My Number?: Planets and Their Numbers

The planets are symbolic characters that live in everyone. They act as guiding allies for the nine numbers and three master numbers. The planetary character is yet another way of expressing the number's vibration. These are suggested associations between numbers and planets. Remember that astrology and numerology are both deep metaphysical systems and their overlay is not a simple equation.

Mars and 1: The Scout Leads the Way

Mars is the scout or warrior who takes charge and gets things started. Like the 1, Mars is a willful kinda guy who takes quick action, yet needs to monitor that he is not leaving tire tracks on people's faces as he zooms forward in life.

Venus and 2: The Lover Cooperates and Balances

Venus is the lover or negotiator who creates and maintains balanced relationships. Like the 2, Venus is a lady of harmony and beauty whose challenge is not to get lost in a partnership but to stay in a fair relationship with self.

The Sun and 3: The Heroine Seeks Joy

The Sun is the heroine enthusiastically on the journey to find out her identity. Like the 3, the heroine wants to express her creativity and be loved and recognized by others. Her challenge is not to think she is the queen of the world and treat others disrespectfully.

The Earth and 4: The Gardener Builds Stability

Earth is the most important planet in our solar system since, without it, none of us would be here. One character associated with the earth is the gardener who lovingly tends to the plants to stabilize the form and function of the garden. And as any human gardener knows, like the 4, the challenge is not to get consumed by all the required detailed work and forget to stop, rest in the sunshine, and smell the flowers.

357

Mercury and 5: The Communicator Explores New Ideas

Mercury is the communicator who loves to explore new ideas and connections with others. He is quick, lively, and a very adaptive kinda guy. Like the 5, the communicator has to guard against burning out his circuits with extremes of activity and mental gymnastics.

Moon and 6: The Nurturer Feels and Connects

The Moon is the nurturer who wants to feel safe and emotionally connected to others. Like the 6, her challenge is to avoid becoming "super mother" whereby she smothers her loved ones with attention while ignoring her own needs.

Pluto and 7: The Transformer Explores Solitary Depths

Pluto is the transformer who catalyzes change and healing by getting to the root of the matter. The transformer says be empowered and clean up your own stuff, and, when it's over, let it go. Like the 7, the transformer must avoid getting caught in illusions and obsessions that lead to isolation and loneliness.

Saturn and 8: The Administrator Leads and Organizes

Saturn is the administrator who keeps things functional and efficient. He leads because he knows the game plan and how to steadfastly accomplish a goal. Like the 8, his challenge is to avoid being a dictator and mistakenly think that the ends justify the means.

Uranus and 9: The Revolutionary Honors Change

Uranus is the intuitive revolutionary who seeks change and new revelations for the good of all. Like the 9, the revolutionary wants the old to end and must guard against being intolerant of others' timing and processes because of things being incomplete.

Jupiter and 11/2: The Philosopher Seeks Truth

Jupiter is the teacher or philosopher who seeks to expand knowledge and growth. The philosopher wants to know the bigger perspectives in life and help others to understand them. Like the 11/2, the philosopher needs to avoid aggressively insisting on its truth as the only valid one.

Earth and 22/4: Gaia Builds the Vision

The earth is also Gaia, the great mother goddess of life on this planet. Gaia wants all her children to survive and prosper. As mother earth, she provides the big vision of unity with the cycles of nature and death and rebirth. Like the 22/4, she is a Master Builder who sustains life, yet at the beginning of the 21st century, she is sorely challenged by the burdens her children have placed upon her.

Neptune and 33/6: The Dreamer Serves the World

Neptune is the dreamer who seeks connection to a quiet and contemplative world within. He has faith in something beyond the material world and can easily lose himself in a belief or idea. Like the 33/6, the dreamer needs to stay focused on spiritual goals and not lose himself in the bigness of his dreams.

Numerology Cycles and Astrology Life Phases: No Mere Coincidence

Just as numerology tracks the cycles of the numbers throughout your life, astrology tracks the cycles of the planets. Astrology determines a planet's cycle by its movement through the zodiac signs as it orbits around the Sun. Planetary cycles help us to understand cycles of human growth and evolution. Astrology tracks the correspondences between what the planets are doing in the sky and what humans are doing on Earth.

When you are under the influence of a particular numerology cycle, the challenges and gifts of the corresponding astrology life phase of that period of your life can help guide you through the numerology cycles. We discuss this more at the end of this chapter.

Astrology Life Phases of Adulthood

Each planet in our solar system moves around the Sun in its unique orbital period (the time its takes to complete one orbit around the Sun). For example, Mars takes about two years to go once around the Sun. In contrast, Uranus takes about 84 years for its orbital period.

Merlin's Notes

Over time, a planet can be in a different spatial relationship to its own position in your natal chart. For example, Jupiter takes 12 years to complete one orbit around the Sun. If Jupiter was in the sign of Gemini at the time of your birth, then approximately six years after your birth (one half of Jupiter's orbital period), Jupiter will be in the sign of Sagittarius and be opposite the location in the sky it held at your birth. In astrology, this is called a Jupiter opposition cycle and defines a phase of your life in which you explore the teacher character within you.

Astrology assigns meaning to specific planetary cycles that occur throughout your life. These are universal life phases that everyone experiences. The most important cycles are

> ➤ **Return:** A planet has moved back to the same place in the sky where it was at your birth.

> ➤ **Waxing Square:** A planet has moved to a place in the sky that is 90 degrees away from where it was located at your birth.

> ➤ **Opposition:** A planet has moved to a place in the sky that is 180 degrees away from where it was located at your birth.

> ➤ **Waning Square:** A planet has moved to a place in the sky that is 270 degrees away from where it was located at your birth.

There are special astrological life phases that correspond to different periods of adulthood. These phases are based on where the planets have moved to in the zodiac since you were born. The life phases occur at specific ages in life. For example, everyone who is age 20 to 21 is experiencing the Uranus waxing square cycle; everyone who is age 43 to 44 is experiencing the Saturn opposition cycle. In the following section, we define these astrological life phases.

To determine your current astrological life phases, find all of the planetary cycles that correspond to your current age. For example, if you are age 60, then you are experiencing both the Jupiter return and Uranus waning square cycles. The ages listed are when the cycle is most potent. Some people experience the effects of the cycles before the ages listed and continue to work with the accompanying life issues after the ages listed.

Because the inner planets (Mercury, Venus, Earth, and Mars) move so quickly around the Sun, their cycles do not carry as much significance as those of the slower-moving planets (Jupiter, Saturn, Uranus, Neptune, and Pluto). So we list only the important life cycles connected to the movements of the slower planets.

Jupiter Cycles: Follow Your Spiritual Truths

Jupiter return cycles are phases of philosophical growth and expansion. During these cycles, you often get opportunities to travel, expand your horizons, and learn about your belief systems. The challenge of Jupiter cycles is not to burn out with too much activity and expansion. In this section, we list only Jupiter's return cycles because they correspond to times in your life when you want to start over with your life direction. The other phases of Jupiter's cycles are not as significant. To determine if you are in any Jupiter return cycles, look to see if your age is listed and read about the issues associated with that cycle.

> ➤ **Return (ages 35–36):** Claiming the wisdom of early adulthood. Consolidate your core belief systems and prepare to transform inauthentic ones. Express your wisdom with confidence and enthusiasm.

> ➤ **Return (ages 47–48):** Musing at midlife about the meaning of it all. Shift and deepen your core belief systems in response to the midlife changes of the last 12 years. Express your wisdom with humility and sensitivity.

➤ **Return (ages 59–60):** Shifting into retirement. Solidify the core belief systems that support the shift into a quieter and more reflective time of your life. As a mentor for younger folks, express your wisdom with maturity and humor.

➤ **Return (ages 71–72):** Sharing the wisdom of the elder. Track the changes in your core belief systems as you age and get closer to death. Share your elder wisdom about aging and trusting the rhythms of life.

➤ **Return (ages 83–84):** Exploring the truth about mortality. Reflect on the core belief systems that assist you to face your mortality. Share your wisdom about surrendering control of the body and the mysteries of mortality.

Sixes and Sevens

Remember that in Greek mythology Jupiter is the god Zeus, ruler of the Olympiads. Zeus is often arrogant and self-righteous as he pursues his own agendas no matter who gets hurt in the process. During a Jupiter cycle, be careful not to get carried away by rigid personal belief systems and thereby hurt yourself and others.

Saturn Cycles: Take Responsibility for Your Life

Saturn cycles are phases in which you take responsibility to manage your life and to be your own authority. The challenge of Saturn cycles is over control, working too hard, and feeling confined and boxed in. To determine any current Saturn life cycles you are in, look for your age to see if it connects to any Saturn cycles near that age. Read about the gifts and challenges of the corresponding cycle to support and guide you in navigating through these cycle.

Merlin's Notes

Ever wonder where the phrase "seven year itch" comes from? Saturn takes about 29 years to complete one orbit around the Sun. That means that approximately every 7 years of your life, Saturn is in one of its key planetary cycles (a return, waning square, opposition, or waxing square) with respect to its position in the sky at your birth. That means you are ready to restructure and make a course correction in your life. So when you are approximately age 7, 14, 21, 28, 35, etc., you are open to making significant changes to your life.

➤ **Return (ages 29–30):** Claiming authority for your life. Claim ownership of your life and cultivate self-responsibility. Confront limitations catalyzed by external authorities. Establish personal authority for life by building a solid foundation in career, relationships, and personal lifestyle.

➤ **Waxing Square (ages 36–37):** Shaking up your foundation. Question the solid foundations established at age 29 to 30. Begin to dismantle inauthentic life structures that are based on family, societal, and cultural rules that are not true to your nature.

➤ **Opposition (ages 43–44):** Redefining your life purpose. Redefine your life direction based on the deep changes you have made since age 36 to 37. Choose authentic ways to be responsible. Make room in your life for the paradoxes and unexpected changes you know will occur in life.

➤ **Waning Square (ages 50–51):** Becoming a mentor. Disseminate the wisdom learned since age 29 to 30. Create solid foundations to support continued healing for self and community. Begin to prepare for the transition into elderhood.

➤ **Return (ages 57–58):** Stepping into elderhood. This is the initiation into full elderhood. An elder is a wise person who mentors younger people by sharing his or her acquired life wisdom. Establish authentic life structures based on the true responsibilities at this phase of your life. Relinquish the obligations to society that are completed (for example, children raised, career goals accomplished, and social tasks handed over to others). Take time to explore and build a spiritual structure in your life.

➤ **Waxing Square (ages 64–65):** Adjusting to time's dance with your body. Explore the status of your physical body. Determine and implement what you need in life structures to sustain and support your body's current aging process.

➤ **Opposition (ages 71–72):** Acknowledging the authority of time. Recognize the authority of the body and its need to continue to prepare for death. Create life structures that support a spiritual foundation for this time of your life. Continue to release responsibilities that are not yours.

➤ **Waning Square (ages 78–79):** Distilling the wisdom of the soul. Surrender more to the changes in your body. Allow your consciousness to rest more deeply on the eternal foundation of your spirit. Recognize that we are not just our physical bodies, but also an eternal soul residing in the body.

➤ **Return (ages 87–88):** Taking it down to the bone. Time to review and honor the past 30 years of your life. Celebrate your accomplishments. Continue to create a spiritual foundation that holds you through your aging process and preparation for death.

Merlin's Notes

Fasten your seat belts for the next part of our ride in the solar system. We're going to the transpersonal planets—Uranus, Neptune, and Pluto. These planets are the farthest away from the Sun and are not visible to the naked eye. Transpersonal means "beyond the personal." The cycles of these planets challenge us to go beyond our conscious ego awareness to explore liberation (Uranus), visioning (Neptune), and death and rebirth (Pluto).

Uranus Cycles: Illuminate and Re-Vision Your Life

Uranus cycles are phases of radical transformation and the quest for individual freedom. During these cycles, you often get opportunities to make sudden changes and to develop hidden or unexpressed parts of yourself. The challenges of Uranus cycles are not to blow up your life as a destructive anarchist or check out with denial because you don't think you can make the necessary changes to live an authentic life.

To determine your current Uranus life cycles, look to see if your age connects to any Uranus cycles near that age. Read about the freedom and liberation issues of the corresponding cycle to support and guide you in navigating through these cycles.

> ➤ **Waxing Square (ages 20–21):** Launching into freedom. Step into early adulthood with courage and excitement. Follow your dreams and explore all the diverse opportunities available to you. You gotta be you and see what's out there.

> ➤ **Opposition (ages 39–40):** Coming out of the closet. Welcome to the phase of the classic mid-life crisis. Integrate radically different aspects of self into your conscious life. Explore other dimensions of you that allow for authentic self-expression. Break free from the self-imposed limitations created so that others wouldn't judge you to be too weird or different.

> ➤ **Waning Square (ages 60–61):** Answering the call of the inner revolution. Confront the ideas about rebellion and liberation that you explored at ages 20 to 21 and ages 39 to 40. Surrender to the inner freedom of being your unique self. Release the need to act out as a cantankerous, angry rebel in your external life.

> ➤ **Return (ages 83–84):** Embracing the ultimate liberation. Time to honor the uniqueness you carry and recognize how you lived your life on your own terms.

Release your hold on the physical world. Recognize that some important task of liberation is complete that weaves together the ages of 20 to 21; 39 to 40; 60 to 62; and now.

Merlin's Notes

And now for something completely different! Uranus is often connected to Prometheus, the figure in Greek myth who stole fire for humankind. In doing so, he rebelled against what he saw as the unjust authorities. Other associations for Uranus are the trickster and the rebel. During a Uranus cycle, reality just isn't what it used to be. Change, chaos, and unexpected surprises often accompany you. If you are under a Uranus cycle, like Prometheus, you may want to rebel against the establishment and what you perceive to be unjust.

Neptune Cycles: Surrender to the Mystery

Neptune cycles are phases of exploring the spiritual and intuitive aspects of reality. During these cycles, you often get opportunities to surrender to the Divine, pursue creative and imaginative projects, and examine issues around personal faith. The challenge of Neptune cycles is to not get caught in unhealthy illusions and become overwhelmed by negative emotions of fear and victim consciousness.

To determine if you are in any Neptune life cycles, see if your age connects to any Neptune cycles near that age. Read about the spiritual gifts and challenges of the corresponding cycle to support and guide you in navigating through these cycles.

➤ **Waxing Square (ages 41–42):** Dissolving illusions, keeping the faith. Explore your relationship to oneness and merging with all life. Forgive yourself and others for past mistakes. Confront self-deceptive patterns. Acknowledge and surrender to the greater mystery of life. Cultivate the artist within. Examine destructive patterns of escapism, addictions, and being a martyr for others.

➤ **Opposition (ages 81–82):** Dream a little dream of eternity. Review the memories and dreams of your life. Just as at ages 41 to 42 when you confronted the dreams that were no longer accurate for you, this is a time to review the dreams and illusions of your life. Surrender more control to the organic rhythms of your body and reflect on compassion and self-forgiveness. Honor your unique relationship to the Divine.

Pluto Cycles: Shed the Old Skins

Pluto cycles are phases of deep life transformation. During these cycles, you often get opportunities to explore sexual and emotional intimacy and to confront your (and others') hidden agendas and manipulative patterns of behavior. You also face your mortality and examine what is truly worth investing in. The challenge of Pluto cycles is not to get obsessed and emotionally violent in your need for change at all costs.

To determine if you are currently in a Pluto life cycles, look to see if your age connects to any Pluto cycles near that age. Read about the issues of power and transformation of the corresponding cycle to support and guide you in navigating through these cycles. Check the information in the Merlin's Notes that follows to clarify how to figure out when the Pluto waxing square cycle occurs for you.

➤ **Waxing Square (ages 36–50):** Metamorphosis. Confront issues of the right use of power. Face and integrate your major shadow aspects (the unexamined parts of yourself that you don't want to look at, like rage, lust, brilliance, and ambition). Begin to deal with mortality. Release the inauthentic self created in response to family and cultural expectations. Tell the emotional truth about who you are and what you want in life.

➤ **Opposition (ages 85–86):** At the gate of mortality. Face your upcoming death with consciousness and honesty. Create ways to feel empowered in your process of preparing for death (no matter how many more years you have left to live). Review and honor the parts of your life that will continue on after your physical death.

Merlin's Notes

Pluto has an unusual orbit around the Sun such that different generations will experience the Pluto waxing square cycle at different times in their lives. For those born in the 1930s, the cycle occurs at age 46 to 48. For those born in the 1940s, the cycle occurs at age 42 to 45. For those born in the 1950s, the cycle occurs at age 37 to 40. For those born in the 1960s and 1970s, the cycle occurs at age 36 to 38. For those born in the 1980s, the cycle occurs at age 39 to 41. For those born in the 1990s, the cycle occurs at age 43 to 50.

The Astrology of Your Personal Year

Use astrology to deepen your understanding of the current Personal Year under which you are living. Match the corresponding astrological sign and planet to the number of your Personal Year. Develop the character associated with the planet as a guide to help you navigate through the challenges of that Personal Year. Use the energy of the sign as a technique or tool for enhancing your ability to live under the number's vibration.

As an example, if you are in a 1 personal year, think of yourself as a scout entering into a brand-new territory of your life. Act like an explorer who is interested in every event or person who crosses your path that year. Cultivate the energy of Aries to take some risks to check out new places in yourself and your world. Be independent and develop your "ram" willfulness.

Easy as 1-2-3

You can explore the link between astrology cycles and your Personal Year. Determine your Personal Year Number. Find the corresponding sign(s) and planets for that number. Determine any astrological life phases connected to your current age.

Also, determine which astrology life phase or phases you are currently living under. Use the key tasks of that phase as supportive actions to perform during your current personal year.

Let's continue the example of the 1 Personal Year. If you are age 57, then you are in a Saturn return cycle. The challenge of this life phase is to release old responsibilities and pursue more spiritual structures in your life. Under the 1 Personal Year vibration, you may decide to retire from your regular work and begin to courageously scout and pursue new interests (like travel, art, volunteer work) that you did not have time for before.

The Astrology of Your Pinnacles

Astrology life phases can give perspective on the current numerology Pinnacle under which you are living. Because a Pinnacle lasts for many years in your life, it helps to know its associated life phases. The key tasks of the astrology life phase give you form and purpose for meeting the challenges of the Pinnacle's lessons.

For example, let's say that you were born in the 1950s and your 7 Pinnacle lasts from ages 35 to 43. First determine the associated astrology life phases for those ages of your Pinnacle. They would include these cycles:

➤ Jupiter return of ages 35 to 36

➤ Saturn waxing square of ages 36 to 37

➤ Pluto waxing square of ages 37 to 40

➤ Uranus opposition of ages 39 to 40

➤ Neptune waxing square of ages 41 to 42

➤ Saturn opposition of ages 43 to 44

Next determine the key themes of your Pinnacle. For the 7 Pinnacle, this means you desire to pull back from life to pursue deeper research and contemplation. The associated challenges of each of the astrology life phases contribute to how you work out and live through the 7 Pinnacle.

For a person in a 7 Pinnacle, during the nine years of their 7 Pinnacle, that person explores his or her inner work and reflection process by

➤ Questioning the belief systems that keep him or her from inner work (Jupiter return)

➤ Changing his or her lifestyle so that he or she can have more time to reflect and pursue research (Saturn waxing square)

➤ Releasing old power games whereby he or she avoids inner work (Pluto waxing square)

➤ Making radical life choices to develop more intuitive and reflective hidden parts of his- or herself (Uranus opposition)

➤ Creating time to dream and reflect by surrendering illusions about his or her identity in the world (waxing Neptune square)

➤ Making significant life-direction changes to incorporate time for contemplation (Saturn opposition)

Using Numerology and Astrology to Help Others

Astrology and numerology are tools to spiritual mysteries that offer profound insight to the uniqueness of a person's life journey. Sometimes you get the opportunity to help others by sharing these insights. You might be a counselor working with clients. You might be a caring friend who opens this book to help someone in a life transition. You might be a person who wants to know and understand more deeply the meaning of your life.

Whatever your reason, you can offer important support to someone by honoring his or her life purpose and cycles. If you have permission to use someone's birth data, determine that person's key numerology numbers and cycles. Look up his or her Sun sign and determine the astrology life phases under which that person is living. Share the knowledge and insights that astrology and numerology can offer to that person about his or her life purpose and cycles. Help that person to know that his or her life has a meaning and is proceeding in accordance with a larger spiritual plan.

The Least You Need to Know

➤ Astrology and numerology are both systems for examining the mysteries of life.

➤ Planets and signs are symbols, like numbers, that help you understand your own nature.

➤ Every astrological planet and sign corresponds to one or more numbers in numerology.

➤ Astrology's cycles and numerology's cycles can help you understand your life cycles.

Relationships by the Numbers

By now, it should come as no surprise that your relationships can be better understood when you look at what numbers you and your family or friends have in common—as well as what numbers are different for each of you. In fact, how you and someone else will act and react in a relationship can be determined if you know how to read the numbers.

Some numbers have natural relationships as well, and, if you know your basic arithmetic, you already know what these Concords are: the 3, 6, and 9; the 1, 5, and 7; and the 2, 4, and 8. Each of these three triads of three numbers has a special emphasis, one more numerological aspect that you can learn to use to your relationship advantage.

Finding Your Soul Mate

There are some really simple formulas to use when it comes to finding the best relationships. For example

➤ When it comes to close, heartfelt relationships, you'll want to look to the Soul Number.

➤ For working with someone, you'll look to the Life Path Number and the Destiny Number.

➤ To see if you'll get along with someone, the Personality Number is the one to check.

Sixes and Sevens

The Personality Number will give you an idea of how someone behaves and comes across in public life, but don't go signing on the dotted line when you're looking for a deep, soul-mate relationship. For that—look to the soul—the Soul Number, that is.

➤ If you're curious about growing old together, look to the Maturity Number and the Personality Number. (After all, if you can't stand your partner's personality, why spend all those years with him or her?)

➤ If you want a spiritual relationship, look to the Soul Number—and especially for numbers 7, 9, or 11/2.

➤ If you want a partner you can count on to bring home the bacon and put a roof over your head, then look for a 4, 6, or 8 Life Path Number, or a 4 Destiny Number.

➤ If you're looking to play, live in a creative environment, and laugh your way through life, then look for a 3 Personality Number or a 3 Soul Number.

Looking for Love in All the Right Places

All kinds of things will affect your relationship choices, including karmic lessons and the Major Cycle and Pinnacle Numbers, which will show what the climate is for settling down for life. In addition, the Challenge Number will tell you what Mr. or Ms. Right is struggling with, and ultimately what he or she must learn and grow into.

Merlin's Notes

When it comes to compatibility, look at the 5 core numbers as indicators of the essential elements of the person you want to understand. If you are trying to find somebody who is compatible, look to their 5 core numbers. If you want to know if the timing is right, or what the future holds, look at the Pinnacle/Challenge, Major Cycle, and Personal Year Numbers.

If you want to know if your new love interest can be loyal, open-minded, and appreciative, look to the numbers in both the Personality Number and the Soul Number. A 4, 6, or 9 would be nice for these qualities, for example. If, on the other hand, you want someone who'll be compliant, supportive, and loving, find yourself a 2 Personality or Soul Number.

When you look at compatibility, there are several ways to examine your compatibility quotient. The most compatible of all is when you're evenly matched—Soul to Soul.

Every number can be counted on to have specific needs, and once you understand what each number's special needs are, you'll understand your potential for compatibility with a person who has that number. Here's a chart to help you evaluate the compatibility quotient of each number.

Sixes and Sevens

People who share a master number can have many similarities, but they will also both share the intensity and sensitivity of the master number. It is not a match made in heaven.

Number	Needs
1	Needs to be an individual and can be willful
2	Needs cooperation and peace
3	Self-expression is a must and is compelled to pursue its creativity
4	Will work hard and expects discipline
5	Wants change and to feel free
6	Needs to feel responsible, to be of service, and to feel needed
7	Focus is on gaining wisdom and is detached, introspective, and silent
8	Focus is on power and achievement
9	Needs to express compassion, is altruistic, and has strong emotions
11/2	Needs to inspire others and is intense
22/4	Needs to have a purpose, to be building something, and is intense
33/6	Needs to be saving the world, rescuing lost souls, teaching others how to love, and is emotionally intense

Master Number Relationships

Master numbers are thought to be more charged, with a stronger energy present. To say the least, a master number is intense. Therefore, the person with the master number most likely won't remain at the intense level of the higher vibration (11, 22, or 33), but will revert to its lower vibration (2, 4, or 6). By operating at the lower frequency, the master number person will be easier to live with, but, be forewarned, that person must address these master level energies, so it will be a life of constant ups and downs.

Merlin's Notes

If you have a master number as one of your 5 core numbers and want to team up with someone else with a master number, expect the relationship to be both intense and volatile. On the other hand, you two will share an understanding that's not available to those who don't have a master number in their charts. Most likely, a two-master-number relationship will be spiritually connected, and you both will be leaders. It could be the most alive, high-energy, intense experience of your life! Remember, all of the master numbers are charming and have a poise about them, which is what attracts people to them in the first place. You just have to be up for intensity if you're going to have a significant relationship with another master number person.

A Match Made in Heaven

In this section, we'll be talking about matching numbers, that is, when your number *matches* the number of someone else who has your same number in the same place in the 5 core numbers.

Easy as 1-2-3

It's simple: If you're looking for someone to be your lifetime companion, choose someone with your same Soul Number. In fact, matching Soul Numbers are the most significant of all of the compatibility indicators. The trick is finding him or her!

If it's a permanent, committed relationship you're looking for, or one where you feel truly understood, then you'll want to look for the Soul Number. Remember, the Soul Number is also called the "heart's desire" number, and it's precisely the matter of the heart we're talking about here.

When the Soul Number is the same for both of you, there's a strong emotional tie. It suggests that you both want the same things in your heart of hearts. When you have the same Soul Number as another, in fact, it strongly suggests a long-time love relationship, and even though other circumstances may cause problems or separation, the bond here goes on, because the tie between two similar Soul Numbers is a spiritual one, and possibly even a past-life relationship.

Note that if you have a similar number in your chart to one of your mate's, but not in the same core position, then there's still a good degree of compatibility, because you both understand each other through the characteristics of that number.

Life Matches

The next most important number to consider for compatibility is the Life Path Number. When two people share the same Life Path Number, it points to a happy relationship with many shared interests. This association may have its roots in work or social interests connected to work, because the Life Path Number indicates successful use for your inherent talents. With similar Life Path Numbers, in fact, you and your partner can expect to find similar talents and abilities. Look to the specific number for details.

Your Life Path Number tells of the path you'll travel in this lifetime, and with a love interest who has the same Life Path Number, you might expect to share a similar journey in life. While this attraction may lead to marriage, however, it doesn't promise smooth waters, because it's what's in your hearts (your Soul Number) that will determine the depth of understanding.

Destiny Matches

The next important number to consider for compatibility is the Destiny Number. When two people share the same Destiny Number, the relationship may be comparatively happy because they live on the same level, have similar backgrounds, come from similar environments, and are headed in a similar direction. Even though this can be a comparatively happy marriage, there will need to be other similar points of attraction in order for this flame to be a lasting fire.

Maturity Matches

The last significant number to consider in finding a true love is the tie between two who share matched Maturity Numbers. Usually, when this is the matching number, it suggests a late-life marriage, so you'd want to share this number with your mate if you're wondering about the later years of life and the ultimate goal for your lives.

Personality Matches?

The Personality Number isn't considered an indicator of successful love relationships because this number shows the external person, rather than what's in the heart. In fact, relationships based on Personality Number compatibility may feel great at first, but generally don't have the staying power of the other combinations. You know the old saying, "Don't judge a book by it's

Sixes and Sevens

While we wouldn't recommend basing a marriage on matching Personality Numbers, we would strongly recommend that you look at your mate's Personality Number anyway, because it will tell you a lot about what it will be like to live with this person.

cover"? Well, we want to encourage you to follow this advice, and to look more deeply than the Personality Number for your soul mate.

Compatibility by the Numbers

What if you add up your and your mate's numbers and find that each of you have all different numbers? Naturally, you're wondering about the degree of compatibility you share. The secret is in the differences—the mathematical difference in your numbers.

> **Numerology Rule #21**
>
> When figuring the compatibility differences between two people, subtract the numbers to find the key to resolving the difference.

Some numerologists call this number the *stress number,* because it shows the nature of the stress in a particular combination. For instance, if you have a 2 Soul Number and your mate has a 9 Soul Number, the stress will be the issues of the difference between these two numbers or $9 - 2 = 7$. The stress number here is 7. Therefore, you'd want to bone up on the number 7 to understand its positive and negative energy and to determine which of each you're exhibiting.

Most likely, negative energy is being expressed if there's conflict between you, so you would want to look at the negative energies of all of the numbers involved, such as the 9, 2, and 7 in our example, and then look to the positive qualities of each of these numbers and begin to emphasize the positive aspects, particularly the positive qualities of your difference number, in this case, the 7.

Let's look at an example. Let's say you have a 4 Soul Number and your significant other has a 5 Soul Number. The difference between these numbers is 1 $(5 - 4)$, so the key to resolving differences will be in understanding that you must work together to honor the characteristics of the 1: independence, desire to lead and do things your way, a need to be self-reliant, and a need to assert yourselves. These are the traits you'll want to foster in each other for the 4 Soul to feel secure, and for the 5 Soul to feel she can be free to change things.

By the Numbers

Finding the **stress number,** the mathematical difference between any of your core numbers and another's, can help you understand which energies you need to focus on to improve your relationship.

Of course, it will help enormously if you study the characteristics of each number. For this, you'll want to review the chapters on the meanings of each of your numbers earlier in this book. In addition to self-knowledge, you can gain valuable insight into your partner's needs. For example, if a 5 Soul doesn't understand that security and stability are vital to the 4, then you won't experience compatibility—at least not on issues such as a steady income, accountability, and doing what you say.

Using Your Differences to Your Advantage

So—what's the difference? Once you know, you can use it to your—and your relationship's—advantage. Consider the following for differences between any of the numbers in your charts.

➤ **When 1 is the difference:** You'll need to honor the need for independence and individuality in the relationship.

➤ **When 2 is the difference:** You'll need to be sensitive to the person with the 2, and minimize conflict in the relationship. Honoring each other's sensitive points and working together as a team is key.

➤ **When 3 is the difference:** You'll need to communicate—communicate honestly, with no pushing anything under the rug. You'll have to say your truth and make it safe for the emotions that have been locked away to surface.

➤ **When 4 is the difference:** You'll need to resist the urge to be inflexible and rigid (especially) if you're the one with the 4 number. Instead, learn to set good boundaries, and keep them with love and kindness. There's hard work here, and you'll have to discipline yourselves to make this relationship work.

➤ **When 5 is the difference:** Change is required here—honest, well-thought-out change. One or both of you may have an extreme need for freedom, and, with this number, you'll have to find a way to give each other that sense of freedom without compromising the integrity of the relationship.

➤ **When 6 is the difference:** You'll have to give up stubbornness and dogmatic opinions. Something's out of balance when a 6 is the difference number. Restore the balance immediately for love is at stake. You may also be learning about the depth and commitment of love and about being truly responsible.

➤ **When 7 is the difference:** You'll need to honor the need to be alone, to have private time, and to examine the spiritual or lack of spiritual consciousness in the relationship.

➤ **When 8 is the difference.** There are power struggles with this number, and you'll need to empower each other rather than struggle with who'll be the boss. You'll want to work on softening your response to each other, and to find a new plan for the business of this relationship.

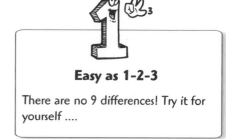

Easy as 1-2-3

There are no 9 differences! Try it for yourself ....

Compatibility with Others

When it's not a love relationship you're analyzing, but rather you're curious about other types of relating, such as sibling relationship, mother/daughter, father/son, father/daughter, mother/son, boss/coworker, or even best friend relationships, examining the other person's numbers will give you tremendous insight into what you can expect (and what you can't expect) from this relationship. You can determine how compatible you'll be with others by looking at the 5 core numbers of someone's chart and comparing them to your own.

Here are the matches to look for:

➤ Personality-Personality

➤ Destiny-Destiny

➤ Life Path-Life Path

➤ Soul-Soul

➤ Maturity-Maturity

Use your differences to your advantage by understanding your numbers. If some of them are similar, there will be a greater basis for understanding and sharing complementary attitudes about life.

Looking at What's Going On in Both Your Lives

After you have both of your 5 core numbers figured out, it's time to look at where each of you are in life. You might then want to look at how this time in life is going: What goals are important, what challenges need to be faced, and what Personal Year each of you is in now. It's especially fun (and informative, to say the least) to look to the following as indicators of what's cooking for your person of interest:

➤ **Personal Year.** This number tells what the immediate issues are, as well as what this year has in store for the other person. Compare this number with your own. Are you able to commit to that person when he or she has this kind of year coming up? What about next year?

For example, if your guy has a 6 year coming up, or is in a 6 year, and you aren't talking marriage yet, you'll want to note two things: First, marriage or making a commitment may be the agenda for this 6 year; second, if marriage isn't it, then you should know that this 6 year will require your love to give most of his time and energy to his family, because family obligations and responsibilities govern this year. And no, it's not negotiable.

➤ **Pinnacle.** For compatibility purposes, it's very valuable to look at what your mate will need to expend his energy on in this cycle in his life. Remember, a Pinnacle is at least nine years long. You'll want to consider what's to be achieved, as well as how to time certain events and plans. For this, consult the Pinnacle Number of your partner. If the number you find on the current Pinnacle is the same as yours, then you'll have greater understanding and similar goals. But if the number is different, then you'll want to study the meaning of his Pinnacle for clues about what to expect.

For example, if you're in a 7 Pinnacle and your love is in a 7 Pinnacle, too, you'll know that this will be a cycle of introspection, soul searching, and carefully evaluating the directions of both of your lives. You shouldn't expect this to be a time for raising a family, building an empire together, or entertaining hordes of people. Instead, it's a quiet time, and anyone with a 7 Pinnacle will be moving toward more solitude, time alone, and quiet activities—at least that's the natural flow of energy. Now, if that's not the way one of these 7s is living it, then you can expect that person to be out of sorts, and possibly to develop health issues.

It is also important to note that other numbers influence this Pinnacle number. Look to the Major Cycle Number, the Challenge Number, and the Destiny Number for clues about other influences.

Merlin's Notes

If you're in an 8 Pinnacle and your sweetie is in a 7 Pinnacle, you'll have to make some adjustments. The 8 Pinnacle will be moving out into the world—especially the business world—and will be working toward accomplishing recognition and material wealth, while the 7 won't find these pursuits to be his or her cup of tea. In this case, it will be best if the two of you honor the compatibility rule: Find the difference between your numbers and work from there. For the 8 and 7 Pinnacles, the difference is a 1, the number of individuality, so let the 8 have its independence to pursue the business world, and let the 7 pursue its introspective analysis. Then, you can meet at the end of the day and compare notes! The key is to honor the individual path each of you is on.

Exploring Your Compatibility Ratings

So which numbers work best together? In the following sections, we've listed each pairing of numbers and give you a quick assessment of how they'll do together. In addition, we thought it would be fun to come up with some compatibility ratings, a grading system you can use to see if you and your potential partner match up when you share the same number—whether Soul to Soul or Pinnacle to Pinnacle. Use the following list to find what each grade means.

You may apply any of the 5 core numbers or the timing numbers: Pinnacle/Challenge, Major Cycle, or Personal Year Numbers to establish a compatibility rating. In fact, why not check out all of them? Then you will have a complete picture of just how compatible you two are.

The compatibility ratings are designed to be used for both love relationships and business relationships. Feel free to use this information for any and all of your many relationships.

➤ A = the best, most compatible

➤ B = good success in the relationship

➤ C = average relationship

➤ D = poor combination for the relationship

The 1s in Relationships

You may notice that the 1s aren't necessarily compatible in an overall sense, unless they can have their own way.

➤ **1:1** Each of you is trying to become an individual of his or her own making. Personal = B, Business rating = B.

➤ **1:2** One person follows, the other leads. Good personal relationship if both of you agree to this type of relationship; excellent business relationship because what one lacks the other provides; excellent combo. Personal = B, Business = A.

➤ **1:3** Lots of creative ideas spring to life with this combination. B.

➤ **1:4** One person leads, the other manages; nice combo for business (see 1:2), but in the personal arena, it doesn't work; they're just too different. Personal = D, Business = B.

➤ **1:5** Both independent, the 1 initiates, the 5 promotes and sells, both move at the speed of light. Great for business but not for a personal relationship, mainly because of the high degree of change that dominates the duo. Four is the difference. Personal = C, Business = A.

➤ **1:6** Both want to be the creative one, but this combo has the potential for a good relationship, both in business and love life. B.

➤ **1:7** Works only if you recognize in one another the need to be alone. C.

➤ **1:8** Need separate areas to be in charge of. Good for a business partnership but not so good for cozying up and making a nest. Personal = C, Business = A.

➤ **1:9**   Brilliant ideas from both, wisdom of the 9 balances the leadership of the 1. Excellent combo for business and a great one for personal relationship—as long as both are secure in their own senses of authority. Personal = A, Business = A.

The 2s in Relationships

The 2 is the number of relationships, so it does well with just about anyone—but especially with another 2.

➤ **2:1**   See 1:2. Personal = A, Business = B.

➤ **2:2**   Evenly matched for harmony, but each is very sensitive. You were meant for each other, because no one understands you like another 2. Personal = A, Business = C.

➤ **2:3**   A winning duo if the 2 is willing to play second to the 3. Very social combo; neither is strong as a business number. Personal = B, Business = C.

➤ **2:4**   Harmonious, 2 covers the details, 4 manages and builds things up, an even flow of energy. Personal = B, Business = B.

➤ **2:5**   One wants to go, the other wants to wait. Personal and Business = D.

➤ **2:6**   The 6 will be in charge at home, the 2 will look to the details and support, but not a great business combo. However, it's a very loving personal relationship. Personal = B, Business = D.

➤ **2:7**   Could make it work if focus is on spiritual, metaphysical relationship, otherwise it conflicts. Personal = B, Business = D (business is too demanding for these numbers).

➤ **2:8**   This duo can live and work well together. They attract money through honesty, industriousness, and reliability. The 8 leads, the 2 follows. Personal and Business = B.

➤ **2:9**   A winning team. Wisdom, insight, and careful management of details with these two. Together, they'll put things right in the world. Personal = A, Business = B.

Easy as 1-2-3

You may recall that the 2 is *the* relationship number, so 2s tend to be compatible with just about everyone.

The 3s in Relationships

The 3 relates in a burst of enthusiasm, and optimism but doesn't necessarily have what it takes to create a long-lasting relationship.

➤ **3:1**   See 1:3. B.

➤ **3:2**   See 2:3. Personal = B, Business = C.

➤ **3:3** A risky venture. Too impulsive, spontaneous, into the enthusiasm of the moment, but no long-lasting aspects to draw from. Flighty, reckless, and trusting too much to luck. This relationship doesn't stand a chance! Personal = D, Business = D.

➤ **3:4** Here's a rub. Serious 4 won't appreciate playful 3, although the 3 will fun up the 4. Personal = C, Business = C.

➤ **3:5** The 5 knows how to market the idea and the 3 knows how to package it in a creative fun way; but for love, hastiness and impatience are the main ingredients. Personal = C, Business = B.

➤ **3:6** This duo can be partners for life, but both are very emotional numbers, which can stress a relationship. Personal = B, Business = B.

➤ **3:7** If space is given, this one works. The 3 gives energy and the 7 gives understanding. Personal and Business = B.

➤ **3:8** The 3 is the communicator, the 8 is enterprising, but their combined big ideas don't make for a solid personal relationship. Personal = C, Business = A.

➤ **3:9** Very compatible, but idealistic in nature, so let's hope you don't have to work for a living. Practicality isn't operative with these two. Personal = A, Business = D.

The 4s in Relationships

You may notice that because the 4 is so solid, it will get along with many combinations, except for those numbers right next to it, the 3 and the 5.

➤ **4:1** See 1:4. Personal = D, Business = B.

➤ **4:2** See 2:4. B.

➤ **4:3** See 3:4. C.

Sixes and Sevens

Here's an interesting tidbit: When two numbers are next to each other, generally they are incompatible. For example, 4 and 5, 6 and 7, or 2 and 3 most likely won't get along well. In any case, there's a rub.

➤ **4:4** Good business partners, but short on emotional expression. Inflexibility can get in the way of romantic relating. You'll share same the same goals and both of you enjoy making a plan and building a relationship based on solid values. Emotions are kept in close control with this duo. Personal = B, Business = A.

➤ **4:5** The 4 is working hard, planning for the future, setting down roots, while the 5 wants to be unencumbered, to travel, to be free of responsibility. D.

➤ **4:6** This is a difficult combination: The 6 is very responsible, and the 4 is disciplined and follows the plan well; but both are doing such hard work they may have very little time to actually relate to each other. Personal = C, Business = B.

➤ **4:7**   Both are serious, so while the 7 is analyzing, the 4 can be working out the plan, but this will be a dull time, so look to the difference. The difference is 3, so what will bring harmony to this relationship cycle is to have fun from time to time and to learn to say what's in the heart. B.

➤ **4:8**   Excellent combo, wonderfully balanced. The 8 sees the big picture, the 4 sees the details, both are productive and practical. They see things from the same perspective and work hard for business, but not a romantic combination. Personal = B, Business = A.

➤ **4:9**   Wisdom and practicality match these two. A better private relationship than business one, but things will move slowly in both situations. B.

The 5s in Relationships

You may notice that the 5s can have trouble with relationships, mainly because of their high need for freedom and their unwillingness to make commitments.

➤ **5:1**   See 1:5. Personal = C, Business = A.

➤ **5:2**   See 2:5. D.

➤ **5:3**   See 3:5. Personal = C, Business = B.

➤ **5:4**   See 4:5. D.

➤ **5:5**   A dangerous combo. With a changeable heart, rebellious nature, and reckless outlook, this potentially explosive relationship should be avoided if at all possible. Personal = D, Business = D.

➤ **5:6**   Excitable 5 meets home-loving 6 and both undergo change. Can bring conflict unless the 5 is older and ready to settle down. Otherwise, a stressful combo. C.

➤ **5:7**   Both will be involved in investigating, examining where they're headed but one will want to be "out there" and the other "in there." Personal = D, Business = C.

➤ **5:8**   Excellent for business; the 5 networks and promotes, the 8 organizes and executes the plan for profit. As a love relationship, excellent while it lasts. Personal = B, Business = A.

➤ **5:9**   Two dreamers but different motives. Both focused on the world stage, this combo has possibilities. B.

The 6s in Relationships

Sixes in relationship blossom (except in the combo 6:7). Nurturing and loving, this number is at home in relating to others.

➤ **6:1** See 1:6. B.

➤ **6:2** See 2:6. Personal = B, Business = D.

➤ **6:3** See 3:6. B.

➤ **6:4** See 4:6. Personal = B, Business = C.

➤ **6:5** See 5:6. C.

➤ **6:6** Domestic bliss for this duo, with interests focusing mainly on the home and family, not on business. While the 6 is a good business number, when teamed with another 6, the focus shifts to being predominately about domesticity. Personal = A, Business = C.

➤ **6:7** The conflict here is that the 6 wants to focus on family and romance while the 7 wants to be left alone to focus inward. D.

➤ **6:8** Goals are clearly defined; 8 leads, 6 supports and nurtures. An excellent pairing for domestic life, and a good prognosis for business. Personal = A, Business = B.

➤ **6:9** An excellent combo—and special relationship. The 6 loves beauty, 9 loves truth, both know how to give and take. This relationship rarely breaks up. Personal = A, Business = A.

The 7s in Relationships

You may notice with the 7s, relating is not their thing. Detached, aloof, and living in a world of their own making, 7s aren't as good at relating as are some of the other numbers, but like all humans, they need love, too.

Sixes and Sevens

The 7:7 couple seldom argues, because they're in tune with each other, but they each live in their own worlds, and as a couple they live in a world of their own choosing—a private one. They'll need a more materialistic view to function well in the real world.

➤ **7:1** See 1:7. C.

➤ **7:2** See 2: 7. Personal = B, Business = D.

➤ **7:3** See 3:7. B.

➤ **7:4** See 4:7. B.

➤ **7:5** See 5:7. Personal = D, Business = C.

➤ **7:6** See 6:7. D.

➤ **7:7** Can be understanding of each other's need for solitude, will give each other space but can also be aloof and detached, therefore not really present in the relationship, but they understand each other like no other. Personal = A, Business = D.

➤ **7:8** Both visionary, excellent for business, especially technology, and research. Good personal duo if the 8 isn't too domineering and 7 gets time alone. Personal = B, Business = A.

➤ **7:9** Both share intuitive insights, and while the 7 will specialize, the 9 will dream of the next phase. Both are spiritual numbers. Personal = A, Business = C.

The 8s in Relationships

Eights are good with relationships as long as they can be the boss, and can fit their partners into their busy plan!

➤ **8:1** See 1:8. A.

➤ **8:2** See 2:8. B.

➤ **8:3** See 3:8. Personal = C, Business = A.

➤ **8:4** See 4:8. Personal = B, Business = A.

➤ **8:5** See 5:8. A.

➤ **8:6** See 6:8. Personal = A, Business = B.

➤ **8:7** See 7:8. Personal = A, Business = C.

➤ **8:8** This combo has the potential to be all about business and can be an unstoppable team; however, with issues of power, authority, and success as top interests, it can be a destructive relationship, with many power struggles and mixed priorities. Personal = C, Business = A.

➤ **8:9** Both can be visionary, both can be involved with projects that affect the larger good. In private, they bring out the best in each other. Good relationship potential here. B.

The 9s in Relationships

The very loving 9 is definitely relationship-oriented, although 9s may be a bit distant and lost in their dreams.

➤ **9:1** See 1:9. A.

➤ **9:2** See 2:9. A.

➤ **9:3** See 3:9. Personal = B, Business = D.

➤ **9:4** See 4:9. B.

➤ **9:5** See 5:9. B.

➤ **9:6** See 6:9. A.

➤ **9:7** See 7:9. Personal = A, Business = C.

➤ **9:8** See 8:9. B.

➤ **9:9** Together, you'll use your wisdom, imagination, and knowledge to benefit humanity. This is an excellent match, and people who share 9s often remain together for life. Personal = A, Business = B.

Remember, you have more than one number to consider when evaluating your compatibility quotient. After all, you are more than one number—and so are your potential partners and current flames!

Numbers That Are Most Incompatible

Some numbers simply don't get along. Here's a quick list of combinations to ponder. You might want to think twice before wandering off into the sunset together with combos like these.

Matches That Aren't Made in Heaven

1:4	4:3	5:6	7:5
1:7	4:5	5:7	7:6
2:5	5:2	6:5	
2:7	5:5	7:1	
3:3			

Some Other Measures of Compatibility

When you're considering compatibility with another, don't forget about the Challenge Number. This number is valuable for looking at the lessons your sweetie is learning: These are his or her weaknesses. It's here you'll find the theme of the person's shortcomings, so you'll want to use the same number analysis we've just shown, to help determine compatible Challenges.

As indicators of large spans of time, the Major Cycles are valuable tools also for understanding where your mate is headed and if you can match lifestyle choices and major decisions for the life you each want. Here's a quick look at what to expect during each Major Cycle.

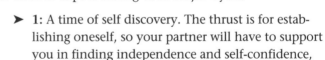

Sixes and Sevens

When there's a 1 and a 6, the issue will be self versus others: The 1 thinks of him- or herself, while the 6 will be concerned for the family and others. Needless to say, this causes all kinds of conflict. Don't forget to figure the difference. In this case, it's a 5, so change and personal freedom are the key to compromise.

➤ **1:** A time of self discovery. The thrust is for establishing oneself, so your partner will have to support you in finding independence and self-confidence, or it will be best for you to go this one solo.

➤ **2:** A time for partnering and learning from relationship. However, it's a very sensitive time as well.

➤ **3:** A time for creativity and self-expression. If your partner can't support you on this, don't expect to stay in relationship.

➤ **4:** A time for putting down roots, building a business or career, having a family, buying a house, and learning the attendant managerial skills.

➤ **5:** A time for exploring what the world holds for you. Change, moving around, and uncertain circumstances dominate this period in your life, unless it's the last cycle, then it's a time for enjoying the world and traveling to all parts of the globe. But you've gotta love travel and change.

➤ **6:** A time for marriage and family, for divorce and children, for teaching/counseling careers, and for creating a happy heart and happy home.

➤ **7:** A time for learning, study, research, specialization, to be with nature, and turning inward to the inner landscape. A great need for solitude, spiritual questing, and gaining of wisdom. Teaching and sharing the wisdom is a part of this cycle.

➤ **8:** A time for expansion, enterprise, and recognition. Business holds the key, as does acquisition of material wealth. A time to come into your own power, and discover your authentic self. You will have metaphysical and spiritual interests as well during this cycle.

➤ **9:** A time for humanitarian service, tolerance, compassion, and universal love. A time of spiritual and artistic development. You are focused on perfecting your ideals under this cycle. You'll receive great rewards and enrichment in this period of life.

Your Overall Compatibility Score

We thought you might enjoy trying an analysis of your relationship with your sweetie, boss, daughter, or whomever. You'll need to have handy the core numbers, Pinnacle Numbers, Challenge Numbers, and Major Cycle Numbers for both of you.

To find your compatibility rating, first set up a chart with each of your number combinations noted. Then, refer to the personal rating grades we gave to the various possible combinations we showed you in the previous section. Enter on your chart the grades we gave your particular combinations. Then, fill in the number equivalent for each grade. We've set up a sample compatibility rating chart to show you how it all works.

First, here's a table showing you the number equivalent for each grade and what each grade means. We call the number equivalent the grade point average or GPA.

How Does Your Relationship Rate?

Grade	GPA	Assessment
A	4.0	Excellent
B	3.0	Good
C	2.0	Average
D	1.0	Poor—don't go there!

Now take a look at this sample chart to see how see how your chart will look after it's completely filled out.

A Sample Compatibility Rating Chart

Position	His:Her	Grade	GPA	Notes
Soul	7:7	A	4.0	
Destiny	5:3	C	2.0	(good business)
Personality	5:7	D	1.0	
Life Path	4:4	B	3.0	(good business)
Maturity	9:7	A	4.0	
Pinnacle	1:7	D	1.0	
Challenge	2:2	A	4.0	
Major Cycle	6:6	A	4.0	
Total		B–	2.8 (23 ÷ 8 = 2.8)	

Here's how we arrive at 2.8 total GPA. We divide the total GPA score (23) by 8, so the total compatibility score for this couple is 2.8. Because 2.8 is not quite a B, this relationship's compatibility falls somewhere between a B and a C. We might say that this couple has a B– or C+ personal relationship (which isn't good enough if you want to be truly happy). It would be an even better business relationship, as our notes indicate. Got the idea?

We're sure you'll want to set up your own chart for major relationships, so we've provided a blank form to do just that.

Personal Compatibilities

	Your Numbers	Your Significant Other's Numbers	Difference
Soul	_____	_____	_____
Destiny	_____	_____	_____
Personality	_____	_____	_____
Life Path	_____	_____	_____
Maturity	_____	_____	_____
Birthday	_____	_____	_____

Concords

In numerology, there are certain groups of numbers that naturally belong together. These are called Concords, and there are three of them. Each Concord has three numbers in it, three numbers which have similar characteristics. For this reason, Concords are another measurement of compatibility.

The *Concords,* three separate groups of numbers that belong together, tell of a natural affinity for one another. Because these numbers go together naturally, it's useful to consider the Birthday Number of a would-be partner to see what group or Concord his or her number belongs to.

The three Concords are:

Group #1 = 3 – 6 – 9

Group #2 = 1 – 5 – 7

Group #3 = 2 – 4 – 8

Look at these three Concords and select the one which reduces to your Birthday Number. This is your Concord, your own number group. It is here that you will find like-minded kindred souls and compatible friends. For example, if your Birthday Number is a 6 or reduces to a 6 and your friend, love interest, or partner is born on the 12th (1 + 2 = 3) of any month, both of you belong to Concord group #1. This suggests that you will have shared interests in the artistic, creative, and inspirational, and both of you will approach life from an emotional perspective.

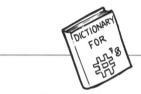

By the Numbers

Concords are three sets of three numbers that naturally belong together. The concords are: 3, 6, 9; 1, 5, 7; and 2, 4, 8. Concords tell where friends can be found.

The Concords

Each of the three Concords is a set of three numbers:						
9			7		8	
3	6	1	5	2		4

Now that you have found your Concord, let's look at the meaning of these number groups.

Inspirational, Spiritual, and Artistic: The Numbers 3, 6, and 9

These are the motivational teachers, the artists, the creative arts people, and the spiritual directors of our world, the numbers of those who resonate to matters of spiritual and artistic interest. Inspired by others with these numbers as well as inspirational themselves, these numbers are creative and emotional. You'll want to look to those who share these numbers for a heart-felt connection.

Anyone with a 3, 6, 9, 12, 15, 18, 21, 24, 27, or 30 Birthday Number will find comfort and kinship in this tribe.

Scientific, Intellectual, and Technological: The Numbers 1, 5, and 7

These are the thinkers, the intellects, and the analytical ones, and they all share an innate love of learning, are curious, and want to be informed. Look to these numbers for the analytical types, the science guys and gals, the techies (and Trekkies), and the computer whizzes. But even without a specialized field, these numbers crave mental stimulation. Look to those who share these numbers for good stimulating conversation—and someone who thinks like you do. When they're at a loss for words, just give them a good book to read—they'll love it.

Anyone with a 1, 5, 7, 10, 14, 16, 19, 23, 25, or 28 Birthday Number will find like minds here.

Business, Money, and Management: The Numbers 2, 4, and 8

These are the workers of the world, and they own, operate, manage, and build the business world. Stable, efficient, and business minded, these are the practical ones. In addition, they're the ones who have trouble expressing their emotions. Look to those with these numbers for compatibility in business, for feeling grounded, for stability, and for career considerations. When your life needs order or you need to get back on track, the numbers in this concord will help you refocus. Members of this concord find solace in each other's no-nonsense approach to life.

Anyone with a 2, 4, 8, 11, 13, 17, 20, 22, 26, 29, or 31 Birthday Number will find similar ability and temperament here.

No matter which of the three Concords you belong to, you will find likeness and similarity with others in your number group. Concord compatibilites show similar approaches to life.

Figuring Your Own Compatibility Quotient

Here's a worksheet for you to see just how compatible—or incompatible—the two of you are. You may want to copy this worksheet to use for more than one relationship.

Compatibilities Worksheet

Concords

My Birthday Number (reduced) is: _____

My **concord** group is _____. My most compatible group is: spiritual/artistic, intellectual, or business (circle one).

My significant other's **concord** is _____ . Most compatible group: spiritual/artistic, intellectual, or business (circle one).

Compatible Cycles

Pinnacles: Mine   1st _____   2nd _____   3rd _____   4th _____

His/Hers   1st _____   2nd _____   3rd _____   4th _____

Areas of concern: _____

Areas where we match: _____

Challenges: Mine   1st _____   2nd _____   3rd _____   4th _____

His/Hers   1st _____   2nd _____   3rd _____   4th _____

My lesson and challenge for this cycle is: _____

_____

My significant other's lesson and challenge for this cycle is:

_____

_____

Major Cycle

My **Major Cycle** at this time is: _____

My significant other's **Major Cycle** at this time is: _____

My next **Major Cycle** is: _____

My significant other's next **Major Cycle** is: _____

Personal Year

At this time I am in a _____ **Personal Year.**

My significant other is in a _____ **Personal Year.**

Five Core Numbers

My **Soul Number** is: _____

My significant other's **Soul number** is: _____

The difference between our numbers is: _____

Our compatibility quotient at the soul level is: _____

continues

continued

My **Destiny Number** is: _____

My significant other's **Destiny Number** is: _____

The difference between our numbers is: _____

Our compatibility quotient at the destiny level is: _____

My **Personality Number** is: _____

My significant other's **Personality Number** is: _____

The difference between our numbers is: _____

Our compatibility quotient as personalities is: _____

My **Life Path Number** is: _____

My significant other's **Life Path Number** is: _____

The difference between our numbers is: _____

Our compatibility quotient for life paths is: _____

My **Maturity Number** is: _____

My significant other's **Maturity Number** is: _____

The difference between our numbers is: _____

Our compatibility quotient for maturity is: _____

*Now that you have filled in the Compatibilities Worksheet, you can see the strengths and weaknesses of your relationship. Keep in mind that all of the numbers have positive and negative aspects. In any partnership, the challenge is to understand the essence of each individual in the duo. Once you know both of your numbers, you can begin to balance your differences and make better unions and better choices.

A Final Note on Relationships and Compatibility Numbers

No one we know of has found the secret formula for the perfect relationship. The mystery of love is truly a mystery. The numbers don't cause things to happen, they merely indicate the energy available for a given period of time, or assist in character analysis. As you know, there are many more factors at work than just the numbers.

For instance, not only are your numbers influencing a situation, but you have personal astrological influences at work, as well as biorhythms, personality preferences, and skill (or a lack of it) in communication. We're only just beginning to understand how the mind-body connection influences our lives, to say nothing of our relationships. After all, if you don't feel well, what kind of a connection will you be able to make with another?

Numerology is only one of a vast array of resources you have available to you to discover how to read the signs for compatibility. Still, using numerology will help you form healthy relationships. Try it and see!

The Least You Need to Know

➤ Looking to the numbers of relationships can help you find the best matches.

➤ Finding compatibility with others is one more potent aspects of numerology.

➤ Concords are numbers that have a natural affinity for each other.

➤ The numbers next to each other usually have conflict.

Chapter 29

Names: A Rose by Any Other Name Might Not Smell as Sweet

In This Chapter

➤ Your name is an energetic force

➤ Your first name: physical and mental abilities

➤ Your middle name: your emotional side

➤ Your last name: your spiritual nature

➤ Maiden, married, adopted, and business names

➤ Choosing names by the numbers

"My name is Ben, so what's the big deal? I mean it's a common enough name." Or so you thought! You may think of your name as just so many words, but there's far more to a name when it comes to numerology.

Instead, we invite you to think of your name as an energetic force field that carries your family heritage, your lessons in consciousness, your destiny, your personality traits, and your soul vibration. In fact, each name you were given at birth provides information about the strengths and weaknesses inherent in each name.

In this chapter, we'll look at what's in your name, including what the first vowel and consonant mean in your name. We'll also show you ways that you can choose names for babies, businesses, and even yourself—to maximize your success.

What's in a Name?

Have you ever met someone whose name just seems "wrong" for that person? Or, does your own name feel as if it should belong to someone else? When it comes to names, a perfect fit can be as important as the right pair of shoes or finding the right relationship.

When we look at a name numerologically, we can explore just how those shoes fit. To begin, each part of your name tells of three different levels of information present within your name. For example

➤ Your first name tells of your physical conditions and mental acuity.

➤ Your middle or second name tells of the emotional aspect of your life.

➤ Your last name tells of your spiritual consciousness.

Merlin's Notes

What if you haven't got a middle name? If that's the case, your last name carries the combined story of your emotional and spiritual consciousness. If, on the other hand, you have more than one middle name, for numerology purposes, you'll treat them as one long middle name, which will give insight into your emotional life. Last, if you have more than one last name, string them together into one long last name. This name will tell of the level of spiritual consciousness you're dealing with.

With that background in mind, let's look at what's behind each of the names you were given at birth.

Your First Name

Numerologically, your first name tells us many things, including

➤ The physical and mental influence of your direction for growth.

➤ How predictably you think, act, and behave.

➤ How you interpret life's experiences.

To understand this information, you'll look to the individual numbers that make up your name as well as the number total. For example, let's consider the first name Anna-Stina. This hyphenated name is considered as one whole first name.

A	N	N	A		S	T	I	N	A	
1	5	5	1		1	2	9	5	1	= 30 = 3

What can we tell about this person from her first name? First of all, notice that there are four 1s in this name. This suggests that she's going to be a very independent person, and, with three 5s, she'll want her freedom. These also indicate her ability. The 2 and 9 tell us that she has mental ability that is good with both details (the 2) and the big picture (the 9). The first name total 3 indicates a happy disposition, humor, quick wit, an emotional nature, and someone who's good with words.

The total from your first name also gives us your *Growth Number*. The Growth Number helps you know how to further grow as you move along your path. We look at this Growth Number in relationship to the Life Path Number. For example, with a Growth Number 3, Anna-Stina can expect to use her special gifts of creativity, self-expression, and way with words to assist her along her 11/2 Life Path, which is about inspiring and uplifting others. This is a nice match.

By the Numbers

The **Growth Number,** sometimes called the **Key,** tells of the growth and development you can expect with this number. The single-digit number total is found in your first name. It's found by adding together the numerical value of the letters of your first name and reducing to a single number total (unless it's a master number—remember, we don't reduce master numbers).

To find your Growth Number we've provided space for your calculation.

1. Write down your first name and assign the appropriate number to each letter.

   First name: __ __ __ __ __ __ __ __ __ __

   Numbers: __ __ __ __ __ __ __ __ __ __

2. Add the numbers together and reduce to a single digit ___ = Growth Number

So, what's your Growth Number? Whatever it is, it indicates where the greatest growth will be as you move down your path in life in relationship to your Life Path Number. Remember, your Life Path Number is found in the sum total of your date of birth (see Chapter 17, "Your Life Path Number: Rules for the Road," for an in-depth look at your Life Path Number).

Now, most numerologists consider the first vowel in your name to have valuable information as well. Let's look at this feature of your first name next.

The First Vowel

It is believed that the ancients thought that the soul entered the body on the vibration of the first vowel of a name. That's not surprising since the Soul Number is calculated from the vowels in a name. No matter what, however, numerologists agree that the first vowel of your name holds great significance.

The first vowel of your first name reveals valuable information: This is the letter that describes your natural and innate approach to life. The first vowel is considered your soul vibration, because it reveals character traits such as sensitivity, will power, and determination. Will you approach life with determination, timidity, or as a pleasure-seeker? In fact, the first vowel is thought to describe your spiritual approach to the experience of life as well.

Easy as 1–2–3

Is your name "Yves" or "Yvonne"? If so, that "Y" is the first vowel of your first name. If your name's "Yolanda" or "Yancy," however, that "Y" is a consonant.

Let's consider the first name Anna-Stina. The first vowel is an "a." When we check the vowel interpretation chart that follows, we find that "a" means that Anna-Stina will innately approach life creatively and independently, demonstrating the value and importance of the individual. Her spiritual approach will be to seek a belief system where individuality is stressed. All of this is told in the number 1, which is the number of the first vowel (the "a") in her name.

What's the first vowel of your name? Use the following chart to see what it means.

First Vowel Interpretation

Vowel	Number	Interpretation
A	1	Stresses individuality, creativity, leadership, the value of one
E	5	Stresses curiosity, investigation, fascination with the mystery of life
I	9	Stresses deep emotional nature, a humanitarian approach, a cosmic consciousness, the soul of the healer, creativity, and highly developed intuitive skill
O	6	Stresses concealed feelings, accepts responsibility, sentimental, protects family and home, mission is to beautify
U	3	Stresses sensitivity, inspired creativity, enthusiasm for life
Y	7	Stresses thoughtful analysis, vacillation, intuition, observation, uses an investigative, possibly skeptical approach, seeks divine guidance, pursues the metaphysical and philosophical for truth

Like Anna-Stina, you can use this chart to determine the meaning of your first name vowel. Simply match the vowel letter to the appropriate number, and then find the meaning for that number.

The first vowel in my first name is ____.

The matching number for this letter is ____.

The meaning of the first vowel of my first name is

_____.

This vowel number indicates my spiritual and philosophical approach to life.

Your Middle Name

Your middle name is thought to govern your emotional life, and reveals your likes, loves, emotions, attraction to certain hobbies, and marriage suitability. Add together the numbers of the letters that make up your middle name. The reduced total number tells the story.

Note that if you have a master number as your middle name number, do not reduce it. When you're ready, use the chart at the front of the book to find the meaning of the reduced number of your middle name.

The reduced number total for my middle name is ____.

The meaning of the my middle name number is

_____.

My middle name number indicates my emotional approach to life.

Your Last Name

The letters of your last name govern your spiritual nature, that is, your inner, subconscious response to life. Some letters in your last name are more conducive to spiritual growth than others. Again, we recommend examining the letters and number equivalents for your last name and then interpreting the meaning of the numbers you find here.

Your Family Name

For many of us, the family name is our last name, which naturally carries with it a history and linkage to ancestral traits. In your family name are certain strengths and inherent weakness. It may seem odd, but just as we can inherit genetic characteristics like hair color and shoe size, we also inherit vibrational traits like attitudinal and ancestral history through our family name. Inherited traits are calculated in the same way we figure any name, except that we work with only the last name at birth.

Let's look at two famous names of our times to see what each has inherited. Here's the first one:

```
K   E   N   N   E   D   Y
2   5   5   5   5   4   7 = 33/6
```

In the Kennedy name, we see the traits of cooperation (2), sudden unexpected change (all those 5s), determination and hard work (4), and a sense of privacy and intellectual analysis (7). In addition, when the Kennedy name is added up, we find a master number 33, which reduces to a 6. This then, would be a name which promotes family closeness (6), while at the same time demands that those who carry this name endure the tests of a master number (33).

Here's a second family name:

G   A   T   E   S

8   1   2   5   1 = 17, which reduces to 8

In the Gates family name, we see the traits of authority and a prowess in the material world (8), independence, self-starting (1), teamwork (2), the need for freedom (5), and leadership—as long as it's "my way" (1). In total, the Gates family name adds up to success, wealth, and power (8).

Figuring Your Family Name

Let's examine your family name.

1. Write down your family name and assign the appropriate number to each letter.

   Family name: __ __ __ __ __ __ __ __ __ __

   Numbers: __ __ __ __ __ __ __ __ __ __

2. Add the numbers together and reduce to a single digit ___ = Family Name Number

Here's a quick guide for checking out what your Family Name Number means:

What Your Family Name Number Means to You

Number	Meaning
1	You have inherited an independent spirit, a forceful nature, a strong will, and the ability to come up with original ideas.
2	You have inherited a peaceful nature, the desire to reduce conflict, a sensitivity to things, and a loving nature.
3	You have inherited an outgoing, optimistic personality, a sense of humor, and a creative spirit.
4	You have inherited a belief that hard work is the right way to work, a sense of cautiousness, thoroughness, and self-discipline.
5	You have inherited a belief that you shouldn't be fenced in, for you are a free spirit. Restrictions, limitations, routine challenge you. Travel and change are easy for you, and you are innately curious and a risk taker.
6	You have inherited a conservative attitude that sees that helping others is the responsible thing to do. You are an excellent problem solver and, of course, are family oriented. You may have inherited a stubborn streak as part of the number 6.
7	You have inherited a desire for knowledge, you value learning, and you respect quality, facts, and theories, as well as spiritual understanding. Your family traits will be those of observation, analysis, and desiring privacy.

Number	Meaning
8	You have inherited an attitude about money and power that will cause you to seek recognition in business and finance. Your family name brings you the qualities of leadership, organization, and possibly an inflated ego.
9	You have inherited concern for others, an emotional nature, generosity, a sense of needing to serve, and an attitude of compassion and sympathy.
11	You have inherited the ability to uplift, encourage, and inspire others. Your family name brings with it a sensitivity to others and the desire for spiritual truth. You will learn from life through many tests.
22	You have inherited the ability to build things that will benefit the masses. Your family name brings you the skills of leadership, management, a good solid work ethic, and the ability to gain material wealth. You have the endurance to bounce back after many difficulties.
33	You have inherited an ability to teach others in a masterful way. Your family name brings a keen sense of responsibility, love for your fellow human, and a desire to serve. You will learn, just as your family has learned, to overcome the many setbacks life will put in your path.

If you have done your numbers correctly, you may have already figured your Family Name when you calculated your Destiny Number. Look for the number total for your last name at birth (last name only if you are looking at the Destiny Number calculations). The reduced total number of your last name is your family name and shows the inherited traits from your family.

For many women, the family name is the maiden name. We discuss the significance of that name next.

Your Maiden Name

Have you noticed that it's the women who do the name changing for the most part? Wonder what that means on a cosmic level, since the original birth name, the original song of the soul, is changed for so many women all over the world?

Your maiden name is the name of your family: It tells of the traits you've inherited down through the family line. Your maiden name is part of your original birth name and therefore part of your original cosmic code and blueprint for life.

Whether you use your maiden name now or not, the energy that is present in that name will be with you all of your life. When you give up your maiden name in favor of a married name (or any other name you may choose), you cannot deplete the energy of that name, for it is your essence and belongs to your energy field. Any new name you assume will merely be an add-on—additional energy you bring to your experience of life. But it won't change the essence of who you are—that story is told in your maiden name.

To calculate your maiden name, follow these steps:

1. Write down the letters of your family name:

   _____

2. Convert each letter to a number:

   _____

3. Add the numbers together, and reduce to a single digit (unless, of course, it's a master number): _____

4. Write your Maiden Name number here:

   _____

To interpret the meaning of your maiden name, you simply use the Family Name table which precedes this section.

Your Married Name

In numerology, we look at the married name as an additional energy. For some, it will be a number that's missing in the original birth name, and in that case, it would also be one of your karmic lessons. If that's the case, the married name may be assumed to be bringing you a karmic lesson which you've needed to round out your learning experience while you are here on Earth.

The married name does not replace your original birth name. The essence of who you are is determined by the name you were given at birth, which determines your major 5 core numbers.

To determine the meaning of your married name, follow these instructions.

1. Write down your married name and assign the appropriate number to each letter.

   Married name: __ __ __ __ __ __ __ __ __ __

   Numbers: __ __ __ __ __ __ __ __ __ __

2. Add the numbers together and reduce to a single digit ___ = Married Name Number

To interpret the meaning of your Married Name Number you'll once again consult the Family Name table we gave you earlier. This will tell you what new energy you've brought to yourself by assuming your married name. It usually will bring another number to your original name and vibration.

So, let us say it again, your original birth name is the most significant name: It tells of the essence of who you are. That never changes—not even if you add a married name, or drop your original birth name.

Your Adopted Name

While we discussed the adopted name briefly in Chapter 18, we want to go into a little more detail here. If you were given an adopted name early on in life, it may be the only name you have known. If that's the case, figure your numerology chart on your given name, although if you are privy to your original name, for our purposes, the original name is best to use.

An adopted name may sometimes replace your original name, as in the case of your mother remarrying and your stepfather adopting you. For example, if you were born David Yale Krug and your mother remarried your stepfather, whose last name is Baker, and he adopted you, your new name would be David Yale Baker. For numerology purposes, your entire numerology chart would be figured on the original name David Yale Krug, but we would want to examine the new name Baker to discover what new energy has come in.

Sixes and Sevens

When calculating a married name, Mrs. is never used—just as Mr., Jr., Sr., or the Third (III) aren't used either.

Let's look at this situation more closely.

D	A	V	I	D		Y	A	L	E		K	R	U	G	
4	1	4	9	4		7	1	3	5		2	9	3	8	
22						16					22				
22/4						7					22/4				Totals for each name

Now we can see that this name has two master numbers, and he also has a karmic debt number 16/7 as a middle name energy. This original birth name is very powerful. What happens when he changes his name?

The adopted name then becomes Baker instead of Krug, and we figure it like this:

David	Krug		B	A	K	E	R
22/4	16/7		2	1	2	5	6 = 19 = 1 (1 + 9)

Several things need to be pointed out in this situation. First, as we've said, the original name remains as the essence and the basis of the numerology chart. David's Soul, Destiny, and Personality Numbers, and eventually his Maturity Number, will all be figured from his original name, David Yale Krug. However, with this new adopted name, a new energy comes into play, the energy of the 1 (Baker).

So we might say that David has an additional vibration of independence, innovation, and self-reliance which has come to him through his adopted name. This new energy will serve him as long as he carries the name of Baker and lives up to the demands of this new name.

Merlin's Notes

It's interesting to note that David Krug's new name of Baker is in fact a 19, which is also a karmic debt number. This means that he now bears two karmic debt numbers (16 from his original name, and 19 from his new name)—and all that those numbers imply. While he has increased his debt load, in keeping with universal law, it would seem that there's no mistake. David must have needed to work with this kind of energy (both the 19 and the 1) to advance his spiritual development.

The message is the same for adopted names as it is for married names. You'll use your original birth name and then figure your new names separately. However, you'll want to note your original last name, for it tells of inherited family traits, strengths, and weaknesses.

When you have no other name except an adopted name, then all of your calculations will be done with the adopted name. This name represents the energy you're presently experiencing, and the strengths and weaknesses that will accompany you through life. Note that there's less of an energetic impact if you change an adopted name than there is if you change your original birth name.

Nicknames

While our nicknames or pet names bring a certain personal response, and carry a vibrational frequency, these names aren't to be considered part of the original 5 core numbers. Like any name you may add to your original set of birth names, it's just that—an add-on. So consider the nickname as an added energy you have brought into your sphere of energy. Of course, it is valuable to figure the number for this nickname and the meaning of that number, just as we have figured the married name or the family name. In short, the nickname is an added energy and is figured separately from your original birth name.

If you were named William but are called Bill or Billy, you might have fun calculating these name numbers to see how the energy changed for you at those times in your life when you went from being one name to being another.

Choosing a Name

At some point in our lives we all have to choose a name—either for a child, a new business, a pet, an e-mail name, and even a new surname (that's your last name) when the old one wears out for one reason or another. As we mentioned earlier in the book, the ancients believed that a name is a mystical code for the essential character of a person, and, because your birth name is your destiny, name changing should not be entered into lightly.

Things to Consider When Changing Your Name

There are several things you'll want to consider when changing your name. For example, there's a mistaken notion that a new name will mean a new life. The main thing to keep in mind if you're going to change your name is that you'll have two sets of numbers operating simultaneously. The first and most significant set is the numbers in your birth name—you're never without this cosmic code and vibrational pattern. The second is that a new name has a vibrational pattern also, and, with careful choice, this new name can enhance your original name energy.

Sixes and Sevens

A new name can bring a new advantage, and even a special purpose, because it's a new tool for the enhancement of your original capabilities and consciousness. But beware—changing your name means you're changing your power. Obviously, you'll want to select your new name with a great deal of care.

If you're changing your name, keep these things in mind:

➤ Choose a name that feels right rather than a name that is cutesy, popular, or to honor your great uncle Alfred. When we say "feels right," we mean using your intuition. Is this a name you would enjoy using, today and in 10 years? Does your energy rise when you think or hear this new name? Use your inner sense of knowing to guide you in a new name choice.

➤ Choose a name that will attract favorable experiences—not more tests, karma, or aggravations. To do this, you'll have to calculate the meaning of this new name using the same steps we've outlined for you in Chapters 18 through 20, especially if you are changing more than one of your names. You'll want to be aware of what your new name means and what kind of energy you're bringing to your life. You'll want to know what the vibration is for your Soul, Destiny, and Personality Numbers. Invest time in this important decision—and take your time, too.

➤ Avoid choosing a name that adds up to one of your challenge numbers or a karmic lesson number, unless you've already conquered these challenges. The same is true for a master-number name—be sure you're willing to live up to the additional demands of the master number.

➤ For best results, select a name that has the same Soul Number and Destiny Number as your original birth name—so the inner motivation and general direction for your life will be the same as your original blueprint.

Sixes and Sevens

Then again, maybe your original name isn't so bad, and through careful calculation, you'll learn a new appreciation for it. After all, you could have been born with the name Romeo Montague—and "A rose by any other name might not smell as sweet."

➤ A new name carries the potential for new opportunities, but it takes approximately five years before the energy of this new name is fully integrated.

➤ Choose a name that harmonizes with your Life Path Number (your birth date). If you have a strong Life Path Number, you won't want to choose a weaker name number—it won't bring you the success promised in your birth date. Choose a new name whose vowels add up to a number that's compatible with your Life Path Number, and then also calculate the total name number (consonants and vowels) to harmonize with your Life Path Number. Taking care to work out these numbers will pay off—you don't need to make life any harder than it already is!

➤ Have fun with your new name but remember, you're expected to live up to your new name vibration as well as your original name. Name changing isn't for the faint of heart. Be sure you understand your original name's meaning before you give it up: You'll want to know who you really are before you become someone else.

Finally, if you're in doubt about choosing a new name, consult a professional numerologist.

Naming Your Baby

Choosing the name for a baby is a very important step. You're choosing for another soul the pattern for his or her time on Earth. Needless to say, this must be done with careful consideration.

Some numerologists refuse to influence the naming of a baby. The child's purpose and destiny in life aren't meant to be put in the hands of a numerologist or a stranger. Instead, it's generally felt that the responsibility for naming the baby is solely the parents'.

In fact, it's hoped that the chosen name for the baby will be an inspiration coming from the parents. That's because it's believed that the parents have chosen to be a channel for this baby's birth and life on Earth, and if they'll only tune in to their own inner guidance, they'll come to a name that's just right for their newborn. This is all part of the great mystery, the secret of creation and belongs to the souls of those directly involved: the new baby and the parents. In other words, we don't recommend that you work on getting the numbers right for your unborn child—the number that results from the name you "choose" will be the one that's right for that soul!

Parents who have kept their own last names and need to decide which name to give the baby might want to work out the family name of each parent. You can use the Family Name Table for interpreting the number of each family name. If both family names are desired, you might want to hyphenate the baby's name.

In the meantime, we suggest you find a time to sit quietly each day prior to the baby's birth, and listen in your own mind. When the right name comes to you, you will know. Your energy will rise when you've hit upon the right name, and your intuition will signal that this is it—you've got the right one. The surname is usually the family name, which brings the new soul into alignment with the family inheritance—traits of similarity—that the newborn will share with those in his clan. In this way, a newborn can be held in the family vibration while it begins to establish its own vibrational pattern.

Easy as 1-2-3

We strongly recommend that the final selection of the name for the new baby not be made until you're in the presence of an incoming spirit. If you can still the inner clamor, the baby will help you to know the perfect name to choose.

Naturally, it's recommended that you set up a full chart for your baby, in order to examine the meaning of the name you choose for your infant. But it's not recommended that you try to select a name that means "money and power" or that sort of thing. In addition

➤ Don't pick a name for the qualities you hope to create with this name, but instead, choose a name that feels right and know that this little soul's path will be just the right one for him or her.

➤ Trust the universal law that says, "Everything works out perfectly in its own way." The soul of this incoming child knows what it needs.

➤ Don't block your inner guidance, your inner sense of knowing, by trying to force a name to fit a certain number. When a name comes to you that feels right, trust it.

The time to check on the numerology of the new baby's name is after you've decided upon a name—and don't be tempted to change your mind just based on the numbers. Instead, use your intuition as your guide.

Naming Your Business

When choosing the name for a business, you'll want to consider the nature of the business. Whether it's a product business, service business, research firm, educational institution, or business for the arts, keep in mind that it's the nature of your enterprise that should resonate to the number of the name.

Here's a quick way to see which numbers would be best for your business:

➤ Product Businesses = 2, 4, 8

➤ Service Businesses = 2, 3, 6, 9

➤ Research Businesses = 2, 7, 9

➤ Educational Businesses = 6, 7, 9

➤ Arts Businesses = 2, 3, 6, 9

Use the same tenets for choosing the name of your business as you would use for naming a baby (after all, your business is your baby, right?). Let your intuition be your guide, and choose a name that feels right first. Only then should you look to see what the name means.

Here are a few other pointers:

➤ Don't use "Inc." in the name calculation.

➤ Examine the Soul Number for this business name as well as the Destiny and Personality Numbers. (See Chapters 18 through 20 for an in-depth discussion of how to calculate these numbers and the interpretation of each number.)

➤ If your business is family owned, the name should harmonize with the Family Name Number.

➤ If your business is a sole proprietorship, then the business name Soul and Destiny Numbers should harmonize with your own Soul and Destiny Numbers.

➤ If the business is a partnership, then you'll want to consider the Soul and Destiny Numbers for each partner and look for a business name that resonates with each of these.

Easy as 1-2-3

The Personality Number of the business name shows its public image (how others will view this business) so you'll want to choose a Personality Number that spells greatest attraction!

Utilize the steps we've outlined for you for choosing a name and you should be able to create a successful choice for your business name. We wish you the very best of luck with your new enterprise. May the numbers guide you to your highest and best!

Names have meaning, whether it is a business name, a married name, or a child's name. There are many resources available for choosing names, and some give numerical meanings for names as well. All names have number equivalents, and all names have a vibrational frequency. Rely on your intuition—but let the numbers guide you as well.

The Least You Need to Know

➤ Your name is an energetic force that reflects your nature.

➤ Your first name reveals your physical and mental abilities.

➤ Your middle name shows your emotional side.

➤ Your last name tells of your spiritual nature.

➤ Maiden, married, adopted, and business names each tell of special meanings.

➤ Choosing names by the numbers should be undertaken cautiously and judiciously.

Chapter 30

Numbers for Daily Living

In This Chapter

➤ Living your life by the numbers

➤ Finding the right numbers for your money and luck

➤ Finding the right numbers for family planning and home improvement

➤ Numbers for spiritual questing, building things, and your dreams

---

Now that you know your own numbers—from your core numbers to your Personal Days, Months, and Years, as well as your Pinnacles, Challenges, and karmic lessons—it's time to have a little fun with the numbers in your daily life.

In Chapters 2, "What Numerology Can Do for You," and 3, "Apartment or House, It's the Number That Counts," we introduced you to some simple daily numbers such as your phone number and house number. In this chapter, we're going to take a closer look at some of the other numbers in your daily life, including your Money Numbers, your Lucky Numbers, your Communication Numbers, your Learning Numbers, your Family Planning Numbers, your Home Improvement Numbers, your Spiritual Growth Numbers, and the numbers of your dreams.

Your Numbers and Your Money

Whether it's about earning money or having your money earn money, we all want to know how to get money and hang on to it. When it comes to numerology and money, there are three areas to consider:

➤ The numbers of your bank accounts

➤ Your lucky numbers

➤ Your personal money numbers

Before we begin, we'd like to remind you that this chapter is largely in fun. If winning the lottery were as simple as knowing your personal Money Numbers, we'd patent the formula! Still, we thought you'd like to have a little fun with numerology, too. And it's always possible that changing a number could change your life.

Bank Accounts Have Numbers, Too!

Every bank account has a number, and it's as simple as adding up the digits of the account. Here's an example:

Bank account number 34567 89012

Add: $3 + 4 + 5 + 6 + 7 + 8 + 9 + 0 + 1 + 2 = 45 = 9$

This 9 bank account adds up to money in the bank, because it knows the importance of completing what one's begun. Nine is also the number of rewards generated through giving to others.

What can you expect with each bank account number? Here's a table to guide you.

Sixes and Sevens

If you're having trouble with money, make sure your bank account doesn't add up to a 5, a 4, or 3. The most stable bank account numbers are 8, 9, or 7. Of course, if you're wanting independence, a 1 is good, too.

Bank Account Number	What to Expect
1	New beginnings, especially if enterprising
2	Good for partnerships and sharing
3	Possible frivolous spending, but there's luck here, too
4	Conservative approach—may be low or no interest to avoid risk-taking
5	Up and down, changeable, and unpredictable, uncertain finances
6	Money going out to family or others who seem needy, but attracts money through service to others
7	Specialization and research can help the money add up
8	Organization and clarity of purpose can make this a winning bank account number
9	Money comes through giving but receive reward for work you've done previously—favors the arts

Lucky Numbers

The number 3 is considered lucky, so it's important to pay attention to your 3s whenever they appear. A 3 day in a 3 month in a 3 year is particularly lucky. Lisa's already got September highlighted on her calendar: It's a 3 month in a 3 year for her. You'll want to be sure to highlight those days or months on your calendar, too.

Even if it's not a 3 year, you can still use your 3 days and months to your advantage, especially 3 days that occur in 3 months. Is there something you need a little extra luck with? Just be sure to schedule it at a lucky time!

Money Numbers

What are the best days for you to make money and keep money? We've created the following table to give you some handy hints. For this table, all you'll need is your Personal Day.

Finding your Personal Day Number:

> Personal month number + calendar day number

By the Numbers

The 3 is considered inherently lucky, so if any of your money numbers is a 3, luck is with you.

Money by the Numbers

Personal Day	What to Expect
1	New ventures will take off.
2	Partnerships and cooperation take a front seat. Take care of details today.
3	Creative activities do well, but watch out for those extravagances.
4	Building strong foundations, set up systems, be thrifty and practical today.
5	Not a good money day! Leave the checkbook at home—but promotion is great!
6	Money comes toward you if you're in service, such as teaching, counseling, any helping profession, or in the service industry—wherever you are giving of yourself.
7	Put your money where your research is—be cautious and analyze carefully.
8	The number of money and manifestation—a great Money Number. Organize, take charge, tend to business.
9	Another good Money Number—rewards for previous work; number for bringing things to completion.

Your Communication Numbers

Good Communication Numbers are 3 and 5. The 3 is the most cheerful and talkative of numbers, so if you're looking for a number to drive away the silence, a 3 is what you're looking for. The 5 is the number to have if you're looking for never a dull moment, so if peace and quiet are what you're after, you won't find it here.

Your Sex Numbers: Not Tonight, Honey

How do you define love? When it comes to your sex numbers, knowing what's what can make or break a relationship. What happens when you're having an optimistic 3 day while your partner's having a brooding 7, for example? We'd guess separate bedrooms (at the suggestion of the 7, of course).

Discovering whether your sex numbers add up is as easy as knowing your personal day and month. If you're in a 5 month, for example, lucky you if your partner's having a 3 day, too (a 2 wouldn't be bad, either). Similarly, if you're on a 1 and your partner's on a 2, it's a good sex day, too. Get the idea? Here's some sex, by the numbers.

Sex Number	What to Expect
1	Wants to take the lead
2	Good partner, wants you to feel good
3	Fun and energetic, playful (sex kitten for the day)
4	Loyal but not very inventive
5	Hot—but that may not last for long
6	Good lovin'—and good cookin'
7	Needs own space, but still waters run deep
8	Strong and supportive, but busy
9	Very loving, passionate, but a bit spacey

Merlin's Notes

When your lover's having a 9 day, she still loves you, but you may not always know it. That's because she can't keep her mind on just one thing, and that includes, unfortunately, sex. You may think it's the best sex ever, but she may well be thinking about anything from earthquake victims to her plan for world hunger. Just remember that your 9's love is of a universal nature; she's got big things on her mind, but you're a part of her universe—a very special part.

Your Alone Numbers: Greta Garbo Was Right

Which numbers do the best alone? The 1 is always out in front, far ahead of the pack, while the 7 naturally prefers solitude. As the saying goes, "Some days are diamonds, some days are stone," and using your alone days to their best advantage can make all the difference in your life. Some things to do when you're having a 1 day are

➤ Start something new.

➤ Assert yourself.

➤ Create new ideas—something original.

➤ Change your image—get a hair cut, buy that dress.

Some things to do when you're having a 7 day are

➤ Meditate and write in your journal.

➤ Take a walk in the country.

➤ Stay in bed all day and read!

➤ Take a long, soothing bath by candlelight—alone.

Numbers to Make the Grade

Making the grade isn't just about school (although we'll be discussing those numbers later), it's also about making sure every "i" gets dotted and every "t" gets crossed. That's why we're also going to discuss Signature Numbers as well as the numbers for study and graduation.

Signature Numbers

Your signature is important because it attracts to itself whatever number energy is being put out. Think about just how often you write your signature. If you're writing your signature for money purposes, you'll want to be sure the signature you use adds up to a favorable number.

Everybody's signature vibrates to a certain energy, because every signature has its own number, which, while good for certain things, is bad for others. What's important is what signature you're using. If your signature adds up to an unfavorable money number, change it. You could, for example, drop the middle initial, or go back to your original first name rather than your nickname.

Here's an example: If you are named William Bradley Pitt, but sign all those 8 × 10 glossy photos, "Brad Pitt," then you'll want to know what it is you're attracting with this signature. After all, numbers are energy, and your signature has a number.

So what's Brad Pitt saying by signing those photos that way? Let's take a look:

B	R	A	D		P	I	T	T
2	9	1	4 = 16		7	9	2	2 = 20

Now, adding both names together we get 36, which reduces to a 9.

With this 9 signature, Brad is attracting rewards for his hard work and is sending out caring energy—remember the 9 favors the arts.

What does your Signature Number indicate? Use the following table to sign away.

Signature Number	What You'll Attract with This Number as Your Signature
1	Full speed ahead, especially for solo ventures—good for independent, innovative ventures
2	Especially good for signing partnership agreements, or if you want to be involved with lots of details
3	Good for creative activities, such as book contracts, speaking engagements, or for the communication industry
4	A good number to sign for building things, conserving, or for practical pursuits
5	Somewhat unstable but good for changing something or if you are wanting your freedom
6	Good for house contracts, home improvement, community service, family oriented living, duty, and responsibility
7	Best for agreements concerning legal matters
8	CEO time—you're the boss here
9	For completion—that last loan payment, for example, or for giving generously to that charity fund

Study and School Number

The number 7 is for times when you want to be alone, study, contemplate, or re-examine things, so it's perfect for research or just the joy of studying. Because 7s love to study, someone with a 7 in her core numbers might just be that "perpetual student" you see on campus, getting her third degree. Seven is usually the sabbatical number (which is the number of years a tenured professor must teach in order to take a paid year off), so if you're going off to research or going back to school on your sabbatical, this is the perfect time.

The 7 is also the number of investigative work as well as the number of metaphysics, so study in any of the metaphysical, spiritual, or esoteric fields is appropriate and comes easily at a 7 time in life.

Easy as 1-2-3

A 4 works if you want stability, and an 8 means being the authority figure and having all the financial responsibility, which is great if you're the boss, but bad if you're struggling to rub two pennies together.

Graduating Number

The big day arrives, and you're finally ready to graduate. Don't be surprised to find that the big day is in fact a 9 or that it's happening in your 9 Personal Year!

Family Planning Numbers

Whether it's getting married, having a baby—or even trying to have a baby—knowing your Personal Year and Personal Month can help you stack the numbers in your favor. We're not Planned Parenthood, but we do know how to add up the numbers to success.

Numbers for Getting Married

For getting married, the 2 and the 6 are ideal, but you can get married in all years. Kay's best friend got married in 6 year, which is a great year for a loving relationship with the home as the focus. If you were finally getting hitched after a long, long relationship on the other hand, a 9 year might be a better time. Ultimately, though, love comes all the time, so it's not beholden to any one number.

Numbers for Giving Birth

This one seems easy—the baby pops out in the 9th month, so naturally, the 9 is the number that signals release, conclusion, completion, and the finale! But remember, there's more than one way to give birth, and every new beginning is a 1.

Even Numbers for Getting Pregnant!

Getting pregnant in a 3 year—a time of creation—is always good. But even better is an 8 year, when it's a time to expand! Then you can deliver in a 9—perfect timing!

Home Improvement Numbers

Buying or selling a home? Remodeling the one you already have? Look to the numbers for the best times to maximize profit. For buying and selling, you'll look to a favorable month to sign contracts and to your Personal Year for the best time overall. For remodeling, you'll look at the entire year, because, as any remodeler (like both Kay and Lisa) can tell you, remodeling is not an overnight activity. (It took two and a half years to finish the upstairs bedroom at Kay's house, and remodeling is an ongoing activity wherever Lisa's living.)

Remodeling Number

You may want to schedule your remodeling in a 6 year. Because remodeling, redoing, reconstructing, and reworking all fall under the 6, it's a time to beautify. In addition, the 4 year is also a good time to work on the home, because the 4 is the number of building foundations, digging in, putting down roots, and doing the hard work.

Selling or Buying a House

The 4 and the 9 are key here: The 9 is the number of endings and reward, so it's a good time for selling a house and getting the money you want. As we've mentioned earlier, the 4 is the number of building foundations, so it's a great time to buy a home and set down roots.

More than the year will be at play here. In fact, you can time a contract right up to the minute, if you want, to maximize your profits. A good time to buy, for example, would be on a 4 day in a 4 month in a 4 Personal Year (at 4:00), while a good time to sell might be a 9 day in a 9 month in a 9 Personal Year (at 9:00). None of this is cast in stone because each of us has our own energy pattern that will influence whatever we engage in.

Of course, if they're offering you *money*—you know, cold, hard cash—forget the day, the time, or the year—just take the money and run!

Growth and Change Numbers

Growth and change come in many guises, but the best numbers for self-improvement are the 1, the number of new beginnings, and the 11/2, the number of self-illumination through spiritual inspiration. As you already know, the 5 is the personal transition number—change personified—but, in addition, the 9 is the number of transformation, and a 9 year can be a good time to end something of major significance. We all know what kind of growth that takes!

Spiritual Questing

Are you seeking an answer that lies within? That's what spiritual questing is all about, and some years are naturally better for this than others. If you're in a 7 Personal Year, you're probably questing already, because examination, contemplation, and analysis are very much a part of what the 7 is all about.

Sometimes, a 5 year will find you curious about mystical matters and drawn to classes and workshops to investigate this material. Similarly, an 11/2 year can bring to light all kinds of spiritual answers, because illumination is what that year is all about. Last, the 9 Personal Year offers promise for those who quest, for it's the year to draw upon your intuition and re-dream the dream.

Easy as 1-2-3

When a number or series of numbers appears in your dream, chances are it has some meaning and is worth investigating further.

Numbers for Building Things

Whether you're building buildings or dreams, no numbers are better than the 4, the 8, and the 22. A 4 year is a year of hard work and endurance, an 8 year of strength and fortitude and building things with vision, while the 22 is the year of the master builder, who builds for posterity.

The Numbers of Your Dreams

Numbers and dreams go hand in hand, and each number has both significance and spiritual power.

While the meaning of each number is largely symbolic, it's precisely that symbolic meaning that causes insight into the potential energy that's a part of our lives.

So what exactly do the numbers in your dreams mean? Let's take a look at them, one at a time.

Numbers in Your Dreams	Interpretation
1	Independence, a new beginning, oneness with life, individuality
2	Balancing of the male/female energies, needing people, relationship to something, putting others before yourself, balance needed somewhere in your life
3	Creativity, happiness, joy, the need for saying what's true in your heart, may be a spiritual message in this dream
4	Hard work, foundation of something, the root of a family issue, need for order and self-discipline; can mean it's time to put things into form or to look to health care
5	Change is taking place now or very soon; feeling of liberation, freedom, wanting to explore and take a risk
6	Looking for self-harmony or needing balance, the number of guidance, the White Brotherhood (teachers of truth), indicates love is present and self-care is needed
7	A mystical number, means wisdom of a spiritual, mystical nature; stands for the 7 chakras, the path of solitude, the cycle of death and rebirth
8	Material wealth, self-power and empowerment, abundance, authenticity, achievement, self-mastery
9	Selflessness, signifies completion and endings, releasing the old
10	Wholeness and perfection, a rebirth with a higher frequency of understanding
11	Master number, means self-illumination, intuition, inspiration
22	Master number, spiritual expression of balance and integration of self and others, self-mastery on both the material and spiritual planes
33	Master number, the spiritual teacher comes into consciousness
0	An open channel to the Divine, unformed energy

When you dream about numbers, a message is being given to you. Learn the language of numbers.

Easy as 1-2-3

Two more things to know about numbers and your dreams (dreams here refers to your hopes and wishes for your life): A 2 suggests you're finding inner peace and a sense of tranquility this year; a 9 is the year to re-vision your personal dreams for the future.

Using Numbers in Your Everyday Life

It's important to remember that numbers are symbols that communicate to our unconscious minds. Not every number has a meaning (that flight number to Tulsa is probably meaningless, for example), so don't get crazed and try to decipher every number you encounter. Instead, surround yourself with energy that will support you in living harmoniously and in the flow of your own natural energy pattern.

In this book, we've tried to show you how you can live harmoniously in your own life by knowing what your numbers' energy reveals about you, those around you, and the things you surround yourself with. The rest is up to you. We wish you much joy and happiness—by the numbers.

The Least You Need to Know

➤ Knowing your Money Numbers can help you hang onto your hard-earned cash.

➤ Knowing your Communications Numbers can help you improve relationships—and your sex life.

➤ Knowing your Family Planning Numbers can help with everything from marriage to having a baby.

➤ Understanding the numbers of your dreams can help you live your waking life to your fullest potential.

➤ Living harmoniously with your numbers can help you keep your energy flowing smoothly in your life.

Further Reading

There are literally hundreds of books about numerology out there. Here are some that we recommend.

Adrienne, Carol. *The Numerology Kit*. New York: Penguin, 1988.

Adrienne, Carol. *Your Child's Destiny: A Numerology Guide for Parents*. New York: Penguin, 1994.

Angeles, Arrien. *The Four Fold Path*. San Francisco: HarperCollins, 1993.

Arnold, Margaret. *Love Numbers*. St. Paul: Llewellyn, 1997.

Balliett, Dow, Mrs. *How to Attain Success Through the Strength of Vibration*. Santa Fe: Sun Publishing, 1905.

Bethards, Betty. *The Dream Book*. Rockport, MA: Element Books, 1995.

Bishop, Barbara J. *Numerology: Universal Vibrations of Numbers*. St Paul: Llewellyn, 1990.

Blyth, Laureli. *The Numerology of Names*. Kenthurst, Australia: Kangaroo Press, 1995.

Bruce-Mitford, Miranda. *The Illustrated Book of Signs and Symbols*. New York: DK Publishing, 1996.

Campbell, Florence. *Your Days Are Numbered*. Marina Del Rey, CA: DeVorss & Co., 1931.

Crawford, Saffi, and Geraldine Sullivan. *The Power of Birthdays, Stars, and Numbers*. New York: Ballantine, 1998.

Deaver, Korra. *The Master Numbers*. Alameda, CA: Hunter House, 1993.

Decoz, Hans. *Numerology: The Key to Your Inner Self*. Garden City Park, NY: Avery Publishing, 1994.

DiPietro, Sylvia. *Live Your Life by the Numbers*. New York: Penguin, 1991.

Drayer, Ruth. *Numerology: The Power in Numbers*. Mesilla, NM: Jewels of Light Publishing, 1994.

Goodwin, Matthew. *Numerology: The Complete Guide*, 2 vols. North Hollywood, CA: Newcastle Publishing, 1981.

Heline, Corinne. *Sacred Science of Numbers*. Marina Del Rey, CA: DeVorss & Co., 1991.

Hesse, Hermann. *Demian*. New York: Harper & Row, 1965.

Hitchcock, Helyn. *Helping Yourself with Numerology*. West Nyack. NY: Parker Publishing, 1972.

Houston, Helen, and Juno Jordan. *Two Guides to Numerology*. North Hollywood, CA: NewCastle Publishing, 1982.

Javane, Faith, and Dusty Bunker. *Numerology and the Divine Triangle*. Rockport, MA: Para Research, 1981.

Jeanne. *Numerology: Spiritual Light Vibrations*. Salem, OR: Your Center for Truth Press, 1987.

Jordan, Juno. *Numerology: The Romance in Your Name*. Marina Del Rey, CA: DeVorss & Co., 1966.

Jordan, Juno. *Right Action Number*. Marina Del Rey, CA: DeVorss & Co., 1979.

Jordan, Juno, and Helen Houston. *Two Guides to Numerology*. North Hollywood, CA: Newcastle Publishing, 1982. (out of print).

Line, Julia. *Discover Numerology*. New York: Sterling Publishing, 1993.

Linn, Denise. *Sacred Space*. New York: Ballantine Books, 1995.

Marooney, Kim. *Angel Blessings*. Carmel, CA: Merrill-West Publishing, 1995.

Miller, Dorcas S. *Stars of the First People*. Boulder, CO: Pruett Publishing, 1997.

Millman, Dan. *The Life You Were Born to Live*. Tiburon, CA: HJ Kramer, 1993.

Montrose. *Numerology for Everybody*. Chicago: Nelson-Hall, 1945.

Pierson, George. *What's in a Number?* New York: Abbeville Press, 1996.

Pond, Lucy, and David Pond. *The Metaphysical Handbook*. Port Ludlow, WA: Reflecting Pond Publications, 1994.

Roguemore, Kathleen. *It's All in Your Numbers: The Secrets of Numerology*. San Francisco: Harper & Row, 1975.

Tognetti, Arlene, and Lisa Lenard. *The Complete Idiot's Guide to Tarot and Fortune-Telling*. New York: Alpha Books, 1998.

Figuring a Chart

YOUR NUMEROLOGY CHART

REMEMBER

All double digit numbers (except master numbers) are reduced to a single digit. For example, 17 = 1 + 7 = 8

Letter Conversion Grid

1	2	3	4	5	6	7	8	9
A	B	C	D	E	F	G	H	I
J	K	L	M	N	O	P	Q	R
S	T	U	V	W	X	Y	Z	

WORKSPACE

Record each number in its own star

Add vowel numbers together. Write numbers for vowel letters above the name.
Vowels:

START HERE

= ___ total = ___ (reduce it) = Soul Number

Full Name _____

Write letters' numbers here. Add all numbers together.

= ___ total = ___ (reduce it) = Destiny Number

Consonants:
Add consonant numbers together. Write numbers for consonant below the name.

= ___ total = ___ (reduce it) = Personality Number

Date of Birth ____ ____ ____ = ___ total = ___ (reduce it)
    Month Day Year
    (use all four numbers)
= Life Path Number

Remember, if you have a master number don't reduce it!

Destiny Number ___ + Life Path Number ___ = ___ total = ___ (reduce it)
= Maturity Number

Major Cycles	Ages
1st Cycle ____ ____	
Day of Birth	
2nd Cycle ____ ____	
Month of Birth	
3rd Cycle ____ ____	
Year of Birth	

MAJOR CYCLES CHART

Life Path	End of 1st Cycle / Start of 2nd Cycle	End of 2nd Cycle / Start of 3rd Cycle
1	26-27	53-54
2	25-26	52-53
3	33-34	60-61
4 and 22	32-33	59-60
5	31-32	58-59
6 and 33	30-31	57-58
7	29-30	56-57
8	28-29	55-56
9	27-28	54-55

Your Birthday Number is ____ (the day you were born) and reduced it is ____

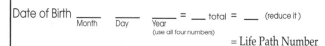

Spanish and French Language Letter Chart

What if you were born somewhere else? We don't have the room here to show you letter charts for every language from Russian to Tagalog, but we thought you might be interested in French and Spanish birth names.

French Language

French uses the same alphabet as English, so that one's easy. Ignore any accent marks and use the standard letter chart.

Spanish Language

Spanish doesn't use every letter English does—and it has a few extra letters as well. So here's the Spanish letter conversion chart for your Spanish birth name.

Spanish Letter Conversion Chart

1	2	3	4	5	6	7	8	9
A	B	C	D	E	F	G	H	I
J		L	M	N	O	P	Q	R
				Ñ				RR
S	T	U	V		X	Y	Z	
	CH			LL				

Laws, Rules, and Lists

We thought it might be helpful for you to have all the Universal Laws, Numerology Rules, along with gems, colors, signs, and flowers for each number, all in one place. That's what this appendix is for: lists!

Universal Laws

Universal laws are the laws of nature which govern human existence on Earth. These laws can not be altered, and they touch all of our lives whether we are aware of them or not. Universal laws are operative in our everyday lives.

Throughout this book, we have interwoven a sampling of some of the universal laws that are operative in our lives. Here, we have grouped together these laws for your convenience.

1. Nothing happens by chance. Everything happens for a reason.
2. Life happens as it should. There are no mistakes.
3. All things happen according to a Master Plan or Master Design. We all have free will by the choices we make about how we live the Master Plan.
4. The number 1 is the universal principle of action. It affirms "I act."
5. You're never given more than you can handle.
6. When it's right for you, it's right all the way around—trust this.

Numerology Rules

As we have with the Universal Laws that were scattered throughout the book, we've collected the Numerology Rules for you here as well, in one handy place.

1. Reduce numbers to a single digit. Add all numbers together to get a single number.
2. Don't reduce master numbers! Our master numbers are 11, 22, 33. They tell of special attributes.

3. The most important numbers in numerology are the 5 core numbers: Soul Number, Destiny Number, Personality Number, Life Path Number, and Maturity Number.

4. Don't add all the numbers straight across!

5. Don't lose your master numbers!

6. From your date of birth, you'll find the Life Path Number.

7. Add your name and birthday together to get your Maturity Number.

8. To find your karmic lesson(s), look for the missing numbers in your birth name.

9. Use the following formula to find your Life Path Number: Birth month + day of birth + year of birth = Life Path Number.

10. Use this formula to find your Destiny Number: First name + second name + third name = Destiny Number.

11. Use the following formula to find your Soul Number: Add together the vowels of your full name.

12. Your Maturity Number is found by adding together the energies of all that you are: Birth name + birth date = Maturity Number.

13. Finding your Pinnacle Numbers:

    First Pinnacle = Month of birth + day of birth

    Second Pinnacle = Day of birth + year of birth

    Third Pinnacle = First Pinnacle + Second Pinnacle

    Fourth Pinnacle = Month of birth + year of birth

14. Finding your Challenge Numbers:

    First Challenge = Day of birth – month of birth

    Second Challenge = Year of birth – day of birth

    Third Challenge = Second Challenge Number – First Challenge Number

    Fourth Challenge = Year of birth – month of birth

15. When subtracting the Challenge Number, it doesn't matter if the result is negative. In numerology, we ignore negatives and convert them to positives.

16. The First Major Cycle Number is found in the month you were born.

17. The Second Major Cycle Number is found in the day you were born.

18. The Third Major Cycle Number is found in the year you were born.

19. The formula for finding your Personal Year Number: Month of birth + day of birth + current calendar year = Personal Year Number.

20. The formula for finding your Personal Month Number: Personal Year Number + calendar month number = Personal Month Number.

When figuring the compatibility differences between two people, subtract the numbers to find the key to resolving the difference.

Colors, Gemstones, Signs, and Flowers, by the Numbers

Every number is associated with a color, gemstone, and astrological signs. We've collected this information for you from the number chapters, so you'll have it all in one place for those special occasions.

Number	Colors	Gemstones	Signs
1	Red, flame	Ruby or garnet	Aries
2	Orange, salmon peach, gold	Moonstone	Libra
3	Yellow	Topaz, gold	Leo
4	Green	Jade, emerald	Taurus
5	Turquoise	Aquamarine, turquoise	Gemini
6	Royal blue, indigo	Pearl, sapphire	Cancer/Pisces
7	Violet, purple	Amethyst, alexandrite	Pisces/Virgo/Scorpio
8	Pink, rose	Diamonds, rose quartz	Capricorn
9	White, clear	Opal	Scorpio/Pisces/ Aquarius
11/2	Silver, glossy silver	Platinum, mother of pearl	Aquarius/Sagittarius
22/4	Red gold	Rose gold	Virgo/Libra/ Capricorn
33/6	Deep sky blue	Lapis lazuli	Cancer/Pisces

In addition, each number has a number of flowers associated with it. Next time you remember your sweetie's birthday at the last minute, we hope you have this list handy to save your day!

➤ **Number 1:** Lily for purity, purple lilac for first emotions of love, sage for esteem
➤ **Number 2:** White jasmine for amiability, white lilac for modesty, hibiscus for delicate beauty, mimosa for sensitivity, and the pansy for timidity
➤ **Number 3:** Yellow jasmine for happiness and elegance, larkspur for lightness and levity, lily of the valley for the return of happiness
➤ **Number 4:** Bluebell for constancy, nasturtium for patriotism
➤ **Number 5:** Ranunculus for radiant charms, gardenia for sensuality
➤ **Number 6:** The rose for love, and honeysuckle for devotion

➤ **Number 7:** Lavender for silence, rose-scented geranium for preference and discernment

➤ **Number 8:** Hollyhock for ambition, camellia for excellence and mastery

➤ **Number 9:** Michaelmas daisy for farewell, magnolia for grief, red poppy for consolation, rosemary for remembrance, woodbine for fraternal love

Glossary of Numbers and Terminology

What the Numbers Mean

1 The number of initiation and action, the self-motivated leader.

2 The number of cooperation and partnership, the most sensitive of the numbers. Gravitates toward living in peace, finding harmonious solutions, and, most important, finding sensitive partnerships. It seeks to live without discord.

3 The number of creativity and joyful self-expression.

4 The number of hard work and tradition. It's the most solid and stable of the numbers.

5 The number of change and exploration. It's the number of freedom and adaptability.

6 The number of nurturing, sympathy, and understanding and responsibility.

7 The number of analysis, specialization, solitude, philosophical thought, and mysticism.

8 The number of power, money, and achievement.

9 The number of completion and transformation.

11/2 master number   The number of illumination and inspiration. Includes all of the qualities of the 1 and the 2.

22/4 master number   The number of vision, organization, and building of lasting foundations for the improvement of humanity. Includes all of the qualities of the numbers 2 and 4.

33/6 master number   The number of the teacher of teachers and healing energy through love. Includes all of the qualities of the numbers 3 and 6.

What the Terms Mean

age vibration   The way your age influences your Personal Year.

archetypes   According to psychoanalysis pioneer Carl G. Jung, archetypes are myths and stories that explain the unexplainable and belong to the collective unconscious. These archetypes have common links to us all.

astrology   Explores the interconnectedness of humans, planets, and stars by studying their interrelationship.

avatar   A Sanskrit term meaning "descent." In Hinduism, an avatar is thought to be a human incarnation of the Divine who mediates between people and God. Krishna, an East Indian deity, is considered the most perfect expression of the Divine, and so is an avatar. In popular usage, this word is used to indicate a person or program of superior spiritual achievement in consciousness development.

base number   The final reduced single digit you get after adding all of the numbers together.

biorhythm   The name for any biological cycle that involves periodic change. Because biorhythms are cyclical, like numerological cycles, they can be predicted.

Birthday Number   The day you were born.

Challenge Numbers   The four Challenge Numbers in your chart outline for you what it is that you must face in order to reach the highest peak of your Pinnacle. You might think of your Challenge Numbers as doors you must go through in order to advance in your personal growth.

Cipher Challenge   Another name for a zero (0) Challenge Number. It contains all or none of the other Challenges, depending on how you look at it—and how you live it!

concords   The three sets of three numbers that naturally belong together. The concords are: 3-6-9, 1-5-7, and 2-4-8.

core numbers   There are 5 of these: the Soul Number, Destiny Number, Personality Number, Life Path Number, and Maturity Number. Core numbers are the basis of your numerological profile. Different numerologists may call these numbers by different names, but they are figured the same no matter what they're called.

Destiny Number   One of your 5 core numbers. Refers to your purpose and direction in life. It is found by adding together the vowels and consonants of your birth name.

Feng Shui   The ancient Chinese art of placement, based on the belief that a home or building is a definable map of energy that has an influence on our daily lives.

Growth Number   Sometimes also called the Key, this number tells of the expected growth and development you can expect with the single-digit-number total found in your first name. It's found by adding together the numerical value of the letters of your first name and reducing to a single number total.

karma   Whether good or bad, it's a playing out of the universal cause and effect, which takes place over many lifetimes of the reincarnated soul.

karmic debt numbers   The numbers 13, 14, 16, and 19, which represent past life abuses that must be addressed in this lifetime.

Life Path Number   Reveals your inherent talents and abilities and shows the best career path for you to follow to utilize those skills. It's calculated by adding together all the numbers of your birth date.

major cycles   Three distinct cycles that show what you'll need to do to advance along the path of your life. They're found in the date of your birth; the month of birth number, the day of birth number, and the year of birth number.

master numbers   The numbers 11, 22, and 33 are called master numbers because they're considered to have more potential than the other numbers. The 11 is considered the most intuitive of all of the numbers, the 22 is considered the most powerful of all of the numbers, and the 33 is thought to be the most loving of all the numbers.

Maturity Number   Also called the True Self Number, this is one of the 5 core numbers and is the ultimate harmonic vibration of your being. It's found by adding together your birth date and your birth name.

myths   Stories that, through the use of archetypal images, often tell of a person's quest to access spiritual power. Myths reflect how an individual relates to the universe or his or her culture.

natal chart   Describes symbolically in which zodiac sign each of the 10 planets were located at the moment you were born. For example, if your Sun sign is Pisces, it means at the time you were born, the Sun appeared to be moving in the sky against the backdrop of the Pisces sign.

numerology   The study of the significance of names and numbers.

old souls   Souls who have returned through many lifetimes. They're thought to be wizened in the ways of spiritual matters.

Personal Day   Adds a certain number's subtle energy to every day of your life. It's found by adding the number of the calendar day to the number of your Personal Month.

Personal Month   Each Personal Month has a theme that is part of the rhythm of your Personal Year. The Personal Month is found by adding the number of your Personal Year to the number of the calendar month.

Personal Year   The theme of the year you are in currently. Represents where you are in the 9-year cycle of personal growth. It's found by adding your birth month and day to the current year.

Personality Number   One of your 5 core numbers. Offers clues to habits, mannerisms, and behaviors of the people you know in your life, as well as for your own self discovery. It's found by adding together the consonants of your birth name.

431

Pinnacle Numbers   Reveal your potential for achievement and success. These numbers show what is possible to attain at a given period in life.

predictive numerology   Uses numbers to look at the future and includes the Personal Year, Pinnacles, Challenges, and Major Cycles.

reduction   In numerology, all numbers are reduced to a single digit by adding their digits together, with the exception of master numbers. The number 27, for example, is reduced as $2 + 7 = 9$.

right action   In Buddhist teachings, it is believed that one must take right action in accordance with the laws of the universe and in keeping with the highest good for all.

Soul Number   One of your 5 core numbers. Reveals what you long for in your "heart of hearts." It tells what you desire for and what your soul wants to express in this lifetime. It is found by adding together the vowels of your birth name.

spiritual numerology   A way to frame an individual's journey on Earth as one of meaning and purpose. The method is based on the idea that each of us carries a set of vibrations, a blueprint for our life. This blueprint can be discovered from a numerology chart.

Stress Number   Found by calculating the difference between your numbers and another's. It can help you understand which energies you need to focus on to improve your relationships.

Yin/Yang   Yin and yang represent the two sides of every whole, according to Oriental tradition. Yin represents female energy, while yang represents male energy. In numerology, odd numbers are considered to be yang and even numbers yin.

Index

How to Order
Numerology Charts

Special offer for readers of *The Complete Idiot's Guide to Numerology!* Ten percent discount on Numerology Consultation or chart interpretation. To order a complete numerology chart, photocopy this page and send the following information.

Name: _____

Address: _____

City: _____ State: _____ Zip: _____

Country: _____ Phone: ( ) _____

To order your chart, fill in your Birth Name and Birth Date—please print.

Complete Numerology Chart

$30.00 (plus tax and shipping)
Your chart information (please fill in the requested information):
Name on Birth Certificate (exact spelling): _____
Date of Birth: Month: _____ Day: _____ Year: _____

Chart Consultation

Interpretation of your numerology chart is available in person, or by phone. Chart Consultation and Interpretations: $125 (two hours). Call for appointment 360-221-2696.
I would like to have my chart personally interpreted. Yes ____

Gift Chart Information

Gift Numerology Chart: $30.00 (plus tax and shipping)
Fill in the requested information about the person you are ordering a numerology chart for.
Name on Birth Certificate (exact spelling): _____
Date of Birth: Month: _____ Day: _____ Year: _____
PRINT mailing address:

Deliver Numerology Chart to:

Name: _____

Address: _____

City: _____

State/Zip: _____

Day Phone: ( ) _____

Evening Phone: ( ) _____

Send Gift Chart directly to:

Name: _____

Address: _____

City: _____

State/Zip: _____

Day Phone: ( ) _____

Evening Phone: ( ) _____

Postage and Handling Charges

	U.S.	Canada	Mexico	All Other International
Each Numerology Chart	$5.00	$6.00	$7.00	$11.00

Payment should be made in U.S. funds

	# of Charts	Price each
1. Name: _____	_____	_____
2. Name: _____	_____	_____
3. Name: _____	_____	_____

Numerology Charts Total $_____

Chart Consultation Total $_____

WA residents add 8.6% sales tax $_____

Shipping (see shipping table above) $_____

Grand Total $_____

Payment by check or money order. Checks must have name, address, and phone printed on check. Make checks payable to Kay Lagerquist.

Mail this form and check or money order to:

Personal Insights—Kay Lagerquist, P.O. Box 1031, Langley, WA 98260
Phone: 360-221-2696; e-mail: insights@whidbey.com

Allow three weeks for delivery. Prices and availability subject to change without notice.

Look for **Kay Lagerquists's** upcoming Web site: http://numerology-insights.com

Special Offer for Readers of
The Complete Idiot's Guide to Numerology!

Twenty percent discount from regular price of Sheila's audio tapes and quarterly newsletter.

Sheila Belanger offers you the chance to order her quarterly newsletter, **Spirit Cycles**, a down-to-earth guide for navigating the astrological cycles of the seasons. Designed for the layperson, it contains information on the current moon phases and major planetary cycles and is filled with insights, humor, and easy-to-use timing information. It is published four times a year at the equinoxes and solstices. In addition, Sheila produces audio tapes from her astrology classes, lectures, and workshops. Tape orders include handouts.

——————————————————————*cut here*——————————————————————

Name: _____

Address: _____

City: _____ State: _____ Zip: _____

Country: _____ Phone: ( )_____

	Quantity	Price	Total
Newsletter			
Spirit Cycles four issues (start with current season)	_____	@ $14.40 each	$_____
Audio Tapes			
Chiron: the Path to Healing (one-tape lecture)	_____	@ $6.36 each	$_____
Key Astrology Cycles at Midlife (1-tape lecture)	_____	@ $6.36 each	$_____
Gateway to the Millennium: Astrology Cycles of 1999–2000 (two-tape workshop)	_____	@ $11.16 each	$_____
Astrology Basics I: Signs, Planets and Houses (complete set of nine-tape class) (separate purchase of textbook *Astrology For Yourself* by D. George and D. Bloch required)	_____	@ $31.96 each	$_____
Astrology Basics II: Aspects (complete set of five-tape class)	_____	@ $17.56 each	$_____
Astrology Basics III: Transits as Tools for Self-Growth (complete set of six-tape class)	_____	@ $21.56 each	$_____
Cycles of the Season (two-hour lecture on astrology cycles of the current season)	_____	@ $8.76 each	$_____

Subtotal $_____

WA residents add 8.6% sales tax $_____

Shipping and handling for audio tapes $_____

(From USA, add $1 per lecture; $2 per workshop; $4 per class set; up to $7 max.)

TOTAL ORDER $_____

Send this form with your check or money order to:

Sheila Belanger, P.O. Box 6, Greenbank, WA 98253-0006

Allow three weeks for delivery. Payment made in U.S. funds. Prices and availability subject to change without notice.